This Land is Our Land

Jan Metzger, Martin Orth and Christian Sterzing

This Land is Our Land

The West Bank Under Israeli Occupation

**Jan Metzger
Martin Orth
Christian Sterzing**

Translated by Dan and Judy Bryant, Janet Goodwin and Stefan Schaaf

Zed Press, 57 Caledonian Road, London N1 9DN.

This Land is Our Land was originally published in German by Lamuv Verlag, Martinstrasse 7, 5303 Bornheim-Merten. First published in English by Zed Press, 57 Caledonian Road, London N1 9DN in 1983.

Copyright © Jan Metzger, Martin Orth, Christian Sterzing
— 1980
Translation Copyright © Zed Press, 1983

Copyedited by Janet Scharf & Urvashi Butalia
Proofread by Mark Gourlay & Anne Hilal
Typeset by Audrey Meek
Cover design by Jacque Solomons
Photo credits: Jan Metzger & Christian Sterzing, Bernd Nanninga, Michael Volke, Manfred Wolf-Maduschka, and UNRWA
Cover photo credit: Manfred Wolf-Maduschka
Printed by The Pitman Press, Bath, U.K.

All rights reserved

British Library Cataloguing in Publication Data

Metzger, J.
This land is our land.
1. Jordan (Territory under Israeli occupation, 1967-)—
History
I. Title II. Orth, M. III. Sterzing, C.
IV. Das ist unser Land. English
956.95   DS153.55.P34

ISBN 0-86232-086-0
ISBN 0-86232-073-9 Pbk

U.S. Distributor:
Biblio Distribution Center, 81 Adams Drive, Totowa,
New Jersey 07512, U.S.A.

Contents

Foreword	i
1. First Glimpses of the Occupation	1
2. Faits Accomplis: The Jewish Settlements	19
Judaization of the West Bank?: Inventory of Settlement Activities	20
Security Considerations and 'Historical Rights': The Zionist Settlement Policy	31
'They Take Our Land': The Settlements from a Palestinian Point of View	41
The Path to Confrontation: Opposition to the Settlements	45
'Re-unification': The Annexation of East Jerusalem	51
3. Administration of Suppression: The Occupation and Human Rights	61
Justice and Politics: The Occupation and International Law	62
In the Name of Security: Political Suppression	65
Exiled from the Homeland: Deportations	67
'Indiscriminate Crackdowns': Collective Punishments	68
The Power of Evidence: Political Prisoners and Torture	70
4. Creeping Annexation: The Economy	82
An Uneven Start: The Background	82
Becoming a Colonial Power: The Economic Policy of the Occupiers	86
The Short Cut to Israel: Employment of Labour	90
Integration or Penetration? Trade Relations	97
Domination and Deterioration: Agriculture	98
A Shadow Existence: Industry	111
The 'Boom'	113
5. New Alliances: The Social Structure	124
Few Winners, Many Losers: The West Bank	124

Nothing to Lose: The Gaza Strip 127
Occupation Policy as Boomerang: Political Consequences 128

6. Birth of National Consciousness: Political Development under the Occupation 133
From the Frying Pan into the Fire: The Historical Background 133
The Occupiers Stay: The First Three Years of Occupation 140
Peaceful Times: From Black September in 1970 to the Elections in 1972 151
From Protest to Resistance: 1972 to 1976 158
A New Leadership Emerges: The 1976 Elections 169
A New Era: After the Elections 173
In the Backyard of History: The Gaza Strip 183

7. Peace Without the Palestinians? International Peace Initiatives 196
A Desperate Mission: The Sadat Initiative 196
The Label Swindle: Begin's Autonomy Plan 201
The Coup: Camp David 205
Complete Rejection: Reactions in the Occupied Territories 211
A Dead End: The Egyptian-Israeli-American Peace Treaty 216
Peace Out of Sight: The Situation in the Occupied Territories 221

8. Dream and Reality: An Independent Palestinian State alongside Israel 237
Homeland and Exile: The Background to Different Palestinian Concepts 238
The Position in the Occupied Territories 241
The Position of the P.L.O. 244
Future Problems: The Viability of a Separate Palestinian State 252

9. 'Better A Land of Peace than A Piece of Land': Israeli Opposition to the Occupation 256

Bibliography 265

Maps

1. Existing and Planned Israeli Settlements in the West Bank and Gaza Strip — 21
2. Israeli 'Security Areas' according to the Sharon Plan — 37
3. Israeli 'Security Areas' according to the Allon Plan — 40
4. Jerusalem — 53

Tables

1. Property Ownership in the Occupied Territories, 1979 — 20
2. Deportations from the Occupied Territories, 1967-78 — 68
3. Workers from the Occupied Territories Employed in Israel, 1970-78 — 91
4. Unemployment in Israel and the Hiring of Workers from the Occupied Territories, 1967-78 — 94
5. Employment in the Occupied Territories, 1970-79 — 95
6. Migration Balance, 1969-78 — 96
7. Trade in the West Bank and the Gaza Strip, 1968-78 — 99
8. Israeli Exports to the Occupied Territories as a percentage of Total Exports, 1966-79 — 100
9. Agricultural Production in the West Bank, 1966-78 — 102
10. Agricultural Production in the Gaza Strip, 1968-78 — 103
11. Agricultural Employment in the West Bank, 1970 and 1977 — 107
12. Registered Refugees and Palestinians Living in Camps, May 1976 — 253

Foreword

This book is, among other things, a way for us to come to terms with a part of our past. We lived and worked in Israel and the occupied territories for over a year and have returned several times since to do research in this region and in neighbouring Arab states. Along the way, we have made friends on both sides of the border. This book is a result of this personal relationship with Palestine and its Jewish and Arab inhabitants.

As Germans, we must not and do not want to shirk our responsibility of solidarity with the Jewish victims of German fascism. Yet this solidarity must not stop us seeing the injustice and misery which Jews have inflicted and continue to inflict on the Palestinians. However, this does not mean we identify with every demand which emerges among the Palestinians or their liberation movement.

In view of the Israeli-Egyptian peace treaty, it might appear that peace in the Middle East is only a matter of time. But appearances are deceptive. Peace will not be possible until a settlement is found which takes the vital interests of all parties involved — those of the Jewish Israeli people, as well as the Palestinians — into consideration.

It is with great scepticism, to say the least, that we have been following the transformation in official U.S. and European Middle East policy during the past few years. There does seem to be growing recognition of the fact that peace without consideration of the Palestinians is impossible, but as far as the American so-called 'peace' policy is concerned, the acceptance of a minimum of Palestinian demands is only viewed as a necessary evil. The growing interest in the Palestinians stems more from the desire to secure economic and political interests in the region than from any perception of the legitimacy of Palestinian demands.

We believe, however, that even if the Palestinians were given 'autonomy' in the West Bank and Gaza Strip as a means of safeguarding the existence of the state of Israel and securing energy sources and markets for the West, peace in the Middle East must encompass more than this.

In our view, there is no way around the recognition and practical realization of the legitimate right of the Palestinian people to self-determination. Today, the establishment of a Palestinian state alongside Israel presents itself as a possible political compromise.

A compromise is necessary if the explosive situation in the Middle East is not to end in a bloodbath. A compromise must, therefore, also be in the interests of Jewish Israelis. In the long run, their physical existence can only be guaranteed within the framework of a comprehensive and just peace. This compromise will not lead to a solution overnight, but it will enable the first step to be taken on the way toward peaceful coexistence between both peoples.

Current press coverage hardly takes notice of the Palestinian population in the West Bank and the Gaza Strip, their situation under the occupation and their political prospects, even though numerically they represent a significant portion of the total Palestinian population; if there can be any talk of an intact Palestinian society at all, it is to be found in the occupied territories. Despite the fact that this segment of the Palestinian people is the key to a peace settlement in the Middle East, there is a lack of publications dealing with the situation of these people in a coherent and comprehensive manner. This book is an attempt at filling this gap.

It is not our aim to add one more book to the already long list of publications dealing with the Middle East conflict. Our book centres, therefore, exclusively upon the Palestinian population in the territories occupied by Israel since 1967. Contrary to common usage and for the sake of brevity, we have used the term 'occupied territories' to mean the West Bank (including East Jerusalem) and the Gaza Strip but excluding the Golan Heights and Sinai.

This intentionally narrow perspective has certain consequences. Anything which goes beyond this limited approach to the subject, yet which appears to us to be essential to an understanding of the political and economic development of this region can only be roughly outlined. For instance, the background to Israeli policy-making and action can, for the most part, only be presented in a fragmented and shortened form, and the reader may feel a one-sided picture of Israel is being depicted. Likewise, limited space has not allowed us to draw a complete picture of the political positions and prospects of the P.L.O.; these are only described in relation to their significance to the situation in the occupied territories. The same is true of political developments at an international level.

Our primary interest is, therefore, to supply a lot of information on the situation of the Palestinian population, rather than interpretations of it. The emphasis is on documentary elements and we have tried to convey the atmosphere of the region and to clarify the points of view of those affected. In the first chapter, we have tried to describe people's experience of daily life under the occupation, in order to awaken understanding in the reader as to the conditions under which the Palestinians in the West Bank and the Gaza Strip have been suffering for 16 years under the Israelis. In the following chapters which deal with the settlement policy, the violation of human rights, and economic, social and political developments

Foreword

during the occupation, we have attempted, in addition to describing and analyzing the changes, to provide the reader with a sense of authenticity by including documents, newspaper articles, interviews, etc.

Each chapter contains extensive notes. Our statements are intentionally based, to a large extent, on Israeli sources; not only because they are more accessible, but because we do not want to make it easy for pro-Israeli critics to dismiss statements in our book as hostile propaganda. However, we have generally avoided citing Israeli propaganda, from which basic facts have been left out in order to make developments in the occupied territories appear normal and positive.

During the lengthy preparation of this book, many friends, particularly from Israel and the occupied territories, have supported us with advice and assistance. Their aid has been invaluable to us. We owe them our gratitude.

Jan Metzger
Martin Orth
Christian Sterzing

1. First Glimpses of the Occupation

Daily Hassles
For those in the taxi, it seems to be part of the usual procedure. The first road block is just beyond the airport between Jerusalem and Ramallah: an armoured car parked across the road, in front of it a double row of long nails pointing upward and a warning hand on a sign reading, 'Stop! Police!' Every car stops. The Israeli soldiers are young, standing around nonchalantly, swinging their machine guns. A few of them sit by the armoured car, relaxed, smoking a cigarette. The task of the guards is to check all the cars that go by. Depending on the situation, the soldiers' temperament and mood, everything is taken care of either in a relaxed way with an occasional smile, without a word, or with curses and insults. Today nobody says a word. The Palestinians who are sitting with us in the taxi hand their worn identification papers to the Israelis. They too are silent; what is there to say? The soldier leafs through the papers routinely, evidently checking to see if there is an Israeli work permit stamp in them. It is only when he sees our West German passports that he hesitates for a moment. 'Where are you going?' 'To Ramallah, to visit friends.' He returns the papers, the driver lets in the clutch of his diesel Mercedes and manoeuvres the car carefully through the narrow opening between the nails.

On the other side, soldiers are checking a bus on its way to Jerusalem. All passengers must get out and line up with their papers in their hands. Meanwhile, a soldier goes through the bus, casting a glance at the luggage.

The press officer for the military governor explains the procedure as he receives us at the press information centre in West Jerusalem. From his point of view, such measures prevent weapons and explosives from being brought into Israel, thereby protecting security. In this respect, they serve to protect everyone.

Occasionally, a different version is presented in the Israeli press asserting that, above all, the check points perform a psychological function. They show the people in the occupied territories that everyone has to bear the consequences for assaults on Israeli citizens. Thus, each time there is an attack in Israel these security measures are drastically increased.

Everyday reality – street control in the West Bank

'Security? – We Are the Ones Who Need Security!'

In the occupied territories one tries to ignore, as best one can, the way in which the army daily demonstrates its presence. Often it is impossible, especially when the authorities exceed the limits, to which one has finally become accustomed and which one has quietly put up with.

> Yesterday morning the Israeli army staged another raid in the centre of Ramallah. They randomly arrested a few dozen people on the street and detained them at the main square. First, our people were forced to undress. Then their clothing was searched. The whole affair lasted over two hours. There was no particular reason for it. They were not accused of having done anything. . . . These things just happen.

We are sitting in the living room of Pastor Rantisi, the deputy mayor of Ramallah. Rantisi vents his bitterness about the incident:

> The Israelis are constantly talking about security. We are the ones who need security! There is no security for us Palestinians in our own country. Things like this can happen at any time. Let me tell you

something: we are fed up with the occupation; we are simply fed up with it.

'The military government is against the city councils,' says Karim Khalaf, mayor of Ramallah:

> Why? Because the political stance of the councils is friendly to the P.L.O. They put stumbling blocks in our path, obstacles in the way of our projects. For example, at the moment, we are working on the sewage system in Ramallah. We started in 1974. The sewage pipes were supposed to pass through some land that is next to a military camp. The military government had already given its approval. While the construction was going on they suddenly enlarged the camp, so that our pipes now pass through their grounds. After we had spent millions, they stopped the work. We went to the military government several times to discuss this. A few times they said, 'Okay, you can continue working.' But when our workers came to the construction site, they were sent away again by the soldiers.

The story of the sewage system shows how the distribution of power often expresses itself in trivial things. Many of the mechanisms through which the Israeli military government rules in the West Bank and the Gaza Strip are also not always visible. 'From 1967 to the present, we have not received one single written decision from them, only oral communiqués,' said the mayor.

> When I negotiate with the military governor and ask him to write down the results of our talk in an official memorandum, he refuses. When I then return the following week and refer to what he said the week before, he maintains, 'No, I never said anything of the kind. You must be mistaken, Mr Khalaf.'

The mayor has received us in his office in Ramallah's city administration building. Our conversation is often interrupted by phone calls. Several people are waiting outside for an opportunity to confer with him, thus lending weight to Karim Khalaf's comment:

> You know, for the people in the occupied territories, the city administration is the most important place for solving their problems. When someone from Ramallah has a problem and wants to speak to the military governor about it, he can't simply go to him. He wouldn't even get into the building. Therefore, the person in question comes to the city administration in order to solve his problem with the military government through us. However, the difficulty now is that the military government avoids co-operating with us as much as possible. There are a great many collaborators who are in the Israelis' good books. They go into the offices, are served a cup of coffee and are treated with all

due respect. They solve the problems of the people better than we do. The elected mayors receive no answer. We are told, 'You are responsible for sanitation and order in the city. Don't get mixed up in the affairs of the people.' In this way, the Israeli authorities try to stop the city administration from attending to the problems of the people. They want the people to think: 'What kind of mayors and city councils are these anyway? They don't do anything at all for us.'

'Freedom' of the Press

The daily newspapers *Al-Kuds, Al-Fajr, Al-Sha'ab* and the weekly newspaper *Al-Tali'ah* are required to lay out each edition of their papers on the military censor's desk. 'As far as freedom of the press is concerned, there is the following difference between Jordan and Israel,' explains the editor of *Al-Tali'ah* to us:

> When someone in Jordan criticizes the regime, the edition concerned is confiscated. In the West Bank, there is military censorship of the press: passages or whole articles are cut, on an average of 30–40% per edition. Because of this, we always have a number of substitute articles ready. Acquiring information is no problem. The Israelis let us run around and collect all the material we want. The censor only needs to make one slash of his pen and all the work has been in vain. In this way we are kept busy.
>
> Everything that appears to support the P.L.O., everything about the P.L.O. and everything containing expressions such as 'legitimate rights of the Palestinian people' is slashed. Censorship applies to all reports about demonstrations and everything about the National Front, to which most of the city council members and mayors belong. Almost all reports about Jewish settlements in the occupied territories become victims of the censorship. For a long time, topics such as Iran were also taboo. We have two possibilities. Either we orient ourselves to the censorship practices and do not write about things that are likely to be censored in the first place, or we run the risk of doing twice the amount of work.
>
> Regardless of their political tendencies, all East Jerusalem newspapers are likewise affected by censorship. One of the editorial staff of *Al-Fajr* explains another peculiarity of censorship: 'There are not only things which, in general, are not allowed to be published, but also things which are not meant for Palestinian readers in particular. Articles or pictures are often censored which have already appeared in the Israeli press and therefore have already passed military censorship for use in the Israeli media in Tel Aviv. What is considered to be freedom of information in Israel is, under certain circumstances in the occupied territories, a danger to the security of the state.

First Glimpses of the Occupation

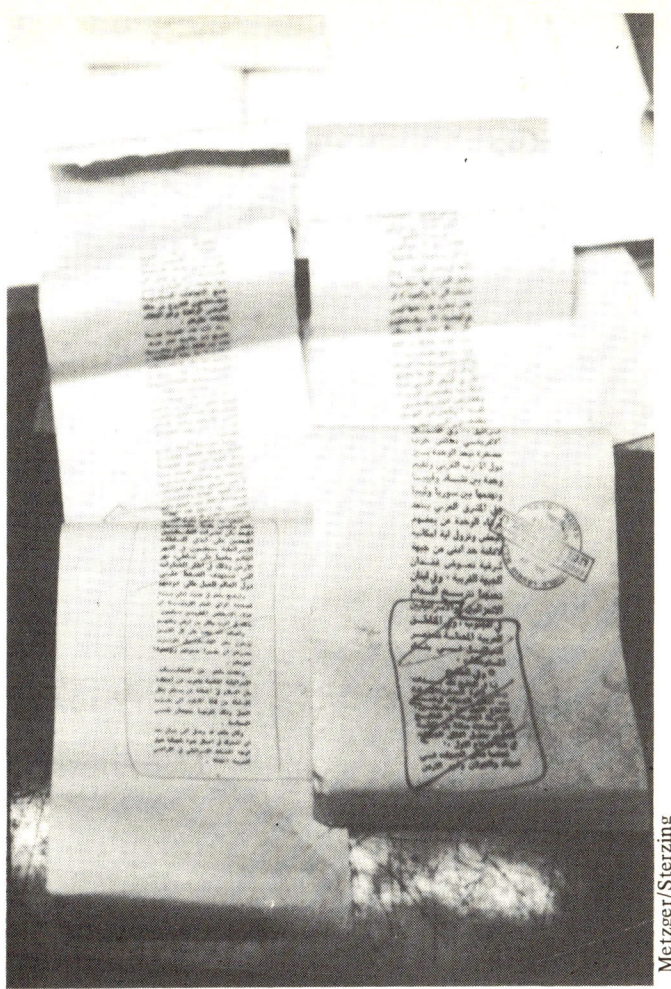

'Freedom' of the Press — censored galley proofs of the Palestinian daily Al Fajr

'Who Will Till the Land?'

Kafr Nameh is a farming village in the mountains west of Ramallah. Until a few years ago there was not even a paved road leading to the town. Going shopping in the city was a whole day's undertaking. The brown houses stand very closely together; the narrow alleys are hot and dusty. In the midday heat, people sit together in shady corners, chatting. A group of strangers attracts attention and is sure to be invited to come in for a cup of coffee.

Abu Yassuf[1] lives with his family in a flat, rectangular, stone house at the entrance to the village. This little, wiry man with a white moustache, dressed in a traditional, long robe, must be 70 years old. After making the opening courtesies, taking the first sip of coffee and telling the children – who loudly insist that a chicken must be slaughtered for the guests – to be calm, he talks to us about farming. 'I have a total of 40 *dunams*,[2] 20 of which I cultivate; the other 20 are too stony.'

'What is grown here in Kafr Nameh?'

> Most people have olive trees. Olives are our most important fruit. We make oil from them: that is, we take them to Ramallah where they are pressed. In addition to that, there are grapes and figs which are dried and, for the most part, sold. For ourselves, we have tomatoes, lentils and chickpeas, also a little wheat. But the wheat – that is another story. There is only a small amount of land here flat enough for wheat to be planted on.

'Can your family live on what you earn from the olive oil?'

> No, we can't. The work takes about three months – ploughing, digging ditches, taking care of the trees. The rest of the year, part of the family has to work off the farm, in Ramallah or in Jerusalem, and since 1967, above all, in Israel. But we do not have the means for improving the harvests. For example, we do not have enough water and, therefore, can only plant the things which grow without irrigation – olives, wheat, tomatoes, each with one crop per year. That is not enough to live on. The family gets bigger, prices rise. Farming simply does not bring in enough money. Today I receive the same amount for the olive oil as I did under Jordanian rule, although everything else has become more expensive. It is simply necessary for my sons to work off the farm.

This is not Abu Yussuf's problem alone. A short time later, we join four old men – three of whom are farmers – sitting in an airy and cool room on the third floor of a house. They tell us that Kafr Nameh, like many villages on the West Bank, is not exactly blessed with good land, as the whole area is mountainous and dry. 'Farming is declining here. I still work my land and try to develop it. But I don't know, for example, if my son will want to take it over some day,' says one of the old men:

> Once you earn I£150 (Israeli pounds) per day in a factory, you never think of returning to farming again. It's only eight hours of work a day and money in your pocket. That's much more attractive. This is why many farmers give up working their land. My brother, for example, has over 100 *dunams* which he no longer does anything with.

First Glimpses of the Occupation

Another agrees with him:

> Many give up their land because there are so few workers. My eldest son, for example, is married and has his own family. The youngest works in Israel. In order to be able to continue, I need someone to help me. I would have to pay a worker. That I can't afford; I don't have the money.

A third says:

> There are still about 100 people who work in the village. But most of the young and strong work outside of the village. One hundred and fifty ride every day to Ramallah and Jerusalem, 200 to Israel. They have to work outside because we in the village need the money. A short time after 1967, it was better than today. Many people could work in Israel and living was cheaper. Today, there is not as much work in Israel and the prices have risen sharply. Today, everything is so expensive that we don't live as well, even though we have more money.

From the window one can see over the stony hills which surround the village. The farmers have toiled all their lives in the fields. Their fathers, from whom they inherited the land, were also farmers. For generations the families, indeed whole villages, have lived off the proceeds of the land. The fact that their sons earn their money somewhere else today perplexes them. 'One bit of our land lies on the edge of the village. We want to build a house there. But the rest has to be cultivated. My son will just have to do something about it. . . . Who will the land belong to someday, if the sons all leave?

The Daily Ride to Israel
In the afternoon, in the neighbouring village of Bila'in, we run into two of sons about whom the farmers in Kafr Nameh had spoken. We sit drinking tea on the terrace with a family whose father also works in Israel. At weekends he takes care of his farm. The conversation becomes lively when two young men from the neighbourhood join us. They drive up in a large car and come in, nonchalantly swinging their car keys — shirts open at the neck, jeans, stylish shoes — at first glance, farther removed from their fathers than from other 20-year-olds in Tel Aviv. Both work in Israel. 'I am paid well there, I£150 per day; in Ramallah they pay less.'

'How long is the drive to work each morning?'

'I leave home at 6:00, and get back at 5:00 in the afternoon — that is eight hours of work and three hours on the road.'

His friend joins in the conversation: 'If you subtract the driving time from the amount we earn in Israel, then it really is a good question as to whether it is worth it. But in reality the question never arises; most of us can't find a job in the West Bank. So, day after day, we go to Israel.'

Since the beginning of 1968, the occupied territories have exported labour

This Land is Our Land

'The short cut to Israel' – market for day labourers in Jerusalem

to Israel. Most of the workers have a stamp from the Israeli 'employment agencies' glued onto their identification papers – the official work permit. Approximately one quarter of those who work in Israel do not go through the official agencies. These workers enter Israel illegally, work under worse conditions than their colleagues and usually only get work from day to day. They can be found every morning gathering at the busy border crossings like cattle at a market.

> **The Human Cattle Market at Ashkelon Junction**
> 3.50 a.m. The dark fields are lit by a single lamp. A loaded truck blocks the entrance to the petrol station. Car horns can be heard. Noises in the darkness. A short column of shabby vans tries to enter. The vans stop for a minute and turn back. It is not for petrol that they came for the petrol station is closed. They came to unload their human load. People spill out of them, like sardines from a can and disperse in the darkness. These shabby vans saw better days in the 60s. Not so their passengers. 20, 25 per van. They all hurry, and in the dim light they look pale and ill. Each of them holds a plastic bag, clutching it like a baby would a

safety blanket. By now 60 men, a few women and some children, ages 12 to 14, are standing in the square. At first only a dozen children are present. The men lean on the closed doors of the station's restaurant. The women are packed in a dark mass of heads and scarfs in the corner. The children gather round the petrol pumps, playing with them and yawning, for they are half asleep. They come from Gaza, Khan Yunis and Rafah, towns in the Gaza strip. The air is heavy with the smell of oil. This is the coastal shore at dawn. In the west, a vague sound can be heard, like a ship's siren in a stormy sea.

At 4:05 the sky begins to brighten. At 4:20 the hills seem red. Twenty minutes later the sun rises. The people pacing in the dark can now see light. By this time there are some 200 people waiting here. 400 working hands. 40 children. 40 pairs of working hands. The petrol station is still closed. Beyond the cotton fields the roses of the Lakhish area can be seen covered with nylon sheets.

A jeep approaches from the north, driving much too fast (but there is no policeman here) and halts by the diesel pumps. The crowd turns to the jeep. The driver's head sticks out above the moving crowd. He is wearing a cap. He shouts: 'Four. I said four.' The crowd shouts: 'Work' 'Master', 'I good work'. The master rises, the master says something. From a distance, his words cannot be heard. Four men climb into the jeep. 'Take me master, I'm for 60 Israeli pounds.' The master begins to drive. The crowd jumps out of the way. The jeep passes in between.

Source: Amos Elon in *Ha'aretz*, 2 August 1978.

Number of Schoolchildren Decreasing

'The primary and secondary schoolchildren are also affected by the general situation.' The young teacher we meet in Ramallah tells us, in detail, about the pressure of the political situation on pupils and teachers. He speaks of outdated teaching curricula and methods, unqualified teachers and those who, because of the meagre wages, have to have a job on the side, and describes how there is no discipline or book that teaches the schoolchildren anything about 'Palestine'. He himself works in a school at a refugee camp.

> The children from the refugee camps used to be the ones who worked the hardest in comparison with those in the city. Before the June War, the only way to get out of their family's miserable economic situation was to work hard in school in order to find a good job after graduation. Today, they don't care. The father works in an Israeli factory and does not have time to look after his children, because he comes home late and is too tired. The youth are also given the opportunity to work in

an Israeli factory. They realize the value of money when they see their peers who work in the factory, running around and smoking Kents. Then they quickly get fed up with school and find some excuse to leave. In this way, we lose about 30 pupils a year in our school. And that really is not so many. In the villages near the Israeli border, the percentage of pupils dropping out of school before graduation is even higher. The schools keep getting smaller instead of larger. And the number of children who leave school early is steadily increasing. That is only part of what happens here.

'They Take Our Land'

> I have lived under three foreign occupations — the Turkish, the British and now the Israeli. Of the three, the Israeli regime rules with the lightest hand and yet is the hardest to bear. Whenever there was a rebellion or unrest under the Ottoman Empire, gallows were erected from here to Jericho. The British, as well, were not averse to occasionally hanging leaders of insurrections. But the Israelis do not make use of the death penalty, not even for murderers. And yet they are our worst enemies, and we fear them most of all. Why? The answer is simple. The Turkish sultans ruled this area here for 400 years. They introduced high taxes, they were often unjust and cruel, but they did not touch our land. The British kept their mandate for 30 years. But the Israelis, only four months after they marched into our territory in June 1967, seized 6,000 *dunams* which belonged to us and which we had cultivated for many generations. They took it to set up a Jewish settlement . . . — a Palestinian *mukhtar* (village elder) from the West Bank.
>
> Source: *Frankfurter Rundschau*, 1 September 1976.

There are now over 100 Israeli settlements with approximately 13,000 inhabitants in the West Bank and Gaza Strip. The government of Menachem Begin speaks clearly: 'Judea and Samaria' — their terms for the West Bank — were 'liberated' in 1967. This region is part of 'Eretz Israel', the Land of Israel which had been promised to the Jewish people in the Bible. 'The Israelis have the right to settle in all of Eretz Israel. This land was promised to us and we have a right to it,' said Prime Minister Begin at the awarding of his Nobel Peace Prize in Oslo.[3]

In almost every conversation the authors had in the occupied territories, the settlement policy of the Israeli government was the main topic. All Palestinians consider themselves affected by the policy, even if it is not their land which was taken for a settlement. The fact that Israelis are settling today on Palestinian land in the territories occupied since 1967 and are taking the place of Palestinian farmers, calls to mind the old experiences with the Jewish settlement of the other part of Palestine in the 20s and 30s. It is in terms of this memory that the Palestinians measure the character of the occupation — a person who builds houses and plants trees, intends to stay.

Each settlement is a step towards establishing Israeli control in the rest of Palestine. 'It makes us despair,' says an old man. 'The Jews won't leave here again on their own. They want the land and, at the same time, they want peace. We don't even exist for them. They say that this land has belonged to them for 2,000 years. So where did we come from?'

The Black Wheat of Akraba

The road leading to Akraba, a small Palestinian village with 4,000 inhabitants in the West Bank, is very bad, full of bumps and potholes. But when one finally arrives, the bad roads are quickly forgotten. The scenery of the hills and valleys spreads out before one as far as the Jordan and radiates a calm which cannot be destroyed.

But, on April 28 (1972), an Israeli Piper Cub, circling above this peaceful scene, sprayed chemical poison on the wheat fields of the Akraba farmers. The wheat, sown last December on approximately 2,000 *dunams* of land, changed colour overnight. Formerly green, it became brown, burned by the chemicals.

When I heard the story in Nablus, I refused to believe it. But in Akraba, I was shown the fields. I was told the story of the long battle the villagers had been fighting against the authorities ever since the day the Israelis decided to confiscate more than 6,000 *dunams* of good land. 'We had been cultivating the land', the *mukhtar* told me, 'ever since the Turkish Sultan, Abdul Hamid, gave it to us.'

Israel does not deny the facts. It admits having destroyed the wheat, to 'teach the villagers a lesson'. They had stubbornly continued to cultivate their fields, although the army had forbidden them to set foot on them. But why were they not allowed to step onto the fields? 'Because for almost five years, these fields have been used for target practice and we were tired of warning the villagers that they were risking their lives by going into the fields,' explained General Shlomo Gazit, the man responsible for the co-ordination of the civil administration in the occupied territories. Mr N. Levi, spokesman for Moshe Dayan, confirmed this version.

What do the villagers say? As to the first phase of expropriations at the end of 1967, when the Israeli army laid claim to about 100,000 *dunams* in the Jordan valley (of a total of 154,000 *dunams* belonging to the village), they say only, 'that was our best

> land, for there is a lot of water in the Jordan valley. But we didn't say anything,' explained the *mukhtar*, 'the army is the army.'
>
> In May 1971, a representative of the Israeli Land Administration came to the village and offered to buy 6,000 *dunams* of land. The *mukhtar* refused. 'These 6,000 *dunams* were the last good arable land we had. What were we supposed to live on if we gave that up, too?' The Israelis came to the village several times regarding this matter, but every time the *mukhtar* refused to sign the deed of sale presented to him. Then one day, a representative of the military government came and told him that the farmers no longer had the right to go into the fields which were under dispute and that they would be better off selling them. Nevertheless, the villagers succeeded in tilling and sowing the land in December. But, in February, the army put a fence around it and in April the wheat was burned.
>
> At the beginning of May, the villagers wrote a ltter to Moshe Dayan and the Minister of Agriculture — no response. Instead, an Israeli came and advised them not to write any such letters again if they ever wanted to receive any compensation for the loss of the land.
>
> In the Ministry of Defence, they speak merely of lands 'confiscated for the needs of the army'. One might ask oneself why, in this overwhelmingly arid region, were cultivated fields — of all places — chosen for a target area? The answer is not a mystery to anyone — the way is being prepared for the arrival of Jewish settlers.
>
> Source: Victor Cygielman, *Nouvel Observateur*, 3 July 1972.
>
> Postscript: The Israeli settlement of Gittit was established on the fields of the Akraba village in August 1972.

'Every Palestinian can be Affected'

Occasionally, we were guests in the shop of Abu Hassan[4] in Hebron. There, one can sit by the hour, talk, drink coffee and watch the customers. During one visit, there were more young people in the shop than usual and the atmosphere was strangely tense. The reason: Mahmud, the 16 year-old brother of the shop owner, has been taken by the Israeli army and kept in prison in Hebron for several days.

'Why was he arrested?'

'They claim he violated the security of Israel,' says Abu Hassan. 'That usually means that the students demonstrated and threw stones at Israeli army vehicles.'

'And what did he do? Why did they arrest *him*?'

First Glimpses of the Occupation

'I have no idea. He was on his way home from the market. As he passed the Patriarch's Tomb they grabbed him — "security reasons". He hasn't had anything to do with the demonstrations in the past few weeks.' Around the Tomb of the Patriarch, a holy place for Islam and Judaism alike, there are continually altercations between Jews and Arabs.

'What will happen to Mahmud now?'

'Either we pay the fine, which amounts to a few thousand pounds, or he will spend several months in prison. We will pay, of course. . . .'

When there are demonstrations in the West Bank, it is usually the primary and secondary school students who are out in the streets. Because of their age, they have the least to fear from the possible consequences — the occupying authorities can neither push the young students across the border nor lock them up for a long time. For this reason, the Israeli military government holds the families responsible. At every demonstration, one to two dozen young people are arrested and brought before the military court for violating the security of the state. They are then either fined or sent to jail. The families prefer to pay for their offspring — and then forbid them to be anywhere near any demonstrations in future.

'The young people of school-going age are very much influenced by the political situation here. They are perhaps the most politically active part of the population in the occupied territories,' explained a teacher to us.

'Every Palestinian can be affected' — a protesting student is led away in Ramallah

In what we call the 'War of Stones' in 1967, the youth threw stones at the Israeli tanks, while the Arab armies fled. Those were brave actions. The young students have often demonstrated since then in the streets, sometimes in the schools too. The Israelis came into the schools, beat the students and punished the teachers. Sometimes, they also arrested pupils who did not take part in the demonstrations, but instead sat quietly in their classrooms. The Israeli soldiers came into the classes and punished those who had not had anything to do with the demonstrations. That was a good lesson for them to learn, that every Palestinian is pronounced guilty, whether he was involved or not. If you are walking down the street carrying vegetables home, walking quietly and not paying any attention to them, you can be arrested anyway and have to pay a fine. There are always school students in the prisons because they have demonstrated. Sometimes, they haven't actually done anything. Sometimes, they have shouted slogans against the occupation, such as 'We want freedom and independence' or 'We are for the P.L.O.' – things that are done in your country too, that are done everywhere. This right is refused us in our country. For these reasons, schoolchildren are punished. The Israelis break the rules as they please. There is no justice here. Every Palestinian can be affected. . . .

'At 1 a.m. the Army Surrounded My House . . .'
Dr Abdul Aziz Haj Ahmad, 35, from Al Bireh, father of three children, was deported on 27 March 1976, two days before he could have himself officially registered as a candidate for the city council elections. He reports on his deportation experience:

At 1 a.m. the Israeli army and intelligence surrounded my house. There were 40 or 50 soldiers and two armoured cars. They knocked on the door with their guns. My wife opened the door a crack. They asked, 'Who owns this house?' She said, 'If you knock at the door at 1 a.m. you must know who owns the house.' She refused to tell them anything. After a while they said, 'We want Dr Abdul Aziz Haj Ahmad. Is he here?' She said yes, and they opened the door. I was about ten metres inside. They told me to put on my clothes. About ten soldiers went with me to the bedroom, they searched it and tore everything apart. After that they took me to jail. When we reached the prison the director refused to enter my name on the prisoners' list because he needed an order from the governor. After some discussion the intelligence officer took a stamped paper from his pocket and wrote my name on it. I asked him, 'What are you doing? You should have my name on this order before you come to my house.' He said, 'No, it doesn't matter, it is stamped with the governor's stamp and we need only to enter your name. This is the way we always do it.'

First Glimpses of the Occupation

At 7 a.m. the intelligence officer came with an order, translated into Arabic, from the military governor of the West Bank to deport me without any charges. I was allowed to contact my lawyer as there was to be a special military committee at 9 a.m. in the governor's headquarters. The officer asked me if I wanted to contact my lawyer. I said yes, although I knew that this special committee would do nothing. In the past they deported many people by taking them directly from their homes to the border, but because of articles in the foreign press and protests made against this deportation procedure, the Israelis try to do something to make it appear legal.

So I said I wanted to contact my lawyer in Ramallah, and to meet him before 9 a.m. They said okay and left. At 9:15 a.m. they came and took me out of my cell, handcuffed and blindfolded me, and sent me in a police car to headquarters. They removed the handcuffs and blindfold, and at 9:30 I met my lawyer who had been waiting since 8:30. He asked what the problem was and I told him everything I knew. At 11 a.m. we went in front of the committee; they asked the lawyer to speak. He said, 'How can I speak if there are no charges. Tell me the charges and I will speak.' They read the order in Hebrew and translated it. The charges were violating security, inciting people against the authorities, organizing and leading demonstrations, and causing danger to the security of the people.

My lawyer said, 'These charges are nothing. You have to state that on that day, at that hour, he contacted so-and-so and told him such-and-such, and you have to give valid reasons.'

After that the head of the committee asked the military prosecutor to give detailed charges and make all the charges clear. So the prosecutor, after speaking to one of the intelligence officers sitting next to him, said, 'I have evidence, not from now but from eight years ago. And I have a big file, but because of security I can't say anything in front of Abdul Aziz or his lawyer or the soldiers who brought him here.' So he asked the head of the committee to send us out, and then he would give his evidence. My lawyer objected, but the head of the committee said that we had to go outside for five minutes and then come back. We went out, and after two minutes the intelligence officer came to take me. My lawyer stood up and said no, stay here and you will go back before the committee. But the officer handcuffed me, put me in a covered military truck and took me away. After half an hour they put me in a helicopter, after that in a truck, (all the time I was blindfolded), and at about 3:45 we were at the Lebanese border in Arquob. When I crossed the border, over the mines and under the barbed wire, they told me to walk straight towards a village in Lebanon, and not look back.

Source: *MERIP Reports*, No. 50, August 1976.

The West Bank and Gaza Strip at a Glance
The West Bank is mountainous and has relatively large amounts of rainfall. Its highest point lies 1,000 metres above sea level (in the Hebron region), and its lowest at the Dead Sea, 400 metres below sea level. The land is rocky and there are few forests. The Gaza Strip is a flat coastal area. The larger part is fertile, arable land; the south is made up of sand dunes.

Population: (Sept. 1979)
	West Bank	786,000
	Gaza Strip	442,300
	Total	1,228,300

43.7% of the population is under the age of 15.[1]

Area:
	West Bank	5,700 km²
	Gaza Strip	367 km²

In the West Bank approximately 210 km² are covered by populated areas and roads. 2,000 km² are farm land. In the Gaza Strip approximately 60 km² are used for human settlement and roads, 200 km² are farm land, barely half of which is irrigated.[2]

Important Cities:
In the West Bank
East Jerusalem	85,000	inhabitants
Nablus	42,000	"
Hebron	38,000	"
Bethlehem	14,000	"
Ramallah	12,000	"

In the Gaza Strip
Gaza	165,000	"
Khan Yunis	154,000	"[3]

Distribution of the Population:

	West Bank	Gaza Strip
Rural	70%	15%
Urban	30%	85%
In refugee camps	73,000	190,000
Population density	110/km^2	1,100/km^2 [4]

Housing Conditions

	West Bank	Gaza Strip
	(% of families)	
1-2 rooms	49.3	54.4
3 rooms	20.4	22.2
4 rooms	30.3	23.4

The average-size family in the West Bank has 6.7 persons and in the Gaza Strip 6.9.

33.5% of households in the West Bank and 13.9% in the Gaza Strip have running water.

45.8% of households in the West Bank and 35.7% in the Gaza Strip have electricity.[5]

Sources: (1) cf. *ILO 1980*, p. 134; the data for East Jerusalem is included in the data for the West Bank, estimated from *Statistics* 1975, p. 23. (2) *Tuma 1978*, p. 52 ff. (3) *Ibid.*, p. 56; statistics from the 1967 census. (4) *Ibid.*, p. 48; statistics for 1975. (5) *Statistics* 1978, p. 779.

Notes

1. The name has been changed.
2. *Dunam* — Arabic measurement of surface area; 1 *dunam* = 1000 m^2; 10 *dunams* = 1 hectare.
3. *Davar*, 12 December 1978.
4. The name has been changed.

This Land is Our Land

A Palestinian family in the West Bank

2. Faits Accomplis: The Jewish Settlements

> Now, my friends, we should spread a net of farmer colonies across the land which we want to acquire. When one makes a net, first one must hammer in the spikes on which the net is to be stretched. Then one spans strong ropes between these spikes. Then one weaves strong strings between the ropes, thereby producing a rough net which can then be refined with finer thread when needed. It is precisely in this way, I feel, we have to proceed. As long as our resources available for that purpose last, we have to acquire large pieces of land in all parts of the country — and, wherever possible, whose soil and water supply assure productive agriculture.
> — Franz Oppenheimer at the Sixth Zionist World Congress in 1902.[1]

What Franz Oppenheimer recommended to the Zionist settlers at the beginning of the century, Israeli governments have put into practice in the occupied territories since 1967. By the end of 1979, about 100 settlements had been built, or were in the process of being built, in the West Bank. In the Gaza Strip, there are twelve.[2] The building of these settlements follows, for the most part, strategic planning. Just as Oppenheimer had envisaged for the settlements of the 20s and 30s, the new settlements secure the Jewish presence in these areas, which are eventually to be incorporated into the Israeli state. The various Israeli administrations have never tried to make a secret of the strategic importance of the settlements. 'If you are asking me if the Israeli government has ever developed a comprehensive concept for the location of these settlements, then I must say such a plan has never been written,' replied Labour Foreign Minister, Yigal Allon, in 1976:

> However, if you look at the many decisions taken by the Israeli government in the past as to the locations of the settlements, then you will recognize that they do add up to a concept. Settlements are established in strategically important areas, along existing borders or near areas which will probably become borderlines in the future. . . . In my

opinion, settlement is one of the largest tools of leverage in our political struggle for defendable borders in the framework of a peace treaty. I see in these settlements . . . a large contribution to the security of our state.[3]

Judaization of the West Bank?: Inventory of Settlement Activities

It is difficult to obtain exact data about land area in the occupied territories, as this information is under Israeli control.[4] 'Concerning land purchases — the less we talk, the more we shall be able to do.' With these words Moshe Rivlin, the chairman of the Jewish National Fund, characterized the policy of the acquisition of land in the occupied territories.[5] Due to the reluctance of official agencies to publish more precise information, much of the data given are based upon estimates.[6] Without taking into account the Israeli measures used to acquire land in East Jerusalem or the conspicuously large areas of land whose ownership has not been settled, Israel has control over approximately 1.3 million *dunams*, more than 20% of the total land area. The occupying authority came into possession of this land through confiscation, expropriation and purchase of property, as well as through the destruction of Arab villages following the war in 1967. However, the Israeli authorities obtained the power of disposition over the largest part by taking over Jordanian and Egyptian 'state land'.

Table 1: Property Ownership in the Occupied Territories (excluding Jerusalem), 1979

Gaza Strip (dunams)	Land Classification	West Bank (dunams)
253,000	Arab private property	2,770,000
8,000	Private property of 'absentees', now under Israeli 'trusteeship'	430,000
40,000	'State land'	696,000
40	Land expropriated by Israel 'for security and military reasons'	61,000
–	Land purchases by Israeli citizens or institutions	80,000
800	Land registered before 1948 in the name of Jewish owners	30,000
63,000	Property with a status of undetermined ownership	1,530,000

Source: *Ha'aretz*, 1 November 1979, with reference to a study of the Defence Ministry.

Faits Accomplis: The Jewish Settlements

Map 1: Existing and Planned Israeli Settlements in the West Bank and Gaza Strip

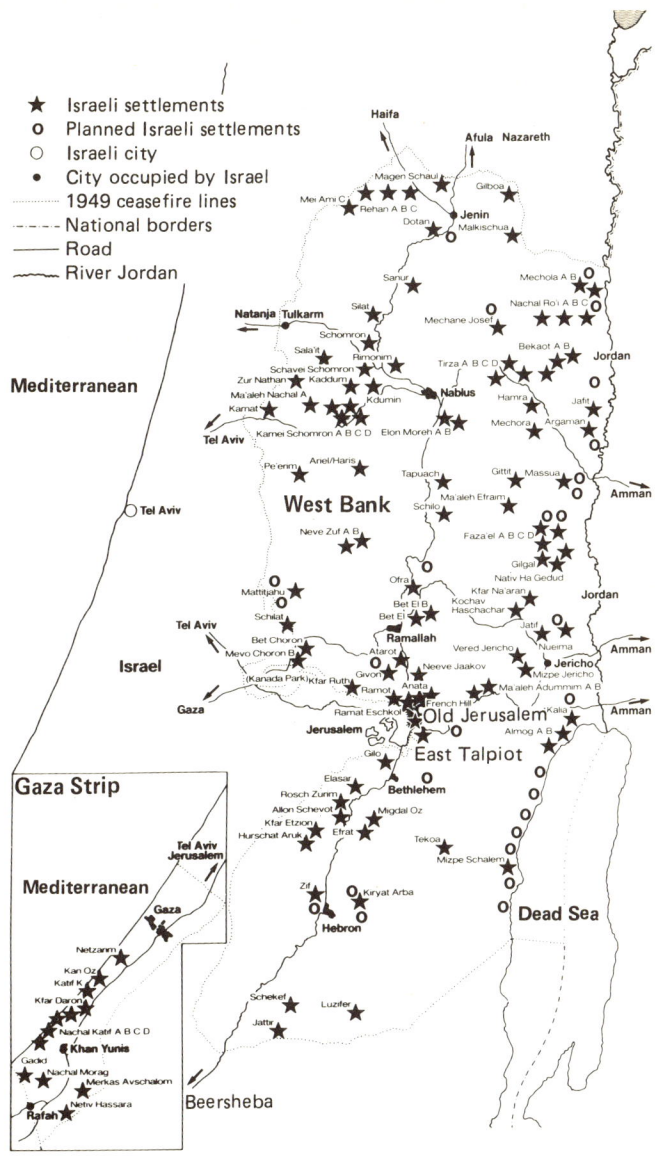

Source: U.N. *Special Committee 1979*, Map No. 3070.

State Land
Israel utilized the so-called 'state land' especially for the establishment of the new Jewish settlements in the West Bank:

> Israel has nominated as 'public domain' what is known as *meri* land — land given, pursuant to Ottoman law, to villages for cultivation. Some of this land was used by the village as a whole, some was divided between village families for their own cultivation. Jordan adopted this traditional system of land tenure. Although technically state land, the state has no right of usage to *meri* land. Such land passes by inheritance to heirs but cannot be transferred at will.[7]

Under the Jordanian government, this state land was not claimed for state use, but was left in private use as it had been for generations; however, the situation changed under Israeli occupation. The military government placed part of the land at the disposal of Jewish settlers. Palestinian farmers were forced out because they could not prove that the land was part of their property.

The takeover of public property contravenes international law, for according to the Hague Regulations (Article 55), state land does not become the property of the occupying authority.[8] On the contrary, the occupying authority is merely to act as administrator and is only to adopt temporary measures,[9] unless, in exceptional cases, urgent military or security matters demand something else. This does not justify transfer of land to Jewish settlers, since the establishment of civilian settlements and agricultural operations obviously creates a situation which cannot be reversed.

An Example: Frush Beit Dajan

Azzat Abu Iash from the village of Frush Beit Dajan owns a total of 100 *dunams* of land on which he built his home and cultivated tomatoes and other vegetables. In an average year he would earn approximately $1,200 from his vegetables. In 1970 the Israeli military government informed him that he did not have clear title to the land that he was farming and therefore the land was not his. All 100 *dunams* were confiscated from him. The Israelis then agreed to let him stay in the house by offering to rent the house and a total of six *dunams* back to him for a yearly fee. Although the house is small, the authorities have informed him that if he attempts to carry out any improvements to the building, it will be torn down. The nearby Israeli settlement of Hamra now cultivates his remaining 94 *dunams*.

Apart from the five *dunams* of 'rented' land which he continues to farm, he now has to work as a day labourer in order to live. He is considered a guest on a fraction of the land which he inherited from his father, and must pay a small rent to the

> Israelis in order to retain this 'privilege'.
> Source: *Quiring 1978*.

Confiscation and Expropriation

Jewish settlements are also being built on private Arab soil. So far, according to the latest Israeli figures, the military authorities have taken over by confiscation and expropriation, 61,000 *dunams* on the West Bank alone, 40,000 of which have been placed at the disposal of the settlers.[10] These official figures are surprising inasmuch as Israel has, up to now, always tried to deny the expropriation of private Arab property.[11]

In the last few years, Israel has tried everything to cover with a veil of legality the expulsion of Palestinian farmers from their land. Israel is a Western-style parliamentary democracy, thus there exists a legal basis for each confiscation, each expropriation, each expulsion.[12] This appearance of legality is provided by numerous laws and ordinances, the origins of which lie, in some cases, more than 30 years in the past.[13] 'Legal' expropriations have the following pattern. On the basis of Article 125 of the British Defence (Emergency) Regulations of 1945 under orders of the military commander of the region, an area is declared a 'restricted area'[14] for 'security reasons', which are never explained in detail. The British Mandate authorities issued these ordinances in order to control the disturbances between Jews and Arabs in Palestine after 1945 by limiting freedom of movement in the troubled areas. Israel has used these regulations in the West Bank and Gaza Strip since 1967 thus making it impossible for Palestinian farmers to cultivate their own land. After three years, during which entry into the restricted area is forbidden, the military administration makes use of a Jordanian law, according to which land that has not been cultivated for three consecutive years must be registered as state land.

This legal trick for covering up expropriations has enabled Israeli politicians to maintain, until recently, that Palestinian private property had not been expropriated for the establishment of settlements. So as not to use the revealing word 'expropriation', Prime Minister Menachem Begin issued the following guideline: 'The government would not expropriate land, but would seize it.'[15] In this way, the occupying authority exempted itself from the burdensome duty of paying compensation, which is required in the case of expropriation but not in that of confiscation.[16]

Nevertheless, in the past there have been 'real' expropriations. Typically, an uprooted family is offered compensation, the amount determined 'without any public hearing and without prior consultation with the community or individuals concerned'.[17] The amount offered as compensation is usually so insufficient that expropriation is practically the same as confiscation for which no compensation is paid. The Palestinian farmers who are affected have almost always declined these payments.

Some fear that accepting compensation might make them liable under

Jordanian law by which the sale of land to Israelis is a capital offence. Others, out of solidarity with their community and the national cause, refuse to accept compensation. Perhaps the majority refuse Israeli money because they do not want to sign away forever claims to properties they do not want to give up.[18]

Hadassah Hospital in Hebron: A Jewish settlement in the centre of an Arab town

> **An example: Kfar Haris**
> In February 1978, the Israeli army closed off 500 *dunams* of land owned by the villagers on a hill adjacent to Kfar Haris. The villagers have *Tapo* certificates (documents dating from the Ottoman period) authenticating their claim to ownership. The confiscated land was partially cultivated with grain and olive orchards. The olive orchard was destroyed by the Israeli army when construction of the settlement began. The military governor of the Tulkarem district told the *mukhtar*, head of the Kfar Haris village council, that the land was to be confiscated for the construction of an army base. The *mukhtar* replied that the

government's intention was to build not an army base, but a civilian Jewish settlement. The military governor denied this, but added that even if a civilian settlement were built on the site, 'this would be good for Kfar Haris since it would bring them new roads, water and electricity'. The civilian settlement of Kfar Haris now occupies a portion of the hill and it continues to expand ...

Hassan Masoud from Kfar Haris owns 36 *dunams* near the site of the settlement of Haris. In February, $33\frac{1}{3}\%$ of this land was confiscated when the army took 12 *dunams* for the construction of an access road for Haris. Hassan had planted cereals on the land; he estimates his loss for seeds, labour and the potential value of the crop he would have harvested to be $200. This is in addition to the value of the land itself, for which he has neither been offered nor would accept compensation.

Source: *Quiring 1978.*

NB: The Israeli settlement Ariel is located today on the private land of the Haris farmers. According to the Sharon Plan, this settlement is to become a Jewish centre in the northern part of the West Bank, where two belts of settlements will cross; 150,000 Israelis are to live there some day.

'Absentee' Property

Another source for the acquisition of land is the property of 'absentees'. According to a decree by the military government,[19] all land areas and buildings, whose legal owners left the country before, during or after the June War of 1967, are considered 'abandoned property'. As a result of the high rate of emigration even before the war, the large number of refugees from the war and Israel's constant refusal to allow them to return in any significant numbers,[20] the military authorities who administer this land as 'trustees', according to Article 8 of the decree, gained control of additional large areas of land in this way.

At first, only Palestinians staying in hostile countries, i.e. Arab countries, were considered to be absentees, even if they had only been on a brief business trip in Amman or Beirut on 7 June 1967.[21] Since 1978, however, the definition has been broadened to include as 'absentees' all former inhabitants of the West Bank who live abroad.[22] According to Israeli sources, 430,000 *dunams* fall under the category of 'trusteeship' by the occupying authority.[23]

This 'abandoned land' of absentees is also used for the establishment of Jewish settlements. The International Commission of Jurists noted that:

> much the greater part of the land for the Israeli settlements has been acquired under legislation giving title to public authorities over 'waste land' or 'abandoned land' or 'absentee property'. In other words the

settlements have to a substantial extent been established through the expropriation or confiscation of private property.[24]

> **Nothing but Problems Ahead**
> Under the Labour Party's administration, Israeli settlements were already being built in the Jordan Valley, which Israel declared a 'security zone.' One Jewish settler relates:
>
> First and foremost — the lands. Here in the Jordan Valley we cultivate thousands of *dunams* of rich, fertile agricultural land. It is — let us tell the truth — land belonging to Arabs. . . . The absentees, residents of Nablus and Tubas who fled to Jordan during the Six Day War cannot come back to Judea and Samaria [the West Bank] because at the bridges there is a list of names. And the people in charge of the bridges are strict, and if you are a landowner considered an absentee — they will not let you enter. Lo and behold, a few years ago one of those absentees managed somehow to return to Tubas. . . . He rushed to a lawyer, appealed to the High Court, and obtained his legal and kosher land back. The piece of land — a few good *dunams* — was situated in the midst of the plots of one of the valley's *moshavim* [settlements]. All the irrigation pipes ran through it. Don't ask how much haggling we had to do with him, with that absentee, before he agreed to exchange it for another plot, and stop being a pain in the neck. Now there will be autonomy. Even if it is agreed that no more Arabs are allowed to enter the West Bank — which is unreasonable and impossible . . . because those 'absentees' will be allowed to come back, by mistake — they will all be here. And then they will all parade to the courts, ours or theirs . . . present their titles, and that will be it: the settlements of the valley are left without land.
>
> And if this does not happen, something else will: some of the absentees' lands were not suitable for the needs of the settlements; they were either rocky, or somewhat remote . . . we exchanged them with land where the owner had remained in occupation. You think they enjoyed it? We exerted pressure, as they say. We, the government, the military government, the military. We pressured them in various ways, and they agreed. With the autonomy — they will go to court and say: 'What we exchanged was illegally exchanged. They threatened us, fired at us.'
>
> Source: *Ha'aretz* (Supplement), 20 October 1978.

Destruction
Property also came into the hands of the occupying authority by their destroying entire villages. It is estimated that as many as 20,000 houses,[25] were blown up in the first ten years of the occupation. In some cases — estimated at about 1,000 — the destruction of houses was imposed on 'suspicious' Palestinians as collective punishment[26] and its purpose therefore was not to annex territory.

Most well-known are the villages of Emmaus, Beit Nuba and Yalu which were razed to the ground after the end of the June War.[27] All three villages lay along the narrow Israeli corridor to Jerusalem. Their destruction served to provide security on the road from Tel Aviv to Jerusalem.[28] Even those critics who take a favourable view of the Israeli occupation policy cannot find justification for these measures[29] since international law only permits destruction when 'military necessity' absolutely requires it.[30]

Today, there are Israeli fields and a newly planted forest on the land where these three villages once stood.[31] Emmaus, Beit Nuba and Yalu were not the only villages to be destroyed.[32] However, after 1968, destruction of entire Arab villages and the subsequent annexation of the land were never carried out again.

Land Purchases
Shortly after the June War of 1967, the Israeli government empowered the Jewish National Fund and the Israeli Land Administration to purchase land in the occupied territories. These institutions privately carried out land purchases, the extent of which cannot be precisely determined. 'We purchase every piece of land, wherever it is and at any price and in any currency', is the motto of these organizations.[33] In an estimate for the American government in 1977, Professor John Ruedy assessed the amount of land acquired in the whole West Bank (including East Jerusalem) at more than 300,000 *dunams*.[34] According to Israeli figures however, the land is a matter of only 80,000 *dunams* in Judea and Samaria (i.e. excluding East Jerusalem).[35]

Private individuals and other institutions besides the two mentioned above were not allowed to acquire land for many years. Still, private land purchases were heard of again and again. Even though these transactions were illegal according to Israeli law, they were silently tolerated by the various administrations.[36] Taking part in these business deals were construction firms and land speculators, who — especially by means of their purchases in the area around Jerusalem — counted on an early annexation or, at least, the subsequent legalization of these deals.[37]

After many years of discussion in the Labour administration,[38] it was the right-wing, nationalist Likud administration under Menachem Begin which carried out another step along the way towards gradual annexation through the legalization of private purchases of land.[39]

The Settlers
In view of the considerable amount of land in the occupied territories already

This Land is Our Land

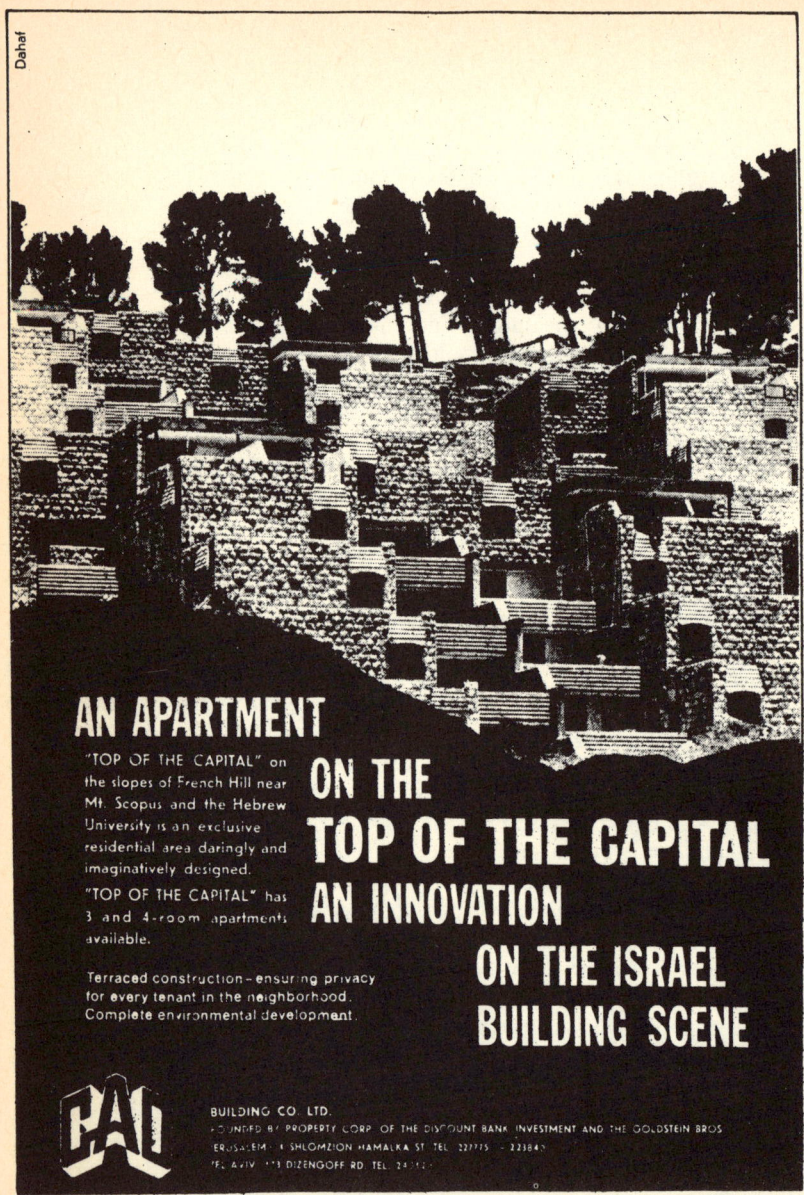

Advertisements for apartments in the ring of settlements around East Jerusalem

under Israeli control, the number of Jewish settlers, outside East Jerusalem, appears relatively modest. At the beginning of 1980, approximately 13,700 Jews were living in settlements in the West Bank and Gaza Strip.[40] To be added to that are approximately 70,000 Jews in East Jerusalem, which, according to Israeli interpretation, is no longer part of the West Bank, but rather part of the 'reunited Jerusalem'.

The organizations which support the settlements, that is those which, above all, send their members there to live and support them financially, represent almost the entire political spectrum of Israel. Only the parties and groups left of MAPAM are missing.[41]. The settlers are, therefore, a thoroughly heterogenous group.

Of all these organizations, Gush Emunim has caused the largest stir. Their belief in the historical Biblical right of the Jewish people to the land of Israel has developed into an explosive mixture of religious zeal and chauvinistic politics in which the Palestinian right to self-determination has no place. The activism of these groups, their 'practical idealism'[42] and their uncompromising political behaviour have evoked the sympathies of many Israelis who see in these men and women the embodiment of the Zionist ideal, pioneers in enemy surroundings who, under the most difficult of conditions, cultivate the land with a plough in one hand and a gun in the other.

> **Oil, the Jewish Mind and Arab Hands**
> We have come here to settle. We know very well that the Arabs don't want us here. On our clubhouse wall there is a picture of five people who died driving over a mine laid by Arabs. All of this won't stop us from staying here and developing a good neighbourhood. They'll get used to us. In spite of all other attempts, they'll have to resign themselves to the fact that we live here and will not yield.
>
> I don't know — maybe these areas belonged to the Arabs before the war. It is certain though, that these areas have not been cultivated during the last five or six years. As a result, the government assumed that they didn't belong to anyone and had people settle here. We are here on the land of our fathers and forefathers. Throughout history, Jews have resided here. Even if there have been occasional wars and these areas have been conquered, we still have enough evidence that Jews have lived in these places. These places belong to the Jews — this is the State of Israel. We don't find ourselves here thanks to someone's mercy but because of the historical past of the Jewish people. The tension between the Arab and Jewish peoples will continue to exist until the Arabs and the world realize that these areas belong to us on the basis of our historical past. First of all, we expect their recognition of the State of Israel, the Land of Israel, and that this land belongs to the People of Israel. This would actually solve the

> problem, for the Jewish people have nothing against an Arab minority living in harmony and peace in their country.
>
> I believe we have the right to live here. I believe it is a question of power. When we didn't have any power, they were on top. ... I believe there is enough room here for both Jews and Arabs. We have a lot of open land here which we can use and live on together! More than that, I believe when we find a way to live in peace, not only with the Palestinians but also with Jordan, Syria, Saudi Arabia and all these countries, then — as far as the way of life is concerned — the first America would come into being. For the oil is here, the Jewish mind is here and Arab hands are here. Therefore, we have everything we need.
> Interview with a Jewish settler from Gittit.
>
> Source: the school television series, 'Alltag ohne Frieden — Menschen in Nahost-Konflikt', (People in the Middle East Conflict'), West Berlin broadcasting station, SFB, printed in part in the book of the same name by Neumann/Seewald/Sterzing, Berlin, 1977, p. 37 ff.;

In other settlements — especially those of kibbutz organizations in the Jordan Valley — the religious component is missing, though they do not doubt the right of Jews to settle there. The Zionist pioneer ideal seems rather distant to other groups; for example, to the orthodox Jews living in Kiryat Arba near Hebron, an urban settlement with light industry. For them, life in Hebron is a religious commandment, the fulfilment of which must be carried out, using force against the resident Palestinians if necessary.

Many of the settlements — especially on the frontiers — are paramilitary, agricultural settlements. At first, soldiers from the so-called Nahal units, serving part of their military duty in one of these agricultural defence villages, establish the necessary infrastructure: water and electrical systems, prefabricated houses, fences and guard installations, and the first cultivation of the soil. After a while these units are replaced by civilian settlers. Former Prime Minister Golda Meir described these defence villages as being not 'ordinary settlements but military agricultural outposts'.[43] Certainly, the terms chosen ('security reasons', 'military purposes'), are necessary in order to retain a veil of legality over the expropriations which made the establishment of these settlements possible. Nevertheless, the International Commission of Jurists is asking, in this context, what Israel's reaction would be, should these settlements be bombed during military disputes.[44] Would Israel accept these settlements being considered military objectives by, for example, the Palestinian Fedayeen?

Financing
The settlements are worth a lot of money to the government. For the fiscal

Faits Accomplis: The Jewish Settlements

year 1980-81 enormous sums of money were again made available for the establishment of new settlements. The Ministry of Agriculture's budget shows a doubling of the funds for settlements — I£1.3 billion for settlement purposes. A further 1.6 billion was given to the Department of Housing for the completion of settlements. The expansion of existing settlements is also covered by an item in the budget of the World Zionist Organization; I£2.6 billion is allotted for the 'maintenance of equipment and temporary structures' in the occupied territories. The Defence Ministry estimates its expenditures for maintaining the military administration, security functions, troops, road construction, etc., at I£1.5 billion. Experts estimate Israel's total expenditures for the territories — including amounts spent by various other departments — to be about I£7 billion.[45] These estimates do not include the substantial sums of money with which other organizations and associations — especially Jewish communities abroad — support Jewish settlements: these sums may run into millions.

Security Considerations and 'Historical Rights': The Zionist Settlement Policy.

'Judea and Samaria [the West Bank] are Israeli lands belonging to the Jewish people.'[46] 'Settlement is a right and a duty. We have and we will continue to fulfil that right and that duty.'[47]

These words of Prime Minister Menachem Begin are characteristic of the settlement policy of his administration. One of his first acts after his election victory in 1977 was to visit the 'wild' (meaning that even as late as the previous Israeli government, this settlement was officially considered illegal) settlement Qaddum. To the religious fanatics of Gush Emunim, Begin stated: 'We are standing here on liberated ground . . . there will be many more Qaddums. We will establish new settlements in Judea and Samaria, along the Gaza Strip and in the Golan Heights!'[48]

The Bible as Land Register

The decisive motivation for the settlement policy of Begin's coalition government consisting of liberal, nationalist, chauvinistic and religious factions, is based upon the 'historic rights' of the Jewish nation. The basis for this belief in the permanent Jewish ties to Eretz Israel (the Land of Israel) is the divine promise of God: '. . . and you shall take possession of the land and settle in it, for I have given the land to you to possess it'. (Numbers 33:53) For the Zionists, this repatriation of the land of their forefathers after centuries in the Diaspora means the fulfilment of this divine promise. In Biblical times it was Judea and Samaria in particular which formed the core of the Kingdoms of Solomon and David.

Today, to realize the 'historic rights' of the Jewish people, it is necessary, above all, by establishing settlements on the West Bank, to create a situation in which it is impossible for any other power to regain sovereignty over this part of the 'liberated homeland'. According to the religious-nationalist forces in the government, whoever relinquishes the 'historical claims' to these areas undermines the basis of legitimacy of the Israeli state. For if the Jewish right to Judea and Samaria did not exist, then they would have even less right to claim, for example, Ashkelon, an Israeli city on the coastal plain, since this area is not part of the Biblical kingdom.

Members of Begin's cabinet as well as Begin himself never tire of repeating these demands at every opportunity. Even today, the motto of Begin's Herut (Freedom) Party stems from a poem by the militant Zionist fighter, Vladimir Jabotinsky:[49] 'Both banks of the Jordan — this side is ours and the other side too.' According to other Zionist parties as well[50] — the 'historical claims' extend to parts of the Jordanian Kingdom, so that for the Jewish people to have the territory of the state of Israel as well as Judea and Samaria represents a political concession on the part of the Arab people.'[51]

Secure Borders
In addition to the supposed 'historical rights', the security argument forms the second important pillar of legitimacy for the Jewish settlements. According to the conception of Israeli politicians, the state still has no final 'secure' border 'capable of defence'. The new defence village settlements should help secure existing and possible future borders, in that they serve as the first military bulwark against possible Arab attacks.

The much praised security argument is not only characteristic of the narrow, political perspective of many Israeli politicians. It also allows political endeavours for peace to degenerate into a mere continuation of the military policy under a different name. An extreme example of this fact occurred in the first hours of the 1973 War, when the Syrian attack on the Golan Heights made the evacuation of settlers necessary. The settlements handicapped the Israeli defence position more than they helped, since the evacuation tied up people and materials, thereby causing valuable time to be lost.[52]

> **Guidelines for Public Relations**
> On 23 September 1977 the Prime Minister's adviser for overseas information announced the following guidelines for public speaking:
> We must put an end to the use of the term *West Bank*. These territories have names, and only these names may be used: *Judea and Samaria*. This usage must be strictly observed both vis-a-vis non-Israelis abroad and in Israel itself. The term 'annexation' as applied to the idea of including these territories in the State of Israel must be wiped out. One can only annex land that belongs to someone else. The use of the term *annexation* only strengthens the false and mendacious claims of the Arabs and their friends regarding Arab ownership of Eretz Israel, and may even appear to grant legitimization to the Jordanian conquest.
> When referring to the idea of including Judea, Samaria and Gaza

> in the State of Israel the terms to be used are *inclusion* or *the application of Israeli law*, according to the circumstances — but on no account *'annexation'*!
>
> The very use of the term *return of territory* has helped the Arab argument that the territory in question *belongs to them*, since one obviously does not speak of *returning* something except to its *owners*. In any event, the idea that Judea, Samaria and Gaza (let alone Sinai and the Golan) belong to the Arabs has taken root among many people (even people of goodwill) in the world — the majority of whom, including journalists and politicians, are not professional historians or experts on Zionism. Since the peace negotiations (on their understanding) will be first about territory, ... settlement in these territories appears to them unnecessary and provocative. ... It is clear to them that Israel will have to return the territories in the end.
>
> In short: the conflict is not a result of territorial conquest but of the refusal of the Arabs to recognize our rights to our motherland. ...
>
> Source: *Israleft*, No. 132, 1 September 1978.

Despite numerous contradictory statements, the Israeli military cannot avoid facing up to the frightening possibilities of modern warfare and its consequences for the strategic importance of the settlements. 'As far as the security of the Jewish state is concerned, the establishment of settlements has no great significance.'[53]

Gush Emunim

From innumerable statements and decisions, it is clear that the current Israeli government is determined to maintain the occupation for an indefinite period of time in order to secure long-term Jewish control in this part of Palestine. On the other hand, the government must defend its settlement policy against criticism from the Israeli opposition, as well as — and this is much more difficult — criticism from abroad. While basically agreeing with the militant aims of the Gush Emunim movement, the Begin government is in a different situation since it also has to pursue foreign policy and in no way wants to endanger the separate peace with Egypt. The international situation, the fear of undesirable consequences American criticism of the settlement policy could have (a cut in financial aid and arms shipments) forced the government to put a damper now and then on the extreme demands of militant groups of settlers. That does not mean that during international negotiations, the activities of Gush Emunim play no part. They put great internal pressure on Menachem Begin, demonstrating the difficulties he would have if he made substantial concessions. Foreign policy tactics actually increase the pressure at home from the militant followers for whom the settlement of the occupied territories proceeds too slowly and who accuse the government of giving in to the Palestinians on the West Bank as well as to the Egyptian negotiators.

Thus, the extreme right wing of Begin's own Likud faction[54] has split due to the 'compromising', even 'traitorous', policy of the government towards Egypt and has formed a new party, the Tehiya Party (Party of National Rebirth). Without hesitation, this party is put by many Israelis into a class with European fascist movements.[55] The Tehiya Party demands not only the dissolution of the peace agreements with Egypt but also 'the closing down of camps and deportation of the refugees to Saudi Arabia and other oil-producing countries in urgent need of labour'.[56]

The growing nationalist enthusiasm finds its most prominent expression in Gush Emunim[57] — the 'Block of the Faithful'.

> **'The Chosen People'**
> We have settled in Eilon Moreh [a wild settlement] since we are chosen to settle the land which God gave our forefathers. Our settling here has in itself no security reasons, but rather serves to fulfil this mission.
> — statement of the representative of Gush Emunim to the Israeli High Court of Justice.
>
> Source: *Davar*, 31 August 1979.

In the settlement concept of Gush Emunim, security arguments play only a subordinate role. In achieving their 'historical right', its adherents consider the establishment of settlements even in the midst of Arab people in the most densely populated areas of the West Bank to be of special importance. Being at variance with the settlement concept of earlier Labour governments, they tried to realize their aims without official permission and by force. The illegal settlements were not only a provocation for the Palestinians living there, they were likewise a challenge to the government, which, under public pressure, could seldom afford to have the 'wild' settlements cleared by the army.

> **Israeli Ethics**
> Interview with Mr. Gershon, political secretary of Gush Emunim:
> *Gershon*: It is impossible for two people to have a right to the same piece of land. We have an absolute right to this land and the Arabs have none whatsoever.
> *Q*: Doesn't the fact that they've been living on this land for centuries give them a right to it?
> *Gershon*: No, not in relation to the importance of our right.

> *Q*: Aren't you afraid that this ethic could hurt us and could, for instance, cause the total isolation of the Israeli state in the world?
> *Gershon*: I prefer Israeli ethics to world ethics.
>
> Source: *Ha'aretz*, 2 November 1979.

The motto of these religious nationalists is 'All of Israel for the People of Israel'. Their followers emphasize their independence from the state and its institutions. They consider themselves to be above the law and claim to be representatives of a divine authority. They, meanwhile, have a number of settlements and receive substantial loans as an officially recognized settlement movement. They possess weapons and communication installations and demonstrate their power in grand style.

Certainly the members of the Tehiya Party and the followers of Gush Emunim represent the right wing in Israel's political spectrum; yet, the latter are much more than a small, non-influential, extra-parliamentary minority. A solid majority of the Knesset deputies — not only members of the right wing and religious government parties, but also many representatives of the labour parties — insists on the historically-based right of the Jewish people to settle in the West Bank and gives political support to the demands of this militant group. Gush Emunim has its most vehement spokesman in the influential Minister of Agriculture, Ariel Sharon, a general and war hero of 1973 who is responsible for the settlement activity in the occupied territories. He holds all of the important offices for settlement issues — cabinet minister, head of the Israel Land Administration, chairman of the government's settlement committee. He is not only the 'strong man' in Begin's cabinet, but also 'the hope of all anti-democratic elements in Israel. . . . His philosophy can be summarized as follows: "Everything that is good for Israel, is also justified."'[58]

The Sharon Plan

Minister Sharon drafted the government's current, official settlement concept which was named the 'Sharon Plan' after him. His plan provides for the construction and strengthening of various Jewish-populated settlement belts; his strategic concept characteristically includes all of Palestine. With regard to the West Bank, this plan calls for a strip of Jewish settlements extending along its western border, an axis of Israeli settlements runs north-south, which would control the passes and intersections in the hills of the northern West Bank. It is bordered on the east by an Arab-populated strip of land — the area between Jenin and Ramallah. Another broad strip in the Jordan Valley forms the last of these Jewish settlement belts running north and south.[59] Of course, in the future the main settlement centres already existing around Jerusalem, in the Etzion region and near Hebron, are to be further expanded. In order to prevent the military isolation of the Jewish belts and to weaken adjoining Arab-populated areas through separation, the settlement strips running north and south are intersected by at least one such belt extending from west to east, thereby connecting the Jordan Valley with the coastal plain and cutting Arab cities and towns between Nablus and Ramallah into two halves. Sharon also has special plans for Jerusalem.

> Jerusalem will not remain the capital of Israel if it does not have a Jewish majority. The answer is to construct satellite cities all around the Arab sections of Jerusalem. . . . Within 20 to 30 years, we must reach the point where there are a million Jewish inhabitants in Greater Jerusalem, including the cities surrounding it.[60]

The perspectives for the Gaza Strip changed when the agreement with Egypt over the return of the Sinai made the dissolution of the Israeli settlements in the Sinai northern region unavoidable. In April 1979, the Jewish Agency made it known that it would found 20 new settlements between the cities Gaza and Khan Yunis within the next three years. This new strip of settlements was named Pithat Shalom (peace corridor). Fifteen of the planned settlements are to replace the 15 settlements of the Yamit territory in northern Sinai, which are to be evacuated. 'We are not evacuating settlements,' said the chairman of the Jewish Agency, Arye Dulzin, 'but transferring them.'[61] This fully incorporates the Gaza Strip, which is densely populated anyway, into the Israeli settlement strategy.

Settlements Without End
Since the signing of the peace agreement with Egypt in March 1979, and parallel to the negotiations over 'autonomy', the Israeli government has carried on its settlement policy, contrary to international law[62] and despite international protest. This occurs at three levels. Firstly, Sharon and other members of the cabinet demonstrate, more than just verbally, their determination to carry on settlement activity in the occupied territories. Large sums of money are allotted for the establishment of new settlements. Almost daily, Israeli newspapers report on new plans and decisions by the responsible committees.[63] Secondly, the expansion of already existing settlements is being worked on. In spite of the economic crisis and protests from the under-privileged classes in Israel[64] who demand more money for social welfare, there is no lack of funds for this expansion.[65] Finally, the consolidation of all Jewish settlements, technically and administerially, is expedited. In the near future, all settlements are to be served by a common water system and are to receive their power from the Israeli electricity system. In April 1979, the forming of 'area councils' in the West Bank and Gaza Strip was begun,[66] uniting the various centres of settlement into a political structure to bring about Jewish self-administration.

In spite — or maybe because — of the autonomy negotiations in progress,[67] Israel, under the centralized control of the cabinet minister in charge of settlements, Ariel Sharon, continues its efforts to change the

Faits Accomplis: The Jewish Settlements

Map 2: Israeli 'Security Areas' according to the Sharon Plan

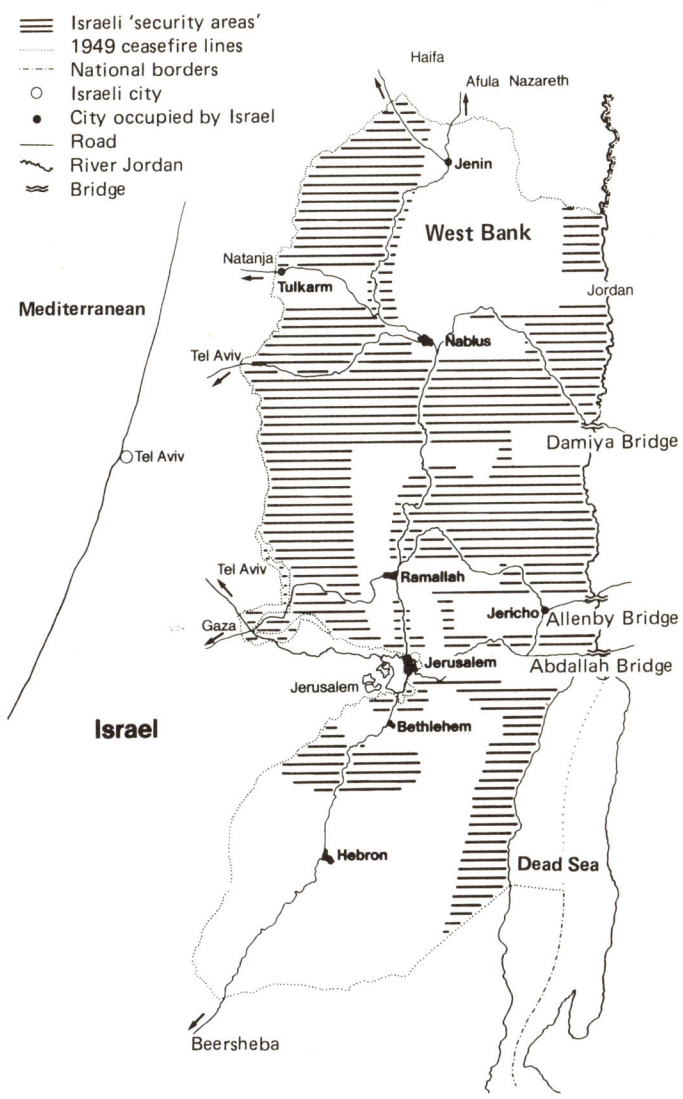

character of the Arab-Palestinian West Bank: where Jewish settlements once stood isolated in an Arab area, Arab settlements will one day stand isolated in a Jewish area. 'It is clear that Jewish and Arab peoples will have to live together,' says Sharon.[68] This sounds peaceful enough but Judaization of the West Bank and Gaza Strip actually means for the Palestinians nothing more than 'living together' on Israeli terms. Israel is spreading out as far as the Jordan,[69] while the Arab population is restricted to enclaves. If it goes the way the Likud government would like, then the Palestinians in the rest of Palestine will suffer the same fate as the Arab people in Israel: an unpopular minority discriminated against in their own country.

Security instead of Peace

Especially since Begin took office, the settlement policy of the Israeli government has appeared prominently in the press in connection with the peace negotiations with Egypt, yet this should not lead one to believe that this administration was the first to begin the Jewish settlement of the occupied territories. The coalitions dominated by the Labour Party, in power until 1977, also established Jewish settlements in the occupied territories. As early as September 1967, the government authorized the first civilian settlement on the West Bank, Kfar Etzion. The establishment of this settlement was justified at that time by 'security reasons'.[70] By 1972, there were almost 50 settlements in the occupied territories, although the majority were in the Golan Heights and in northern Sinai.[71]

The governments' priorities within the settlement policy clearly show that the strategic aspects were of the utmost importance. Once the establishment of the first Jewish settlement became known, the Israeli government tried to play it down. The United Nations Israeli ambassador gave to understand that the few settlements of little importance were no indication of any decision as to the final status of the occupied territories.[72] Even the reference to the purely military character of the settlements had the function of dispelling fears regarding a possible Jewish takeover of the occupied territories.

At least by 1968, after the legalization of the 'wild' settlement by religious Jews in Hebron[73] (which later became the settlement of Kiryat Arba), it became clear that statements made by cabinet members about the legalization only represented half the truth. This urban settlement lacked any military characteristics and, without a doubt, demonstrated the intention of its inhabitants to settle permanently. Actually, the only real reasons for the establishment of Kiryat Arba were religious ones — the right of the Jews to settle in their 'historical homeland'.

The ideology of the Labour government at that time which made its settlement policy legitimate was not essentially different from that of its successor. Whereas the governments of the Labour Party normally emphasized pragmatic arguments (for example, 'the settlements ensure the security of Israel'), representatives of the current administration usually stress the national aspect ('we have the right to settle in all of Eretz Israel, the land of our forefathers'). There is no basic difference or contradiction between the two arguments — they are simply the expression of two different trends within the Zionist movement. The Labour faction emphasizes the principle of 'liberation of the Jewish people', while the ideology of the reactionary, middle-class faction emphasizes the principle of 'liberation of Jewish soil'.[74]

The Allon Plan
A plan designed by Yigal Allon, Foreign Minister in the Rabin administration, shows where, in the opinion of the social democratic, Labour faction of the Zionist movement, settlements should be established for security reasons. This settlement concept, known as the Allon Plan, although never officially accepted by the administrations of Golda Meir or Yitzhak Rabin, virtually determined the policy of the Labour Party when in office, and represents, even today, the basis of their policy in opposition. According to his concept, as Allon again outlined in June 1979, the southern Jordan Valley and the desert region parallel to it, with the exception of one or two Arab enclaves, were unpopulated areas and could form a 'solid, continuous defence wall'.[75] Kiryat Arba near Hebron could be connected in the east to the Israeli 'security area' in the Judean desert and in the northwest to the settlements in the Itzion block. Adapting his concept to fit in with the Begin government's autonomy plan, Allon suggested that, on the West Bank, the populated sections of the northern districts (i.e. the region from Ramallah to Jenin, including Nablus), and in the south, the cities of Bethlehem and Hebron, as well as the mountain villages, would lie in the sphere of autonomy. The annexation of East Jerusalem, or the 're-unification', is also considered to be irreversible and 'forever' by the Labour Party. In Allon's opinion, Israel needs the Gaza Strip as a buffer zone in the south and as a mini-substitute for the settlements in the Rafah area given up after the Israeli-Egyptian peace agreement.

> In other words, all the areas densely populated by Arabs will be included within the territory under Palestinian autonomy. . . . The security areas . . . will remain under Israeli control by means of the military government's authority, . . . the Israeli Defence Force's formations, and the integration of existing and new settlements in the territorial defence.[76]

Allon's plan has always been disputed, even in the ranks of his own party, although one could see in it a little of what the Labour-dominated governments had wanted to offer the Arabs as a 'territorial compromise'. According to Allon, the Arab-populated areas in the West Bank should not be entitled to autonomy of any sort, but should be returned to Jordanian sovereignty, while the 'security areas' should, by whatever means necessary, remain in Israeli hands. Criticism of such plans for peace came from both the 'hawks' and the 'doves'. To the 'hawks', such as the then Defence Minister, Moshe Dayan, and the current leader of the Labour opposition Shimon Peres, this

This Land is Our Land

Map 3: Israeli 'Security Areas' according to the Allon Plan

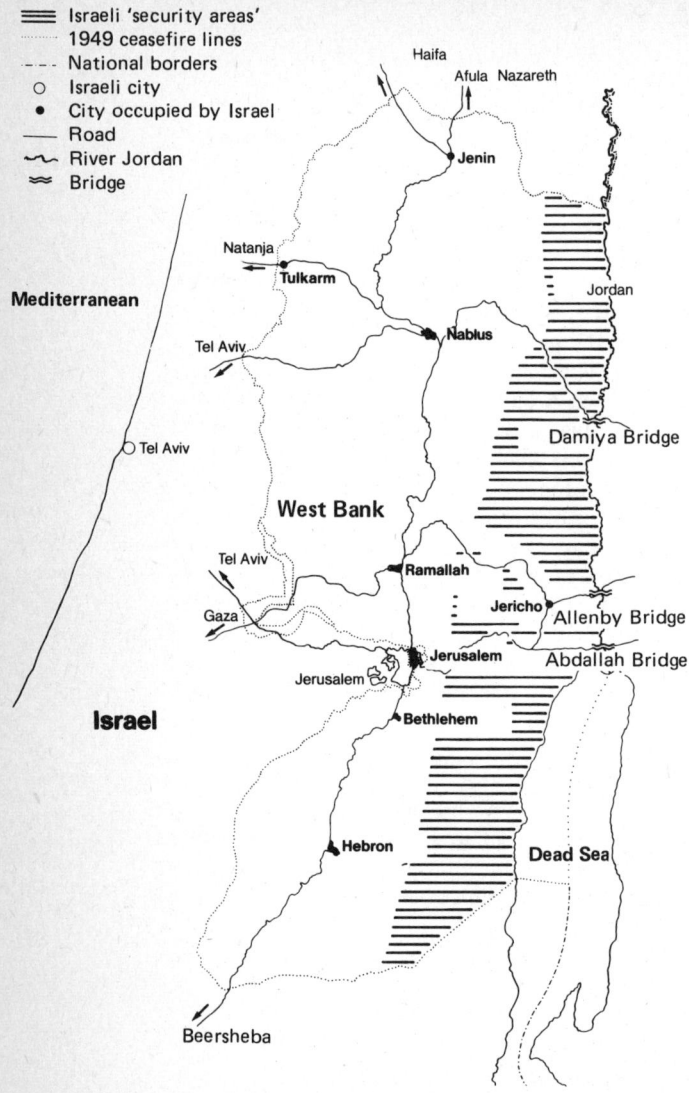

plan demonstrates too great a willingness to compromise. The few 'doves' to speak out for more concessions to the Arabs could not hold their own, especially since the Nationalist Religious Party, as a coalition partner in the government, was pleading for a forced settlement policy in the occupied territories.[77] Further, the Labour governments were subject to the pressure of Gush Emunim and its followers in the government, so that the policy of Rabin's cabinet toward the illegal settlements of this fanatical group always had the character of brinkmanship: giving the army the command to clear the settlements would always endanger the already shaky consensus in the coalition; yielding to the settlers meant the loss of government authority and international difficulties.

'They Take Our Land': The Settlements from a Palestinian Point of View

Although relatively few people in the West Bank are directly affected by the expropriations, every Palestinian feels threatened by the establishment of settlements. The population is confronted daily not only with the occupying authority, which it does not accept and to which it will never submit, but also with the settlements which are evidence of the fact that the occupation is not temporary, but planned to last. Whoever takes land away from the Palestinians strikes the vital nerve of this still predominantly agricultural society. It is abundantly clear that the Israelis are not settling on Palestinian soil merely to give up houses, fields and gardens just a few years later. Using the argument of their historical right and the Biblical promise, the Jewish settlers dispute the Palestinian people's right to live there too. In the Jewish settlements, the Israelis' determination to take away the Palestinians' right to their own land is manifested in the efforts of the Israelis to make the Palestinians guests in their own country. This denial of the Palestinians' right to their homeland is not an abstract process, it makes itself apparent in the daily life of the Arab population on the West Bank.

Water
For the Palestinians, the Israeli settlers are not only competitors for the soil but also for another vital resource — water. The military government takes the lead in this dispute as well. The Palestinians receive whatever is left over by Israel and have no influence over the securing or distribution of water.

Mekorot, the Israeli National Water Authority, has been responsible for the public water supply in the West Bank and Gaza Strip since 1967. Control of the water is a key factor to the political and economic control of the territories. In the first years of the occupation, the water rights of the Palestinian farmers were already encroached upon by the Israeli authorities. In the Gaza Strip, as well as in the Jordan Valley, wells for Israeli settlements were dug right next to springs which Palestinian farmers used for watering their animals, irrigating their fields and obtaining their own drinking water. In some cases, these new wells, for the exclusive use of the new settlements, literally drained the water away from the Palestinians; the farmers affected have not had enough water ever since.[78]

'They Take Our Land' – the first step, *'Land Reclamation'* signs of the Jewish National Fund

According to figures from Mekorot, at least 17 new wells have been drilled in the West Bank since 1968, wells which supply not only Jewish settlements but also Israel with water. In addition, four springs belonging to 'absentee owners' were taken over for Israeli use. Since 1967, the Israeli National Water Authority has not approved the construction of a single well by the Palestinians for agricultural purposes. In the last 12 years, the construction of only seven wells for drinking water has been permitted.[79] Thus, the Palestinians' water provisions have worsened because of the occupation. As long as the water is administered by the Israeli National Water Authority – according to the 'autonomy' plan, this will remain the case in the future – and new wells may only be dug with Israeli permission, the Palestinian farmers will continue to be dependent on the generosity of the Israeli occupying authority.

Land

The loss of arable land also has drastic economic consequences for the Palestinian farmers. The uprooting of farmers whose land had been expropriated and the change in the trade structure of entire villages can clearly be seen by reference to one example, the Rafidiye village near Bethlehem.
In 1970, 70% of all workers here still made a living for themselves and their families by the farming of 3,000 *dunams* of land south of the village. In 1973, almost the entire 3,000 *dunams* were declared 'closed off' for the establishment of the Tekoa settlement. Now, Rafidiye only has a few hundred *dunams* of relatively poor land left. The *mukhtar* of the village says no one can live from farming any more. Most of the village workers must now earn their living as day labourers in neighbouring Bethlehem or in Israel.[80]

By having their land taken from them, the Palestinian farmers lose that which defines their existence to the greatest extent and that which is, therefore, most valuable to them. Their economic base is pulled out from under them. The people continue to live in their villages and have perhaps even found remunerative employment at another location. But they no longer have the possibility of returning to their land, even if the political and economic situation changed or if they could no longer find work somewhere else. Like so many other Palestinians, the only alternative remaining to them is emigration.

Jewish-Palestinian Coexistence

The Jewish settlers often let the Palestinians know who is boss in the occupied territories. A particularly extreme example of this is the Jewish orthodox settlers living in Kiryat Arba in the immediate proximity of Hebron. According to an Israeli newspaper: 'In their view, they maintain law and order. The Arabs complain that the settlers beat them whenever they like, that the settlers occasionally shoot to scare the people and that they damage Arab property.'[81] The settlers do not simply make their presence felt but understand themselves to be a legitimate 'security force'. In the middle of March 1976, Rabbi Levinger, the 'spiritual leader' of Kiryat Arba, said on Israeli television that he had 'ordered' the inhabitants of the settlement to 'shoot to hit' whenever they had stones thrown at them while 'patrolling' in Hebron.[82]

Relations between the Jewish and Arab people have deteriorated rapidly in the last few years. There have been repeated incidents of radical Jewish settlers provoking fights, setting fierce dogs loose on Palestinian residents, blocking streets and damaging Arab property.[83] The settlers have even made use of their weapons, shooting at demonstrating Palestinians and harmless passers-by.[84] In the Patriarch's Cave, sacred to Moslems and Jews, which the patriarch Abraham allegedly bought as a tomb for his wife Sarah, Jewish zealots occasionally desecrate Muslim sacred relics and provoke the Palestinians to acts of revenge.[85]

The Israeli military forces usually look on and do nothing. Palestinians would be locked up for a long time for such acts of disturbing the peace or insurrection, but Jewish persons are hardly ever punished.[86] Jewish settlers who shot and killed two Arabs during a fight with Palestinian youths in the town of Halhul near Hebron were set free after only a few days in jail.[87] On the other hand, drastic measures are taken in cases of infringement of the law by Palestinians. For example, the occupying authority reacted to days of violent altercations between Jews and Moslems at the Patriarch's Tomb with 200 arrests, 74 of those arrested were sentenced in a summary hearing to long terms of imprisonment; a 16-day curfew was imposed on Hebron, and after five days residents were permitted for the first time to leave their homes for one hour to go shopping.[88] Not one of the Jewish participants was arrested. In another instance, following the murder of a young Jewish settler in February 1980, the 35,000 inhabitants of Hebron were confined to quarters[89] while the Jewish perpetrators, who had shot and killed several Arab citizens, received minor sentences, if they were arrested at all.[90]

The Jewish extremists can carry out their anti-Arab activities knowing that they will not be held responsible and that they 'are not far removed from Prime Minister Begin's opinion'.[91] Up to now, the Israeli government has done nothing to put an end to these provocative acts. On the contrary, approving a Jewish settlement in the heart of the Arab city Hebron contributed to a heightening of the tensions which, on 2 May 1980, reached a bloody climax with an attack by Palestinian residents on Jewish theology students.[92]

Coexistence from an Arab Point of View

In the following interview, three mayors from the West Bank respond to Israeli claims that the Jewish settlers and Arab population live together peacefully:

Q: Moshe Dayan once said that the establishment of Jewish settlements in occupied territories would establish coexistence between Jews and Arabs. What kind of relations exist between the Jewish settlers and Arab inhabitants living near them? What is the attitude of the settlers to the people of the localities they settle in?

Shak'a: I really have to laugh at this. I cannot see any kind of relationship between Jewish settlers and the Arab inhabitants. The settlers come with their guns and force themselves into an area. They destroy property and enclose themselves with barbed wire and electric fences. There can be no coexistence in this way. The settlers' hostility to the Arab people is deeply ingrained, and is reflected in their conduct. They are the most fanatical of all Zionists. In Elon Moreh, the settlement outside Nablus, they were saying 'we shall hang Bassam Shak'a'. I personally told Defence Minister Weizman that settlements only cause hatred.

> With regard to Nablus, no inhabitants from Nablus work in Jewish settlements for the Zionist settlers.
>
> *Milhem*: Dayan and his settlements have proved that settlements decrease the chances for peace, because the settlers in the last 12 years have proven that they have come here, not to co-exist but to take our land, terrify us and shout at our children and students. The girl killed last March in Halhul was shot by a Kiryat Arba settler. During October 1976, seven people from Halhul were injured by Jewish settlers from nearby settlements. Is this co-existence when they have to fence themselves in behind a two-fold electrified fence?
>
> *Qawasmeh*: The settlers are taking land here by force. How can we trust them when they take away our land? Officially, there exist no relations whatsoever between the people of Hebron and the settlers in Kiryat Arba just outside our town. I have never dealt with them. I told the military governor that we will accept Jews living in Hebron if they do the same, and allow our Palestinian Arab people to return to Ramleh, Jaffa or Haifa.
>
> Postscript: Fahad Qawasmeh and Mohammed Milhem were deported by the Israeli authorities in May 1980 following an attack on Jewish settlers in Hebron; precisely one month later, Bassam Shak'a lost both his legs in a bombing apparently carried out by Israeli extremists.
>
> Source: *Journal of Palestine Studies*, No. 33, Autumn 1979, p. 118 ff.

The Path to Confrontation: Opposition to the Settlements

The inhabitants of the West Bank and Gaza Strip have used widely differing means of defending themselves against the establishment of settlements, expropriation of their land and Jewish takeover of their homeland. The mildest method takes the form of open letters and petitions to Israeli politicians and military authorities, as well as reports and appeals to international organizations. In the past few years these have been written by a wide variety of persons and institutions in the occupied territories.

> **A Memorandum from Nablus concerning the Israeli Government's Settlement Policy**
> His Excellency the Defence Minister
> c/o The Honourable Military Governor of the City of Nablus
>
> The decision of the Israeli Ministerial Special Committee concerned with new settlements was no surprise to the Nablus City Council nor to any of the patriotic Councils signatory to this Memorandum. This decision was only a reflection of the expansionist settler-state policy, the implementation of which started immediately after the June War with the annexation of Jerusalem, contrary to and in defiance of U.N. resolutions, international law, and the Geneva and Hague Conventions.
>
> This policy, which has continued throughout the period of occupation, deprives Palestinian citizens of their property and encircles their cities with a ring of settlements designed for still further expansion at the expense of our people. Regrettably, all this creates 'new facts', and leads us further away from peace.
>
> After the establishment of numerous settlements in the Jordan Valley, settlement and expansionist attempts commenced in the proximity of the city of Nablus. The first was the attempt of a group of Jewish extremists to establish a settlement near Sebastia. The citizens' steadfast rejection of settlement policy in principle, and their continued protest and resistance prevented that fanatic group from carrying out their objectives. A similar attempt was made in Kafr Kaddum, where the extremists established a settlement by force of arms with the encouragement and protection of the authorities.
>
> The claim that existing or yet-to-be-established settlements are only military outposts should not be accepted because of the agricultural nature of these settlements.
>
> The City Council of Nablus and all the patriotic groups signed below condemn in principle the idea of establishing settlements in the occupied Arab territories, and demand of the occupation authority:
> 1. Respect of and compliance with the U.N. resolutions and principles of international law.
> 2. Return of all expropriated lands to their owners.
> 3. Abandonment of the settler-expansionist policy.
> 4. Stopping the extremists from carrying out provocative actions.
> 5. Heeding the appeals of the international community and moving toward establishment of a just and durable peace in the area.
>
> Nablus, 23 April 1977

Mayor of Nablus
Nablus City Council
The General Confederation of Workers' Union — Secretary
 General
Red Crescent Society — President
Nablus Pharmacists
Representative of Engineers — Nablus
Nablus Chamber of Commerce
For Dentists of Nablus
For the Doctors of Medicine — Nablus
Arab Women's Federation
For the Lawyers of Nablus
Private citizens — Former mayor

Source: *NLG Report.*

Not until the end of 1978 did the Palestinian farmers affected by the land expropriation try another way, — appealing to the Israeli courts. Palestinians from the occupied territories have the right to appeal to the High Court against regulations handed down by the military administration. However, this apparently legal possibility of recourse against arbitrary actions by the occupying authority has one catch — recognition of the authority of the High Court to administer justice over the occupied territories would mean recognition of Israeli control over their land. For this reason, only a few Palestinians have chosen so far to appeal to the High Court. It has only been in the past few years that this court has become the most important showcase in the battle against the expropriations.

The most recent case, Eilon Moreh, appeared in the headlines of the world's press. For years, Gush Emunim settlers have tried to settle near Nablus, an Arab centre of population. Finally, the government could no longer ignore the growing pressure from nationalist and religious circles, and gave the settlement its blessing and justified the decision with 'security reasons'. Seventeen landowners were dispossessed of their property to enable construction of a road to a newly established settlement on a hill near Nablus. The landowners went to the High Court, contested the confiscation ruling, and won. Although this was a bad defeat for Begin's administration, it was only a Pyrrhic victory for the Palestinians — at the beginning of 1980, the settlement was re-established a few hills farther away. That Eilon Moreh, of all places, was the victim of the High Court's decision has double significance. On the one hand, it was clear to the whole world that the Gush Emunim group had not pitched their tents in Eilon Moreh for 'security reasons', but rather to show once again their conviction that the West Bank belongs to the Jewish people. When the government went out on a limb and legitimized expropriations with flimsy, security arguments, when everyone knew and the settlers left no doubt[93] that the reasons behind the selection of the location were actually very different, the legalistic fog surrounding the whole

Creating faits accomplis – a construction project in the ring of settlements around East Jerusalem

settlement policy evaporated once and for all.

On the other hand, the court's decision meant a great loss in prestige for the Likud government. The go-ahead for Eilon Moreh is the most important step the government has taken towards realizing its ambitious settlement plans since Camp David and the lifting of the alleged settlement ban. Eilon Moreh was to demonstrate that Israel, even under great American and international pressure, does not forgo the chance to create 'new facts'.

> **Excerpts from the Eilon Moreh Decision by the Israeli High Court of Justice**
>
> ... We must therefore examine the legal validity of the requisition order under discussion according to the international law from which the military commander, who issued [the order], derives his authority.
>
> But even without this we have enough indications from the evidence before us that both the ministerial committee and the cabinet majority were decisively influenced by reasons lying in a Zionist world-view of the settlement of the whole Land of Israel.
>
> The view concerning the right of the Jewish people, as

mentioned at the outset of the above remarks, is based on the fundamentals of the Zionist doctrine. But the question which is before this court in this petition is whether this view justifies the taking of private property in an area subject to military government – and, as I have tried to make clear, the answer to this depends on the correct interpretation of Article 52 of the Hague Regulations. I am of the opinion that the military needs cited in that article cannot include, according to any reasonable interpretation, national security needs in their broad sense, as I have just mentioned them.

... I do not doubt that the Chief of Staff's opinion was taken into consideration among the rest of the committee's considerations. But in my view this is not sufficient in order to place the decision within the bounds of Article 52. The following are my reasons for this view: When military needs are involved, I would have expected that the army authorities would initiate the establishment of the settlement precisely at that site, and that it would be the Chief of Staff who would, in line with this initiative, bring the army's request before the political level so that it could approve the settlement's establishment. ...

The initiative came from the political level, and the political level asked the Chief of Staff to give his professional opinion, and then the Chief of Staff expressed a positive opinion, in accordance with the conception he has always held ... The political consideration was, therefore, the dominant factor in the Ministerial Defence Committee's decision to establish the settlement at that site, though I assume that the committee as well as the cabinet majority were convinced that its establishment also fulfils military needs. ...

... But a secondary reason, such as the military reason in the decisions of the political level which initiated the settlement's establishment does not fulfil the precise structures laid down by the Hague Regulations for preferring the military need to the individual's rights of property. In other words: would the decision of the political level to establish the settlement at that site have been taken had it not been for the pressure of Gush Emunim and the political-ideological reasons which were before the political level?

Source: *Israleft*, No. 157, 1 November 1979.

Gush Emunim's reaction to this ruling was to state that the High Court was an 'instrument in the hands of terrorists'.[94] Agriculture Minister Sharon also criticized the court by saying that the Jews' right to settle was above any law.[95]

The quintessence of the decision does not justify, however, the propagandists' excitement over an expanded settlement of the occupied territories. The court reprimanded the government in the case of Eilon Moreh, but the underlying meaning of the verdict was: you can settle anywhere on the West Bank and you can even expropriate private Arab property for this purpose, but the military authorities should try a little harder in stating their security reasons.

To the ears of the Palestinians, it must have sounded like mockery when the judges concerned themselves with the interpretation of 'divine right' and warned against making the Israeli people's sovereignty over the whole land absolute. They remind one emphatically 'of the high regard for the right of the foreigners [i.e. the native Palestinians!] spoken of in the Bible and Torah'[96] and they quote the Bible: 'When a stranger sojourns with you in your land, you shall not do him wrong. The stranger who sojourns with you shall be to you as the native among you, and you shall love him as yourself; for you were strangers in the land of Egypt.' (Leviticus 19:33-34)

An armed resistance aimed at Jewish settlements has just recently been instigated. The resistance by Palestinian guerillas in the Gaza Strip during the early years of the occupation was directed at the presence of Israeli occupying troops and at Arab collaborators.[97] In the 70s, there were repeated bomb attacks in the West Bank to which civilians and the Israeli military fell victim. However, these assaults were less the expression of an organized struggle than the result of isolated activities which, however, increased periodically. There were also repeated demonstrations which led to violent altercations with the occupying authority.

Jewish settlements did not become the targets of resistance activities until the Israeli government began to establish settlements in increasing numbers in close proximity to Arab towns and villages. These settlement activities which provoked anger led to growing tension between Arabs and Jews, especially in Hebron, where houses have been occupied by Jewish orthodox settlers in the middle of the city since April 1979.[98] These settlers want to prove through constant unrest that Jewish and Arab people cannot live together peacefully and that consequently, only driving out the Palestinians can permanently guarantee peace.[99]

This thrust of the extremist settlement groups represents a new phase in the settlement policy. Here again, the Gush Emunim movement acts as the vanguard in the Israeli settlement movement and forces the controlling administration to act. First of all, the 'wild' settlement attempts by the settlers produces from the government a slight reprimand which, however, soon yields to silent tolerance. After some months or years, the settlement is eventually legalized. In this way, the religious settlement in Kiryat Arba was established in 1968. In the second half of the 70s, two other settlements, Qaddum and Eilon Moreh, were also established in this manner in close proximity to the Arab city, Nablus. A fourth Jewish settlement was established in this way in the middle of Hebron in 1979. Each of these settlements marked an important step in the escalation of the settlement activity.

In this new phase of the settlement strategy, no longer contenting itself with with Arab land but grasping at Arab cities, lies one of the causes of the growing resistance in the West Bank. Following the bloody assault in Hebron in which six Jews were killed and 17 wounded, Israeli Defence Minister Weizman said, 'We now find ourselves in the middle of a battle over the future of the Israeli state.' The Arab mayor of Nablus, Bassam Shak'a, declared: 'We now find ourselves in a battle over the Palestinian state.'[100] The Palestinians called for a general strike. The Israeli authorities reacted with Draconian measures — deportation of two mayors, blowing-up of houses, curfews, searching of homes, mass arrests, increased censorship of the press, restrictions on travel and trade, etc. Both sides obviously felt themselves challenged to a fight.

'Re-unification': The Annexation of East Jerusalem

The old section of Jerusalem — part of the Arab eastern half of the city — was taken by storm on 7 June 1967 by Israeli troops. The military 're-unification' of Jerusalem was soon followed by the judicial one. On 27 June 1967, the Knesset passed two laws in summary proceedings empowering the government to: 1) extend the boundaries of any city or district at will by means of ordinances;[101] and 2) expand Israel's laws, jurisdiction and administration to 'every part of Eretz Israel' by means of ordinances.[102] On the following day, the government immediately made use of this authority by greatly extending the existing city limits of Jerusalem[103] — nearly to Ramallah in the north and almost to Bethlehem in the south — and by declaring the Israeli laws and the ordinances of the city administration to be applicable to the 'united Jerusalem'.[104]

This annexation (euphemistically called 're-unification') of Arab East Jerusalem was strongly condemned by the United Nations General Assembly on 4 July 1967.[105] Foreign Minister Eban attempted to deny the annexation by saying: 'The term annexation ... is out of place. The measures adopted relate to the integration of Jerusalem in the administrative spheres, and furnish a legal basis for the protection of the Holy Places in Jerusalem.'[106]

A Jewish Fortress

Despite protests by the local population[107] against the annexation, the Israelis continued the process of integration. The desire to make the annexation permanent is clearly shown by construction plans already prepared for the city in 1967.[108] This plan called for:

> a population of 400,000 Jews out of a total population of 500,000 in Jerusalem by 1980, requiring a doubling of the Jewish population in Jerusalem. The political intention behind it is clear. Given the high Arab birth rate, the proportion of Jews to Arabs in 1967 (200,000 Jews : 66,000 Arabs) would have changed to the extreme disadvantage

of the Israelis within a short time. This would undoubtedly influence the political distribution of power. The new Israeli citizens in Jerusalem are to be gained from approximately 10–15% of the most recent Jewish immigrants who will be settled in the newly built Jewish quarters around East Jerusalem. By 1975, at least 65,000 Jews are to be settled in the former Jordanian section of Jerusalem.[109]

However, these ambitious plans could not be realized in their entirety. Far fewer Jews moved to the Holy City than had been hoped — the few Jewish immigrants in the last few years have been drawn to the urban centres on the coastal plain. But — and this is the most important point, in Israel's opinion — the proportion of Jews to Arabs developed 'favourably', since the Arab population only grew to a small extent. The Jewish planners attribute this development not only to a declining population growth (down from 3.4% to 3.0%) and the high rate of emigration (1.1%) but also to the ban on immigration for West Bank residents, in force since 1967.[110]

For the Palestinians, Jewish control manifests itself in the new Jewish quarters that surround the Arab residential areas like an insurmountable fortress wall. No longer do the golden dome of the Omar Mosque and the silver dome of the Al-Aqsa Mosque dominate the skyline of the Holy City. Now it is dominated by the monotonous yellowish-grey, four to eight story apartment buildings which were built on the hills (formerly Jordanian) surrounding the old Arab quarter. The Jewish ring around Jerusalem has turned the old section into a sort of 'native-ghetto'.

The newly established residential areas are reserved for Jewish residents. In the old part of the city, the government did not hesitate to destroy hundreds of houses and force out thousands of Arab families. Today, a large, wide square lies in front of the Wailing Wall — nothing remains to remind one that Arab families once lived there.[111] Likewise, 6,000 Palestinians had to make room for the complete reconstruction of the former Jewish quarter in the old part of the city.[112] The government made a permanent decision that Arab families may not purchase housing in this quarter. The courts declared the decision valid. Even Israeli newspapers have criticized this policy of making entire residential areas 'Arab-free' and point out 'the violence of a regime which makes claims of Jewish–Arab coexistence, and which, in the very days it tries to allow Jews into the heart of Hebron, insists on the expulsion of the last Arab family in the range of an arc from the reconstructed old quarter of Jerusalem'.[113]

Faits Accomplis: The Jewish Settlements

Map 4: Jerusalem

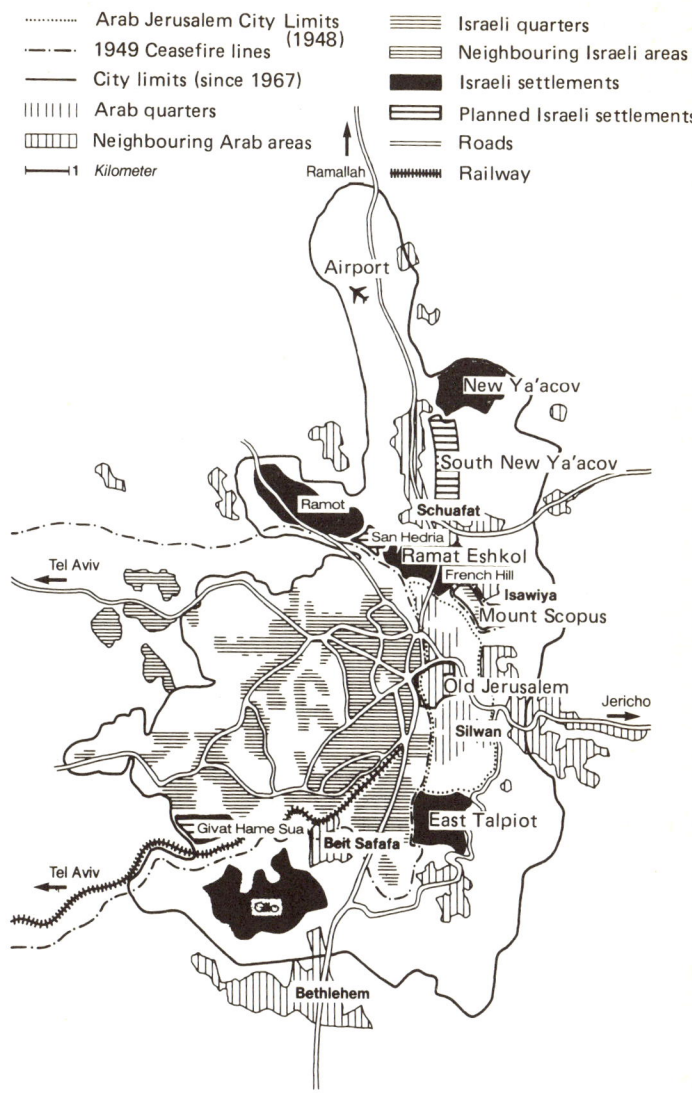

Source: *Ansprenger 1978*, p. 314.

Encircling Arab East Jerusalem – a part of the Jewish ring of settlements

Notes

1. Stenographed minutes (in German) of the Sixth Zionist World Congress in 1902, Vienna, 1903.
2. *U.N. Special Committee 1979*, Appendix III.
3. *Yediot Aharonot*, 14 May 1976; for an analysis of the Israeli settlement policy, cf. e.g. *Abu-Ayyash 1976*, p. 86ff.; *Davis 1976*, p. 12ff; *Lesch 1977*, p. 26ff.; *Decter 1979*, p. 20ff.; *Darin-Drabkin 1978*.
4. See the attempt to compile such information in a documentation of *The Jerusalem Post*, 2 May 1977: and *Ha'aretz*, 1 November 1979, an article based on a study of the Defence Ministry.
5. From a radio interview on 17 September 1977, quoted in the *NLG Report*, p. 7.
6. Cf. Prof. John Ruedy in his testimony for the U.S. Congress, 'Israeli Land Acquisition in Occupied Territories, 1967–1977' in *U.S. Senate Hearing*, p. 124ff. The inexactness of the numerical data is due further to the following factors: a) Until 1979, the purchase of land was only permitted to two Jewish institutions, The Jewish National Fund and the Israel Land Administration (or their subsidiaries) which gradually

acquired land privately through middle-men in the territories. The figures on the purchases transacted were only sporadically made public; b) Officially, many private purchases, which were forbidden for Israelis until 1979, are neither known nor registered; c) Because of the ban on buying and selling, there is probably a Jewish 'behind-the-scenes person' who is behind many transactions between Arabs; d) The available numerical data for the West Bank often do not include East Jerusalem which, despite annexation, still belongs to the occupied territories.

7. *NLG Report*, p. 7; cf. also the statements of Paul Quiring and Don Peretz before an investigating committee of the U.S. Congress in *U.S. House Hearing*, p. 43ff./49ff.
8. The 'Laws and Customs of War on Land' (the Fourth Hague Convention), passed on 18 October 1907, commonly known as the Hague Convention, contains an appendix with the individual regulations for the conduct of states engaging in war (referred to here as the Hague Regulations); the 'Convention Relative to the Protection of the Civilian Persons in Time of War' from 12 August 1949 (referred to here as the Geneva Convention), which is an extension and new formulation of the Hague Convention, was ratified by Israel on 6 July 1951, by Jordan on 29 May 1951 and by Egypt on 10 November 1952, in *Commission 1977*, p. 30.
9. Article 55 of the Hague Regulations must be seen in connection with Article 23g of these Regulations and with Article 55 of the Geneva Convention. These generally allow certain actions by the occupying authority, when absolutely required for 'military or security reasons', i.e. 'required by the military'. What 'military or security reasons' means is strongly disputed in the pertinent literature. (Cf. as introduction to this subject, *Gerson 1978*, p. 160ff. for further references).
10. *Ha'aretz*, 1 November 1979.
11. E.g. the former Israeli U.N. ambassador, Chaim Herzog, stated on 26 October 1977, before the U.N. General Assembly, '. . . we are discussing moves by the Government of Israel which have not displaced one single individual, which have not removed one single Arab from his property. . . .' Quoted from *Commission 1977*, p. 29.
12. Cf. the *NLG Report*, p. 4ff. and *Commission 1977*, p. 29ff.; this question is also handled in different reports of the *U.N. Special Committee*, cf. e.g. 1970, p. 30ff.
13. E.g. The Abandoned Areas Ordinance (1948), Cultivation of Waste Lands Regulations (1948), Absentee Property Law (1950), Development Authority (Transfer of Property) Law (1950), Security Provisions Order (1967); cf. *Israel Yearbook on Human Rights* (1971), p. 428ff.
14. Based on Article 125 of the Defence (Emergency) Regulations of 1945 or Article 90 of the Security Provisions Order of 1967, published in *NLG Report*, p. 5, footnote 8.
15. *The Jerusalem Post*, 26 April 1979.
16. The crucial differences in these two forms of land requisition are: a) expropriation is with compensation and seizure is without, and b) by expropriation, the title is transferred to the Israeli state, whereas by seizure, the title is retained by the former owner, but the property,

17.   i.e. the actual control and the right of use, is transferred to the state. Cf. *Gerson 1978*, p. 140; also *The Jerusalem Post*, 26 April 1979.
17. Cf. *NLG Report*, p. 5.
18. Prof. John Ruedy, in *U.S. Senate Hearing*, p. 126.
19. Cf. 'Abandoned Property of Private Individuals Order' of 23 July 1967, printed in the *Israel Yearbook on Human Rights* (1971), p. 443ff.; this order is practically identical to the Absentee Property Law, valid in Israel since 1950.
20. See Ch. 6.
21. Generally, these absentees are also no longer allowed to return to their own home country; cf. e.g. the case described in the *Frankfurter Rundschau*, 3 August 1978; also *The New York Times*, 25 May 1978.
22. Cf. *The New York Times, ibid.*
23. Cf. *Ha'aretz*, 1 November 1979; here it is only a question of the land which actually falls under this regulation. Other estimates (cf. Prof. John Ruedy, in *U.S. Senate Hearing*, p. 126) give of a total of approximately 700,000 *dunams* of 'absentee property'. A large part of this land is concealed in the Israeli figures in the category, 'land whose ownership is still undetermined', of which 1,430,000 *dunams* are in the West Bank alone.
24. *Commission 1977*, p. 31; the use of 'land abandoned by absentees' for settlement purposes is contested by *Gerson 1978*, p. 164.
25. Cf. the varying figures of Lesch in *U.S. House Hearing*, p. 12; *U.N. Special Committee 1971*, p. 45; *Langer (a)*, p. 24; *Cattan 1969*, p. 109; *The Jerusalem Post Magazine*, 14 April 1976; *ICRC 1970*, p. 486; according to estimates of the 'Israeli League of Human and Civil Rights' more than 7,500 houses were destroyed by 1969 and a total of 16,312 by August 1971 (cf. *Amad 1973*, p. 17).
26. See Ch. 3.
27. For a portrayal of these events cf. e.g. *Gerson 1978*, p. 139 ff.; an Israeli soldier who took part tells of the course of events in *Israel and Palestine*, No. 43, October 1972; cf. also *Le Monde*, 5 July 1969.
28. Cf. the position of the Israeli representative to a delegation of American church representatives in July 1968; cf. *NCCC 1968*, p. 6ff.
29. Cf. *Gerson 1978*, p. 162ff.
30. Cf. Article 23g of the Hague Regulations and Article 53 of the Fourth Geneva Convention; authors who have concerned themselves with this question include *Gerson 1978*, p. 162ff. for further references and *Dershowitz 1971*, p. 377.
31. Cf. *Gerson 1978*, p. 140.
32. For further references to the destruction of villages see *Amad 1973*, p. 95ff.; *U.N. Special Committee 1970*, p. 56ff.; there were also hundreds of houses belonging to Arabs destroyed in Old Jerusalem, see Ch. 2.
33. Quoted from Shulamit Aloni (a member of the Knesset) in an article from *Yediot Aharonot*, 26 March 1976. Further information on the lan land purchases can be found in *Ma'ariv*, 19 September 1977; *Ha'aretz*, 18 February 1977 and 2 March 1977; *The New York Times*, 12 April 1976; in detail in *Gerson 1978*, p. 141ff.
34. *U.S. Senate Hearing*, p. 127; Prof. Walter Lehn estimates the entire area

acquired by the Jewish National Fund in the occupied territories (including the Golan Heights and Sinai) at 2.7 million *dunams* (cf. *NLG Report*, p. 4).
35. Cf. *Ha'aretz*, 1 November 1979.
36. Cf. *Gerson 1978*, p. 142; *The Jerusalem Post*, 13 April 1973; *Ha'aretz*, 4 April 1973.
37. This gave rise to the apparent disunity in the social democratic government, cf. *Gerson, ibid.*
38. Cf. *Gerson ibid.*, describes this dispute in detail.
39. Governmental decision of 16 September 1979, cf. *Ha'aretz*, 17-18 September 1979.
40. Cf. *Süddeutsche Zeitung*, 29 February 1980: only contradictory figures on the number of settlers are available. According to a census of September 1977 there were 8,900 settlers in all territories. The former Israeli U.N. ambassador, Chaim Herzog, gave the number of settlers as 6,000 in a U.N. speech on 26 October 1977 — however, he did not give any figures for East Jerusalem. In her testimony before a U.S. Senate Committee (*U.S. Senate Hearing*, p. 7ff.), Ann M. Lesch estimated the number of settlers in 1977 to be about 10,000 plus around 50,000 in East Jerusalem. New estimates, according to a U.N. official in 1979 (U.N. Doc. A/34/536 p. 8), suggest 90,000 settlers in all occupied territories; the Israeli U.N. representative in Geneva, Yoel Barromi, gave a figure of 7,800 for 'Judaea and Samaria' (the West Bank excluding Jerusalem) to the U.N. Human Rights Commission in February 1980.
41. See also Ch. 9.
42. Cf. Bernstein in his introduction to *DIAK*, p. 3.
43. *Newsweek*, 17 February 1969, p. 49.
44. Cf. *Commission 1977*, p. 31.
45. *Al Hamishmar*, 14 March 1980.
46. Quoted from *NLG Report*, p. 12.
47. *The Jerusalem Post* — international edition, 3/9 June 1979, p. 1.
48. *The Jerusalem Post* and *Ha'aretz* from 20 May 1977.
49. Vladimir (Zeev) Jabotinsky, 1880-1940, leader of the so-called Revisionist Party, the ideological forerunner of Begin's right-extremist Herut Party.
50. E.g. the left social democratic party MAPAM in its party platform from January 1980.
51. Quoted from *DIAK*, p. 2.
52. Cf. *Middle East International*, November 1978; for the security doctrine cf. also *McPeak 1976*, p. 426ff.
53. *Dayan 1969*, p. 179.
54. Likud — an election coalition of various conservative parties was founded in 1974 and includes Begin's own Herut Party, the State List, Free Centre and Israel Liberal Party (from the General Zionists). The Likud block together with the National Religious Party and the remainder of a citizens' protest party (the Democratic Movement for Change) form the governing coalition. For an introduction to the Israeli party structure see *Peretz 1977*, p. 251ff.; *Etzioni 1977*, p. 281ff.

55. E.g. Amos Elon, well known Jewish journalist, in *Ha'aretz*, 12 October 1979; cf. also *Kapeliouk 1979 (b)*, p. 1ff.
56. *Ha'aretz*, 16 October 1979.
57. For the history, forerunners, ideology and political influence of Gush Emunim, cf. *DIAK* o.J. with an introduction from Bernstein; also Moshe Kohn, 'Who's afraid of Gush Emunim?', *The Jerusalem Post Topic*, 1977.
58. *Yediot Aharonot*, 30 October 1979.
59. Cf. e.g. *The Jerusalem Post*, 8 August 1978; *Davis 1979*, p. 13ff.; *Lesch 1977*, p. 26ff.
60. *Ha'aretz*, 20 October 1979.
61. *The Jerusalem Post* — international edition, 15/21 April 1979.
62. For the international assessment of the settlement policy, see Ch. 3.
63. Cf. the collection of the corresponding reports in the Israeli press in the respective reports of the *U.N. Special Committee*, most recently in the *1979 Report*, p. 14ff.
64. As a result of the economic policies of the Begin administration, there have been repeated periods of unrest. At demonstrations in November 1979 giving financial support to the settlements in the occupied territories instead of to the Isreali slum areas was strongly criticized. Cf. e.g. *Ma'ariv* and *Ha'aretz*, 21 November 1979.
65. See Ch. 2.
66. Cf. the most recent Report of the *U.N. Special Committee 1979*, p. 34ff.
67. See Ch. 7.
68. *The Jerusalem Post* 8 August 1978.
69. See Ch. 7.
70. Cf. *The Jerusalem Post*, 27 September 1967; press conference of the Israeli Ambassador to the United States, cf. *The New York Times*, 29 September 1967; there was already a kibbutz in Kfar Etzion (between Hebron and Bethlehem) before 1948, which was destroyed by the Jordanian army in the first Middle East war, cf. *Gerson 1978*, p. 136; *Sinai/Pollack 1977*, p. 207.
71. Cf. *The Jerusalem Post Magazine*, 8 September 1972; *Fried 1975*, p. 314.
72. Cf. *The New York Times*, 27 September 1967.
73. Cf. *Gerson 1978*, p. 137ff., *Fried 1975*, p. 315ff. Hebron is one of the four holy cities of Judaism because it was here that David was appointed king and Abraham bought the tomb for his wife, Sarah. A Jewish congregation lived here continuously from the Middle Ages until 1929, when an Arab pogrom led to the expulsion of the Jews.
74. Cf. Ch. 9.
75. Cf. *The Jerusalem Post* — international edition, 3/9 June 1979.
76. *Ibid*.
77. The Labour Party could not do without this coalition partner, since they would otherwise have lost the majority. The background and historical reasons for this coalition policy cannot be detailed here; cf. Ch. 2, n. 54 and *Diskin/Wolffsohn 1979*, p. 33ff.; *Lexikon 1979*, pp. 106ff. and 119ff.

78. Cf. Ch. 4.
79. Cf. *Quiring 1978*, p. 14.
80. *Ibid.*
81. *Davar*, 8 October 1976.
82. *The Jerusalem Post*, 22 March 1976.
83. For a description of these constantly occurring incidents, see e.g. *Ha'aretz*, 24 March 1976; Documentation on the tense situation in Hebron can be found in *Israleft*, No. 164, 15 February 1980; *Stern*, No. 17/80, 17 April 1980, p. 240ff.
84. Cf. *Stern, ibid*; e.g. also *Al Hamishmar*, 5 October 1976.
85. See Ch. 6.
86. For the criticism and revolt which were triggered by the pardon of Jews who had killed Arabs, see *Israleft*, No. 155, 1 October 1979 and No. 164, 15 February 1980; for individual cases, cf. also *Yediot Aharonot*, 20 April 1979; *Ha'aretz*, 22 April 1979; *The Jerusalem Post*, 23 April 1979.
87. Cf. *Stern, loc. cit.*
88. Cf. report of the former deputy military governor of Hebron, Zwi Bar El, in *Stern, loc. cit.*, p. 245.
89. Cf. *Israleft*, No. 164, 15 February 1980.
90. Cf. *Süddeutsche Zeitung*, 5 May 1980.
91. *Ibid.*
92. Cf. *Frankfurter Rundschau*, 5 May 1980.
93. Cf. *Davar*, 31 August 1979; see also Ch. 2.
94. Interview on Israeli radio on 27 October 1979, quoted from *Le Monde diplomatique*, December 1979.
95. Quoted from Dr Werner Kaegi, 'Ein Gerichtsentscheid von grösster Tragweite' (A Judicial Decision of Enormous Consequences), in *Neue Zürcher Zeitung*, 16-17 February 1980.
96. *Ibid.*
97. Cf. Ch. 6.
98. Cf. *The Jerusalem Post*, 20 May 1979.
99. According to a leader of Gush Emunim, Hanan Porat, in *The Jerusalem Post*, quoted from *Tageszeitung*, 8 May 1980.
100. *Frankfurter Rundschau*, 5 May 1980.
101. Municipal Corporations Ordinance (Amendment) Law (1967).
102. The Law and Administration Ordinance (Amendment No. 11) Law, quoted from *Fried 1975*, p. 198, who also points out that 'Eretz Israel' is used as a Hebraic synonym for the Palestine mandate with the borders of 1922 which included Transjordan.
103. Cf. *The Jerusalem Post*, 27/28 June 1967.
104. Law and Administration Order No. 1 from 28 June 1967, cf. *MER 1967*, p. 290.
105. Cf. Resolution 2253 of the General Assembly (U.N. Doc. A/6798).
106. U.N. Doc. A/6753; S/8052 (1967), quoted from *Gerson 1978*, p. 211; cf. with the efforts to play down the annexation ('The measures are solely to bring about the equal municipal and social services for all residents of Jerusalem.'); also *Mansour and Stock 1971*, p. 24ff; also in detail in *Brecher 1978*, p. 25ff.
107. See Ch. 6.

108. Cf. *The Israel Economist*, 23 July 1967; also Rabinovich, 'On building a fortress [*sic!*] around Jerusalem' in *The Jerusalem Post Magazine*, 8 November 1974; *Al-Khatib 1970*, p. 32.
109. *Fried 1975*, p. 307.
110. Cf. *Fried 1975*, p. 309; cf. also *Ansprenger 1978*, p. 269.
111. Lesch in *U.S. House Hearing*, p. 10; *The Guardian* (London), 4 March 1968; *U.N. Special Committee 1976*, p. 8; even Mayor Kollek stated that 'some Arab families were removed from their homes at too short notice without replacement housing for them having first been found'. Cf. *The Washington Post*, 2 May 1968.
112. Cf. *U.N. Special Committee, loc. cit.*; cf. also *The Jerusalem Post*, 26 December 1975.
113. Cf. *Ha'aretz*, 3 March 1980.

3. Administration of Suppression: The Occupation and Human Rights

The Israeli occupying authority has repeatedly been accused of violating human rights in the occupied territories. A U.N. Special Committee continually examines violations of human rights in the occupied territories and regularly issues strong accusations against the occupiers,[1] which are generally confirmed by the investigations of other institutions.[2]

> **Grave Concern at the Violation of Human Rights**
> The General Assembly ... expresses its grave concern at the violation by Israel of the Geneva Convention relative to the Protection of Civilian Persons in Time of War as well as the other applicable international conventions and regulations, and in particular the following violations:
>
> (a) The annexation of certain parts of the occupied territories;
>
> (b) The establishment of Israeli settlements in the occupied territories and the transfer of an alien population thereto;
>
> (c) The destruction and demolition of Arab houses, quarters, villages and towns;
>
> (d) The confiscation and expropriation of Arab property in the occupied territories and all other transactions for the acquisition of land between the Government of Israel, Israeli institutions and Israeli nationals on the one hand, and the inhabitants or institutions of the occupied territories on the other;
>
> (e) The evacuation, deportation, expulsion, displacement and transfer of the Arab inhabitants of the Arab territories occupied by Israel since 1967, and the denial of their right to return to their homes and property;
>
> (f) Administrative detention and ill-treatment inflicted on the Arab inhabitants;
>
> (g) The pillaging of archaeological and cultural property in the occupied territories;
>
> (h) The interference with religious freedom, religious practices and family rights and customs;
>
> (i) The illegal exploitation of the natural wealth, resources

> and population of the occupied territories ...
>
> Source: U.N. General Assembly, Resolution 3092 (XXVIII), quoted from Wilhelm Wengler and Josef Tittel, eds., *Documents on the Arab Israel Conflict: The Resolutions of the United Nations Organization*, Berlin Verlag, Berlin 1978.

Israel has always contested the accusation that it violates human rights in the occupied territories and even denies that international law applies at all.[3]

Justice and Politics: The Occupation and International Law

For decades, the international community has had regulations which determine the rights and duties of a military occupation in occupied territories. Decisive in this connection are Articles 42-56 of the Hague Regulations, and Articles 47-78 of the Fourth Geneva Convention.[4] Almost all governments of the world and jurists outside Israel proceed on the assumption that these regulations must also apply to Israel in the occupied territories, for Article 2 of the Geneva Convention states, they 'shall apply to all cases of belligerent conflict' and 'all cases of partial or total occupation of the territory of a High Contracting Party'.

Israel considers the West Bank and Gaza Strip to be 'liberated' and not 'occupied', since the Jews have a 'historical right' to Eretz Israel.[5] Israel asserts that it owes its control of the area to a 'defensive conquest' so that it 'has a better entitlement to the territory of what was Palestine, including the whole of Jerusalem, than do Jordan and Egypt'.[6] Since the West Bank and Gaza Strip were illegally occupied in 1948 by Jordan and Egypt respectively, Israeli troops did not drive out the troops of a legitimate sovereign in the 1967 June War, but rather those of an illegal occupier. In addition, it is argued, the West Bank had been annexed by the Hashemite kingdom which was not recognized by any country except Pakistan and Great Britain. Therefore, the West Bank was not even a 'territory of a High Contracting Party', for it never really belonged to Jordan. The Geneva Convention, the argument continues,[7] was meant to protect the 'legitimate sovereign' from the occupying authority, but since Israel is not an occupying authority and neither Jordan nor Egypt a legitimate sovereign, the Convention is not applicable. The Convention applies more to short-term and temporary occupations; however, this is claimed to be a special case (*sui generis*).

The Israeli arguments are not convincing. Biblical promises are not recognized as being internationally binding. Even the fact that the people of Israel inhabited this region in Biblical times, cannot be a basis for claims to the occupied territories. An argument of that type questions the entire political world map.

Even if one assumes that Israel conducted a 'legitimate war of defence' in

1967, that does not affect the validity of the Geneva Convention. A 'territory of a High Contracting Party', as defined by Article 2, is subject to the Geneva Convention even when the legal claims to the territory are disputed.[8] The main purpose of the Geneva Convention is not the protection of the 'legitimate sovereign' but rather, as its name indicates, the 'Protection of Civilian Persons' in the area in question.[9] If it were not for this convention, the civilian population would remain completely unprotected in all of the many cases in which disputed claims to land lead to armed conflict.[10] Treating the occupied territories as a special case is unacceptable, since this legal evasion makes a mockery of all international regulations. 'No war or military occupation is precisely like another. Legal rules are established in advance to be of general application.'[11] It is 'unacceptable that the duly ratified treaty may be suspended at the wish of one of the parties'.[12]

The Israeli viewpoint has been criticized throughout the entire world. The United States,[13] the Security Council and General Assembly of the United Nations,[14] the International Red Cross[15] and other international organizations and associations have repeatedly reinforced their stand that the fourth Geneva Convention must be applied to the occupied territories.

The Victors on top – Jewish settlements overlooking Jerusalem

If the Geneva Convention is applicable in the West Bank and Gaza Strip, it should be examined at this point how Israel measures up against this international standard in her treatment of the Palestinian population. This is especially important since the occupiers continually stress that, in spite of the alleged inapplicability of the Fourth Geneva Convention, they adhere to it in their daily practice.[16]

Settlements and International Law

However, the Israeli government has, to this day, not shown any evidence of willingness to adhere to the Geneva Convention. Article 49 of the Fourth Geneva Convention prohibits the occupying authority 'from deporting or transferring any of its own civilian population to the occupied territories'. Advocates of Israel continually point out that this regulation has to be understood in the context of the Nazi expulsion of the Polish population in World War II. They explain that the German occupying authority had wanted to replace the native Polish population with Germans. In their opinion, Article 49 of the Geneva Convention was meant to forbid this and only this. Israel, they continue, does not practice this type of policy in the occupied Arab territories; no Arabs have been driven out by the Jewish settlements.[17]

Such a restrictive interpretation of Article 49 is, however, unjustified. Certainly, the experiences of World War II had an effect on the drafting of the Geneva Convention of 1949. Yet the wording of this particular section lends no validity to such a limited interpretation.

Analysis of the Israeli settlement policy and its consequences for the resident Arab population refutes the Israeli statement that Palestinians have lost neither land nor place of residence.[18] Especially considering the court proceedings of the past few years, such an assertion defies all the facts.[19]

In view of their permanent character, the Jewish settlements contradict the basic principles of the international law of occupation. Generally, it is the duty of the occupier to administer the occupied territories, not just for their own military use, but as much as possible in the interests of the native population. When making regulations, they are also to bear in mind the basically temporary character of a military occupation.[20] The establishing of civilian settlements not only runs counter to the interests of the Arab population, it actually perpetuates the Jewish presence.

Jerusalem

If, in view of the Jewish settlements, the Israeli government policy in the occupied territories can be considered a 'creeping annexation', then this annexation has already been completed *de jure* in Jerusalem. This fact cannot be obscured by semantic and legal hair-splitting. The Israeli laws and decrees, which form the legal foundation for the annexation,[21] painstakingly avoid the word 'annexation'. However, the application of Israeli laws coupled with their absolute claim to sovereignty[22] over Jerusalem, represents what is known in international law as annexation, particularly since the Israeli governments have never tried to conceal their determination that Jerusalem is never again divided.

Incorporating the occupied territories in this way violates the principle of inadmissible acquisition of land by war. The Judaization of the Arab part of the city through the construction of Jewish districts, the expulsion of the Arab population from the old part of the city and the settling of Jewish people are contradictory to Article 49 (6) of the Geneva Convention.[23]

In the Name of Security: Political Suppression

Under Israeli occupation, the populations of the West Bank and Gaza Strip are crucially restricted in their possibilities for political expression. Political parties and organizations are forbidden; political meetings and assemblies are not allowed; newspapers and magazines are taken out of circulation; and politically active Palestinians face arrest, imprisonment and deportation.

The military government, with its unpredictable reactions, acts more strongly to suppress political activities in the occupied territories than the 'iron hand' that quells all anti-Israeli activity. In this way, political meetings, such as those of the Palestinian mayors of the West Bank and Gaza Strip, are generally forbidden. However, the occupying authority does allow this type of meeting whenever it is politically opportune.[24]

The Fine Difference

Permission is given to mayors, trade unionists and others to hold meetings, if these meetings will bring us closer to peace and build bridges to our neighbours. But if they only want to discuss settlements, land and the electric company,[25] and if they say to us, 'We support the P.L.O., and you Israelis must talk to the P.L.O., not with us', this will not help to build bridges. If the meetings are to speak against normalization and about politics, then we will not give them permission to hold their meetings.
— spokesman for the military government

Source: *The Middle East*, March 1980, p. 19.

Anti-Israeli statements in the occupied territories' Arab press are in no way suppressed as a matter of course. In the daily newspapers *Al-Kuds* and *Al-Fajr*, numerous sharp attacks on the occupying authority[26] have appeared, untouched by the censor. Yet, on other occasions, such an attack can fall victim to the censorship. 'Agitation' and 'incitement' are prohibited topics, yet the definition of these terms obviously depends on the censor's mood.

Travel permits are issued by the military government equally arbitrarily. The Palestinian mayors, for instance, cannot simply travel abroad whenever they wish. Their applications for travel are decided upon individually

This Land is Our Land

In the saddle – street scene in Hebron

according to the political climate.[27]

Since political work is prohibited, it is done underground. Again and again, members and leaders of illegal political organizations are arrested, tried, deported or placed under house arrest. Yet, the person affected usually never learns the exact grounds on which he is charged, nor the basis on which his punishment is decided. Even the possession of anti-Israeli literature is punishable.

Of course, the military government has legal foundations for all measures of repression at its disposal. First of all, it can utilize the legal instruments that the Hashemite monarch had already created and used to suppress political developments in the occupied territories which would have been dangerous to the throne. Whenever these instruments were not sufficient, the occupying authority issued hundreds of ordinances to provide for 'security and order'.[28] A further legal basis for Israel's political suppression in the occupied territories is provided by the Defence (Emergency) Regulations of 1945. These regulations, issued by the British Mandate authority, disregard many human rights and enable the military government to rule arbitrarily.[29]

The legal grounds for the occupation are thus a mixture of Jordanian, Israeli, British and international laws. This creates an atmosphere of legal uncertainty and political arbitrariness. On the pretext of 'security interests', the occupying troops have practically unlimited authority. In addition to the legal uncertainty, there is the political unpredictability. Periods of drastic punishments are followed by relatively liberal periods. Some people can publicly voice their political protest, while others are immediately arrested for similar statements.

The constant threat of arrest and the unpredictability of the occupying authorities, who can, and do, arbitrarily single out and arrest any Palestinian, is an essential element in the strategy to intimidate the Palestinian people and make them feel insecure. Informed sources in Israel estimate that by 1977 approximately 60% of the male population between the ages of 18 and 50 in the West Bank and Gaza Strip had spent at least one night in prison after being arrested.[30]

Exiled from the Homeland: Deportations

The expulsion of Palestinians from the occupied territories is prohibited by the fourth Geneva Convention. Article 49 forbids the deportation of civilian persons to any country, and Article 76 obligates the occupying authority to hold arrested and sentenced persons in prisons in the occupied territories.

Israel has never complied with these regulations, preferring to quote Article 112 of the Defence (Emergency) Regulations of 1945 which permit deportation.[31] Thus, by 1978, far more than 1,000 Palestinians[32] had been deported, usually accused of 'agitation', 'endangering public security' or 'terrorist activities'. Many of those deported were in prison for 'security offences' before their deportation, yet, just as often political undesirables were deported more or less overnight without any court proceedings.[33] In such cases, it has seldom been possible for legal steps to be taken against the deportation order, because the person accused has often been taken from his bed and to the border before a lawyer or judge could be reached.[34] Only a few were able to stop their deportation by appealing to Israeli courts.[35]

Table 2. Deportations from the Occupied Territories, 1967-78

Year	Number
1967	5 (+ one Bedouin tribe)
1968	69
1969	223 (+ one Bedouin tribe)
1970	406
1971	306
1972	91
1973	10
1974	11
1975	13
1976	2
1977	6
1978	9

Source: *Lesch 1979*, p. 103.

For the most part, victims of deportation from the West Bank were members of the political leadership, whose violations of security could not be concretely proven. Usually the grounds for the deportation stated by the occupying authority were refusal to co-operate or agitation. Typically, these deportations were justified to the public by an all-inclusive reference to alleged connections with 'terrorist organizations' such as the P.L.O. Until the beginning of 1970, those deported were usually important teachers, doctors and lawyers, as well as journalists, chairmen and activists from professional organizations; but they also included mayors, village elders and religious dignitaries.

In addition to eliminating political leadership of the West Bank, the Israeli authorities, in the first years of the occupation, apparently intended to deter the public from further political activities by means of their deportation policy.[36]

In the Gaza Strip, in contrast to the West Bank, there was a significant armed resistance against the occupation until 1971. Those deported were almost exclusively members of Palestinian organizations; hardly any were political leaders.

'Indiscriminate Crackdowns': Collective Punishments

Collective punishment, especially the destruction of houses, the imposition of curfews and economic sanctions, is designed to act as a general deterrant.[37] As early as the British Mandate, houses belonging to alleged terrorists or those in which they lived had been blown up as a means of general deterrence. Even today, houses are blown up (or doors and windows shut and boarded) without court proceedings and regardless of innocent family members or other residents of the home[38] The extent of the effects of these measures cannot be exactly determined; yet the number of houses destroyed is certainly in the thousands, since the Israeli authorities themselves confirmed the destruction of 1,224 houses up to 1977.[39]

Collective punishment — a demolished house belonging to a Palestinian family at Kafr Nameh (West Bank)

As justification for these measures, Israel again refers to the Defence (Emergency) Regulations of 1945[40] and the Fourth Geneva Convention (according to Article 53, the destruction of property is allowed for military reasons). Since the military conflict in June 1967, however, there has been general international consensus[41] that these destructions can no longer be justified by Article 53, especially since such acts of punishment almost always affect innocent people as well. Article 33 of the Geneva Convention prohibits the punishment of civilian persons for violations of law which they have not personally committed.[42]

The following are examples of other forms of collective punishment used by the occupying authority: weeks of curfews;[43] closing of universities;[44] travel restrictions for residents of entire cities;[45] weeks of trade restrictions for merchants of a city;[46] ban on foreign currencies for the administration and residents of a city;[47] closing down of businesses.[48] Such measures are part of the military administration's normal repertoire. Incidents of completely arbitrary, humiliating treatment of individual citizens and entire villages are continually reported in the press.[49]

The Power of Evidence: Political Prisoners and Torture

Of course, the arresting and sentencing of Palestinians accused of violating the security of the state are also part of the legal apparatus used by the military administration to control political activities in the occupied territories.

Administrative Detention
Especially feared in this connection were the old British Defence (Emergency) Regulations. According to Article 111, any Palestinian could be imprisoned for cumulative six-month terms.[50] So far, the longest time any Palestinian is known to have been detained under these regulations is four years.[51] The number of these so-called administrative detainees is difficult to ascertain, since precise data are not made public. In addition, the frequency of this type of arrest varies according to the political situation. For instance, former Defence Minister Moshe Dayan spoke of 1,131 detainees in May 1970, when guerilla activities were still relatively intense in the Gaza Strip; in June of the same year, the number is supposed to have fallen to 560.[52] For subsequent years, official estimates have been limited to averages of about 40.[53] However, there is reason to question the legitimacy of these 'averages'. In the period from April to June 1974 alone, 150 Palestinians were put under administrative detention during a wave of arrests aimed particularly at members of the Communist Party.[54] In July of the same year, another 100 were detained.[55] Article 111 was utilized as grounds for detaining political opponents, especially during large waves of arrests, for example, in 1978 when Israel's invasion of southern Lebanon set off large demonstrations in the West Bank. The resulting wave of arrests was described by critics as an 'indiscriminate crackdown'.[56]

Detention without due process of law is permitted according to Article 78 of the Fourth Geneva Convention, but only when 'imperative reasons of security' leave no other choice, and only during the first year following the armed conflict.[57] Israel was still applying the Defence (Emergency) Regulations 12 years after the occupation began, thereby violating the Geneva Convention and Articles 9 and 10 of the Universal Declaration of Human Rights. A more precise examination of some cases shows that the reason for many of the arrests was not imperative security concerns, but rather lack of evidence, which made winning properly conducted court cases appear hopeless to the military authorities. Therefore, Article 111 of the Defence (Emergency) Regulations was used to rob the Palestinians concerned of their right to due process of law. The nature of this practice, clearly contrary to international law, has repeatedly been condemned by international bodies.[58] Not until 1979 did Israel replace the infamous Article 111 with Article 87 of the Security Provisions Order, which provides for judicial and ministerial control over the practice of administrative detention.[59] To what extent these charges are actually carried out cannot yet be determined.

Legal Proceedings
The vaguely formulated penal code used by the Israeli occupying authority and based on the Defence (Emergency) Regulations of 1945 and the Security Provisions Order issued in 1967, have caused considerable insecurity.[60] These provisions prohibit membership of illegal organizations, contact with the enemy', sedition, propaganda and agitation, possession or distribution of illegal literature (including the writing of national slogans on public buildings or distribution of privately recorded Palestinian songs). In the hands of the occupying authority, this sort of penal code is an appropriate means of putting a stop to all types of resistance and national self-assertion.

Even though certain minimum prerequisites for due process of law are guaranteed, not only by the Fourth Geneva Convention, but also by the Security Provisions Order of the military government from 1967, they are often only empty words on paper.[61] Israeli lawyers who defend Palestinians in such cases (best known are Felicia Langer and Lea Tzemel) and international observers of the trials continually report grave violations of legal proceedings. The following are examples of violations: 1) months of solitary confinement without notification of family or lawyers; 2) exclusion of the public at court proceedings (for 'security reasons'); 3) exclusion of family members, the press or certain persons at court proceedings; 4) inadequate translation into Arabic of all statements and proceedings; 5) denial of the right to obtain a lawyer during the period of investigation; 6) prohibiting of visits to prisons by defence attorneys and family members; 7) various obstacles to the defence of the accused; 8) inadequate medical examinations;[62] 9) inadequate possibilities to appeal.[63]

Prison Conditions
There are approximately 3,000 to 4,000 Palestinian prisoners serving sentence for 'security offences'. Each has an average area of 2.6^2 metres in the Ramleh Prison or 4.2^2 metres in the Beersheba Prison, not even half of the international average.[64]

The International Red Cross,[65] Amnesty International[66] and other organizations have condemned these conditions in the 14 detention centres divided equally among Israel and the occupied territories.[67] Even the Israeli commissioner of the prison system, Chaim Levi, admitted in 1977 that 'overcrowding in the prisons has reached a level which can no longer be tolerated'.[68]

The overcrowding has resulted in degrading, unhygienic conditions, as there are often as many as 80 prisoners cooped up in one room without a toilet.[69] In addition, medical care is completely inadequate; the daily exercise period in the court yard is often limited to half an hour; the cells are often too dark and damp;[70] and the food provided is meagre.[71] The Arab 'security prisoners' are not allowed to change their clothes and do not have bedsteads – for 'security reasons', as the Police Minister in 1977, Shlomo Hillel, did not hesitate to explain.[72]

Although the Fourth Geneva Convention prescribes in Article 76 that these security prisoners can only be held in the occupied territories, many Palestinians from the West Bank and Gaza Strip are serving sentences in Israeli prisons, and are in with Israeli prisoners, contrary to Article 76.

These unsatisfactory prison conditions along with the lack of proper legal proceedings, result in situations which 'enhance the possibility of mistreatment'.[73]

Torture

The most serious accusation directed at the occupying authority is the torture of prisoners. A large number of respected organizations and institutions have engaged in very extensive and thorough investigations into these charges.[74]
Amnesty International: As early as February 1969, a delegation from Amnesty International was allowed to visit some Israeli prisons. In their report they stated: 'At the present point in time, Amnesty restricts itself to claiming that the serious nature of these allegations warrants immediate inquiry so that their truth can be tested and the practice of torture, if it exists, can be brought immediately to an end.'[75] However, years of trying to persuade the Israeli authorities to permit such an investigation brought no success. Not until 1978 was a small delegation from Amnesty again allowed to enter Israel.[76]

In the latest report, dated 1979, Amnesty appears very alarmed at 'grave violations of human rights' in the occupied territories and Israel.[77] Referring to the report of a U.S. consular official in Jerusalem,[78] who had determined that the mistreatment of prisoners was not restricted to the practices of a 'handful of "rogue cops" exceeding orders', but was carried out systematically and was at least silently tolerated by higher-ranking officials, Amnesty replied that it had received credible declarations from other former prisoners, which confirm the conclusion drawn by the American official.[79]
U.N. Special Committee: The 'U.N. Special Committee to investigate Israeli practices affecting the human rights of the population of the occupied territories',[80] created in December 1968, has also made a careful study of the torture accusations. Contrary to Israeli claims that this committee was biased and one-sided from the very beginning, it can be shown that it was very cautious at first in its judgment on the mistreatment of prisoners. The Special Committee stated, for example, in its report from 1975,[81] '. . . despite the compelling nature of the evidence it had received, it was unable to reach a conclusive finding. . . . Nevertheless, in these reports the Special Committee has stated its conviction that . . . interrogation procedures very frequently involved physical violence.' Even though during the course of

years, the admonitions of the Special Committee became more and more clear,[82] it was not until its latest report in 1979 that it stated its 'inescapable conclusion that there is indeed in Israeli prisons a systematic practice of torture'.[83] The Committee's conclusion was based on testimonies given by former Palestinian prisoners, medical examinations of those concerned and the evaluation of other reports and statements made by defence attorneys of the tortured detainees.[84] To this day, this Committee has not yet been permitted entry into Israel.

International Committee of the Red Cross: According to the Geneva Convention, it is the duty of the International Committee of the Red Cross to investigate prison conditions in occupied areas. Israel has permitted the Red Cross access to prisoners, but not to the extent specified in Articles 30 and 76, despite constant requests and warnings.[85] The Red Cross very seldom publishes critical reports, since its work relies on direct contact with the authorities concerned, and in the interests of the detainees, it does not want to endanger its right of access. Although the Red Cross technically enjoys exceptionally good access rights in the occupied territories,[86] it could not conclusively refute the torture accusations for a number of reasons: 1) The Red Cross is allowed to visit only prisons, not police stations or military camps where the torturing supposedly occurs;[87] 2) The Red Cross is not always immediately informed of the arrests;[88] 3) The detainees are not allowed to be visited during the so-called interrogation period, yet it is precisely during this time (the first days following the arrest) that most of the torturing allegedly occurs;[89] 4) The Red Cross only looks into complaints of a prisoner if he has complained directly to the Israeli authorities;[90] 5) Access to certain cells is still being denied to representatives of the Red Cross.[91]

Such restrictions have not, however, prevented the Red Cross from discovering some very disturbing facts, and despite the well-known discretion of the organisation, internal memos have leaked out which report serious mistreatment of prisoners. For example, there is the following report about a prison in Nablus:[92]

> A number of detainees have undergone torture during interrogation by the military police. According to the evidence, the torture took the following forms:
> 1) suspension of the detainee by the hands ...
> 2) burns with cigarette stubs
> 3) blows by rods on the genitals
> 4) tying up and blindfolding for days
> 5) bites by dogs
> 6) electric shocks at the temples, the mouth, the chest and testicles.

Sunday Times Report: In the summer of 1977, the report of a five-month investigation made by the London *Sunday Times* Insight team caused a stir.[93] Based on extensive material, the team stated the following: 1) The Israeli security forces and intelligence services ill-treat arrested Arabs; 2) Some forms of ill-treatment are primitive, but more refined techniques are also used, such as electric shocks and confinement in special cells. This ill-treatment goes beyond brutality and reaches a level which can only be called torture; 3) Torture is carried out in at least six centres. All Israeli security forces and intelligence authorities participate; 4) Torture of Arab prisoners is so widespread and methodical that it cannot be dismissed as a handful of 'rogue cops' exceeding orders. Torture is systematic. It appears to be sanctioned at some level as deliberate policy; 5) Torturing is done for three purposes: to obtain information; to induce people to make confessions, be they true or false; and to deter the Palestinians in the occupied territories from resistance activities.

Naturally, this report did not remain uncontradicted[94] and it triggered a whole set of further Israeli reports; yet their denials were unconvincing.[95] *National Lawyers' Guild of the U.S.*: An extensive report was also made available by the American Lawyers' Guild with the conclusion '. . . that torture has been used in numerous instances against detained Palestinians by Israeli police, military, and intelligence authorities'.[96] Access to prisons or to detainees was also refused the delegation of this guild. In addition to statements from former prisoners, they based their evidence on conversations with Israeli and Palestinian lawyers,[97] on contradictory denials by Israeli agencies of all existing torture accusations, and on many reports of other reputable organizations. The Lawyers' Guild points out in particular that Israeli administration of justice in the occupied territories encourages the extortion of confessions by means of torture, as the sentences of most security prisoners were based solely on confessions.[98] There have been no cases so far in which a court has accepted the retraction of a confession, because this would mean the confirmation of the torture accusations.

> **'I Can No Longer Remain Silent'**
> Victor Cygielman, a respected Jewish journalist, describes his difficulties with the torture accusations as follows:
>
> I have kept silent up to now for several reasons. In particular, because I could not prove these accusations. I had neither formal evidence nor the inner conviction that these accusations were founded. Certainly, the lack of political freedom in the occupied territories and the climate of violence — brought about by bloody assassination attempts and the violent reprisals — produce all sorts of deviations from the usual standards of human rights by the prosecuting authorities.
>
> I was able to detect exaggerations, even fantasies, on the part of the Palestinians. . . . There was also the constant testimony by the Arab, or generally anti-Israeli propaganda which described Israel as using 'Nazi methods' or as being a 'Nazi regime', which caused me to be even more cautious. Not because I felt that the

> Jews . . ., who were the victims of the Nazi regime, were themselves incapable of becoming racists, but because such a comparison either reveals an incredible ignorance of the reality of the Nazi regime or shows the unscrupulous willingness to use the most demagogical argument of all, in order to give credibility to a frightening image of Israel. . . . The Israelis also believe, often rightfully so, that the criticism aimed at the government actually challenges the right of the state of Israel to exist. . . . But Israel, because it is Israel, must not let its survival be accompanied by totalitarian and colonialistic practices. . . . Power corrupts. Absolute power corrupts absolutely. Likewise, any control exercised by one people over another corrupts.
> I feel I can no longer remain silent.
>
> Source: Victor Cygielman, 'Les bavures de l'occupation'. *Nouvel Observateur*, 22 March 1976.

Whoever still denies mistreatment and torture in Israeli prisons in spite of the reports and investigations, closes his eyes to reality. Yet, whoever refers to these violations of human rights as the only standard for judging the occupiers, paints too gloomy a portrait of a regime of terror.

Reading reports about violations of human rights in all parts of the world sometimes gives one the impression that there is no difference between Israel and, for example, Chile or Guatemala. In the occupied territories, one is not immediately murdered, executed or sentenced for publicly speaking out against the occupiers. Many newspaper readers in unoccupied countries would be thankful for the amount of freedom of press and opinion which can be observed in the West Bank and Gaza Strip. The Red Cross would be happy if it could work in all countries under the conditions it is granted in Israel.[99]

However, the fact that there are worse offenders against human rights does not make Israel's activities legitimate. Israel is quite rightly indicted for the countless violations of human rights and arbitrary acts of injustice which have characterized the long period of the Israeli occupation.

Today, the occupying authority still refuses to adhere to the regulations of the Fourth Geneva Convention. The Palestinians suffer daily under the arbitrary acts of the occupying troops, which do not allow the Palestinian people to determine their own future.

The conclusion that the Israeli occupying authority is not a murderous, terrorist regime does not ease the suffering of those under occupation, nor does it affect the legitimacy of political resistance. Brutality and torture are neither denied nor justified by it. Yet solidarity with the victims must not exclude justice towards the perpetrator.

Notes

1. On 19 December 1968, the U.N. General Assembly resolved to set up a permanent special committee (U.N. Doc. G.A. 2443 (XXIII)), the U.N. Special Committee to Investigate Israeli Practices Affecting the Human Rights of the Population of the Occupied Territories. This special committee submits an annual report on the results of its investigations (cf. *Gerson 1978*, p. 151). Based on its reports, the General Assembly passed a number of resolutions, e.g. U.N. Doc. G.A. Res. 2727 (1970), 2851 (1971), 3005 (1972), 3092 (1973), 3240 A to C (1974), 3525 A to D (1975), 31/106 A to D (1976), 32/91 A to C (1977), 33/113 A to C (1978), in which Israel's violations of human rights are condemned, cf. *Sharif 1979*, p. 21ff.
2. An abundance of other reports, investigations and documentations made by various organizations also exist. Cf. below.
3. Cf. *Shamgar 1971*, p. 266; *Lorch* (former Israeli ambassador) *1971*, p. 366; *Blum* (current Israeli ambassador to the U.N.) *1978*, p. 49ff.; *Blum 1968*, p. 279; Blum in *U.S. Senate Hearing*, p. 24ff.
4. Cf. Chapter 2, note 10. Only the most important aspects and arguments regarding the problems of occupation and international law can be dealt with here; for more details cf. *Moore 1977*, p. 239ff. for further references, and *Gerson 1978*, p. 2ff.; *Dinstein 1978*, p. 104; *Drori 1978*, p. 144.
5. Cf. Chapter 2.
6. Chaim Herzog, former ambassador to the U.N. in New York, in a speech before the General Assembly on 26 October 1977, quoted from *Commission 1977*, p. 33.
7. Cf. *Blum 1978*, p. 50.
8. See *Commission 1977*, p. 33; it is therefore a situation of *de facto*, not *de jure*. Cf. the references to pertinent international literature in *Commission 1977*, p. 30.
9. Geneva Convention Relative to the Protection of Civilian Persons in Time of War, of 12 August 1949, cf. Mallison, *U.S. Senate Hearing*, p. 51; *Boyd 1971*, p. 258; *Commission 1977*, p. 34; *NLG Report*, Introduction, p. XV.
10. Israel's qualifying Jordan and Egypt as illegal occupiers is contradictory at the very least. Through the ceasefire agreement at Rhodes on 3 April 1949, and the exchange of territory connected with it, as well as through the conclusion of a secret partial non-aggression pact in the first Middle East war with Jordan, Israel at least implicitly recognized the Jordanian claims to the territory. Even today it still considers the Hashemite monarch and the Egyptian president to be the natural and legally legitimate participants in peace negotiations on the future of the occupied territories. In view of Israel's absolute refusal to accept a Palestinian state between Jordan and itself and the willingness expressed by the Labour administrations until 1977 to return at least part of the occupied territories the question arises as to which sovereignty this part of the territory should be returned to, if not to the allegedly 'illegal sovereign'. Therefore, Israel is negotiating, or rather wants to negotiate, with countries which it explicitly feels are

not authorized for such negotiations. For details cf. *Kapeliouk 1977*; *Feinberg 1977*, p. 60.
11. *Commission 1977*, p. 34.
12. The Red Cross in its annual report from 1975, quoted from *Commission 1977*, p. 34.
13. Since July 1967, the U.S. has pointed out to the Israeli government numerous times that the Fourth Geneva Convention must be applied (cf. the speech by Charles Yost, former U.N. envoy from the U.S. to the Security Council on 1 July 1969, quoted from *NLG Report*, Introduction, p. XV). The U.S. has always voted for the U.N. resolutions in connection with this, e.g. in the U.N. Economic and Social Council on 4 February 1978 and in the Security Council on 29 February 1980 (Res. 465/1980).
14. For example, the resolution by the U.N. General Assembly from 7 December 1973, (U.N. Doc. A 3092) in paragraph A 1; also Security Council Resolution 465 (1980) from 29 February 1980.
15. Cf. *ICRC 1970*, p. 426; cf. *ICRC* Annual Report 1978, p. 33ff.
16. Moshe Dayan in the Knesset on 10 July 1968, quoted from *Israel Information Centre 1976*, p. 3; *Shamgar 1971*, p. 151.
17. Cf. *Blum 1978*, p. 49.
18. Cf. Chapter 2,
19. The decisions in the court cases of Beit El, Baqaot B and Eilon Moreh confirm — independent of the issue legality — that private land was confiscated from Arab farmers (see Chapter 2. It is unquestioned that hundreds of Palestinians lost their places of residence when Arab houses were torn down in the old part of Jerusalem (see Chapter 2,
20. Cf. *Commission 1977*, p. 30 for further references; *Gerson 1978*, p. 170.
21. See Chapter 2. Cf. *Nahumi* 1968, p. 35.
22. Cf. *Gerson 1978*, p. 211; *Pfaff 1977*, p. 270ff.; *Jones 1977*, p. 224; *Blum 1978*, p. 52.
23. See Chapter 2. On the status of Jerusalem cf. *Schroeter 1972*, p. 26ff.; *Feinberg 1977*. p. 60.
24. Also see Chapter 7.
25. In the beginning of 1980, the attempted Israeli takeover of the East Jerusalem power stations led to fierce protests in the occupied territories, as this would have meant a further act towards annexation (cf. *Middle East*, March 1980, p. 18ff).
26. For the press situation cf. the well-meaning description by *Ansprenger 1978*, p. 255ff; more critical is *Mathiot*, pp. 27, 30ff; also cf. *Rejwan 1973*, p. 15ff.
27. Cf. for examples the report of the *U.N. Special Committee 1979*, p. 39.
28. According to Article 43 of the Hague Regulations, the occupying authority is entitled to issue ordinances for this reason, cf. *Gerson 1978*, p. 122, *MER 1967*, p. 285 for further references.
29. Israel is of the opinion that these ordinances are part of the Jordanian legal system (cf. *Shefi 1973*, p. 344; *Dershovitz 1971*, p. 310ff.; *Shamgar 1971*, p. 274); whereas Jordan disputes this (cf. *U.N. Special*

Committee 1970, Appendix 5; also see *NLG Report*, p. 61 ff.).
30. Cf. *Monroe 1977*, p. 407; other sources say that approximately 28,000 Palestinians had been in Israeli prisons by 1976 (cf. *Problems of Peace and Socialism* (French edition), No. 6/76, p. 190).
31. Israel never denied the deportations; cf. e.g. *Cahana 1972*, p. 9ff.; *Lesch 1979*, p. 101, a comprehensive study for the American Friends Service Committee examines the extent and practices of the deportation, also cf. the abridged version by *Khouri 1978*, p. 23ff.
32. Concerning the varying numerical data cf. *Lesch 1979*, p. 103; *Financial Times*, 9 December 1977, which refers to official Israeli sources: *Shefi 1973*, p. 348; Israeli figures range from 80 to 200 persons.
33. See the protocol of a deportation in Chapter 1.
34. Cf. *Lesch 1979*, p. 106; *Amad 1973*, p. 18ff., for further references; *U.N. Special Committee 1979*, p. 100; also see the report on the deportation of Dr Hanna Nasir, President of Bir Zeit University, *NLG Report*, p. 75.
35. Cf. *Yediot Aharonot*, 30 January 1979; the most famous case, which circulated in the world press, concerned the mayor of Nablus, Bassam Shak'a, who was in an Israeli prison for a few weeks until the High Court finally declared the ordered deportation to be illegal (cf. the documentation of this case in *Israleft* No. 158 (15 November 1979), 159 (1 December 1979) and 160 (15 December 1979) with a compilation of the coverage from the Hebrew press.)
36. For an analysis of those affected cf. *Lesch 1979*, p. 108ff.; *NLG Report*, p. 75.
37. 'The destruction of houses inhabited or owned by terrorists . . . has proven to be a very effective deterrent and to be a humane method. . . . There can be no doubt that the destruction of a few dozen houses of convicted terrorists . . . has saved the lives of thousands of innocent people.' The Israeli argument for justification does not lack a certain cynicism, 'It is obviously more humane to destroy houses which serve as bases for murder and sabotage than to impose the death penalty.' *Israel Embassy 1978*, p. 5.
38. See the documentation of many cases in *Amad 1973*, p. 15ff.; *NLG Report*, p. 63ff.; *U.N. Special Committee* e.g. 1971, p. 45; *ICRC 1970*, p. 466; Lesch in *U.S. House Hearing*, p. 12/71; also e.g. *Ma'ariv*, 21 March 1974; *The Jerusalem Post*, 5 December 1978; *MER*, 1969/70, p. 361; *The New York Times*, 17 December 1969.
39. *The Jerusalem Post*, 28 October 1977 (excluding East Jerusalem and the destroyed villages).
40. Concerning the validity of these ordinances cf. Chapter 3, note 29.
41. Based on international law, the Red Cross has continually condemned these practices, cf. *ICRC 1970*, p. 483; also see *NLG Report*, p. 66 for further references; *Gerson 1978*, p. 162 for further references to international literature. Gerson himself is, however, of a different opinion.
42. *NLG Report*, p. 65ff.
43. Cf. e.g. *Amad 1973*, p. 15; *NLG Report*, p. 68ff.; *U.N. Special Committee* e.g. 1976, p. 38ff; 1977, p. 25ff.; also concretely in *Ma'ariv*, 26 April 1974; *Ha'aretz*, 8 May 1974; *Gans 1979*, p. 66ff.
44. Cf. e.g. on closing of a UNRWA teachers' college, the *Jerusalem Post*,

1 November 1975; of the Bir Zeit University, *Palästina Bulletin* (Bonn) No. 14/80 from 18 April 1980; of a school in Al Bireh and in Tulkarm, e.g. *Ha'aretz*, 29 February 1976; in Ramallah, *Yediot Aharonot*, 8 January 1978; also the *Jerusalem Post*, international edition, 6/12 May 1979.

45. For instance, the residents of Ramallah, Nablus and Al Bireh were not allowed to travel to Jordan for a period of weeks in 1976, cf. *Al Hamis Hamishmar*, 16 February 1976; similarly as early as 1974, cf. *Davar*, 22 November 1974.
46. For instance, bans on merchants from Al Bireh and Ramallah regarding trade with Jordan in the autumn of 1974, cf. *Davar*, 22 November 1974; e.g. the complete ban on trade for Hebron, *MER* 1969/70, p. 365.
47. For example, Ramallah, *Za Haderekh*, 27 November 1974.
48. The *Jerusalem Post* and *Ha'aretz*, 8 June 1977; the *New York Times*, 6 August 1971.
49. The countless incidents in which soldiers of the occupying authority humiliated Palestinian residents cannot be listed here; cf. e.g. the reports of the *U.N. Special Committee; Amad 1973; NLG Report*, p. 71ff. For further references: *Time*, 3 April 1978, p. 32; the *Christian Science Monitor*, 23 April 1978.
50. For details cf. *Goldstein 1978*, p. 35; moreover *Hadar 1971*, p. 284ff.; *Dershovitz 1971*, p. 310; *State Department 1978*, p. 367.
51. *NLG Report*, p. 80; cf. *A.I. Report 1979*, p. 281.
52. The *Jerusalem Post*, 15 June 1971; Shloma Hillel, minister of police at that time, stated the number of prisoners for 1970 was 1,400, the *Jerusalem Post*, 30 April 1974.
53. Shimon Peres, the defence Minister at that time, the *Jerusalem Post*, 22 January 1976.
54. *Ha'aretz*, 19 June 1974.
55. The *Jerusalem Post*, 26 July 1974.
56. *Time*, 3 April 1978; in February 1980, there were allegedly 21. See statement by Israel's U.N. envoy in Geneva, Yoel Barromi, 7 February 1980, before the Human Rights Committee, p. 13.
57. For the prerequisites cf. *NLG Report*, p. 79.
58. Cf. e.g. *U.N. Special Committee 1970*, p. 50; *State Department 1977*, p. 39, and *1978*, p. 367; Swiss League for Human Rights printed in *U.S. Senate Hearing*, p. 183; *A.I. Report 1979*, p. 281.
59. Cf. *A.I. Report 1979*, p. 281. Yoel Barromi, *op. cit.*
60. For more details see *NLG Report*, p. 86; *A.I. Report 1979*, p. 280.
61. Cf. Articles 64, 66, 71, 73 and 76 of the IV Geneva Convention; Articles 8, 11, 12, 18 and 31 of the Security Provisions Order; for details also cf. *NLG Report*, p. 88.
62. Cf. *U.S. Senate Hearing*, p. 191; *NLG Report*, p. 89; *U.N. Special Committee 1976*, p. 62; *A.I. Report 1979*, p. 282; arguing against this is the Israeli U.N. envoy in Geneva, Yoel Barromi, *loc. cit.*
63. *A.I. Report 1979*, p. 282.
64. Cf. *Ma'ariv* and the *Jerusalem Post*, 4 February 1977.
65. As early as 1970 in *ICRC 1970*, p. 504, and in addition in *ICRC* annual

report 1975, p. 21.
66. *A.I. Report 1977*, p. 303.
67. Cf. e.g. *U.N. Special Committee 1974*, p. 9; *State Department 1978*, p. 366; the *Sunday Times* (London), 19 June 1977.
68. *Ma'ariv* and the *Jerusalem Post*, 4 February 1977; the High Court also confirmed this, *Davar*, 6 December 1977; plans for the construction of prisons repeatedly became known, the *Jerusalem Post*, 8 August 1977; *Ma'ariv*, 21 September 1977; *Israel Magazine*, June 1972. However, up till now, no decisive changes have taken place.
69. *NLG Report*, p. 94.
70. Cf. *Ha'olam Hazeh*, 14 May 1975.
71. Cf. Jehuda Litani in *Ha'aretz*, 11 March 1977, who, amongst others, reports that the subsidy for Arab detainees in 1977 was reduced from I£30 to 20 per month, whereas for Jewish prisoners, it amounted to I£70 per month. The Swiss League for Human Rights also points out this 'questionable differentiation' in its report; cf. *U.S. Senate Hearing*, p. 181.
72. *Ha'aretz*, 11 March 1977.
73. *A.I. Report 1979*, p. 284.
74. Only the most important investigations and documentations can be described here; other reports are those of the State Department on the human rights situation in countries on friendly terms with the U.S., cf. *State Department 1977, 1978; Amad 1973*, Swiss League for Human Rights printed in *U.S. Senate Hearing*, p. 181; moreover *U.S. Senate Hearing* and *U.S. House Hearing*; documentation of individual cases, *Dib 1970*.
75. Report on the treatment of certain prisoners and interrogation in Israel, press release from Amnesty International, April 1970, p. 5; also cf. *A.I. Report 1970* in *Al-Abid 1970*, p. 111ff.
76. Cf. *A.I. Report 1979*, p. 284; also see the *Christian Science Monitor*, 3 April 1970; the *New York Times*, 4 April 1970; *State Department 1978*, p. 370; the *Washington Post*, 7 February 1979.
77. *A.I. Report 1979*, p. 279.
78. Cf. the *Washington Post*, 7 February 1979; *Bishara 1979*, p. 10ff., who depicts the background for these reports in detail.
79. *A.I. Report 1979*, p. 282.
80. Cf. for the history of origins, of the political and legal assessment, *Gerson 1978*, p. 151ff.
81. Cf. *U.N. Special Committee 1975*, p. 34.
82. Cf. e.g. *U.N. Special Committee 1976*, p. 59; *1977*, p. 40: 'The Special Committee has no option but to state that a strong *prima facie* case has been established that detainees in occupied territories are subjected to treatment which cannot be described as other than torture.'
83. *U.N. Special Committee 1979*, p. 117; for the Israeli counter-representation to the most recent U.N. report, cf. Yoel Barromi, *loc. cit.*
84. Cf. e.g. *U.N. Special Committee 1979*, pp. 77-94, 101-03.
85. Cf. *ICRC Annual Report 1978*, p. 33; the *Sunday Times* (London), 'What the Red Cross Secret Reports Show', 18 September 1977.
86. Cf. the *Jerusalem Post*, international edition, 22/28 April 1979; *A.I. Report 1979*, German edition, p. 283.

87. Cf. the *Sunday Times* (London), 18 September 1977; 19 June 1977; differently, Krivine, 'Flawed Insight on Torture', the *Jerusalem Post*, 5 August 1977.
88. *A.I. Report 1979*, p. 283.
89. On 1 February 1978, the International Red Cross made known that Israel would now permit visits to detainees within the first 14 days, even if the interrogations were not yet concluded. This ruling was then introduced on a trial basis; whether or not it actually upholds Israel's international obligations and the wishes of the Red Cross satisfactorily is not known (cf. *ICRC Annual Report 1978*, p. 33; Yoel Barromi on Israel's new agreement in *ICRC, loc. cit.*, p. 11.)
90. In 1970, the Red Cross agreed to this ruling. Since then, the number of the complaints has reduced considerably since the detainees were understandably reluctant to file a complaint with the government that, in their view, authorized their torture. Today, the Red Cross also expresses doubt about this ruling (cf. *ICRC Annual Report 1978*, p. 33).
91. Interview with the ICRC representative in Israel, the *Jerusalem Post*, 5 August 1977.
92. Cited in *U.N. Special Committee 1970*, p. 50.
93. The *Sunday Times* (London), 19 June 1977.
94. Cf. the Israeli reply to this in the *Sunday Times*, 3 July 1977; and in turn, the reaction of the *Sunday Times* Insight team in the newspaper of 10 July 1977, by David Krivine with an interview with the Red Cross representative in Israel at the time, Tschiffeli; the *Sunday Times* Insight team reacted with a special report on the ICRC activities and complaints, 'What the Red Cross Secret Reports Show', the *Sunday Times*, 18 September 1977, where Krivine again published two reports, 'An inexcusable smear', the *Jerusalem Post*, 20 September 1977, and 'More insight on torture', the *Jerusalem Post*, 28 October 1977.
95. For details, cf. *NLG Report*, p. 102.
96. *NLG Report*, p. 116.
97. Among these are also Moshe Amar (MAPAM), a member of the Knesset, and Mordechai Bentov, former minister of housing (cf. *NLG Report*, p. 116), who knew of physical and psychological mistreatment in their districts but repudiated accusations of systematic torture.
98. Cf. the *NLG Report*, p. 109; Amnesty International also criticized this administration of justice in *A.I. Reports 1979*, p. 280; however, this is disputed by Yoel Barromi, *loc. cit.*
99. Peter Küng, the director of the Red Cross in Israel, in an interview with the *Jerusalem Post*, international edition, 22/28 April 1979, p. 13.

4. Creeping Annexation: The Economy

An Uneven Start: The Background

The first Middle East war divided the region into three separate areas and destroyed the Palestinian economic structure. The Negev Desert, the coastal plain, Galilee and the northern Jordan Valley became Israeli territory. The west bank of the Jordan River was annexed by Transjordan (the territory of Jordan prior to the establishment of the Kingdom of Jordan in 1945). The southern tip of Palestine on the Mediterranean coast, the Gaza Strip, came under the supervision of an Egyptian military government.[1]

The West Bank: Cut Off
In 1948, the West Bank was cut off from its ports, Haifa, Yafo and Gaza, thereby losing some of its supply sources and markets. As a direct result of the war, one quarter of the West Bank's inhabitants no longer had access to their jobs in the coastal plain cities nor to fields on the other side of the ceasefire line.

In addition, there were refugees: 600,000 to 900,000 Palestinians fled from the Israeli territory in 1947 and 1948. Of these, more than 400,000 settled in the West Bank, almost doubling the population.[2] Their integration into society was a necessity. The only connection with the outside world was via the East Bank.

The Jordanian Kingdom on the East Bank had been set up under King Abdallah by the British colonial power. Even poorer than the West Bank, the East Bank had always been an appendage to the Palestinian economy.

In 1950, the West Bank was formally annexed. Thus, from that time on, the Hashemite Kingdom of Jordan consisted of the East and West Banks. The Jordanian regime had its own plans for this area, the West Bank was to be the vegetable garden of the kingdom; employment opportunities other than in farming were not promoted. According to the Jordanian economic plan for the years 1964 to 1970, the West Bank economy was to be limited to the agricultural sector; the development of an industrial infrastructure was not planned.[3] New industrial plants were only approved for East Jordan. Although East Jordan's need to catch up economically with the West Bank was originally given as justification for the policy, it soon became evident that it actually served a different purpose, namely to ensure King Hussein's control over the West Bank. Thus, in addition to the already difficult situation following the war, the West Bank was put at a disadvantage by the Amman government.

The development of new employment opportunities did not keep up with the natural growth of the population and only some of the refugees from 1948 could be integrated. Open unemployment was widespread as was the hidden unemployment in the agricultural sector. The employment situation would have been even worse had it not been for the large number of people that emigrated. From 1949 to 1967, an estimated 200,000[4] left to seek work in the East Bank and in other Arab countries or overseas.

From Trade Centre to Enclave: The Gaza Strip

The problems created by the 1948 war were even greater in the Gaza Strip than they were in the West Bank. At the time of the British Mandate, the city of Gaza was the trade centre and port for the area south of Tel Aviv and Yafo and for the area surrounding Hebron and Beersheba. The Gaza markets played an important role in selling goods from all over the country and a considerable amount of import-export business was conducted through the port. In addition, there were also a number of private craftsmen.

During the war, the Egyptian army occupied Gaza and an area surrounding it, 42 kilometres long and 8 to 10 kilometres wide, which was inhabited by approximately 60,000 people. The 'Gaza Strip' was cut off from its hinterland, which had become part of Israel; the Egyptian centres, which lay on the other side of the virtually unpopulated Sinai Desert, could only be reached by a long train ride. Arable land and water were scarce in the Gaza Strip itself. Moreover, in the years 1948-49, approximately 150,000 people fled from the Israeli territory to the Gaza Strip, more than tripling its population. The local economy – which could barely feed the indigenous population – was unable to absorb the refugees. In 1967, almost 400,000 people were living in the Gaza Strip,[5] unemployment and underemployment were widespread and the average income was lower than in the West Bank.

Birth of a Superpower: Israel in the Middle East

After the 1948 war, the Jewish state, unlike the West Bank and the Gaza Strip, was able to build upon existing economic structures. In the 20s and 30s, Jewish settlers acquired some 100,000 *dunams*[6] of arable land, located mainly in the coastal plain and in the northern Jordan Valley.[7] Zionist organizations saw to a favourable distribution of their property and settlements by means of strategic land purchases. The success of this policy was evident in 1947 when the U.N. Partition Plan awarded the fertile regions of Palestine to the Jews.

Another decisive part of Zionist policy, in addition to the land purchases, was to create a purely Jewish economic sector in Palestine.[8] This was necessary to create jobs for the Jewish immigrants who had to compete with the cheaper Arab labour. Despite the opposition of Jewish entrepreneurs, the organizations of the Zionist workers' movement, which greatly influenced the most important phases of the Jewish settlement, led a campaign for *avoda ivrit* (Jewish labour), by which Jewish businesses were supposed to hire only Jewish workers. In order to strengthen their own economic sector, Jews were supposed only to buy Jewish products, even if Arab goods were cheaper.

The creation of a purely Jewish economic sector also had an ideological basis for the socialist Zionist workers' movement who were against the exploitation of Arab labourers. They established a system of co-operatives (settlements, consumer and commercial co-ops, banks, construction companies and transport co-ops), from which Palestinian Arabs were excluded.

By 1948, a complete Jewish entity, separate from traditional Palestinian society, was formed on this Jewish economic base. There were schools, political parties, a trade union, parliaments and the nucleus of an army.

During the military conflicts between 1947 and 1949, about 80% of the Arab population had to leave the Israeli territory. Their property (land, orchards, houses, entire villages and city districts) was classified by the Israeli authorities as 'absentee' property, and, for the most part, passed into Jewish hands. Out of 370 new Jewish settlements established between 1948 and 1953, 350 were located on property belonging to refugees. In 1954, more than one-third of the Jewish population was living on 'absentee' property and almost one-third of the new immigrants (250,000 people) were settled in the city districts the Arabs had left. In 1952, 20,000 *dunams* of land belonging to 'absentees' was leased for industrial sites by the Office for Absentee Property.[9] Ten thousand shops passed into Jewish hands. In 1949, olives from abandoned Arab orchards were Israel's third largest export product (after citrus fruits and diamonds) and in 1951–52 the citrus harvest from Arab orchards brought in almost 10% of Israel's export proceeds.[10]

With the construction of the Jewish economic sector and the benefits from the acquisition of Arab property, the politically independent Israeli economy was in a fundamentally different situation from that of the West Bank or the Gaza Strip. The West Bank had to acquiesce to Jordanian interests, and the major stumbling-block to development in the Gaza Strip was its isolation. The Israeli economy, on the other hand, had a state protecting and promoting it by every conceivable means, as well as considerable support from abroad.

After the state of Israel was founded, its economy could have gone one of two ways — further development of the Jewish economy independent of Arab countries or integration into surrounding markets. The latter, in view of the Israeli level of capital, know-how and productivity, would have led to Israel's economic dominance in the Middle East. Integration promised great advantages and Israeli politicians were already designing appropriate concepts by the time the Israeli state was founded. For example, a U.S. magazine reported in 1950 that Chaim Weizman, Israel's first president, 'talks of Israel's becoming "the new Switzerland", supplying consumer goods to the untapped markets of the Middle East'.[11] Foreign Minister Aba Ebban described possible trade relations between Israel and the Arab nations in a 1952 speech before the U.N. as follows: Israel could import raw materials from Arab nations; for example, produce from Syria, Lebanon and Jordan, meat from Iraq and cotton from Egypt. In return, Israel could supply industrial goods to the Arab countries. Israel's relations with these countries should be 'akin to the relationship between the United States and the Latin American continent'.[12]

However, the Arab boycott blocked these dreams. No one had really believed in the effectiveness of the boycott during the first few years of Israel's statehood, yet it held until 1967 when the newly occupied Arab territory became integrated into the Israeli economy.

Economy and Occupation: Israel in 1967

Even before 14 May 1948, the Jewish sector was dependent on financial aid from abroad — capital from new immigrants and subsidies from Zionist organizations.[13] One of the most important tasks of Israel's first finance minister was to obtain short-term loans from every possible source at any price. The problems did not diminish until new sources of money began coming in from abroad. In 1949, the U.S. government approved the first in a series of loans and in 1951 the first subsidy. In September 1952, the West German Reparation Payments Agreement for Nazi crimes was signed. Added to this were the loans and donations from Jews and Zionist organizations all over the world, especially from the U.S.

It became clear between 1965 and 1967 — the years of recession — that foreign aid would decrease. The U.S. government cut back on its subsidies and converted aid into long-term loans. West Germany's reparation payments, which went directly to the Israeli government, ended in 1966. The volume of pension payments to Holocaust victims and their offspring peaked in 1963 and was already beginning to decline slightly. The influx of capital from abroad was also decreasing. A continuation of this trend would have certain inevitable effects in the long run — the foreign exchange reserves would be exhausted, the balance of trade would deteriorate and the enormous debts would grow. Israeli politicians began to aim at achieving economic independence through a gradual cutback in foreign aid and an expansion of exports.

However, efforts to increase exports soon ran into difficulties. For example, in the important export of citrus fruits further expansion was not possible, since the best land was already being used, and moreover, water was scarce. Israeli exports also met with stiff competition on the European markets; citrus fruits from North Africa and Spain were offered at lower prices due to lower labour costs and shorter transportation routes. Until 1970, three-quarters of all Israeli exports went to developed capitalist countries, chiefly to western Europe, the U.S. and Canada. In the early 70s, when these countries adopted a more protectionist policy, the market for Israel's traditional export products became seriously restricted.[14] Under these circumstances, Israel increased its efforts to enter into trade relations with Third World countries, but only a moderate growth rate was possible. Still its natural markets — the Arab countries — were closed to Israel because of the boycott.

This dilemma was the basis for the Israeli government's policy toward the territories occupied in June 1967. The military government's first economic planner in the West Bank saw in Israel's control over the West Bank and the Gaza Strip the weakest point in the Arab boycott which could be exploited. He hoped to create economic, cultural and even political contacts with the Arab nations through the West Bank. When asked whether promoting exports from the West Bank to East Jordan was worthwhile, he is said to have replied:

> Exports worthwhile? Don't you realize where this could lead to? They are selling in the East Bank — that's export. They get money and can buy goods — that's import, which means credit. Credit means banks, agreements on both sides; agreements between banks are almost like agreements between governments, economic agreements. Commercial agreements will follow ... perhaps delegations .... Don't you see how far things could go?[15]

Becoming a Colonial Power: The Economic Policy of the Occupiers

After six days of war, the amount of territory under Israeli control had tripled. An additional one million Palestinian Arabs found themselves under an Israeli military administration. For the first time, after 19 years of isolation from the neighbouring Arab states, the opportunity to establish contacts with an Arab region presented itself. Whether or not to take advantage of this opportunity was the big question in Israel and, especially during the first few years following the war, developing a policy towards the West Bank and the Gaza Strip became a main concern.

Zionist Tradition or Capitalist Exploitation?

Within the Labour Party faction, which at the time determined Israeli government policy to a large degree, and within the general trade union Histadrut, there were two main positions. The traditionalists feared for the Jewish nature of the state and were, therefore, against integration of the occupied territories and were in favour of long-range plans to 'clear' at least the densely populated areas. This position did not exclude the possibility of annexing 'strategically important' areas. The 'integrationists' saw in the conquests a unique possibility for further consolidating Israel and for opening up at least a small portion of the Arab market to Israel's economy.

There were also those who 'look back to the exclusiveness of the past and those who look forward to exploitation of the Arab people in the future'.[16]

The problem of integration of the West Bank and the Gaza Strip as viewed by the traditionalists, such as Pinhas Sapir or Yigal Allon (Finance Minister and Deputy Prime Minister in Golda Meir's cabinet), was a demographic one. In the long run, the integration of one million Palestinian Arabs would lead to an Arab majority in Israel. The Jewish majority in the entire region of Palestine (the territory which had been under British Mandate) was only 60% and the birth rate of the Palestinian Arabs was more than double that of the Jewish Israelis.

A further issue in the dispute was the tradition of *avoda ivrit* — the principle of Jewish labour — a cornerstone in Zionist ideology. The former secretary general of the Histadrut, Yitzhak Ben Aharon, stated in this regard: 'We shall soon hear that anyone who says he does not want to get rich on the work of the Arabs from the territories questions the realization of Zionism and holds back redemption and development.'[17]

According to the traditionalist view, the complete integration of the occupied territories would eventually lead to dissolution of the structure of the state of Israel. An Arab majority would mean either that Israel would no longer be a Jewish state or that it would cease to be a democratic one, since the Jewish minority could only maintain its control by dictatorial means. Once tens of thousands of Palestinians came from the occupied territories as cheap labour, worked in Israeli factories, built Israeli houses and roads and cultivated Israeli fields, the idea of establishing a Jewish state through Jewish labour would have failed, and with it, the concept of Labour Zionism. 'Labour Zionism never assumed that the Jewish people in their own land could become a nation ruling over other nations,' declared Ben Aharon.[18]

Yet the traditionalists were well aware of the strategic and economic advantages of integrating the occupied territories into Israel. Former Prime Minister Levi Eshkol expressed their hesitation succinctly: 'The dowry is sumptuous, but the bride is so plain.'[19]

The integrationists, led by Defence Minister Moshe Dayan, felt the dowry thoroughly outweighed the disadvantages of the bride. Instead of hanging on to old ideals, they were for the pragmatic use of economic opportunities which had arisen, namely expansion of the market for Israeli industrial products and tapping of a labour reservoir that the Israeli economy needed urgently during the post-war boom. Yet the integrationists avoided any reference to a formal annexation of the territories. The status quo — military occupation — with economic integration seemed to offer every conceivable advantage. According to Moshe Dayan, the question of borders was of secondary importance and did not need to be discussed until peace treaty negotiations were held.

What to Do with the Tomatoes? The First Months of Occupation

Although the war had caused only relatively minor damage in the West Bank, economic life was virtually paralysed for some months. Two hundred thousand people[20] (approximately a quarter of the population) fled to the East Bank during the war and in the first few months following it. In the first 12 months following the war, an estimated 12% of the male labour force was without work.[21] Agriculture had suffered little during the war, but it was unclear where the year's surplus was to be sold. The Jordanian bridges had been destroyed; the route to the East Bank and other Arab countries was closed.

The situation was similar in the Gaza Strip. Although fighting had taken place in the city of Gaza, damage was limited. The employment situation, which, owing to the many refugees of 1948, was even more difficult than in the West Bank, deteriorated further. The jobs in the service sector of the U.N. forces and the Egyptian army were gone. Trade with Egypt and smuggling were stopped. The fishing and construction industries were almost completely shut down. Local trade and industrial output declined along with demand. The war robbed an additional 20,000 people[22] of their jobs, raising the number of unemployed in the first 12 months following the war to 13.3% of the male labour force.[23] Between September 1967 and July 1968, 35,000 to 40,000 people left the Gaza Strip for Jordan. The Israeli government provided their transportation until Jordanian authorities started sending the emigrants back.[24]

The 1967 harvest in the West Bank was a particularly good one. Since the route to Jordan was closed, other markets had to be found. This was not only a problem for the farmers, but also for the military government. If the crops were left to rot in the fields, the entire West Bank economy would collapse. Unrest and increased resistance to the occupation would be the direct result. Selling the harvest in Israel was unthinkable, since the West Bank farmers could have underbid the Israelis by 20 to 25%, thereby disrupting prices in Israel.[25] For this reason, the Israelis initially forbade any import of goods from the West Bank. The crops which could not be sold on the local market amounted to 100,000 tons.

A solution to the problem was improvised. In summer, the Jordan River is quite low and in the middle there are several fords where trucks can cross it easily. The Israeli army permitted hundreds of trucks to ford the river and the Jordanian border patrol had instructions not to interfere. This continued for weeks. First tomatoes, watermelons and grapes were sent, then almonds, dates and olives. Finally, in October, the Jordanian government allowed two bridges to be built, one near Jericho and the other in Damiya on the road from Nablus to Amman, in order to sustain the border traffic in winter when the Jordan was too high to cross.

Right after the war, consideration was also given to the possibility of opening Israeli borders to workers from the occupied territories. At first, the authorities for economic planning opposed this idea. Not until 1968, when labour became scarce, did the government approve the hiring of workers from the West Bank and the Gaza Strip under the express condition 'that Israeli citizens are not affected'.[26]

Taking the Chance

In November 1968, in a Knesset debate on the economic integration of the occupied territories, Moshe Dayan cited the following measures (which had already been taken in the first 15 months of the occupation) for integrating the occupied territories: 1) the employment in Israel of labourers from Judea and Samaria and of tradesmen and limited numbers of other workmen from Gaza; 2) establishment of joint enterprises in Judea and Samaria; 3) permission to set up an Israeli-owned citrus packing plant near Gaza and for joint vegetable-growing projects in the Gaza Strip; 4) integration of transportation between Judea and Samaria and the coastal plain by means of Arab and Israeli bus companies; 5) abolition of customs dues on goods entering Israel from Judea and Samaria; 6) permission to sell agricultural produce from Judea and Samaria in Israel; 7) integration of Gaza citrus exports with the operation of the Israeli Citrus Marketing Board; 8) joint measures for pest control and against the spread of cattle and poultry diseases; 9) also, steps had been taken or were under consideration to link Gaza and parts of Judea and Samaria to Israel's electricity grid.[27]

These measures reflect the political and economic interests of Israel, which wants to control and exploit the resources of the West Bank and the Gaza Strip, but cannot formally annex these regions due to the international balance of power and demographic factors. On the one hand, in Dayan's words: 'The whole area [Israel and the occupied territories] should be regarded as one unit, so that in time the concept of the 4th June lines will be cancelled.'[28] Yet this is to be '. . . an economic integration and not a political integration. In other words: not an annexation; we should not make them [the inhabitants of the occupied territories] citizens of the State of Israel.'[29]

By creating 'new facts' Israel is pursuing a policy which, in the long run, will mean the same thing as annexation. The definition of autonomy which dominates the current debate on that subject had already been anticipated in 1968: 'autonomy of the people', but not of the land and its resources.[30]

The facts show that the dispute between the traditionalists and the integrationists remains an ideological conflict. A realistic appraisal of Israel's relations with the West Bank and the Gaza Strip comes from the Ministry of Defence: 'The areas are a supplementary market for Israeli goods and services on the one hand, and a source of factors of production, especially unskilled labour, for the Israeli economy on the other.'[31]

An Uneven Start

After the occupation in 1967, the Israelis started a series of economic transformations, not with a view to the economic progress of these areas, but in order to annex the West Bank and to integrate it fully into Israel. The evidence is sufficient. This act is in contravention of the Geneva accords and United Nations resolutions, but Israel started implementing that programme from the very first day of the occupation, with the intention of linking these areas to Israel at the economic level. What does this mean?

First, there is the question, was any harm caused by linking the occupied territories with the Israeli economy? My answer is yes, for many reasons. The linking of the West Bank economically

> with Israel means that Israel has ambitions on the West Bank and designs on the land in this area, and consequently we rejected these ambitions and we oppose this economic linkage.
>
> Secondly, the economic linkage between the West Bank and Israel is an unequal, unbalanced and unjust one, because the Israeli economy, compared with the economy of the West Bank, is advanced, and the difference is enormous. The Israeli economy has its bases and its foundations, whereas the economy of the West Bank is still weak. Consequently, an economic linkage would only lead to a further weakening of our economy and transform our territory into a market for Israeli products. This is what has actually taken place.
>
> Moreover, the economic linkage is overwhelmingly in favour of the Israelis, for it is they who formulate and implement the production programmes, with a view to making the Palestinians a profitable market for their output and continuous consumers of the products of their economy, with the benefit accruing to the Israelis.
>
> Our industries, for example, cannot compete with the Israeli industries, which are very much more advanced than ours. The policy of dependence imposed by Israel is not restricted to marketing and production but also covers services, and, in accordance with this policy, the inhabitants of the municipalities of the West Bank have been prevented from having autonomous units to provide them with any services [water and electricity supplies].
>
> The only conclusion I can draw is that the Israeli authorities want to control everything that goes on in the West Bank.
> — excerpts from Mayor Qawasmeh of Hebron's submission to the investigating committee of the U.N. Human Rights Commission.
>
> Source: U.N. document A/AC 145/RT. 279, dated 17 September 1979.

The Short Cut to Israel: Employment of Labour

Today, more than one-third of the labour force[32] in the occupied territories does not work there.[33] This is the most obvious consequence of integration into the Israeli economy. Between 1968 — when the occupying authority began to procure jobs in Israeli companies for Palestinian workers from the West Bank and the Gaza Strip — and 1974, the number of migrant workers rose from year to year. The recession in Israel which followed the October War in 1973 caused the number of workers from the occupied territories to decrease. This trend did not reverse until 1978; the number of workers

Creeping Annexation: The Economy

travelling daily to Israel in that year nearly reached the level of 1974.

Table 3
Workers from the Occupied Territories (excluding Jerusalem) Employed in Israel, 1970-78

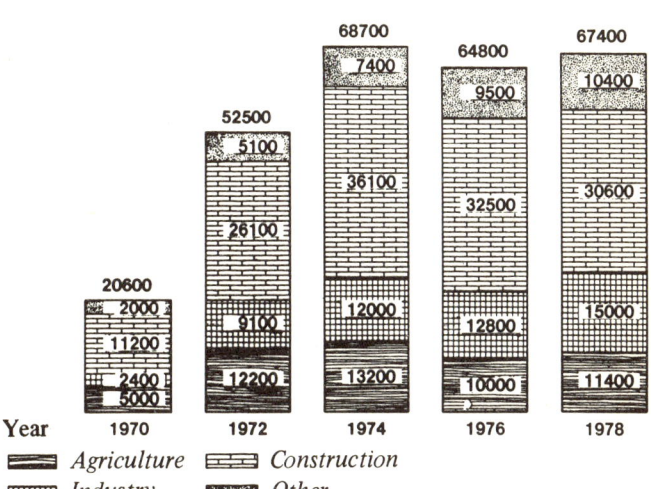

Source: *ILO 1979*, Appendix, p. 31; Israeli Ministry of Defence, 'A Twelve Years Survey, 1967-1979'.

> **'Division Along Ethnic Lines.'**
> For the most part, Arab workers from the occupied territories continue to be employed at the lower end of the occupational scale, in many of the more menial temporary or seasonal jobs to which the Israeli labour force seems less and less attracted. To some extent, therefore, the manpower from the occupied territories seems to be used as a substitute for Israeli workers, which probably indirectly increases the latters' chances of promotion. Once again, the mission would like to draw attention to the threat which the introduction of a kind of division of the labour market not only on the basis of the type of jobs but also in fact, to a large extent along ethnic lines, poses for the achievement of industrial peace and social justice. Action must be taken to combat any tendency for a secondary labour market, partitioned off from the other and affording little prospects for the future,

> to become institutionalized.
>
> Source: *ILO 1979*, Appendix, p. 30.

Between 1968 and 1972, 23 employment agencies were set up in the West Bank and 12 in the Gaza Strip. Israeli firms report their needs for labour from the occupied territories to their domestic employment offices. They, in turn, contact the employment agencies in the West Bank and the Gaza Strip, where all applicants are registered. After the person in question has been checked by Israeli security, the employment agency issues a work permit, a stamp which is pasted onto the identification papers. The work permit must be renewed at least every four months.

Officially, these employment agencies are to regulate the job market in the interest of the job-seeker. Above all, however, they perform a function for the Israeli job market. For example, in December 1968, only 56% of all job-seekers in the West Bank were sent to Israel. In March 1971, this figure rose to 99%.[34] The first criterion for job placement: the demand in Israel.

In addition to the regulated job market, there is the 'free' market. Every morning the border crossings between Israel and the occupied territories are

Palestinian construction workers on their way to work for Israel

loading docks for illegal workers. These workers either look for work on their own from day to day or are forced to go through an Arab employment agent, who makes a living by daily procuring employment in Israel for entire labour crews. According to Israeli authorities quoted in an International Labour Office report, 'about 20,000 workers — over a quarter of the total officially employed — many more according to other sources'[35] evade the employment agencies. (Other sources put the figure as high as 35,000.). A remarkable number of the 'illegal' workers are young people under 17 years of age, for whom jobs may not officially be procured; during checks made by Israeli authorities in the months of September and October 1978, 20% of the 'illegal' workers who were seized in Israel were children.[36]

The Palestinians from the occupied territories make up a reservoir of labour from which the Israeli market can draw according to its own needs.

> **'A Bargain for the Israeli Economy'**
>
> Economists say that the Israeli economy can learn much from the Arab workers who come to us daily from the occupied territories. These workers have many advantages over Israeli workers: Israeli workers shun industry and production whereas workers from the territories are becoming concentrated more and more in industry. Among Israeli workers there exist problems of low work productivity and invisible unemployment while workers coming from the territories possess a high productivity, and hidden unemployment can hardly be found amongst them. It is almost impossible to fire an Israeli worker, impossible to re-locate him without his permission and without a wage increase; on the other hand an Arab worker is exceptionally mobile, can be dismissed without notice and moved from place to place, does not strike and does not present 'demands' as does his Israeli counterpart. In short, from many economic considerations, workers from the territories are a bargain for the Israeli economy. It is a labour force which economists are able to define as responding in an economically healthy manner to the demands of the economy: they exist when and where required and make a full contribution to the production cycle. As long as one does not speak in social or political terms, the workers from territories display an excellent economic flexibility.
>
> Source: *Davar*, 18 May 1976.

The labour market with its great 'flexibility' — a euphemism for having no rights — clearly reflects Israeli business fortunes. During the boom which lasted until 1973/74, increasing numbers of workers from the occupied territories were employed in Israel. During the recession in the years after

Table 4
Unemployment in Israel and the Hiring of Workers from the Occupied Territories (excluding Jerusalem), 1967-1978.

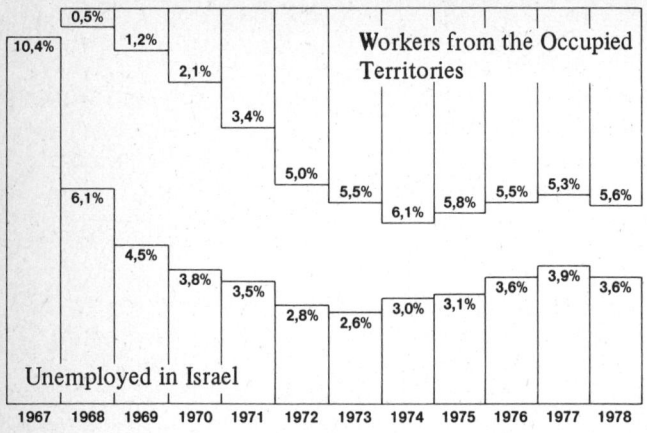

Source: *Statistical Abstract*: 1974, p. 705; 1975, p. 705; 1977, p. 726; and p. 302 ff.; 1979, p. 355 and p. 744.

the 1973 October War, this number fell once again (see Table 4).

Especially dependent upon the level of business activity are the illegal workers, who are normally hired by the day. It is estimated that in 1974, 15,000 illegal Palestinian workers were no longer able to find employment in the Israeli market. It is most probable that only some have since found work in Israel through the employment agencies.

The statistics (see Table 3), point to the role the illegal workers have played as a 'buffer' in Israeli business. The recession began in Israel in 1974, a few months after the October War. The official number of workers from the West Bank and Gaza Strip employed in Israel, excluding the illegal workers, does not begin to fall until 1975. In 1974, i.e. the first year of the recession, this number actually increases by 12.5%. It is clear, therefore, that before the recession has an effect on the number legally employed, the number of illegal workers decreases.[37]

Employment in the Occupied Territories

In 1978, 146,700 people were employed in the West Bank and in the Gaza Strip. Agricultural employment has declined in absolute terms as well as in

Table 5
Employment in the Occupied Territories (excluding Jerusalem), 1970-79

	1970		1979	
	in thousands	%	in thousands	%
TOTAL	152.7	100.0	137.7	100.0
Agriculture, forestry, fishing	59.2	38.8	38.4	28.0
Industry	21.0	13.8	23.2	16.8
Construction	12.9	8.4	13.9	10.1
Services (total)	59.6	39.1	65.7	45.1
Commerce and tourism	21.7	14.2	22.0*	15.0*
Transportation, storage, communication	7.9	5.2	10.2*	7.0*
Public services	23.0	15.1	25.3*	17.2*
Banking, public utilities, private services	7.0	4.6	8.2*	5.6*

Source: *ILO 1979*, Appendix, p. 44; *Statistical Abstract*, 1980, p. 696.
* Figures from 1978, first and second quarters.

relation to other sectors (see Table 5). Many of those who left farming are now employed as wage earners in Israel. Employment figures in the industrial and construction sectors have changed little since 1967.

More remarkable is the ever-increasing importance of the service sector. In 1978, about 45% of all those employed in the occupied territories were working in this sector. Such a large proportion is unusual in an economy where agriculture predominates and industry is of minor importance. It can only be explained by the fact that a significant number of agricultural and industrial workers are employed abroad, mainly in Israel but also in various Arab countries. Moreover, considerable sums of money annually flow into the occupied territories from abroad (e.g. from exiled Palestinians and international relief organizations).

The economy of the West Bank and Gaza Strip today can be described as a 'dormitory economy'.[38] Many workers are not involved in local production, and are only consumers of goods and services in the occupied territories. This unusual, inflated form of the service sector is the other aspect of the absorption of labour into the Israeli economy.

Despite steady growth of the working population, the number of jobs in the occupied territories decreased by 6,000 between 1970 and 1978. The explanation for this lies in an increase of over 40,000 of those working in Israel. This leaves the economy of the West Bank and Gaza Strip in even less of a position to employ all of its inhabitants than it was before. It is even more impossible to retain the workers who have lost their jobs in Israel because of the recession. The old dilemma prevails for anyone losing their job: they can either stop working completely, which is only possible for those who do not have to support a family, such as women who return to their traditional role in the home, or emigrate. A.R. Husseini, an economics expert on the West Bank states:

> We are now losing about 20,000 workers a year across the bridge, most of them skilled — teachers, doctors, engineers. This process has accelerated particularly among educated youth. Unlike unskilled labourers, college graduates are paid relatively poorly, that is if they find jobs at all. In the last couple of years there has also been a marked increase in the outflow of skilled labourers. They can earn a lot more in Saudi Arabia and Amman. Our experience here is bitter; the ones who leave don't come back. They always rationalize in the beginning, that they are leaving for just one or two years to make enough money and come back. But somehow they settle where they are.[39]

Table 6
Migration Balance, 1969-78

Gaza Strip		West Bank (excluding Jerusalem)	
1969	− 2,900	1969	+ 1,200
1970	− 3,300	1970	− 5,000
1971	− 2,400	1971	− 2,500
1972	− 3,900	1972	− 5,100
1973	− 1,600	1973	+ 300
1974	− 1,900	1974	− 2,700
1975	− 3,800	1975	− 15,100
1976	− 4,300	1976	− 14,500
1977	− 3,000	1977	− 10,200
1978	− 4,900	1978	− 13,400
Total	− 32,000	Total	− 67,000

Source: *Statistical Abstract*, 1978, p. 765. Israeli Ministry of Defence, 'A Twelve Years Survey 1967-1979', Appendix.

Emigration is not a phenomenon new to the last 12 years. For decades, the lack of jobs and training has been driving Palestinians from the West Bank and Gaza Strip. In 1967, the Israeli military government estimated the number of Palestinians working abroad but whose families still lived in the occupied territories at 100,000.[40] Added to this is the number of families who have left the country for good. The extent of this exodus is revealed in the following example: there are more people from Ramallah living in the U.S. today than in Ramallah itself.

Integration or Penetration? Trade Relations

Trade relations between Israel and the occupied territories and the conditions under which they have developed clearly show the extent of economic integration. They indicate the same pitfall as was seen in developments in the other sectors of the West Bank and Gaza Strip economy. The determining factor is Israel's interests. Normally, Israel can completely realize its goals in the occupied territories by using its apparatus of military, political and economic power.

According to the Bank of Israel in a 1971 report, 'The rapid development of the trade between Israel and the administered territories can primarily be attributed to the remarkable level of economic integration which has occurred since the 1967 war.'[41] The rapid development in trade can also be attributed to the Israeli economy's need to gain access to a neighbouring market in a less industrialized country. The political situation in the West Bank and Gaza Strip at the time of their economic integration into the Israeli economy also offered another advantage: the occupied territories did not have the national economic/political structure with which to protect local industry from competition and penetration from the far superior trading 'partner'.

Even before 1967, the West Bank and the Gaza Strip had a considerable deficit in their balance of trade. A major part of industrial consumer goods and a significant proportion of foodstuffs were imported, while exports consisted primarily of produce (e.g. citrus fruits), part of which had already been processed (e.g. olive oil and olive soap).

The 1967 war cut deeply into both territories. East Jerusalem, the centre of banking and trade, was annexed by Israel. Trade between the Gaza Strip and Egypt was suspended and after the bridges had again become passable, West Bank trade found itself faced with Israeli as well as Jordanian restrictions. All imports were subject to duty in Israel. In 1968, this restriction was only lifted for some types of goods, mainly grain. In the other direction, Amman allowed everything to pass at first. Not until the West Bank production became more dependent on raw materials imported from or through Israel did Jordan — as part of the Arab boycott — cease to allow certain industrial goods into the East Bank. The Jordan-Israeli bridges are always referred to euphemistically as 'open'. Compared with the way it had been before, the opening was now more like a mousehole.

Through its integration policy, Israel has succeeded in fundamentally changing the occupied territories' trade relations. Today, their most important trade 'partner' is Israel. By 1968, the occupied territories were already buying 12 times as much in Israel as in Jordan.

The Palestinian consumer bears the cost of this development in various ways. As Israeli industry is protected by high tariff barriers, all imported goods cost much more than they actually do on the world market. The high level of prices for imported goods enables Israeli producers to manufacture and sell their products at equally high prices (almost two-thirds above net import prices).[42] In the occupied territories, Israel has replaced Jordan as the country of origin and transfer. As a result, consumers are primarily offered either Israeli goods at high Israeli prices or import goods made expensive by the high Israeli duty. Since 1967, the Palestinians have also had to pay for the protection of Israeli industry from foreign competitors.

The burden imposed by this development on the Palestinians is severe also in its deep effect on the entire economic structure of the territories. Local industry is inferior to the Israeli competitor and because it is unprotected, it develops either to complement Israeli production, or not at all. Agriculture is also subject to these conditions.

Having an economy which almost exclusively produced agricultural goods and which had to import most of its industrial products, the West Bank and Gaza Strip were the most suitable trade 'partners' for Israel whose politicians had long been looking for ways to increase the export of industrial goods. In the past few years, 85% of all Israeli goods sold in the occupied territories have been manufactured goods. Due to the increase in purchasing power in the first half of the 70s (a result of the wages earned in Israel), the sale of durable consumer goods, such as radios, televisions, gas and electric stoves, has increased, providing Israeli industry with numerous sales possibilities. The Israeli industry has almost complete control over this market. Consequently, most of the wages earned in Israel flow back into the Israeli economy and contribute to its growth.

As a matter of fact, since 1967, the West Bank and Gaza Strip has developed into one of the two most important export markets Israel has — equal to the U.S. and above Great Britain.[43] In 1975, Israel sold 16% of its total exports in the West Bank and Gaza Strip. Thus, Israeli exports to the occupied territories have become an important support for its industry.

Domination and Deterioration: Agriculture

Prior to the 1967 war, the most important sector of the economy in the occupied territories was, as in all developing countries, agriculture. At that time, half of the labour force was engaged in agriculture and an additional fifth made its living in agricultural services and the sale of agricultural products. A quarter of those employed in the Gaza Strip were working in the agricultural sector, and seasonal work in the citrus groves was often the only

Creeping Annexation: The Economy

Table 7
Trade in the West Bank (excluding Jerusalem) and the Gaza Strip, 1968-78

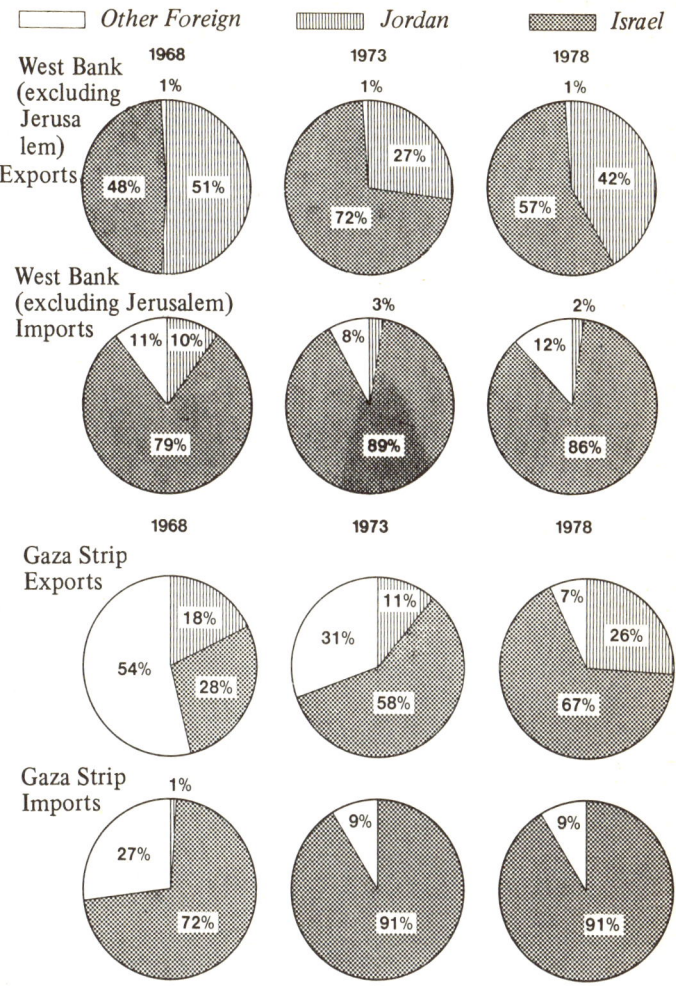

Source: *Statistical Abstracts*, 1977, p. 711; *Bregmann 1976*, p. 84; Israeli Ministry of Defence, 'A Twelve Years Survey 1967-1979', Appendix.

Table 8
Israeli Exports to the Occupied Territories (excluding Jerusalem) as a Percentage of Israel's Total Export Volume, 1966-79

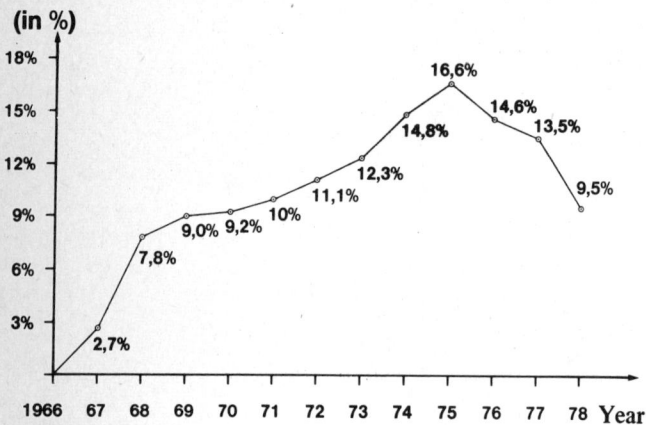

Source: *Statistical Abstract*: 1979, p. 211; 1980, p. 198.

possibility of employment for those from refugee camps.

Characteristic of the agriculture in both territories was the labour-intensive production[44] and its extremely low degree of mechanization. Irrigation was used extensively in the Gaza Strip but not in the West Bank. Under Jordanian rule, the modernization of agriculture, especially the development of irrigation systems, was reserved for the eastern part of the Kingdom. Agricultural production in the West Bank was therefore subject to large fluctuations, according to the climate.

Most farmers in the West Bank grew several crops,[45] chiefly for their own needs. Only a fraction of their produce ever reached the market.[46] The major crops were wheat, grapes, vegetables and the most important commercial product, olives, which were canned or made into oil and soap. The majority of those employed in agriculture farmed their own land (70%) while the remaining third was made up of tenant farmers and farm hands. But most of the farms were quite small, so they were hardly able to provide basic subsistence. Approximately a quarter of the farmers had to lease additional land or supplement their income by working as farm hands.[47] Citrus plantations run on capitalist lines dominated the agricultural sector of the Gaza Strip, whose products were mostly for export. There were a few large landowners and a large number of small farmers.[48]

Four developments characterize the changes that took place in agriculture in the occupied territories, particularly in the West Bank, since 1967.[49] They are: 1) a decline in production and in the total amount of cultivated land; 2) a partial re-orientation of the range of products; 3) a sharp reduction in the number of those employed in the agricultural sector; and 4) the mechanization of individual fields, especially those producing crops for export through Israeli marketing companies or for processing in Israeli industry. In the process of modernization, the agricultural sector in the occupied territories became a limited market for Israeli machinery and chemical fertilizer.

All four developments are based on the policy of economic integration, which, in itself, is an expression of Israel's economic interests. As far as agriculture was concerned, Israeli economic planners were mainly interested in protecting their own agriculture from Palestinian competition and in integrating the export segment of Palestinian agriculture into the Israeli export system. Moreover, Israel was in need of labour from the occupied territories, which came mainly from the agricultural sector.

Without a doubt, the now shrunken agricultural sector of the occupied territories, particularly in the West Bank, has 'developed' during the years of Israeli occupation. However, the direction of this development has been determined by Israel's economic interests and not by the Palestinians. Israel's grip on the most important resources — water and soil — limits any further development of Palestinian agriculture.

Increase in Production?

As shown by an analysis of the figures for the West Bank and Gaza Strip published by Israel itself, the much claimed increase in agricultural production in the occupied territories since 1967 did not actually take place.[50] Israeli publications always use the harvest from the first year of occupation as the basis for comparison, instead of the last pre-war harvest. Only in the first publications on the subject issued by the Israeli Ministry of Defence and the Central Bureau of Statistics[51] are there figures which can correct the picture — the yield of the 1968 harvest was about 40% below that of the pre-war year, 1966.[52] Weather factors and the minor destruction of fields during the war as well as the flight of many farmers during and immediately following the 1967 war were responsible for this.[53] Even the 1974 harvest, the biggest since 1967, did not equal the yield of 1966. Only by excluding the pre-war harvests in the West Bank can one talk of an increase in production.

When examining the production figures, one qualification must be made. Olive groves in the West Bank cover more land area than any other crop but their yield is subject to extreme fluctuations from year to year.[55] For this reason, olive production has been singled out in Table 9 and is not taken into consideration in the interpretation of changes in the West Bank agriculture.

A second reason for the production increase after 1968 is the steady growth in the citrus harvest. This increase can be attributed to new groves planted

Table 9
Agricultural Production in the West Bank (excluding Jerusalem), 1966-78[54]

	1966	1968	1973	1974	1976	1977	1978
			(in thousands of tons)				
Field fruits	85.9	23.5	43.3	63.9	34.9	41.8	46.0
Vegetables and potatoes	131.1	60.0	93.4	136.3	147.3	149.4	156.3
Melons and gourds	64.7	36.0	3.3	4.2	4.5	8.9	11.4
Olives	29.5	28.0	21.0	110.0	50.0	17.0	85.0
Citrus fruits	38.5	30.0	58.6	61.5	74.1	76.1	80.8
Other fruits	71.0	47.9	61.8	69.0	76.6	78.8	95.4
Total	420.7	225.4	281.4	444.9	387.4	372.0	474.9
Total *excluding* olives	391.2	197.4	260.4	334.9	337.4	355.0	389.9

Source: *Statistical Abstract*: 1970, p. 637 (for 1968); 1975, p. 710 (for 1973/74); 1978, p. 793 (for 1976/77); 1979, p. 745 (for 1978); *Israel Defence 1969*, p. 42 (for 1966).

during the Jordanian rule but which did not bear fruit until 1967.[56] Therefore, one cannot speak of an overall increase in production in the West Bank under the Israeli occupation. A relative increase in production did result, however, in that fewer farms produce more today than in 1968.

The production increase in the Gaza Strip's agricultural sector[57] is also almost exclusively due to the rise in the yield of citrus fruits. As in the West Bank, new groves were planted between 1957 and 1967. The Israeli Information Agency noted that '42,000 *dunams* planted since 1963 have reached, or are now reaching, maturity, so that, whereas 106,000 tons were produced in 1969, in 1972 there was a rise to 175,000 tons'.[58] The changes which apply to production volume also hold true for production value. Although the nominal value in Israeli pounds rose steadily in the Gaza Strip and West Bank, when this value is adjusted to the inflation rate and the citrus and olive yields are disregarded, the real increase in value from 1966 to 1977 was a total of I£6.7 million in the West Bank (less than 1%) and only I£4.3 million in the Gaza Strip (approximately 2%).[59]

These insignificant increases in the agricultural production under the occupation can hardly be attributed to the stimulation measures of the Israeli occupying authority; they are much more the result of development before the occupation. Of course, Israeli measures taken in the agricultural sector, particularly in the West Bank, did have results, but these are reflected very little in the overall production figures.

Table 10
Agricultural Production in the Gaza Strip, 1968-78

	1968	1973	1974	1976	1977	1978
			(in thousands of tons)			
Field fruits	—	—	—	—	—	—
Vegetables and potatoes	31.8	40.5	38.1	48.0	54.9	53.4
Melons and gourds	12.5	5.0	6.1	3.0	3.7	2.8
Citrus fruits	91.0	205.2	211.9	243.7	232.3	180.6
Other fruits	19.0	21.4	26.4	20.9	19.7	24.8
Total	154.3	272.1	282.5	315.6	310.6	261.6
Total *excluding* citrus fruits	63.3	66.9	70.6	71.9	78.3	81.0

Source: *Statistical Abstract*: 1975, p. 710 (for 1968, 1973 and 1974); 1978, p. 793, (for 1976 and 1977); 1980, p. 701 (for 1978).

Changes in the Spectrum of Products

Immediately following the June War, and shortly before the harvest in the West Bank and Gaza Strip, the Israeli authorities were concerned that agricultural surpluses in the occupied territories would flood the Israeli market, thereby spoiling prices, or would remain unsold, causing a collapse in the economy of the occupied territories. The 'open bridge' policy with Jordan solved this problem during the first year of the occupation.[60]

In the long run, however, the problem of selling the agricultural surpluses had to be tackled more fundamentally; trust in a continuation of the 'open bridges' would have placed Israel in a position of dependence on Jordan, which it wanted to avoid. Israel could not afford to be an alternative market for West Bank exports, especially for those goods which competed with its own products and which West Bank farmers could offer at a lower price.[61] Israeli agricultural plans were, therefore, primarily designed to reduce the volume of produce such as vegetables and melons in favour of crops requiring processing such as legumes, sesame, tobacco and cotton.[62] The changes in the spectrum of products affected mainly those goods consumed not in the West Bank itself but which were exported to Jordan.[63]

The future agricultural production of the West Bank was planned according to Israeli export strategy and Israel's requirements. 'The first step was to reduce future crops of watermelons (of which there are large surpluses) and some types of vegetables, substituting sesame and legumes, for which there is a great demand, as well as some items in short supply in Israel.'[64]

Agriculture on the West Bank, after supplying local requirements, was restricted to those products which were unprofitable to produce in Israel or which fitted into Israel's range of export products.[65] 'The immediate plan

'You have been warned . . .' – Signs found everywhere before entering the West Bank

increases the area producing sesame by 15,000 *dunams*, chickpeas by 10,000 *dunams*, tobacco by 5,000 *dunams*, and sorghum by 5,000 *dunams*, while reducing the area under watermelons by 35,000 *dunams*, i.e. to half its present size.'[66] Besides the effect it had on melons, the reduction in farmland also affected wheat (by 9%) and barley (by 23%).[67]

In order to carry out these production changes, the Israeli military government reorganized the agricultural counselling services for its use.[68] Seed for the new produce, free or at reduced prices, and training programmes support the introduction of this new branch of production. Furthermore, the marketing of agricultural goods from the occupied territories via Israel is used as a means of directing the course of production. This particularly holds true for citrus fruits from the Gaza Strip. The range of products in the Gaza Strip, unlike the West Bank, has only undergone minor changes under Israeli influence. Only the production of strawberries and certain vegetables for the off-season export to Europe was promoted. Citrus fruits from the Gaza Strip supplement Israeli exports, as was the case in 1971 when grapefruit from the Gaza made up for a shortage of Israeli grapefruit.[69]

Assael Ben-David, who began his service as the man in charge of the West

Bank for the Israeli Ministry of Agriculture in 1972, summarized his impression after his first inspection tour through the West Bank as follows: 'When one crosses through the fields of Judea and Samaria, one can see crops which were never grown there before — tomatoes for processing, early onions for export, as well as, among others, sugarbeet, peanuts and cotton.... Today in Judea and Samaria one can see tractors ploughing and the introduction of chemical fertilizers.'[70]

This change in the pattern of production also has an effect on the balance of foreign trade in the West Bank. Even though the export of produce has been increasing since 1967, it has still become more and more difficult for the agriculture to satisfy local needs.[71] Whereas in 1965 the West Bank exported a third more produce than it imported, in 1977 agricultural imports exceeded exports by I£44 million or 11%.[72] The production changes are not alone responsible for the rising percentage of imports[73] needed to supply the population with agricultural products: the growth in consumption in the occupied territories has led to a rise in demand. But the rise in imports (80% come from Israel) characterizes the increasing adaptation of agriculture to Israeli needs. It also shows that local agriculture has not even been able to take advantage of the chance to develop in line with its own domestic consumption.

According to the Israeli agricultural policy, which seeks to integrate the occupied territories' agriculture into its own,[74] the occupied territories are to grow those products which are labour-intensive[75] and permit only relatively low profits. The fact that these newly introduced products are almost completely processed in Israel underlines the disintegration of the agricultural sector within the West Bank economy and its growing dependence on Israel.

Colonial Policy in the Territories?

Claiming that the Agriculture Ministry's policy in the territories contradicts governmental policy and causes an increased hatred for Israel among their residents, the engineer A. Agmon, until recently staff officer for agricultural matters in the Gaza Strip and northern Sinai, is now speaking out. In a memorandum which he plans to distribute soon to Knesset members, he accuses the Ministry of Agriculture, where for many years he was among the senior officials, of running a 'colonial policy' in the (occupied) territories.

The total value of agricultural produce from the territories presently is hardly 10% of Israel's agricultural produce, and most of this produce from the territories is marketed for export (citrus, olive oil, grapes). Also, limitations of land and water, and the agrotechnical lag — it may be assumed — will cause a future lag in the territories' agriculture, and the present situation will continue (due to natural increase and improvement in the standard of living), in which Israel supplies the basic produce to residents of the territories, like dairy products, meat, fowl, fruit and vegetables, and surplus products without an Israeli demand, like laying-hens' meat and low quality fish.

[On the other hand, Agmon claims,] the Ministry of Agriculture has built up a legislative structure and mechanism of separation, to prevent the free marketing among us of typical produce from the territories, like Gaza fish, Hebron grapes, El-Arish dates, etc. It is also preventing development of livestock branches in the territories for local use, by means of limited financing, while the leftover produce from Israel is flooding the territories, without regard for the interests of local agriculture.

Hawks and doves alike agree, that whether the Arabs of the territories will be our neighbours in the future, or residents of Israel, every possible effort must be made to lessen their hatred of us and to increase our understanding of each other. But we do not always do this.

The past agricultural staff officer complains of the development programmes prepared by the Ministry of Agriculture for the territories, like growing castor-oil plants, for which the gross price is six lirot a *dunam*, sesame, a few vegetables for export herds in the framework of 'supplementary agriculture', that is, agriculture which would not harm a single Israeli farmer.

The West Bank and Gaza Strip buy tens of thousands of tons of Israeli produce. Sales in the other direction amount to only a few hundred tons, devoid of economic significance. Marketing of Israeli produce on the West Bank is free and the reverse is restricted. The starting point of Agmon is — 'good for the Jews.' Therefore he regrets that thousands of Arab farmers in the territories, who know and feel discrimination, come to conclusions opposite from those our information agencies would like.

Source: *Davar*, quoted from *New Outlook*, July/August, 1975, p.41 ff.

Changes in the Structure of Production

The two major developments in the production structure of the occupied territories are the decline in the number of people engaged in agriculture and the 19% decrease in the amount of cultivated land in the West Bank between 1966 and 1973.[76] Three factors were responsible for these developments: 1) the farmers who fled during and directly following the June War of 1976;[77] 2) the rising employment of ex-farmers from the West Bank in Israel;[78] and 3) the growing number of expropriations and seizures of land for Jewish settlements and military purposes (the exact number of these is very difficult to determine).[79]

The number of people engaged in agriculture sank by a good third between 1969 and 1977.[80] As shown in Table 11, self-employed workers as well as wage earners left the agricultural sector. The alternative employment opportunities in Israel caused a rise in labour costs which West Bank agriculture could not bear.[81] The second group affected consisted of tenant and small farmers who had given up their land or who now farm only a part of their land in addition to working in Israel.[82]

Table 11
Agricultural Employment: West Bank (excluding Jerusalem), 1970 and 1977

	1970	1977	
Self-employed and small employers	33.8	28.3)	thousands
Wage earners	8.6	2.6)	

Source: *Statistical Abstract*: 1975, p. 789; 1978, p. 704.

Although the number of those engaged in agriculture has fallen steadily since the occupation, production has risen, without, however, ever reaching the pre-war level. Israel attributes this relative increase in production to the success of its agricultural policy. Productivity did, in fact, rise during the post-war years, but only in a very specific way. Responsible for the increase in the wheat yield per *dunam* was new seed, which doubled or tripled the wheat harvest of non-irrigated fields in the first few years.[83] In addition to wheat, where better seed was able to make up for the decline in the amount of farmland, production improvements primarily involved those products which were destined for export through the Israeli marketing firm, Agrexco. Among these were early onions, tomatoes, peanuts and sugarbeet (for the Israeli industry) — all products for which larger areas of land were allocated.[84]

The modernization and mechanization measures propagated by the agricultural department remained limited to these areas as well as to a small number of farms. The number of tractors in the West Bank rose from 459 to 1,534 between 1970 and 1977. In the Gaza Strip, this number increased tenfold during the same period of time.[85] However, this development is largely due to the sharp rise in wages in the West Bank after 1967. In view of the extremely low wages prior to the June War, a tractor was not an essential investment for farmers who, considering the size of their farms, could conceivably have made use of one. The relatively insignificant modernization measures and their limitation to certain sectors is also revealed by the expenditure on production input (tractors, fertilizers, seed, depreciation, etc.), which rose only at a rate equal to that of production.[86]

The rise in agricultural productivity does not appear significant enough for one to be able to speak of a 'green revolution', as Israel does.[87] Thus, between 1966 and 1977, productivity per worker, taking into account the decrease in the amount of cultivated land area in the West Bank, rose 75% (6.2% annually).[88] In view of the extremely low yield per *dunam*, the high number of workers and the low level of mechanization in 1967, this is a relatively insignificant rate of growth. Such progress as has been made goes hand in hand with an increasing dependence on the Israeli economy and is limited to only a few farms and agricultural sectors. Sectors producing the basic food for the population's daily requirements were, except for the use of better seed, only marginally affected by the modernization measures[89]

The growing dependence on Israel is revealed not only in the changing range of products but also in a specific relationship between the Israeli economy and the agricultural sectors in the West Bank which produce either for export or for Israeli industry. There is a 'marketing officer' of the Ministry of Agriculture who is linked to the military government. His job is to conclude commercial contracts between farmers and either the Israeli export firm, Agrexco, or Israeli canneries. This arrangement is only possible because of Agrexco's monopoly. For the farmers, the only way to European markets is through this export firm. So far, attempts to set up a Palestinian marketing organization in the West Bank have been prevented by the military government. In its marketing contracts, Agrexco agrees to purchase the produce at the price and on the date stipulated, and the farmer agrees to grow the specified produce, guarantee its quality, and to then sell it to Agrexco. The farmers' contractual partner who, in the West Bank takes the form of agricultural counselling service, delivers the necessary input (such as seed, fertilizer, loans and counsel) to production.

Exactly the same process of agricultural production is increasingly used in the Third World,[90] by multinational corporations or within the framework of foreign aid. Apart from the effects of production re-orientation, critics continually point out that the farmers' contractual partner carries none of the risks involved in production, such as poor harvests, inferior quality crops or the effects of political change. Some analysts go so far as to view the farmers under contract as being no more than wage earners.[91]

The changes within the structure of agriculture in the occupied territories have, along with the limited progress which has taken place, led to a growing dependence during the years of the occupation. An economist from the West Bank made the following comment on this development: '... they are actually gearing production patterns along lines which are not compatible with the long-term interests of West Bank agriculture.'[92]

West Bank agriculture is faced, however, with an even more urgent problem, which limits its development possibilities decisively, namely, Israel's amassing of the most important resources — land and water.

Development Opportunities for West Bank Agriculture
'Every additional *dunam* they irrigate means a *dunam* less for us.'[93] The chairman of the supervisory board of Tahal, the Israeli water planning corporation, described thus the importance of the West Bank water reserves to Israel. According to Meir Ben-Meir, the water commissioner, one-third of the water reaching Israeli kitchens and farms originates in the West Bank.[94] A Tahal official described Israeli water policy in the West Bank as follows: 'The military government protected Israel's interests by restricting drilling on the western slopes of the hills of Judea and Samaria. Permits were issued grudgingly, where water would be used only for human consumption and only where there was no alternative.'[95]

Not a single application for the drilling of wells for irrigation has been approved since 1967.[96] Dr Paul Quiring, for many years the representative of the Mennonite Central Committee in East Jerusalem, sums up the water situation for Palestinian agriculture: 'This lack of water resource development, together with the confiscation of wells on "absentee" property,[97] means that there are fewer wells providing less water for Palestinian agriculture in the Jordan Valley today than there were available on the eve of the 1967 war.'[98] Not only the ban on the drilling of new wells, but also the increasing consumption of water by the Israeli settlements and their farms have adversely affected Palestinian water resources. Seventeen wells dug for Jewish settlements in the Jordan Valley today pump 14.1 million cubic metres of water to Israeli settlements and fields in the region per year, 43% of the amount drawn from Arab sources for the entire West Bank.[99] Again and again, there are reports on new Israeli wells which literally drain the water from the older Arab wells.[100]

> **Water Policy**
> In 1968, when the Israeli settlement of Mehola was established near the villages of Bardalah and Tel el-Bada, Mekorot [the Israeli National Water Authority] advised the settlement authority that the drilling of a planned well to supply water for the settlement would adversely affect the five wells and springs used by neighbouring Arab villages. Fully aware of this report, the Israelis dug the well. Until 1970 little effect was registered. However, in 1970 villagers from Bardalah, Tel el-Bada and Kardalah began reporting a decline in the output of their springs and a lowering of the water level in their wells. For example:
>> Before 1970 the central spring in the village of Tel el-Bada supplied 80 cubic metres of water per hour which the villagers used for drinking, watering their livestock and irrigating their croplands. In 1973 the village undertook a project to make more effective use of their water by constructing a small reservoir and building cement canals to carry water to their fields. The investment soon proved pointless. By the summer of 1976 the output of the spring had declined to five cubic metres of water per hour, a quantity insufficient to operate the newly constructed irrigation system.
>>
>> In 1973 village leaders from Bardalah began complaining to the water authority that the water level in their community well was falling at the rate of one metre per month during the summer. In 1975 the water table fell below the level of the well's pump and the pump turbine had to be reset to a depth below the new water table. At the time the well went dry, Mekorot offered to connect the village to the settlement's water system in exchange for closing the village well. The

> villagers refused, preferring the independence of their own water source.
>
> Faced with an ever worsening problem in the Arab villages, and with a water shortage at the settlement caused by its expansion, Mekorot recently completed the drilling of a second well for the settlement adjacent to the village well. This well will cause the closure of the Bardalah well and, in addition to the needs of the settlement, will provide water to the Arab villages. Water will be sold to the villagers on a per person basis. . . .
>
> Source: *Quiring 1978*, p. 15 ff.

In April 1979, Moshe Dayan, Foreign Minister at the time, again clarified the Israeli position on the water issue: 'The Arabs in Judea and Samaria will not receive any more water than they have today.'[101] The limitation of water resources affects, above all, the development possibilities of West Bank agriculture. Even though the amount of irrigated land increased as a result of using the given quantity of water more efficiently through substantially improved water technology under Israeli occupation, the limit has now been reached, making any further increase in productivity of West Bank agriculture doubtful. An agrarian system which is first and foremost dependent on an uncertain rainfall, is not in a position to risk large investment (such as for machinery or chemical fertilizers) or to afford the costs of labour. Therefore, the rise in productivity per farm since the occupation, due to the developments mentioned above, can hardly continue. In this situation, it is doubtful whether workers, whose jobs are in jeopardy in Israel due to the serious recession, can be re-absorbed into the West Bank economy.[102]

Further changes, which are closely related to recent developments in the agricultural sector, make the problem worse. Firstly, the Israeli confiscation[103] has reduced the available amount of arable land. Secondly, more and more land is becoming unusable for farming because it is no longer being tilled, the terraces are not being taken care of, and during the years of the occupation, investment in new seedlings has steadily gone down.[104] The grave consequences of these changes become clear, for instance, in the condition of the olive and other fruit trees. Approximately 40% of the olive trees in the West Bank are 100 to 150 years old and have to be replaced.[105] This represents an investment in the future which only few are willing to make in light of the uncertain situation. West Bank economist, A.R. Husseini remarked, 'Neglect is approaching the point of no return.'[106]

The agricultural situation is analogous with changes in the other sectors. The short-term improvement in income for the reduced number of farmers is outweighed by structural changes which have an adverse effect on the economic development of the West Bank. The most obvious improvements have been related to a growing dependence on Israel. This results in a division of labour and an unequal exchange which is typical of the relationship between industrial and developing countries. Israel's amassing of the most important agricultural resources effectively impedes development. It remains to be seen whether the agricultural sector is in a worse position today than prior to the Israeli occupation in 1967. The fact is that new structural problems have arisen.

Dr Paul Quiring summarizes his analysis of the effects of Israel's settlement and water policy for West Bank agriculture as follows:

> As the controversy over the construction of Jewish colonies in the territories continues, it is important that the settlements do not merely become a part of our political and diplomatic vocabulary. They are more than a theme for newspaper headlines. It is important that they be understood in terms of their legal and human rights implications. The Palestinians have been and continue to be dispossessed of their land, of their jobs, and of their natural resources. It would appear that it is not enough that a people should be brought under military occupation, subjected to the arbitrary whim of a military government, and imprisoned for their political beliefs, but that they must also be shown that they have no right to the land on which they live.[107]

A Shadow Existence: Industry

Even under Jordanian rule, industry played a subordinate role in the West Bank. The industrial sector contributed only 10% to the GNP in the entire Jordanian Kingdom, and the West Bank's portion of this was smaller than that of the East Bank. As stated previously, this was the result of the Jordanian policy which had promoted industrial expansion almost exclusively in the East Bank.

The most important branches of industry in the occupied territories are the food processing and textile industries. 21,400 people (14.6% of all those working in the West Bank and Gaza Strip) are employed in industry. Under Israeli rule, there has been no industrial progress in the occupied territories. On the contrary, Israel's influence tends more to hinder the development of Palestinian industry. The West Bank and Gaza Strip are flooded with Israeli industrial goods, which have found a market there that has been growing for some time. Local industry cannot compete with Israel.

Today, part of the industrial production is directly dependent on Israel. Many Israeli firms have made contracts with farmers and with middlemen for cottage industries in the occupied territories. Israel supplies raw materials or partially-finished products and the Palestinian enterprises process them and return the end products to Israel. Sub-contracting is a common practice in the textile and clothing industries as well as in the furniture business. This entails the same disadvantages as the migration of labour to Israel; people earn their livelihood from these short-term, sub-contracting jobs, even though these pay the lowest wages.

'Subcontracting' – Palestinian seamstresses in the West Bank

This means of production has no positive effect on industry in the occupied territories. Arie Bregmann of the Bank of Israel, a leading Israeli analyst of economic development in the occupied territories, writes:

> The system's usefulness could be in the replacement of sub-contracting jobs with the full production of the same products. This would most probably call for measures to protect at least part of the administered areas' domestic production from competition by Israeli products – as is common for infant industries. It would also require finding new export outlets.[108]

None of this has occurred.

Since 1969, the Israeli government has been encouraging Israelis to invest in the occupied territories. As the result of a decision made by a committee of the Israeli cabinet, a centre for trade and industry was founded on the northern border of the Gaza Strip. In August 1969, the government publicized the benefits for those who invested in the occupied territories – these were tax reductions, sureties and possible lower prices for raw materials. The reaction was very reserved, probably due to the uncertain future of the territories, so the Israeli government offered new investment incentives in

1972. In October of that year it was announced that from then on Israeli companies in the occupied territories would have the same status as firms in Israel's 'developing zones'. This means low-interest loans for up to 50% of the working capital; government subsidies with a value of up to one-third of the cost of construction sites and company buildings; double the usual inflation subsidy; a five-year tax-free period; and a ceiling on the tax rate on profits (28%).[109] This created the most favourable conditions conceivable for Israeli investment in the occupied territories. Today, the Jewish settlements in the West Bank take the most advantage of these conditions and could become the heart of a Jewish economic sector in the rest of Palestine. The political and economic conditions for such a nucleus have already been established.

This selective system of promoting the economy reflects Israel's economic objectives with regard to the occupied territories, namely, to penetrate and control the West Bank and Gaza Strip economically and to hold off competition from this market.

Palestinian businessmen continue to invest very little. For instance, in 1972-73, investments in the West Bank comprised 15% of the GNP, a small amount compared with an investment rate of 17% in Arab countries and 33% in Israel.[110] Taking loans is not a common practice; investments are usually financed instead by recent surpluses or family savings. The occupied territories lack a developed banking system and a functioning capital market. It is estimated that cumulative savings far exceed investments.[111] There are several reasons for this kind of caution: Israel's inflation rate; strong, partially subsidized Israeli competition, which handicaps Palestinian businesses; and the political climate, which cannot guarantee a smooth course of business.

None of the changes described have had a stimulating effect on Palestinian industry. Characteristic of the development in the past 12 years is the stagnation of the industrial sector. Yet the occupation hardly allows for any other prospect for the future. Lacking a national framework which would be capable of protecting domestic industry against foreign competition and which would promote the development of industry by making use of the know-how and capital of Palestinians working abroad, it appears impossible for the industrial sectors of the occupied territories to develop in their own right.

The 'Boom'

There have been many and varied evaluations of the results of Israel's integration policy. Israel views its economic influence on the occupied territories as a type of foreign aid. According to Israel, this is evidenced by the 'boom' in the occupied territories, i.e. the rise in the standard of living over the past few years and the 'green revolution' in agriculture. Yet on the other side of the 'green line' (the 1967 borders) economists speak of the growing problems of farmers and the difficult conditions under which the commuters work. They present as proof of the continuing structural problems in the economy the fact that, for years, the educated segment of the West Bank and Gaza Strip population has had to emigrate because of the lack of job opportunities.[112]

Israeli economic policy in the occupied territories bears the characteristic traits of a 'developed' country that has penetrated an 'underdeveloped' one. The division of labour which has developed between Israel on the one hand and the West Bank and Gaza Strip on the other is typical of this situation. For instance, the production and/or supply of industrial goods of all kinds is controlled by Israel, while the occupied territories specialize in the export of the instruments of production, in this case labour. Many economists from rich countries praise this type of division of labour as 'economic', even though (or maybe precisely because) it is at the expense of the weaker partner.

The most important source of income for the occupied territories comes from Palestinians working abroad (in Israel). In turn, the money brought home by the commuters must be spent abroad — in Israel — to buy a sizable portion of the goods required daily. Under Israel's influence, agricultural production is becoming less and less oriented to local needs. Instead, through sub-contracting, it produces for remote markets and, at least partially for the benefit of the employer, namely Israel.

The 'common market' of Israel and the occupied territories reveals similar structures. Its advantages accrue to the stronger partner, Israel. This becomes very clear in the case of Palestinian industry. Palestinian industry depends on selling its goods chiefly on the domestic market. It is forced, however, to relinquish the field to the stronger Israeli competitor. Under these conditions, industrial growth is always drawn to the Israeli side of the border. For this reason, among others, Palestinian industry has made no progress in the past 13 years.

When looking at this division of labour, one must not lose sight of the characteristics which differentiate the relationship between Israel and the occupied territories from a typical post-colonial relationship. One such trait is the way Israel controls the territories. The military occupation has given the West Bank and Gaza Strip the character of an 'Israeli colony'. The Palestinians have no part in the decision-making process; the 'mother country' always has the final say.

Another special feature is the speed and totality with which economic relations have developed between the occupied territories and Israel. One does not find here, as in other cases, the gradual penetration of foreign capital into a country, until it reaches the point where the key economic positions in the country are managed by heads of businesses of a foreign country. This is much more a matter of an economy undergoing a radical change in direction within a few short years. In 1967, the West Bank and Gaza Strip were still completely isolated from Israel. After 13 years of occupation, the one-sided integration and adaptation of the economy in the occupied territories to Israel's needs has today reached a level where, out of

Creeping Annexation: The Economy

The 'Boom' — TV aerials above the Old City of Jerusalem

economic considerations, Israel will be increasingly reluctant to return the occupied territories.

In the event that the Palestinians achieve political independence, the rapid changes which their economy has undergone will not provide a favourable basis on which to rebuild an economy which is independent, or at least not dependent on just a single partner. Whereas other 'developing' countries have at least the limited structural benefits of national sovereignty, the Palestinian economy does not even have basic economic mechanisms such as customs duties and subsidies at its control.

Being exposed to Israel's economic policies, the West Bank and Gaza Strip are affected by inflation, gradual devaluation of the Israeli pound and the fluctuations in the Israeli business cycle.

What do High Prices have to do with the Occupation?
About one year after the June 1967 war, the Israeli authorities formulated their policy towards the conquered territories on two principles. Firstly, the real permanence of the conquest should be concealed in order to avoid arousing the Arab national feelings; secondly, establishment of mutual economic relations between

the Arabs of the West Bank and Gaza Strip, which could not be reversed.

Although Israel clearly failed in the realization of the first principle, because of specific circumstances (this is not the place to describe these) it has, to a very great extent, succeeded in establishing the second, economic principle. The success of the Israeli economic intervention in the economies of the West Bank and Gaza Strip, has linked them so intimately with the Israeli economy, that the situation has reached the present status: the Arab economy has lost its individual characteristics and has been annexed as a marginal part of the Israeli economy, so that its own development and growth is completely paralysed.

When the conqueror directed his aims towards the Arab economy, destroyed it, and bound it to the margins of the Israeli economy, he did so only for his political aims. We do not need to explain it, even if we should remember that there is always a connection between the economic and political realities, and there is no possibility of separating them. This assumption is important, because any other explanation for the high prices in the conquered Arab territories would be an illusion. We mean here the opinion which claims that the cause for the high prices is the difference between the incomes in Israel and the conquered fatherland, or the claim that the only cause is in the war. The media, including newspapers which try to explain the high prices by those causes, are only serving the conqueror, by misdirecting the public from the single cause of high prices — the conquest — and by directing it towards misleading or marginal causes.

Thus, to the questions which are often asked about how the 'monster' of high prices can be stopped, and how the prices of basic necessities can be prevented from rising, the answer is simple, and it does not lie in any request to the conquering authorities for helping Arab bakeries or the return of the subsidies to the importers of rice, sugar, etc.

The only cause is the stubbornness of the Israeli conquering authorities in their continuation of the economic annexation of the conquered Arab territories, and in the absence of custom-borders across what is called the 'green line'.

The true cause is the stubborn Israeli attempt to bind our territories into an all-Israeli electricity company, an all-Israeli water company, and in the limitation of our imports only through the Israeli importers. Those are the real and important factors. Had we kept the economic characteristics of our conquered territories, and if we could defend ourselves from the economic plans of the conquest, we would not have had to suffer so from those factors which cause the high prices.

> Source: *Al-Fajr* (East Jerusalem), 2 February 1974.

When one observes the advantages and disadvantages that the developments of the past 16 years have brought to the Palestinians, one sees the same pattern again and again. The integration of the occupied territories into the Israeli economy has brought with it direct, short-term advantages. Yet these are always accompanied by long-term structural disadvantages. The development of the labour market and, closely related to it, the debate over the higher standard of living in the occupied territories show this very clearly.

Nearly half of the West Bank and Gaza Strip labour force works in Israel and another indeterminable number are under sub-contract to Israeli firms. The advantage of this situation can be stated as follows: after 1968, the high unemployment figures in the occupied territories disappeared due to openings in the Israeli job market. The jobs in Israel brought a rise in income and, for part of the population, a higher standard of living.

Being at the mercy of job opportunities in Israel may be regarded as the lesser evil, compared with the prospect of being at home without work. However, workers from the occupied territories are employed as unskilled labour and are concentrated at the poorest end of the Israeli job market. They are especially vulnerable to fluctuations in Israeli business activity. Furthermore, while a large part of the local labour force works in Israel, the occupied territories have developed into an important market for Israeli goods.

These facts exert considerable pressure on various sectors of the population and the economy. First of all, those people who do not receive their income from Israel are at a disadvantage: although they only earn the lower wages paid in the West Bank and Gaza Strip they must pay the steadily increasing prices which result from adaptation to Israel price levels. The appeal of the Israeli job market is a problem for farmers and entrepreneurs. Labour has become scarce in the occupied territories, particularly in agriculture, which is generally a family-oriented business, and the wage level has risen markedly. Moreover, local industry is defenceless against Israeli competition in the West Bank and Gaza Strip markets. The resulting stagnation has, in turn, an effect on the job market. Local firms are unable to offer jobs to qualified workers who are not needed in Israel either. Thus, a growing number of qualified workers are forced to emigrate.

This imbalance in the job market makes the occupied territories heavily dependent. The immediate advantage of increased wages and a higher standard of living brings with it structural changes in the job market, which, in the long run, will turn the occupied territories into a dormitory for workers who seek employment in Israel.

The argument that the standard of living has improved considerably under Israeli rule is repeatedly presented in a damaging manner, as proof of the positive effects of the occupation for the well-being of the people. Yet at the same time, the structural arguments and long-term economic prospects, which will determine the well-being of the people in the future, are left out.

It is true that the access to employment opportunities in Israel eliminated unemployment in the occupied territories and that the GNP in the occupied territories grew for several years by 15-20%.[113] Furthermore, it is true that due to the wages, which are higher in Israel than in the occupied territories, the average standard of living rose, as shown by the expenditures for private consumption, durable consumer goods and housing construction.[114]

In order to comprehend the nature of this development one must be aware of what happened after 1967 when Israel began integrating the economies of the West Bank and Gaza Strip. At first, wages and prices in the occupied territories were substantially lower than in Israel. Workers, who earned their money in Israel but used it to support their families in the occupied territories, profited at first from the difference between the Israeli wage level and the lower price level in the occupied territories. However, the Israeli integration policy brought not only the possibility of earning a living in Israel, but also Israeli inflation and the influx of consumer goods produced in or imported through Israel. In addition, Israeli job opportunities have exerted pressure on wages in the occupied territories. With the duration of the occupation, prices as well as wages have risen steadily and are approaching the Israeli level.

Thus, the advantages enjoyed by a Palestinian worker who commutes to Tel Aviv every day, over his colleague who works in Ramallah for example, have decreased in proportion to the wage and price differences between Israel and the occupied territories. The commuter earns no more than he would at home and both workers have to bear the higher cost of living and the inflation imported from Israel. It has turned out that the 'boom' was just a transitional phase in which the Palestinian economy was adjusting to the conditions dictated to it by Israel. Now, at the end of this phase, the Palestinian workers in Israel and in the occupied territories once again find themselves at the low end of the Israeli wage scale. Their limited possibilities as consumers correspond to those of the most disadvantaged groups in Israeli society. However, there is no doubt that, in purely material terms, their situation has improved.

Today, if one looks at wage and price trends, at inflation rates and the 'retarded' growth in, for instance, the purchase of durable consumer goods, the end of this transitional phase has virtually been reached. As a result, workers in the occupied territories no longer have the prospect of improving their situation but face rather the prospect of losing their jobs in Israel during the next crisis.

Future prospects for the Palestinian economy are, on the whole, similar because of Israel's drastic policies. From the viewpoint of a balanced structural development, it is even weaker than before; now it is dependent on Israel and has reduced chances for development. The structural 'deformation' and dependence has been the basic feature of the economic development in the West Bank and Gaza Strip during the past 16 years. The 'boom' offered and offers no future.

Solving the economic problems in the West Bank and Gaza Strip depends on solving their most important problem — the Israeli occupation. The longer the occupation lasts, the more difficult it will be to terminate the dependence on Israel. The occupation runs counter to everything which is defined in the West Bank and Gaza Strip as the political goal: to gain the right of the Palestinian people to self-determination.

Notes

1. This chapter is based on *Kanovsky 1970, Ryan 1974* and *Arkadie 1977*, and Israeli statistics on the occupied territories.
2. Regarding the figures, compare *Neumann 1977*, p. 30; *Dodd/Barakat 1968*, p. 35.
3. In 1965, there were five factories in the West Bank: a cigarette factory in El Azarije, a factory for plastic articles (e.g. sandals) in Beit Sahur, a furniture factory in Bethlehem, a chocolate factory in Ramallah and a soap factory in Nablus.
4. Cf. *Shahar 1971*, p. 19.
5. Cf. *Arkadie 1977*, p. 29 ff.
6. 1,000 *dunams* = 1 km^2.
7. An insignificant amount in terms of area; in 1945, the amount of land owned by Jews in Palestine was 5.6% of the total area (1.4 million *dunams*). Cf. *Hollstein 1977*, p. 130.
8. For a more detailed study of the history and practice of Zionism, cf. *Laqueur 1975* and *Hollstein 1977*.
9. Regarding the legal basis, see Chapter 2, cf. also *Peretz 1956*, pp. 143, 146.
10. Cf. *Peretz 1956*, p. 143 ff.
11. 'U.S. Capital in Socialist Israel', *Fortune*, June 1950, quoted from *Ryan 1974*, p. 4.
12. Aba Ebban, 'Nationalism and Internationalism', *Voice of Israel, a Blue-Print for Peace*, New York 1957, p. 111, quoted from *Ryan 1974*, p. 5.
13. Cf. *Hollstein 1977*, p. 69 ff.
14. For further details, cf. *Bruno 1970*, p. 54 ff.
15. *Teveth 1969*, p. 146.
16. *Ryan 1974*, p. 7. 'Traditionalists' and 'integrationists' are not common expressions for describing the political spectrum in Israel. For the sake of clarity, we are employing them as *termini technici* from Ryan.
17. *Ma'ariv*, 2 February 1973.
18. *Ibid.*
19. *Becker 1971*, p. 53.
20. U.N. Document A/6713/Supplement 13.
21. For the figures from the first six months of 1968, cf. *Bank of Israel 1971*, p. 33.
22. *Ma'ariv*, 24 August 1967.
23. *Bank of Israel 1971*.

24. Cf. *Kanovsky 1976*, p. 181.
25. Cf. *Lesch 1970*, p. 34.
26. *New Outlook*, October 1968, p. 54.
27. Divrei Haknesset (Knesset protocols) of 18 November 1968, quoted from *MER* 1968, p. 444.
28. *Lamerhav*, 27 September 1968, quoted from *MER* 1968, p. 257.
29. *Ha'aretz* and *Ma'ariv*, 2 December 1968.
30. Cf. *Kapeliouk 1979 (a)*.
31. Israel Defence 1970 (a), no page number.
32. Of the 1.128 million inhabitants of the occupied territories (June 1978), only 19% are considered to be gainfully employed, i.e. 215,400 people. Only 56% (631,800) inhabitants of the occupied territories are of working age (i.e. at least 15 years of age); of this number, barely half are between the ages of 15 and 19. Only a small percentage of this age group is employed because many have not yet finished their education. Few women are 'gainfully employed' as defined by the statistics, even though their number has grown steadily since 1967. Cf. *ILO 1979*, p. 25.
33. Two-thirds of these workers find a job in Israel through official channels, the rest circumvent the Israeli employment agencies and, in this sense, are working illegally in Israel. Only the workers who obtained employment legally are listed in the official statistics. Unless otherwise noted, the figures which follow only refer to these workers.
34. Cf. *Ryan 1974*, p. 13.
35. *ILO 1979*, p. 29.
36. Cf. *ILO 1969*, p. 29; see also Chapter 1.
37. As a result of the 1980 recession in Israel, jobs are once again in danger. The Israeli daily, *Ha'aretz*, quoted Finance Minister Yigal Hurvitz as saying that approximately 50,000 workers from the occupied territories were expected to be laid off. Cf. *Coone 1980*, p. 19.
38. Cf. *Arkadie 1977*, p. 74.
39. *MERIP Reports*, No. 60, September 1977.
40. Cf. *Arkadie 1977*, p. 58.
41. *Bank of Israel 1971*, p. 177.
42. Cf. *Arkadie 1977*, p. 89; net import prices = import prices excluding customs duty and taxes.
43. Cf. *Statistics* 1977, p. 184.
44. The authors feel it is important, however, to point out that in countries where jobs are rare (except in the agricultural sector) and low wages are paid, a labour-intensive form of agriculture could be a good economic policy.
45. Cf. *Census 1967*, p. 20.
46. Cf. *Bull 1975*, p. 70.
47. On land distribution in the West Bank, cf. *Shahar 1971*.
48. Cf. *Ryan 1977*, p. 4. Yet, due to existing irrigation systems, more can be produced in the Gaza Strip on smaller areas of land than in the West Bank. Regarding land distribution in the Gaza Strip, cf. also *Shahar 1971*, p. 46.
49. The changes in the agricultural sector of the occupied territories are concentrated in the West Bank. In the Gaza Strip, which already

produced for export anyway, there was little Israeli intervention.
50. As far as the statistical data are concerned, we refer exclusively to Israeli material (Defence Ministry and the Central Bureau of Statistics) in this analysis. Furthermore, only plant production is being examined. Livestock and livestock products only play a subordinate role and data which would permit an analysis of this are not available.
51. Cf. *Israel Defence 1969* and *Census 1967*.
52. The harvest of 1967, for which no detailed figures are available, is listed by the Israeli Defence Ministry at I£200 million. Although livestock and livestock products are included here, plant production, which accounts for 85% of the total value of production, still amounts to I£170 million, a sum which exceeds the 1966 harvest by almost a quarter (cf. *Israel Defence 1969*). Therefore, the 1966 harvest can be taken as an average, even compared with earlier years. Also cf. *Arkadie 1977*, who has drawn similar conclusions.
53. Many of the 250,000 refugees were farmers, cf. *Census 1967*, pp. XII and XV, as well as *Dodd/Bakarat 1968*.
54. On the selection of reference years: 1966 was the last harvest before the occupation (see n. 52), 1968 was the first harvest following a full agricultural year under the occupation and is also the reference year used in Israeli studies. 1974 was the year with the biggest harvest since the occupation. This year corresponds with a recession in Israel, causing many of those employed in Israel to return to farming. Also see Chapter 4.
55. The following figures illustrate this fact: the Jordanian olive harvest, the largest part of which comes from the West Bank, amounted to 114,000 tons in 1961; 7,000 tons in 1962; and 98,000 tons in 1964. Cf. *Arkadie 1977*, p. 128.
56. Israeli sources also point out this fact. In the 1967 census, the area of newly planted trees which did not yet bear fruit amounted to 162,000 *dunams*. (Cf. *Census 1967*, p. XIII and *Bull 1975*, p. 69). Citrus trees require five to eight years before they bear fruit.
57. There are no figures published by Israel for the Gaza Strip before 1967. Yet there was very little change in the structure of the agricultural sector under Israeli occupation.
58. *Israel Information Centre*, p. 98. Cf. also *Nahumi 1972 (a)*, p. 20: 'The citrus area expanded after 1957, so that over 60% of the plantations do not yet give a full yield.' Cf. here also p. 27. On the criteria according to which the years shown in Table 9 were chosen, see n. 54.
59. In the West Bank, the plant production value amounted to I£192.6 million (excluding citrus fruits, cf. *Statistics 1978*, p. 793). The prices for fruit and vegetables had risen since 1967 8.5 times (cf. *Statistics 1977*, p. 42 and *1978*, p. 774). If 1967 is used as the base year for the West Bank instead of 1966, this would even result in a decline in the value of production. (For the figures for 1967, cf. *Israel Defence 1969*, p. 41).
60. Cf. Chapter 4.
61. From 20% to 25% below the Israeli prices! Cf. *Lesch 1970*, p. 34.
62. Cf. *Lesch 1970*, p. 35, and *Bull 1975*, p. 74.
63. These were fruit and vegetables, in particular. The West Bank produced

65% of the vegetables and 60% of the fruit, but only 30% of the grain within all of Jordan. (Cf. *Dajani 1969*, p. 2).
64. *Israel Defence 1969*, p. 47.
65. Cf. Israeli Ministry of Agriculture, 'Activities in Judaea and Samaria June 1967 to January 1970' (undated) and concerning the new products also *Bull 1975*, p. 83 ff.
66. *Israel Defence 1969*, p. 47.
67. Cf. *Israel Defence 1969*, p. 42 ff. and *West Bank Agriculture 1973* (Ramallah: Agricultural Department of the West Bank, No. 147, August 1974, p. 6 ff.).
68. Cf. *Israel Defence 1970 (b)*, p. 24.
69. Cf. *Ryan 1974*, p. 20 and *Bregmann 1975*, p. 44.
70. The *Jerusalem Post*, 2 June 1972.
71. Before 1967, the West Bank was practically self-sufficient with regard to produce, cf. *Bull 1975*, p. 89.
72. Cf. *Bull 1975*, p. 70 and *Statistics 1978*, p. 773.
73. In 1966, imports accounted for only 7% of the total consumption of produce in the West Bank. Cf. *Israel Defence 1969*, p. 41 and *Bull 1975*, p. 70.
74. Cf. *Bull 1975*, p. 84.
75. Cf. *Bregmann 1976*, p. 43.
76. From 2,073,000 *dunams* in 1966 (cf. *Israel Defence 1969*, p. 43) to 1,693,000 *dunams* in 1973 (cf. *Arkadie 1977*, p. 129).
77. See n. 53.
78. 73.2% of those from the West Bank who are employed in Israel come from villages (cf. *Israel Labour 1979*).
79. Cf. Chapter 2, particularly regarding the various methods of confiscating formerly cultivated land. From the beginning of the occupation, only one example was mentioned, which was documented by the *Jerusalem Post*. It concerns the Israeli settlement Mehola in the north of the West Bank; 'The 1000 acres of land which was placed at their disposal belonged to absentees or the Jordanian government.' (Quoted from the *Jerusalem Post*, 20 November 1968.) The largest part of the land which is no longer tilled by Arab farmers is in the Jordan Valley. Cf. Chapter 1,
80. In 1969, 47,000 (cf. *Bregmann 1975*, p. 32), in 1977, 30,700 (cf. *Statistics 1978*, p. 788).
81. Cf. *Bull 1975*, p. 74. Bull points out, in particular, that the employment of wage workers has become more difficult due to the new relation between costs of and proceeds from new products on the market.
82. Cf. *Bull 1975*, p. 74 ff.
83. Cf. *Israel Defence 1972*, p. 44, and *Bull 1975*, p. 82.
84. Cf. *Bull 1975*, p. 81 ff. and *Israel Defence 1972*, p. 43 ff.
85. Cf. *Statistics 1978*, p. 802.
86. Cf. *Statistics 1975*, p. 710, and *1978*, p. 793.
87. Cf. e.g. *Weigart 1975*.
88. Cf. *Israel Defence 1969*, p. 42 ff., and *Statistics 1978*, pp. 788, 789 and 793.
89. Cf. *Bregmann 1976*, p. 43.

90. Cf. *Ruthenberg*, 'Landwirtschaftliche Entwicklungspolitik', *Zeitschrift für ausländische Landwirtschaft,* Materialsammlung Heft 20, Frankfurt 1972, and Bittner/Orth, 'Das Dévloppement Communautaire Programm der voltaischen Regierung', *Studie für die Kübel-Stiftung, Bensheim,* Mainz/Berlin/Bensheim 1978.
91. Cf. e.g. Baumgartner, Ulf M., and Poppinga, Onno-Hans, 'Grundzüge der Agrarstruktur im peripheren Kapitalismus', *Handbuch II, Unterentwicklung,* edited by Bassam Tibi and Volkhard Brandes, Frankfurt 1975.
92. A.R. Husseini in *MERIP Reports,* No. 60, July 1977.
93. The *Jerusalem Post*, international edition, 6/12 May 1979. Tahal is responsible for general planning and carrying out Israeli water projects. The Israeli state owns 52% of this company, the rest is divided between the Jewish Agency and the Jewish National Fund.
94. *Ibid.*
95. *Ibid.*
96. Cf. *Quiring 1978*. The drilling of a few wells was approved solely to provide drinking water.
97. On 'absentee' property cf. Chapter 2, pp. 00–00.
98. *Quiring 1978.*
99. Figures from a report by the water department of the military government, quoted from the *Journal of Palestinian Studies,* No. 34, p. 21.
100. Cf. *Quiring 1978* and the statement by Mayor Qawasmeh before the U.N. Committee on Human Rights (U.N. Document A/AC. 145/RT.279, dated 17 September 1979).
101. *Hotam* (weekly supplement to the newspaper, *Al Hamishmar*), 20 April 1979.
102. Cf. Chapter 4, pp. 000–00.
103. Cf. Chapter 2, pp. 000–00.
104. 1.5% in 1968 and 1969; 0.4% and 0.5% in 1976 and 1977, respectively. Cf. *Statistics 1970,* p. 637, and *1978,* p. 793.
105. In addition to olives, above all, dates and almond trees as well as the vines. Cf. U.N. Document A/34/536, p. 12.
106. Interview in *MERIP Reports,* No. 60, July 1977.
107. *Quiring 1978.*
108. *Bregmann 1975,* p. 84.
109. *Ryan 1974,* p. 15.
110. *Bregmann 1975,* p. 26.
111. *Ibid.*
112. Concerning the decisive conclusions of this section, cf. *Arkadie 1977,* p. 37 ff. and p. 137 ff.
113. *Statistics 1980,* p. 680 ff.
114. *Statistics 1980,* p. 683 ff.

5. New Alliances: The Social Structure

Since 1967, Palestinian society has been confronted with the Israeli occupation. The occupiers have plainly left their mark on the economic structure in the occupied territories and economic change has brought about social change. Certain social classes perceive their material existence as being threatened and their development as being handicapped, while others have profited from the occupation. If one analyses these changes in the social structure of the occupied territories, the fundamental political developments of the last 16 years become evident. One is the new alliance of parts of the ruling class, the petit bourgeoisie and the emerging working class based on nationalist politics. Another is the fact that Israel cannot find any collaborators for its 'autonomy plan' in the occupied territories today.

As in other developing countries, an analysis of 'class structure' is laden with difficulties arising from the fact that although the capitalist mode of production is dominant, pre-capitalist modes of production continue to exist as subordinate and parallel structures. The social reality can only be captured in part by the class-concept model. A further obstacle in the case of the occupied territories is the incomplete statistical data.

The following description of changes in the social structure and the assessment of their political consequences can be little more than a rough sketch. It illustrates the connection between the political struggle of the Palestinians and the economic changes under the occupation.

A Few Winners, Many Losers: The West Bank

The Upper Class
The statistical composition of the upper class has not changed significantly under Israeli occupation. It is a small and diminishing minority. In 1967 the top echelon of landowners consisted of 135 families, who possessed more than 500 *dunams* each, a mere 30 of whom had more than 1,000 *dunams* each.[1] Today in the industrial sector, there are only five employers who employ more than 100 workers. Big business is also concentrated in a few hands.

Members of the upper class still generally belong to the traditionally powerful clans of the West Bank. During the time of the Jordanian rule, they were closely connected to the royal dynasty.

The large landowners have become neither poorer nor richer under Israeli occupation. Nevertheless they have been dependent on Israeli goodwill, inasmuch as the export of their products is subject to Israeli control. This explains the role they played as 'moderates'.

In view of the sharply rising wage costs, some large landowners have invested in machinery for their businesses and today use improved seeds and chemical fertilizers. Competition from superior Israeli production has pressured the West Bank agricultural businesses into developing production. Ultimately, this has created a dependence which is intensified by the threat of losing land through Israeli expropriations and the military government's water policy.[2]

In the past few years, the power exerted by the upper class over other parts of West Bank society has changed noticeably. Owing to the number of job opportunities in Israel, substantially fewer tenant farmers and farm workers are today dependent on this class.

The only part of the upper classes to profit from Israeli occupation have been the merchant classes.[3] The growing purchasing power in the occupied territories and the sharply rising volume of foreign imports (chiefly from Israel) have greatly expanded their trade and have brought them immense profits.[4] However, the uncertain political situation at home, encourages them to invest their profits abroad. The merchant classes have contributed little to the accumulation of industrial capital.

Rising wage costs and, more especially, Israeli competition, have limited the accumulation of capital and investments in the industrial sector. The industrial bourgeoisie (already impeded in its development under Jordanian rule and, for that reason, often on the side of the Hussein critics) has not been able to develop under the occupation. This particular section of society could have been expected to play a dynamic part in the transformation from an agricultural society to an industrial one, and to have secured the leading role within its own class. The fact that it has nonetheless remained weak points clearly to the lack of possibilities for the upper classes to develop themselves under the occupation. Its leadership role has visibly decayed.

Farmers

The number of self-employed farmers has decreased under the occupation (from 33,800 in 1970 to 28,300 in 1977).[5] Rising wage costs have forced many farmers to give up their land because they can no longer pay enough workers. In addition, the rising cost of living has forced small farmers to abandon farming, which brought in little profit, and to take up work in Israel. The proletarianization of the farmers is one of the clearest results of the economic development under the occupation. But because of the additional source of income still brought in by farming, one cannot speak, in this case, of a complete proletarianization.

The Petit Bourgeoisie

The largest section of the petit bourgeoisie consists of teachers, administrative assistants and technicians as well as doctors, lawyers, pharmacists, etc., in private practice. Even though their numbers have risen slightly in the past few years, the number of job opportunities available to the most highly qualified has declined by more than one-third between 1972 and 1977.[6] Scientists and academics are most affected by the backwardness of the West Bank and the worsening situation under the occupation. For them, the choice which the entire professional petit bourgeoisie faces, is particularly clear: either they leave the country for jobs abroad or they remain under difficult political as well as economic conditions — emigration or protest.

The second largest group in the petit bourgeoisie is made up of self-employed businessmen in the commercial and service sectors. Noteworthy is the increase in the number of merchants.[7] They have profited from the higher income of many West Bank families.[8] The small number of employment agents for Palestinians working in Israel, as well as businessmen acting as middlemen for sub-contracting jobs, have grown and flourished as a direct result of the occupation. People who are self-employed in the service sector (e.g. hauliers, restaurant and hotel owners) are also included in the petit bourgeoisie. They have profited from the increased consumption by the West Bank population, and their numbers have grown.[9]

Another part of the petit bourgeoisie is made up by the small factory owners and private craftsmen who usually run their businesses as family endeavours and seldom employ more than three or four workers.[10] The craftsmen have been more severely affected by the economic development than any other group; between 1970 and 1977, 15% of them closed their businesses.[11] Lack of capital and the large quantity of Israeli goods which flood the West Bank market rob them of the basis for their existence.

The Working Class

The number of labourers has increased under the occupation in absolute figures as well as in its percentage of the employed West Bank population.[12] Those who have joined this group recently include farmers and members of the petit bourgeoisie who had to lower their social status, and women and young people, who were previously not employed. Industrial workers make up only 13% of all employed in the West Bank. This percentage has increased in the past few years through growing employment in the industrial sector in Israel.[13]

Growth of the working class is entirely due to employment in Israel and not to economic development in the West Bank. For the following three reasons, the socio-economic situation of these workers is not very solid and a clear class consciousness does not exist. Firstly, many of them are still working part-time in agriculture. Secondly, their working experience is dominated by factors within Israeli society rather than their own: Israeli employers and Israeli institutions, e.g. army, police and military administration. Thus, social awareness is pushed into the background by the feeling of national incongruity. Finally, employment in Israel has a temporary, provisional character. In a recession, the chances are very great that the Palestinians will be the ones to lose their jobs. Most Palestinian workers now employed in Israel would once again have to earn their living from farming.

Nothing to Lose: The Gaza Strip

The Upper Class

The upper class in the Gaza Strip is made up of a very small group of large landowners and capitalist farmers, as well as important merchants and representatives of foreign trading firms, who are descendants of the original inhabitants of the Gaza Strip. Its size and composition has not changed under the occupation. The owners of the capitalist citrus plantations depend on exporting, which is controlled by Israel.

The merchant class in the Gaza Strip, unlike that in the West Bank, has not profited very much from the occupation. The trade sector, which became oversized in relation to the economic capacity of the territory during Egyptian rule (as a result of smuggling and trade with Egypt), has increased insignificantly, as foreign customers have simply been replaced by local ones.

Farmers

This group consists of small farmers and tenant farmers who produce partly for the market and partly for their own subsistence. The percentage of farmers in the Gaza Strip who farm less than five *dunams* (about the size of a soccer field) is noticeably large. Although the yield in the Gaza Strip is higher than in the West Bank as a result of widespread irrigation, most of these farmers have a second source of income.[14]

Small farmers take on work in Israel — at least temporarily and in addition to their farming. Their numbers are smaller today than in 1967, which means many of them have gone into the Israeli economy.[15] The oscillations in the numbers which appear in the statistics as 'self-employed in agriculture' (most are small farmers) show how unstable their jobs in Israel are. Up till the recession following the October War their numbers sank, only to almost double again between 1974 and 1977. Farmers who had had jobs in Israel until the recession returned to agriculture during the crisis.

The Petit Bourgeoisie

Unlike in the West Bank, the Israeli occupation has not changed the size or make-up of the petit bourgeoisie in the Gaza Strip. There is no vocational group in the petit bourgeoisie which could profit from the occupation.

Professional people form the largest group in this class in the Gaza Strip. They are primarily teachers and administrative assistants employed by UNRWA (United Nations Relief and Welfare Agency for Palestinian Refugees). As in the West Bank, the job market for scientists and academics has shrunk by more than one third.[16]

The second largest group is the self-employed in commerce and service occupations. Not much has changed in this group either. The increase in the number of jobs in Israel has balanced the decrease in the domestic market caused by the abolition of trade in duty-free goods. In the Gaza Strip, merchants have simply replaced their foreign customers with local ones, yet have been unable to improve their total turnover, as has been the case in the West Bank.

In small industry and trade, the number of self-employed declined between 1970 and 1977 by about 20%.[17] Contractors and craftsmen have had to close down their businesses for reasons similar to those in the West Bank: lack of capital and the overwhelming Israeli competition. This competition has also been responsible for the local producers not being able to profit from the increased purchasing power of those who earn their money in Israel, for the Gaza market also is predominantly supplied with Israeli goods.

The Working Class

Since 1970, the working class in the Gaza Strip has risen in percentage terms as well as in absolute figures. This increase can be explained exclusively by the new job opportunities in Israel, since in the Gaza Strip itself, the number of positions has decreased. However, most of the jobs in Israel are only short-term or seasonal.[18] The new labourers from the Gaza Strip come mainly from the marginal refugee population in camps, but also from among the small farmers and proletarianized craftsmen.[19]

The portion of industrial workers in the Gaza Strip has increased since 1970. This increase can also be traced exclusively to employment in Israel.

The same things which characterize the working class and its class consciousness in the West Bank hold true for the Gaza Strip — its proletarianization is not very solid and national incongruities take precedence over social ones.

Occupation Policy as a Boomerang: Political Consequences

Some of the political differences between the Gaza Strip and the West Bank can be explained by these changes in the social structure.

In the West Bank, the proletarianization of farmers and members of the petit bourgeoisie created a large potential for protest against Israeli occupation; at the same time, the power base of the traditional leaders over the villages was weakened by the ability of tenant farmers, land workers and small farmers to find jobs as labourers in Israel. The vicious circle which made indebted farmers even more dependent on the large landholders and merchants, had been broken. When jobs became available in Israel, the economic monopoly on power held by the employers in agriculture and the moneylenders almost completely disappeared.[20] The workers' standard of living had caught up with that of the more powerful farmers and the traditional village leaders. Israel relied politically on the traditional leaders in the West Bank but did not realize that due to their own economic policies these leaders would quickly lose their power base which was primarily an economic one. Changes in the social structure resulted in 1976 in the changeover from the traditional leaders to a new political élite. The elections destroyed the influence exerted by the old élite in the West Bank institutions; that is, they also lost their political power.

The composition of the new political élite clearly reflects the economic changes under the occupation. The National Front (P.N.F.), which won a landslide victory in 1976, is a broad alliance of members of the petit bourgeoisie, workers, and industrialists. These are the groups which have lost or at least not gained anything under the occupation. They have daily been directly confronted by Israeli occupation and their integration into the Israeli economy has robbed them of any chance to develop. This new leadership group has wide support in private and professional associations and trade unions — something completely new for the West Bank where political structures had, up till that time, related entirely to the most important clans.

In comparison to the West Bank, it remained relatively quiet in the Gaza Strip during the first years of the occupation, except for the activities of the Fedayeen. Even though the Gaza Strip was also under Israeli occupation, a wide alliance of groups, which could have protected themselves against the occupation, never emerged there. Two reasons for this can be found in the social structure. First, the composition of the population in the Gaza Strip is neither homogeneous nor indigenous. On the one hand, there are the original inhabitants and, on the other, there is the mass of refugees. Not previously integrated into the production process at all, the refugees today are only partially integrated and generally lead a life of misery in the camps. Each group has different interests and political views. The former are at home in the Gaza Strip and have invested their future in the territory; an Israeli withdrawal would be in their interests. The latter are foreign to the Gaza Strip and have no prospects of being integrated; they come from villages and cities which today lie in Israel. There is no purpose in them fighting for an Israeli withdrawal from the territories since it would not solve their problem. An alliance of two such groups, whose situations are so totally different, is hard to imagine.

Secondly, the economic development under the occupation has not involved the same threat to the interests of wide sections of the population in the Gaza Strip as it has in the West Bank. The petit bourgeoisie has not lost much; industrialists have never played a large role, anyway; and the proletarianization of the small farmers is in no way a completed process .

All in all, the growth of the working class in the Gaza Strip has not been a symptom of social decline, as has been the case in the West Bank, but rather a result of the integration of part of the formerly marginalized refugee population.

Another difference between the political situations in the Gaza Strip and the West Bank has been the strength of the Fedayeen. Until 1972, they had a broad base in the Gaza Strip refugee camps, whose inhabitants had nothing to lose and who sought improvement of their situation by means of an armed struggle with Israel. So far, there has been no broad base for an armed resistance in the West Bank. The integration of the refugees (which, in view of the current recession, could prove to be a temporary one) has certainly stripped the Fedayeen in the Gaza Strip of part of its social foundation, even though the 'pacification' of the territory has chiefly been the result of the Israeli battle against the commando units.[21]

In the Gaza Strip, for a number of reasons the power of the traditional leaders does not seem to have diminished. Firstly, since there have been no elections in the Gaza Strip so far, there has been no opportunity for their rule to be challenged nor has there been any need for them to defend it. It is difficult to say, whether or not they would be able to come through elections unscathed, since such elections would start a political polarization similar to the way the 1976 city council elections did in the West Bank. Secondly, a broad alliance of the petit bourgeoisie, industrialists and workers, which could jeopardize the traditional rule, is missing in the Gaza Strip. Thirdly, their power (unlike that of the traditional leaders in the West Bank) is not based on economic and personal relations of dependence, but rather on the stability of the citrus export economy, which has not suffered any losses under the occupation. The economic interests of the ruling class bind it very closely to Israel and Jordan. The export of their citrus crops is controlled by Israel, and the part which is sent to the Arab world passes through Jordanian customs.[22] Since the world recognizes the P.L.O. as the representative of the Palestinians, the traditional leaders have to pay lip service, at opportune moments, to the Palestinian liberation movement while pursuing their own economic interests.

The integration of the occupied territories into the Israeli economy has been a decisive step in the formation of a Palestinian proletariat. However, it is hardly possible to speak of the Palestinian workers as a fully conscious working class. The highest percentage (60%) works in Israel. Their incomplete proletarianization and the uncertain work situation in Israel have already been cited as reasons for limited class consciousness. The situation of the Palestinians who work in the occupied territories (just as that of Palestinians who work in Israel) is very greatly influenced by the occupation and by the national conflict between Palestinians and Jewish Israelis. For them, too, the national question overrides social awareness. The West Bank employer is not the class's enemy; he is a possible ally in the battle against the occupation.

The unions view this struggle as their most important task. There are 24 individual unions in the West Bank, which are joined together under a single umbrella organization. The number of their members is estimated at 40,000,[23] most of whom work in the West Bank and only a few in Israel. Their political importance goes far beyond the number of members. They co-operate with different professional organizations, (for example, engineers, bar and medical associations). They took part in the elections of 1976 on the

P.N.F. ticket and are represented in a number of city councils.[24] One of their most prominent representatives, the vice president of the umbrella organization, George Hasbun, is the deputy mayor of Bethlehem. As well as in the city administrations and professional associations, the unions play an important role in the National Guidance Committee for the West Bank and Gaza Strip, formed at the end of 1978 to co-ordinate all political activities against the occupation.

The political consequences of the emergence of a working class are still difficult to assess. The refusal of the Palestinian labourers employed in Israel to go to work during the October War and the growing participation of the trade unions in the political process in the occupied territories point to a possible development.

Yet another consequence can be observed in the changes in the social structure. Today no leadership group in the occupied territories is willing, or in a position, to collaborate with Israel. Such a group would have no social base and certainly no political one. That is also true for the Israeli autonomy plan whose success depends on finding persons in the occupied territories who are willing to co-operate. Interesting in this connection is the Israeli proposal to try out 'autonomy' in the Gaza Strip first; there is no broad base of support for it here any more than in the West Bank, but there is not as much resistance to it either.

The groups which profit from the occupation and, therefore, would have reason to co-operate with Israel, are in a dilemma. They can only gain political backing from the population, whose help or at least tolerance is needed even for the implementation of the limited 'autonomy' concept of the Israeli government, if they advocate nationalist goals. If they advocate a national Palestinian policy, they are persecuted by the occupying authority. It is the few wholesalers, employment agents and also the small businessmen who are extremely dependent on Israel and vulnerable to the repression of the military government. They can either pursue their businesses, which are dependent on the goodwill of the Israelis, or get involved in nationalist politics and risk being impeded in their businesses. That is their choice.

The traditional, pro-Jordanian leaders — often striving to co-operate with the Israeli authorities and also courted by them for lack of other 'moderate' negotiators — have rapidly lost power and respect in the past 14 years. They are no longer in the position to accomplish anything in the occupied territories in the interests of Israel. Because they are aware of their own weaknesses, many see it as advantageous today to work with the P.N.F., a tendency which has strengthened since the 'reconciliation' between the P.L.O. and the Jordanian regime.

There are those willing to collaborate. On the other hand, there is the new élite whose power is more political than economic, which shows little inclination to work with the military government. It has its base in the weak industrial bourgeoisie, the small farmers, the greater part of the petit bourgeoisie and parts of the working class, who have understood that the occupation hurts them and see their only chance in an independent Palestinian state.

The current economic and social structure might be the biggest obstacle to an 'American solution' in the region. Those who have the support of the general public in the occupied territories are neither friends of the U.S. nor of Israel, nor are they supporters of Jordan. The Israeli policy has led to a situation in which only the continuation of the occupation can guarantee Israel the type of stability it wants.

Notes

1. Cf. *Hilal 1975*, p. 156.
2. Cf. Chapter 4.
3. Cf. *Bull 1975*, p. 70.
4. Cf. *Hilal 1975*, p. 67.
5. Their percentage of the total number of self-employed decreased from 58.2% to 53.1%, cf. *Statistics 1975*, p. 704; *Statistics 1978*, p. 789. The average size of farms in the West Bank is 44 *dunams*. However, approximately two-thirds of all farms are smaller than the average, cf. *Shahar 1971*, p. 38.
6. The number of scientists and scholars: 3,600 in 1972, 2,200 in 1977, cf. *Statistics 1975*, p. 708, and *Statistics 1978*, p. 790.
7. Jordanian sources give 6,000 businesses in 1967; Israeli sources give 10,400 farms in 1972 and 11,800 in 1977, cf. *Statistics 1975*, p. 708, and *Statistics 1978*, p. 790.
8. For the temporary nature of the boom cf. Chapter 4.
9. Between 1970 and 1977, to 2,300 or 15%, cf. *Statistics 1975*, p. 704, and *Statistics 1978*, p. 789.
10. *Sheskin 1967*, p. 22.
11. One thousand artisans went out of business, cf. *Statistics 1975*, p. 704, and *Statistics 1978*, p. 789.
12. Cf. *Statistics 1975*, p. 704, and *Statistics 1978*, p. 788 ff.
13. Data for 1977, cf. *ibid.*
14. The average size of farms amounts to 26 *dunams*. More than two-thirds of all farms here are also smaller than the average, cf. *Shahar 1971*, p. 46.
15. Self-employed in the Gaza Strip agriculture: 6,200 in 1972, 4,600 in 1973, 7,200 in 1977, cf. *Statistics 1975*, p. 704 and *Statistics 1978*. p. 789.
16. Cf. *Statistics 1975*, p. 708, and *Statistics 1978*, p. 790.
17. Cf. *Statistics 1975*, p. 704, and *Statistics 1978*, p. 789.
18. In 1977, 46% of those from the Gaza Strip working in Israel were employed less than one year by the same company; 65.7% less than two years, cf. *Israel Labour 1979*, p. 23.
19. In 1977, 50% of those from the Gaza Strip working in Israel came from the refugee camps. If one counts the refugees no longer living in the camps, the percentage is even higher, cf. *Israel Labour 1979*, p. 22.
20. Cf. *Bull 1975*, p. 71.
21. Cf. Chapter 6.
22. Cf. *ibid.* and the *Jerusalem Post*, 4 January 1978.
23. Cf. *Coone 1980*, p. 19.
24. Cf. *ibid.*

6. Birth of National Consciousness: Political Development under the Occupation

From the Frying Pan into the Fire: The Historical Background

Until the withdrawal of the British in 1948, the West Bank had been part of the British Mandate territory of Palestine. The U.N. Partition Plan provided for the West Bank to be a part of the Arab Palestinian state. The borders, which were newly formed following the first Palestine war (1948-49), defined the West Bank as a geo-political entity for the first time. They consisted of the Jordan River to the east and the borderline between Israel and Jordan laid down in the Rhodes ceasefire negotiations to the west

The West Bank under the Jordanian Regime

On 1 April 1949, King Abdallah of Jordan annexed the West Bank.[1] There, the Jordanian authority encountered a political and administrative vacuum. The Palestinian national movement had not been able to recover after having been suppressed in a rebellion against the British (1936-39) and, therefore, had dissolved itself.[2] On 1 October 1948, a Palestinian national assembly in the Gaza Strip met and elected Haj Al-Husseini, the former *mufti* (expounder of Muslim law) of Jerusalem, president of the newly formed Palestinian government in exile.[3] The following day, a group of Palestinian notables met in Amman and demanded annexation to Jordan. This demand was repeated on 1 December 1948, at a conference in Jericho, called by the mayor of Hebron, Ali Al-Ja'abari.[4]

After the April 1950 election in the East and West Banks for a parliament of a united Jordan, the new parliament confirmed the annexation previously declared by the King in his Law on the Unity of the Two Banks. All Palestinians living within the territory of the new Jordanian state automatically received Jordanian citizenship. The annexation of the West Bank was only recognized by Pakistan and Great Britain. After a long protest, the Arab League accepted the annexation, but only with certain restrictions: King Abdallah waived his right to sign a separate peace treaty with Israel and, in return, the League granted him the right to temporary administration of the West Bank.[5]

In his selection of leaders who were willing to collaborate with Jordan and take over responsibilities in the West Bank or positions in the Jordanian parliament and cabinet, King Abdallah profited from disputes among the Palestinian clans, which had split at the first onset of opposition to the annexation. The King recruited these political representatives essentially from the following three groups: 1) Rivals of the former *mufti* of Jerusalem, Haj Al-Husseini, who had earlier made himself known as an opponent of King Abdallah's policy of co-operation with the British and who now led the insignificant Palestinian government in exile in Gaza;[6] 2) Large local landowners, a typical representative of whom was Ali Al-Ja'abari, the mayor of Hebron. This group was of greater political value because of its loyalty to King Abdallah. By the end of the Ottoman Empire, they had already lost their influence over large urban landowners as well as over the rising commercial and industrial bourgeoisie; and 3) Palestinians who had served under the British in the Palestinian Civil Service Mandate Administration and who, for this very reason, were useful (as administrators) to an unpopular government.

The Jordanian monarch restricted the sphere of influence of the Muslim institutions, which had been an important instrument in the hands of the opposition during the time of the British Mandate. He named Raghib Bey Nashashibi, the main opponent to the former *mufti* of Jerusalem, successor to this high Muslim office.

The Jordanian regime's policy toward the West Bank was characterized by economic and political oppression. With the rise of Arab nationalism, opposition to the Jordanian King, based on the ideas of Abd Al-Nasser, developed in Jordan in the middle of 1955. In the struggle for pan-Arabism, the establishment of a Palestinian state slid into the background. The goal of the opposition to the Jordanian regime, whose centres were mainly located in the West Bank, but also in north Transjordan, was to change the orientation of Jordanian policy.[8]

One of the first high points in the opposition movement involved negotiations over accession to the Baghdad Pact, which Jordan led in 1955. Following demonstrations in the West Bank (which had had certain characteristics of a revolt), free elections were held in 1956, the only ones Jordan had ever experienced. It was chiefly due to the votes from the West Bank[9] that a National Front (a union of the National Socialist Party, the Ba'ath Party and the Communist Party) under the leadership of Sulayman Al-Nabulsi was able to emerge. However, this new government with its policy of non-alignment[10] was only able to last half a year. Under pressure from, and with the support of Western diplomacy, King Hussein (who had succeeded to the throne after the assassination of Abdallah) had Nabulsi arrested (April 1957), dissolved the parliament and declared two years of martial law. Thousands of intellectuals and nationalists, especially those from the West Bank, were thrown into prisons and concentration camps without due process of law.[11] Demonstrations which flared up in the West Bank were suppressed by the Jordanian regime with the help of the army, a pattern of control which was to characterize Jordanian policy toward the West Bank up until the Israeli occupation.

The economic policy of the Jordanian authority was also notable for its measures to handicap the West Bank and its attempt to make it economically dependent on the East Bank.[12] Various measures to control investments were used to force West Bank industrialists to establish their businesses in the East Bank. Major agricultural projects, mainly irrigational, were concentrated in the East Bank. The result of this economic policy was, on the one hand, the combining of interests of the traditional leaders with those of the Jordanian royal family, and on the other hand, in comparison to Transjordan, 20 years of decline in the standard of living of the West Bank population under the Hashemite reign.[13]

On the eve of the June War in 1967, the West Bank inhabitants were 'second class citizens' within the Jordanian Kingdom, discriminated against politically and economically. In a final wave of arrests following demonstrations against the Jordanian King in 1966, the leaders of the opposition in the West Bank were imprisoned, leaving the opposition virtually without leadership.

The Occupiers Settle In

The population's impression of the Israeli occupying authority was greatly influenced, not only by the speed with which the Jordanian army was eliminated,[14] but also by the actions taken following the military victory. The ceasefire between Israel and Jordan did not stop Israel's military actions. On 12 June 1967, two days after the ceasefire began, three villages, Yalu, Beit Nuba and Emmaus, were destroyed by the Israeli army.[15] Still other West Bank villages became victims of similar actions.[16] Whereas the residents of these other villages were eventually allowed to return and rebuild their homes or received a small compensation, the residents of Yalu, Beit Nuba and Emmaus became refugees.

> **Yalu, Beit Nuba and Emmaus: an Israeli Soldier Reports**
> The commander of my platoon said that it had been decided to blow up the three villages in the sector — Yalu, Beit Nuba and Emmaus. For reasons of strategy, tactics, security.
>
> We were told it was our job to search the village houses; that if we found any armed men there, they were to be taken prisoner. Unarmed persons should be given time to pack their belongings and then told to get moving — get moving to Beit Sira, a village not far away. We were told also to take up positions around the approaches to the villages, in order to prevent those villagers who had heard the Israeli assurances over the radio that they could return to their homes in peace — from returning to their homes. The order was: shoot over their heads and tell them there is no access to the village.
>
> The homes in Beit Nuba are beautiful stone houses, some of

them luxurious mansions. Each house stands in an orchard of olives, apricots and grapevines; there are also cypresses and other trees grown for their beauty and for the shade they give. Each tree stands in its carefully watered bed. Between the trees lie neatly hoed and weeded rows of vegetables.

At noon the first bulldozer arrived, and ploughed under the house closest to the village edge. With one sweep of the bulldozer, the cypresses and the olive trees were uprooted. Ten or more minutes passed and the house, with its meagre furnishings and belongings, had become a mass of rubble. After three houses had been mowed down, the first convoy of refugees arrived, from the direction of Ramallah.

We did not shoot into the air. We did take up positions for coverage, and those of us who spoke Arabic went up to them to give them the orders. There were old men hardly able to walk, old women mumbling to themselves, babies in their mothers' arms, small children, weeping, begging for water. The convoy waved white flags.

We told them to move on to Beit Sira. They said that wherever they went, they were driven away, that nowhere were they allowed to stay. They said they had been on the road for four days now, without food or water; some had perished on the way. They asked only to be allowed back into their own village, and said we would do better to kill them. Some of them had brought with them a goat, a sheep, a camel or a donkey. A father crunched grains of wheat in his hand to soften them so that his four children might have something to eat. On the horizon, we spotted the next line approaching. One man was carrying a 50 kilogramme sack of flour on his back, and that was how he had walked, mile after mile.

More old men, more women, more babies. They flopped down exhausted, at the spot where they were told to sit. We did not allow them to go into the village to pick up their belongings, for the order was they must not be allowed to see their homes being destroyed. The children wept, and some of the soldiers wept, too. We went to look for water but found none. We stopped an army vehicle in which sat a lieutenant-colonel, two captains and a woman. We took a jerry can of water from them and tried to make it go round among the refugees. We handed out sweets and cigarettes. More of our soldiers wept. We asked the officers why the refugees were being sent back and forth and driven away from everywhere they went. The officers said it would do them good to walk and asked 'Why worry about them? They are only Arabs!' We were glad to learn that half an hour later they were all arrested by the military police, who found their car stacked with loot.

More and more lines of refugees kept arriving. By this time there must have been hundreds of them. They couldn't understand why they had been told to return, and now were not being allowed to return. One could not remain unmoved by their entreaties. Someone asked what was the point of destroying the houses, why didn't the Israelis go and live in them instead? The platoon commander decided to go to headquarters to find out whether there was any written order as to what should be done with them, where to settle them and to try and arrange transportation for the women and children, and food supplies. He came back and said there was no written order, we were to drive them away.

Like lost sheep they went on wandering along the roads. The exhausted were beyond rescuing. Towards evening we learned that we had been told a falsehood: at Beit Sira, too, the bulldozers had begun their work of destruction, and the refugees had not been allowed to enter. We also learned that it was not in our sector alone that areas were being 'straightened out'; the same thing was going on in all sectors. Our word had not been a word of honour, the policy was a policy without backing.

The soldiers grumbled. The villagers clenched their teeth as they watched the bulldozers mow down trees. At night we stayed on to guard the bulldozers, but the entire battalion were seething with anger; most of them did not want to do the job. In the morning we were transferred to another spot. No one could understand how Jews could do such a thing. Even those who justified the action said that it should have been possible to provide shelter for the population, that a final decision should have been taken as to their fate, as to where they were to go The refugees should have been taken to their new home, together with their property. No one could understand why the fellah should be barred from taking his oil-stove, his blanket and some provisions.

The chickens and the pigeons were buried under the rubble. The fields were turned to desolation before our eyes, and the children who dragged themselves along the road that day, weeping bitterly, will be the Fedayeen of 19 years hence. This is how, that day, we lost the victory.
— report of Israeli journalist, Amos Kenan.

Source: *Israel & Palestine*, No. 43, October 1975.

NB: Today, on the land where these three villages once stood, are the Canada Memorial Park and Israeli fields. (Cf. *Le Monde*, 5 July 1969.

Such measures of destruction (including shooting over the heads of the people[17] and making public announcements over loudspeakers attached to vehicles, recommending that they flee,[18] contributed to the exodus of hundreds of thousands of inhabitants from the occupied territories. Even explicit orders given over Arab radio stations commanding the Palestinians not to leave their homes could not stop the flow of refugees.[19] Statistics on the number of refugees who left the occupied territories after the war are contradictory. According to Jordanian figures, which correspond with UNRWA statistics, the number of refugees from the West Bank and Gaza Strip amounted to about 250,000.[20] Even the agreement between Jordan and Israel, reached after long negotiations with the International Red Cross acting as mediator, was able to change very little. The number of refugees granted repatriation remained under 20,000. As noted in the UNRWA report, the return of refugees who had lived in East Jerusalem or in refugee camps was denied in almost every case.[21]

Standing before the Wailing Wall on the evening of 7 June, Israeli Defence Minister Moshe Dayan commented on the end of the dispute with the Jordanian army after Jerusalem had been captured. He stated; 'We have united Jerusalem . . . . We have returned to the holiest of our holy places, never to be apart from it again.'[22] In the eyes of the population, the annexation of Jerusalem on 28 June 1967, was the clearest sign that the Israeli occupation was to last a long time, particularly since it was based on a law passed the previous day by the Israeli parliament, which enabled the administration to extend the application of 'the law, jurisdiction and administration of the state [of Israel] to any area of Eretz Israel designated by the government by order'.[23]

Israeli intentions were demonstrated not only by measures taken during the first days of the occupation, but also by a psychological campaign carried out in the Gaza Strip which was aimed at convincing the population that 'Israeli troop withdrawal was not planned for any time in the near future'.[24]

The occupying authority regarded the statements of Israeli politicians and leading personages as having a decisive role to play. General Dayan stated: 'While waiting, we must – without formally proclaiming the annexation of the occupied territories – create *faits accomplis* in these liberated areas.'[25] Both of Israel's chief rabbis demanded that the conquered territories never again be returned. They said: 'The land was promised to us by the Almighty, and all the prophets foretold its return to us. Therefore, it is forbidden for any Jew ever to consider returning any part whatsoever of the land of our forefathers.'[26]

To those who, directly after the war, saw the occupied territories (excluding Jerusalem) as a bargaining card for peace, the dispute in Israel soon became only a question of how much booty one should acquire.[27] The Allon Plan, presented only one month after the fighting ended, received broad support. It provided for the annexation of Jerusalem, the Gaza Strip and a 10–15 kilometre wide strip along the Jordan and the Dead Sea. Kibbutzim were to be established in this area and a large city, between Jerusalem and

Jericho. If a peace agreement was reached, the rest of the West Bank was to be returned to Jordan.[28]

Some proposals went even further. General Dayan felt peace negotiations were impossible and, therefore, demanded that, as far as possible, 'new facts' (*faits accomplis*) should be established to make future annexation easier.[29] The proposals of the conservative parties, with future Prime Minister Menachem Begin at the head, were simple and even more to the point. Not even a small piece of Eretz Israel should ever be returned to the Arabs, as it is 'our fatherland and we have the rights to it'. At that time, Begin envisaged Jews settling in all Arab cities rather than the founding of settlements.[30] Debates in Israel on the annexation of the occupied territories were mainly supported with demographic arguments. While some in the Labour party felt that annexation endangered the Jewish character of Israel,[31] the supporters of a 'greater' Israel believed this problem could be solved through intensified Jewish immigration and through the encouragement of Arab emigration. This hope was expressed by Shimon Peres, former Defence Minister and leader of the opposition during the Begin administration, when he said in November 1967: 'There is the phenomenon in the modern world, of roaming from village to city and from agriculture to industry. In the Arab world, industrial development was delayed by several generations . . . . Why prevent the movement of emigrants from underdeveloped agriculture in Judea and Samaria to the oil industries of Kuwait and Bahrain?'[32]

The combination of the policy of *faits accomplis* begun immediately after the occupation,[33] the plans discussed by Israel, and the views of leading Israelis, soon gave the Palestinians of the occupied territories the impression that they were 'unwanted guests in their own land'.[34]

Local city administrations served as the connection to the military government, installed (on 6 June in the Gaza Strip and 7 June in the West Bank) immediately following the occupation. Their tasks, defined by Jordanian law, were restricted to administration. From the beginning, political functions, such as those of the governors of three Jordanian administrative districts in the West Bank, were not recognized by the military government. General Dayan further recommended that the development of political leadership on a regional level be prevented.[35]

In a series of security regulations, the military government listed the following, among other things, as punishable acts: membership of an organization which intends to disturb public order; agitation and hostile propaganda; publication of political papers which have not previously been cleared by the military government; contact with foreigners of enemy countries; possession, manufacture and use of explosives and weapons; and interference with the Israeli defence forces.[36]

The security regulations were soon followed by action. Leaders and members of nationalist and leftist organizations were arrested and deported, in the meantime, the military government tried to promote a so-called third force in the political spectrum in the West Bank. Prominent persons who spoke out for establishment of a Palestinian entity connected to Israel could count on Israeli support, for example, through the Arab newspaper *Al-Anba* which is financed by Israel.[37] But Israel never undertook concrete steps to realize these plans. Rather, the purpose of the verbal support seemed aimed at splitting the West Bank leadership and to some extent countering radical demands.

The Occupiers Stay: The First Three Years of Occupation

Protest and Collaboration
Immediately following the takeover of the West Bank, there was no widespread resistance among the population. This is attributable to the shock produced by the takeover of the West Bank by Israeli troops, and to political conditions under the Jordanian regime. Political power in the West Bank had been vested in a few hands, and some of the Jordanian political functionaries had fled to the East Bank when the fighting started. Most of the opposition leaders were in prison or were not released until during the war. Political parties were prohibited and the Fedayeen had not been able to gain a firm foothold in the West Bank (as it had in the Gaza Strip) under the Jordanian regime. Thus, West Bank leadership which could have organized a resistance movement did not exist.

The records of the Jordanian police and intelligence authority fell into the hands of the Israeli army, quickly providing them with a survey of the opposition forces. Among the factions of the traditional leadership, Israel found those willing to co-operate with the occupiers as loyal partners. One of these was Sheikh Ali Al-Ja'abari, mayor of Hebron. At the first city council meeting immediately following the end of the war, he assured the Israelis of 'full co-operation in the maintaining of peace in the city and in the resumption of important services'.[38]

Not until it became clear that the occupation would be of long duration, did a first wave of protests arise, mainly directed at measures taken under the Israeli *faits accomplis* policy. Characteristic of the protests in the first months was that they occurred within a Jordanian context. The aim of the protests was to reverse the occupation, and its leaders were mostly former Jordanian functionaries, judges, teachers, city councillors, and also Muslim dignitaries. The acts were almost always done with the approval of the Jordanian authorities or were in response to Jordanian summons to protest. The protest against the annexation of East Jerusalem was led by a group of 25 dignitaries, founded on 24 July 1967, that called itself a 'body for Muslim affairs in the West Bank including Jerusalem'. This group drafted a resolution against the annexation, named a successor to the *qadi* (Muslim judge) who had fled during the war, and organized a general strike in East Jerusalem for 7 August. The signatories of the resolution were chiefly pro-Jordanian notables, but a few also belonged to the opposition movement against the Jordanian monarch.

Birth of a National Consciousness

Memorandum of the West Bank Muslim Leaders

Jerusalem, 24 July 1967

To His Excellency the Military Governor of the West Bank

... We hereby declare that the decisions issued by the Israeli legislative and administrative authorities to annex Arab Jerusalem and its outskirts to Israel are null and void, for the following reasons:

a) Because Arab Jerusalem is an integral part of Jordan ....

b) Because the United Nations, in its resolutions issued at the emergency session held between 17 June 1967 and 21 July 1967, ruled that the annexation of Arab Jerusalem to Israel was illegal.

c) Because the Israeli Knesset has no authority to annex the territory of another state.

d) We also declare that the people of Arab Jerusalem and its outskirts, together with the other inhabitants of the West Bank, enjoyed complete freedom of choice when they opted for union with the East Bank, thus forming the Hashemite Kingdom of Jordan by virtue of the unanimous decision of the Jordanian National Assembly on 24 April 1950 ....

We hereby record that the annexation of Arab Jerusalem is an invalid measure taken unilaterally by the occupation authorities against the will of the inhabitants of the City, who reject this annexation and insist on the continued unity of Jordanian territory ....

Signed:
Anwar al-Khatib	Muhafiz of Jerusalem
Ruhi al-Khatib	Mayor of Jerusalem
Abdul Hamid al-Sayih	President of the Shari'a Appeal Court
Hilmi al-Muhtaseb	Member of the Shari'a Apeal Court
Said Sabri	Qadi of Jerusalem
Sa'aduddin al-Alami	Mufti of Jerusalem

Kamal al-Dajani, Lawyer, Ibrahim Bakr, Lawyer, Arif al-Arif, Director of the Jerusalem Museum, Fuad Abdul Hadi, Notable and Lawyer, Abdul Rahim Al-Sharif, Notable and Lawyer, Hafiz Tahbub, Lawyer, Sa'id Alauddin, Lawyer, Omar al-Wa'ri, Lawyer, Abdul Muhsen Abu Maizar, Lawyer, Ishq Darwish, Ishaq al-Duzdar, Hasan Tahbub, Director of Waqfs, Jerusalem, Dr Daud al-Husaini, Dr Subhi Gawsha, Ali-al-Taziz, President of the Chamber of Commerce, Nihad Abu Gharbiya.

Source: Institute for Palestine Studies, *The Resistance of the West Bank of Jordan to Israeli Occupation*, Beirut, 1967, p. 19ff.

Israel reacted to these first protests with repressive measures to hinder the establishment of an opposition to the occupying authority. This repression came in the form of exile to cities of northern Israel and house arrest for the signatories of the resolution and deportation of the new *qadi*, the first of many expulsions to come under the occupation. The religious jurisdiction over East Jerusalem was withdrawn from the Muslim institutions there and was delegated to the *qadi* of Yafo.

By eliminating this Muslim body, Israel wanted to prevent any resistance to the occupation which could be organized by religious groups, as had happened during the time of the British Mandate. Defence Minister Dayan commented on the protest against the annexation of East Jerusalem with these words:

> We are not in Jerusalem on condition or by someone's approval. We are there because it is vital to our security. Jerusalem is not Aden, and its administration is not dependent on co-operation from the Arabs. We shall be glad if they will be loyal partners in a united [i.e. Israeli] Jerusalem. But if not, we intend to run the services ourselves.[39]

Another point which caused protest in the West Bank to spread on a large scale was a change in school books and curricula. At first, the plan was to replace curricula and textbooks in the occupied territories with those of the Arab schools in Israel. After fierce protest from the population, which interpreted this as a move to consolidate the occupation, this decision was retracted in the occupied territories, with the exception of East Jerusalem. Instead of this, Jordanian textbooks were censored, revising passages 'found to be deprecatory of Jews, Zionism or Israel'.[40] This censorship lay mainly in the hands of the Education Ministry, which demanded very extensive changes, leading to a long-lasting strike by school students and teachers.[41]

'This is Palestine' — Conversation with a Palestinian Teacher

Q: Can you please give us an idea of the the curriculum and books used in the West Bank schools and tell us the meaning of the changes?

A: The Jordanian books were already very poor. The Israelis combed through these books and took out what didn't suit them. Take the following situation. Once, I taught fifth grade English and we were studying a map of our region. Only a few cities were marked on the map and the word 'Palestine' was not on it at all. We looked at the English words for the neighbouring Arab countries and Palestine. I pointed to Jordan, Syria and Lebanon and gave the English names for them. The students could guess the meanings of the English words because the names sound very similar in Arabic. Then I pointed to Palestine and said, 'This is Palestine.' The children could not guess what the English word

> 'Palestine' meant. The history and geography books don't contain anything about Palestine. Nothing about Palestine as a geographic concept, nothing about Palestine as a political concept!
> *Q*: Which map is actually used in the geography books then?
> *A*: Syria, Jordan and Israel are indicated on the maps in the geography books. Israel with the borders after the 1967 war, therefore including the occupied territories (the West Bank, Gaza Strip, Golan Heights and Sinai). They don't make any distinctions. On the maps, which were put into the books by the Israeli authorities, everything is Israel — no ceasefire boundaries from the war, nothing, absolutely nothing.
>
> Source: Interview by the authors, September 1978.

In 1968-69, the protest movement entered a new phase. Only at the very beginning of the occupation had the traditional leaders taken part with the Jordanian government in initiating demonstrations and strikes. On the grounds that the notables had set the population against the occupation, the curfew in Nablus was extended and the licences of local bus companies were revoked. This form of collective punishment[42] and the deportation of traditional leaders, enabled the Israeli military government to successfully intimidate the notables. Even Jordan granted its supporters limited collaboration with the military government after the first deportations.[43] In this new phase, the organization of protest action was almost completely left to the groups in opposition to the traditional leaders. This was soon reflected in the slogans and goals of the demonstrations. Slogans such as 'we shall not yield to the occupiers'[44] were aimed not only at the Israeli occupying authority but also increasingly at the notables.[45]

The centres of protest lay in the north of the West Bank: Nablus, Ramallah, Tulkarm and East Jerusalem. Occasions for protest were anniversaries or concrete steps taken by the Israeli military government, such as arrests, blowing up of houses, establishment of settlements or expropriations. The acts of protest during these years never amounted to the popular revolts depicted in some Arab propaganda. Yet their continuity and the harshness of the Israeli reaction to them disproves the assertion that life in the occupied territories was normal. Foreign observers confirmed this. In 1969, the *International Herald Tribune* commented: 'The escalation of reprisals, the movement toward establishing collective responsibility [i.e. collective punishment] both bring the region closer to those horrors which Lidice, Hué and Pinkville represent.'[46] Similarly, *The Times* reported: 'The Israelis are at least as determined as are the Russians in Czechoslovakia to crush all opposition and are in a better position to do this.'[47]

> **Acts of Protest: Some Examples 1968-69**[48]
> *1968*
> January: In Nablus and Hebron, committees formed in protest against the detainment of West Bank residents.
> February: Petition to the Israeli Defence Ministry, the General Secretary of the U.N. and the International Red Cross signed by 300 women from the West Bank and Gaza Strip.
> June: Demonstrations in Ramallah and Nablus; strikes in shops and businesses in Nablus and Tulkarm.
> August: Demonstration by 200 women in Nablus against the annexation of East Jerusalem and against the arrest of residents of the occupied territories.
> September: 500 schoolgirls demonstrate in Nablus against the destruction of houses by the Israeli occupying authority.
> October: School strike and demonstration in Nablus involving more than 1,000 school students; student strike in Qalqilya; demonstrations in Ramallah and Al-Bireh.
> November (anniversary of the Balfour Declaration): Demonstrations in numerous cities in the West Bank and also in the south. End of a two-month school strike in Nablus.
> *1969*
> February: School strikes in Ramallah and Nablus and on separate days also in Jenin, Bethlehem and Tulkarm. Demonstrations in Nablus, Ramallah, Al-Bireh, Qalqilya, Tulkarm, Bir Zeit and Jenin. Businesses strike in Nablus. Sit-in strike by 200 girls in Ramallah. Demonstration by 400 schoolgirls in Bethlehem.
> March: Large demonstrations with 1,000 participants in Nablus. Sit-in demonstration by 400 women in Nablus.
> April: School strikes in Nablus continue.
> May (Israeli Independence Day): School and business strikes in Nablus, Tulkarm, Qalqilya, Bethlehem and Hebron.
> June (anniversary of the June War): General strike in Nablus.
> August: Demonstrations and general strike in the West Bank.
> September: Demonstrations and school strikes in Nablus and Jenin.
> October: School strikes in Nablus.
>
> Source: *Middle East Record*, 1968 and 1969.

The military administration had a wide range of legal provisions still valid from the time of the Mandate plus Jordanian laws and their own security provisions to draw on when dealing with the protests. The measures included collective punishment, for example, curfews following demonstrations and the closing of schools following school strikes, as well as trade restrictions such as the closing of Jordanian bridges for export from certain regions.[49] The military government acted against individuals by imprisoning, deporting or heavily fining ringleaders. The basis for this policy toward the protests can be seen in a letter from the Defence Minister addressed to the notables of several cities. They were asked to prohibit protests and it was pointed out to them that 'anyone dissatisfied with Israeli rule could leave the area'.[50] The number of deported persons rose sharply in 1968 and 1969. While there had only been five persons exiled in 1967, 62 inhabitants of the West Bank were expelled in 1968, 187 in 1969 and 260 in 1970.[51] The actual causes were usually demonstrations. Protests in the autumn of 1968 as well as in February and June 1969 led to large waves of deportations which affected all members of the opposition to the traditional leaders and even pro-Jordanian notables.[52]

Formation of Public Opinion in the West Bank

Public opinion in the West Bank was shaped by several factors. The absence of political structures under Jordanian rule was remarkable. Political parties were prohibited and only a limited amount of public awareness could be promoted in the newspapers, which in any case reached only the élite in the urban centres. Village authorities were elected in only a few cases. More and more, however, the leadership of those whose power had been legitimized through tradition and economic dependence was being questioned.[53] Traditional leaders in the West Bank, the majority of whom were closely tied to Jordan, were confronted by a growing opposition which was still affected by the political suppression of Jordanian rule (some of the leaders were still in prison or had not been released until during the war). In addition, their freedom to act was restricted through bans on organizing and assemblies; demonstrations, strikes and other forms of protest were prohibited; and leaders were arrested or deported.[54]

Israeli plans for the future of the West Bank were also decisive in the formation of public opinion. Israel continually emphasized that it would be prepared to negotiate only with Jordan over the West Bank; precise plans, however, concerning the future of the occupied territories were never put forward. The occupying authority's actions (i.e. the 'new facts': the annexation of East Jerusalem, settlements and economic integration) were, therefore, all the more important as an indicator of its plans. Jordan continued to play an important role for the Palestinians, too — possibly as a negotiating partner they could not afford to do without, as the only 'bridge' to the Arab world and as a market for West Bank exports.

Finally, the Palestinian liberation movements gained increasing importance. After the defeat of the Arab states in the June War, they became more and more prestigious and influential, and, while the political/military goals of the P.L.O. appeared to many to be unrealistic, daily confrontation with the occupation increased the necessity for a solution in the eyes of the population.

The political groups and the leadership had to grapple with the following three problems in developing a political perspective: 1) the fight against Israeli occupation; 2) their attitude toward King Hussein of Jordan; and 3) the development of solutions and prospects for the future.

The Traditional Leaders
The members of this group had in common their claims to leadership which stemmed from the traditional social structures. Most of them were leaders of the most important families of the West Bank. In the south, a predominantly agricultural region, Sheikh Ali Al-Ja'abari was the dominant personality for a generation and in 1967, his influence was not in question. The south was involved in protests during Jordanian rule only to a very small extent. But in the north the situation was different. In addition to agriculture, the few industries, larger cities and trade centres were concentrated there. In this region loyalty to King Hussein was the most effective guarantee for maintaining the status of the traditional leaders. Particularly in the north, many of the notables were personally and economically connected to the Hashemite dynasty.

Al-Ja'abari was the first traditional leader to break with King Hussein. The fact that he vehemently supported the annexation of the West Bank by Jordan in 1948-49 and switched over to Israel immediately in 1967, allows only one interpretation — that Al-Ja'abari was always ready to collaborate with whomever happened to be in power. He summarized his new stand with regard to Jordan thus: the residents of Hebron had neither asked King Hussein for the war nor for his withdrawal from the West Bank. 'Jordan proved itself incapable of defending the West Bank, therefore, we owe it nothing.'[55] Al-Ja'abari, along with a few other West Bank leaders, soon made the suggestion that the West Bank leaders themselves should negotiate with Israel. (These included, for example, the lawyer Aziz Shehadeh from Ramallah, who had already rejected the annexation of the West Bank in 1949, and the veteran Palestinian politician Nimr Al-Hawari, who had been especially active during the period of the British Mandate.) In October 1967, followers of Al-Ja'abari distributed leaflets suggesting the formation of a 'Palestinian entity'. This entity would be connected to Israel in the form of a federation.[56] Al-Ja'abari continually provided evidence of his willingness to collaborate with the military administration. Even when Jewish settlements were established on expropriated Arab land in the southern West Bank (provoking fierce protests from other traditional leaders), Al-Ja'abari was against organizing protest demonstrations.[57] His caution was based on the conviction that 'correct' relations between Israel and the West Bank were essential in order to prove that a 'Palestinian entity' would not endanger the Jewish state. Thus Al-Ja'abari hoped to win Israeli support for his plan.

But the Israeli government never made any concessions, let alone took any concrete steps which could have led to the realization of such a minimal solution. These plans contradicted many of the premises upon which Israeli policies were based. The annexation of parts of the West Bank and the establishment of settlements would have been more difficult and such a Palestinian entity would have claimed East Jerusalem as its capital instead of Amman.

Al-Ja'abari could not find much support in the West Bank for his plan. It was labelled as having been initiated by Israel, and the population doubted that the occupation would end voluntarily without political pressure from the Arab nations. In addition, they feared becoming second class citizens (similar to the Arabs in Israel) in a Palestinian entity bound to Israel. Because of criticism from the West Bank, the P.L.O., the Arab nations and particularly Jordan, and for lack of any signs of willingness on the part of Israel to help realize his plan, Al-Ja'abari finally also considered the possibility of a federation with Jordan. Beginning in early 1969, he again spoke of a possible re-annexation of the West Bank to Jordan,[58] above all, to avoid the danger of total isolation.

Jordan vehemently attacked the idea of a Palestinian entity, depicting it as a move designed to turn the Palestine problem into a local matter thereby divesting it of its status as an Arab concern. While labelling Al-Ja'abari as a traitor, Jordan attempted to mobilize the rest of the traditional leaders (most of whom had remained loyal) against the concept of a Palestinian entity.[59]

Most of the opponents of Al-Ja'abari's concept were located in the north of the West Bank. The traditional leaders' most important representatives were the mayor of Nablus, Hamdi Kana'an, his deputy and successor, Hikmat Al-Masri, as well as a relative of his, the former president of the Jordan parliament and minister, Haj Ma'zuz Al-Masri, both tied to Jordan by financial commitments. Other traditional leaders opposing the entity idea were the governor of East Jerusalem, Anwar Al-Khatib, who is related to the royal dynasty, and other traditional leaders (such as Qadri Tuqan and Anwar Nuseibeh), who had all, at one time, held Jordanian offices. They all firmly advocated re-annexation to Jordan.

Supported and encouraged by Jordan to refuse co-operation with Israel, they helped organize the first protest demonstrations. At the beginning of the occupation, the Israeli measures of repression, especially deportations, also affected this group. The most prominent victims were Sheikh Abdul Hamid Al-Sayih and the mayor of Jerusalem, Ruhi Al-Khatib.[60] Their deportation put an end to all protests organized by traditional leaders. Even the Jordanian government had given up its hard line by the beginning of 1968. Probably out of fear that this hard line could lead to the decimation of the pro-Jordan leadership, the government let its adherents know that it would not undertake anything against 'limited collaboration' with the occupying authority.[61] From that point on, two factors determined the policy of the traditional leaders; first, their connection to the Jordanian King whom they represented *in absentia*; and second, a developing opposition which questioned their power. If they intended to maintain their power, they had to be careful not to betray the population opposed to the Israeli occupation too openly and also to display a moderate criticism of King Hussein.

They presented their rejection of the entity idea and with it the related demand for re-annexation to Jordan, with apparently unchallengeable technical arguments. Hikmat Al-Masri, for example, put economic considerations into the foreground. He emphasized that the West Bank could not exist without the East Bank, and would be dependent on agriculture and 'Israeli goodwill' alone. He said: 'Those who talk of it [the concept of a Palestinian entity] are only making fun of us. The unity of the two Banks is a fact.'[62] Similarly, mayor Hamdi Kana'an said: 'Such a state could not exist independently and the Israelis would swallow it up.'[63] In order to avoid isolation, they cautiously criticized King Hussein and demanded that he carry out reforms within the Jordanian state. However, these reforms in no way threatened the Hashemite power and were not to be implemented until after the end of the Israeli occupation.[64] Growing difficulties for those loyal to King Hussein in the West Bank and sinking support for the Jordanian King, made concessions necessary. Towards the end of 1968, an 'authorized source' of the royal court let it be known that the King had 'plans for the future of the West Bank — to decentralize the government after the liberation of the territory as a step towards modernizing Jordan'.[65] In their conduct towards the Israeli military administration, the traditional leaders sought a compromise between collaboration and concessions to the public. Unlike Ali Al-Ja'abari in the south, who prohibited demonstrations and acts of protest, the attitude of the pro-Jordan leaders in the north was more complex. Verbally they granted the public the right to protest. At the same time, however, they tried to check any acts of protest and to attribute them to 'extremist circles'.[66]

The Israeli military government had no interest in allowing even more radical leaders to come to power. For this reason, their demands never went so far as to endanger the position of the traditional leaders. On the contrary, they tried to make it clear to the public through small concessions to these leaders how useful they were.

The Nationalist and Leftist Opposition

The opposition to this traditional group of leaders and to the Jordanian King was made up of Communists, Ba'athists, Arab nationalists and followers of the various Palestinian liberation movements and was concentrated in the north of the West Bank. Immediately following the war, these organizations were only capable of limited action, as they were chiefly busy with reorganization. Their political position was limited to the demand for Israeli troop withdrawal; only then could the future of the West Bank be decided upon.[67] This demand, which was directed against the entity concept, enabled them to work with the pro-Jordan notables in the first few months following the war, especially since, at that time, the latter still resolutely opposed the Israeli occupying authority.[68]

All nationalist and leftist forces had the following three things in common: their resolute opposition to the Israeli occupation, their rejection of King Hussein's regime and their fundamental opposition to the traditional leaders. The progressive groups denied the traditional leaders the right to speak for the West Bank population and reproached them for their co-operation with the occupying authorities, for their connection to the Jordanian monarch, and for the fact that their power was not legitimate.

> **Criticism of the Traditional Leaders**
> It is an open secret that the present traditional Palestinian leadership attained its status in Jordanian government circles by diligently serving the interests of the Hashemite throne. Since an autonomous Palestinian State was anathema to the well-being of the monarchy, they did all that was possible to stifle any flicker of support for Palestinian independence that may have survived the 1948 defeat. In return for their services, the King showered upon them financial emoluments and entrusted them with the running of the affairs of the West Bank.
>
> The aftermath of the Six Day War created new political realities that endangered their position of leadership. Should Israel undertake the creation of a buffer state in the occupied territories designed to secure her eastern flank, there was a possibility that their allegiance to Amman might cause Israel to proceed without their blessing and active participation. To circumvent this possibility they attempted an impossible manoeuvre. Continued support for Amman and the 'three nos' of Khartoum would be evinced now and then, but in the meantime overtures would be made to their new masters in Tel Aviv, just in case the Israelis were serious about their plan. Such a course of action, so they thought, would assure them a continued role of leadership no matter what the future brought.
> --Yassuf Nasir, an East Jerusalem teacher.
>
> Source: *New Outlook*, February 1969, p. 39 ff.

The opposition in the West Bank tried to express its criticism of King Hussein in co-operation with opposition groups in East Jerusalem.[69] They demanded that the monarchy be democratized and that more power be given to Palestinians in Jordanian politics and in the army as well as a change in Jordan's pro-Western policy.[70]

There were two groups within the opposition which differed in their political goals and in their strategies. The members of the Ba'ath Party and the sympathizers of the Palestinian organizations advocated a 'true revolution' which would lead to the liberation of all of Palestine and to a secular democratic state. They emphasized the necessity of armed struggle and opposed all dialogue with Israel, whether it be with government officials or political parties.[71] The Communist Party's central demand was to put an end to the occupation, leaving any goals beyond that open in the first few years after 1967. It recognized the 1947 partition plan and later also recognized Israel. The Communist Party was the best organized of all groups and was rooted in professional, student and social associations as well as in the labour unions.[72] In contrast to the other two groups, i.e. the Ba'ath and Palestinian organizations, it emphasized political forms of struggle and did not take part in armed actions.[73] Furthermore, the Communists saw no reason not to carry on a dialogue with leftist Israeli groups which they perceived as 'friends in the struggle against the ruling "military junta" in Israel'.[74] Among the progressive organizations, the Communist Party was the main one to organize demonstrations and strikes against the occupation. At the same time, it attempted to bring all the opposition groups together in order to broaden the base of the protest against the occupying authority as well as the political disputes with it.[75]

A first attempt in this direction was the founding of the Higher Commission for National Guidance in September 1967. The three leading figures were the lawyer, Ibrahim Bakr, the journalist and poet, Gamal Nasir from Ramallah and Faiq Muhammed Warrad from Al-Bireh. All three were considered to be members of the Communist Party[76] and had taken part in the Nabulsi revolts in 1957. Leaflets, for which the Committee had claimed responsibility, circulated in the West Bank in mid-September 1967. They protested against the annexation of Jerusalem, called for a strike against the occupying authority and resolutely criticized plans for a Palestinian entity. A functioning organizational structure was never attained mainly because of Israeli counter-measures — all three initiators were deported in December 1967.[77]

At the end of 1968, members of the Communist Party attempted to form a National Front, in which all nationalist and leftist groups were to join forces. In Nablus, a stronghold of the progressive opposition, the Committee for National Solidarity was founded to co-ordinate all activities against the occupying authority. The founding of similar committees in other West Bank cities followed. The National Front was to emerge from the alliance of these committees.

The Israeli military administration's reaction to these attempts to organize, which were illegal according to Jordanian laws and the Israeli security regulations, was either the deportation of those who had taken part, or their administrative detention (without being charged or put to trial),[78] as occurred, for example, after the founding of such committees at the end of 1968 in Nablus[79] and in March 1969 in several other West Bank cities.[80]

These organizational attempts made by the opposition failed not only because of Israeli counter-measures, but also because of differences of opinion among the various factions. In an interview with the Beirut newspaper, *Al-Anwar*, an exiled participant, described such an obstacle as follows: 'The Communists had supported the formation of a wide National Front, and had taken initial steps in this direction, but could not continue because of premature use of extreme slogans by the Ba'ath Party.'[81] The newspaper further commented that the difference of opinion between the Ba'athists and Communists had existed shortly after the June War and, therefore, had already stood in the way of an alliance. In the eyes of the commentator this, as well as deportation and imprisonment of progressive leaders, had enabled the 'followers of defeatism and collaboration' (as for example, Hamdi Kana'an and Ali Al-Ja'abari) to present themselves in the first few years of the occupation, as the only representatives of the Palestinians in the West Bank.[82]

A major factor in the political development in the West Bank was the quickly growing sympathy for the P.L.O., especially after the Fedayeen's successful fight against the Israeli army in Karameh (in the East Bank) in 1968.[83] After the crushing defeat of the Arab armies in 1967, the P.L.O. gained increasing prestige in the eyes of West Bank residents. 'The Fedayeen has saved our honour' was a frequently expressed opinion. This, however, did not change the fact that the military acts of Palestinian groups in the West Bank were welcomed by only a small minority and were actively supported by even fewer. Unlike similar groups in the Gaza Strip, they only played a subordinate role in the West Bank and were discontinued, for the most part, in 1970.

Peaceful Times: From Black September in 1970 to the Elections in 1972

In the years following the widespread protests of 1968-69, there were only smaller demonstrations in the West Bank. There were two main reasons for this. First, the Israeli methods of repression, particularly deportation and administrative detention, prevented attempts to organize political resistance. There was a sense of resignation amongst the people who, after three years, still found themselves under Israeli occupation. Secondly, the standard of living in the occupied territories has risen because of the job opportunities in Israel. Although this development could not eliminate the resistance potential, it certainly diminished it.

It was not until September 1970 (Black September) with the Jordanian massacre in refugee camps and the crushing of Palestinian organizations in Jordan that large demonstrations again took place, this time primarily against the Jordanian King.[84] Throughout the West Bank, relief committees were set up to collect donations of money and items needed to support Palestinians in the East Bank. Associations and professional organizations as well as the mayors signed a memorandum to the Arab nations, urging them to put a stop to the bloodshed. During demonstrations in several West Bank cities at the end of September, King Hussein was called the 'Butcher of Jordan' and the 'Hashemite Nero'.

There were, however, substantial differences in emphasis between the statements made by the traditional leaders and the various petitions and slogans of the demonstrators. The demonstrators and national organizations (education, medical, bar and women's associations) led by the opposition claimed Hussein was responsible for the massacre, demanded his overthrow and openly expressed their sympathies for the Fedayeen.

The traditional leaders were more reserved in their positions. The Higher Muslim Council in Jerusalem merely demanded a ceasefire. The mayor of Hebron demanded that both Yasser Arafat, leader of the P.L.O., and King Hussein lay down their weapons. The mayor of Nablus, under pressure from the anti-Hussein sentiment in the city, signed the message from all the mayors to Hussein and the Arab heads of state, but he did not sign the more harshly formulated petition from the city's residents, which was directed at the Arab nations and signed by thousands.[85] As early as a month after the massacre, the traditional leaders retreated a

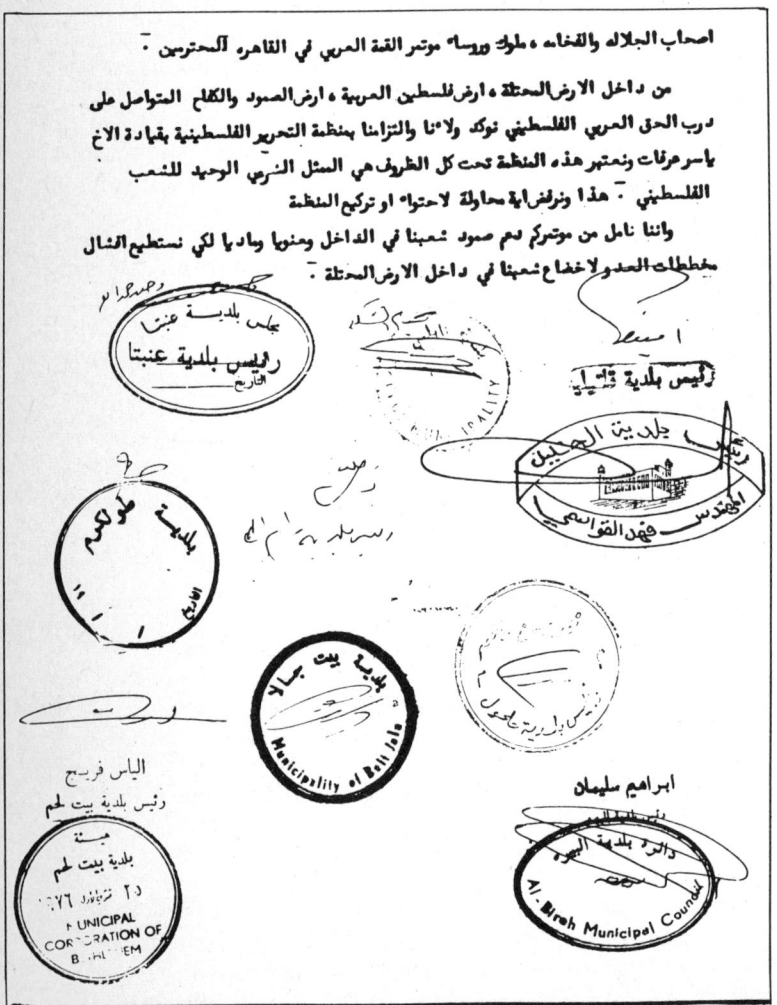

Letter from the West Bank mayors to the Arab heads of state

step further. In a conversation with journalists, the notable Qadri Tuqan from Nablus gave the following answer as to the future of the West Bank: 'We will return to Hussein .... We know how to deal with him, we will manage with Hussein. As for what happened recently in Jordan, one can only be sorry. This is a fairly natural phenomenon in the light of the nationalist awakening of the Arab nation.'[86] Other traditional West Bank leaders loyal to Hussein (e.g. Dr Anwar Nuseibeh, former Defence Minister and Jordanian ambassador) recommended to King Hussein that he make some concessions to the population.[87] These people were concerned about their financial commitments in the East Bank. In their eyes, the only way to secure their power was re-annexation to Hussein's Jordan.

Black September had two consequences for the West Bank. First, the opposition to King Hussein increased; and second, the confrontation with the Hashemite regime led to the realization that the Fedayeen's possibilities within Jordan were limited and that prospects for a change in Jordan had dwindled.

In the same period of time, there was another attempt at organizing the opposition, significant mainly because of its detailed plans for the future. The initiative came from a number of young intellectuals. On 8 October 1970, the National Palestinian Gathering was founded in East Jerusalem. A leading figure in the group was Yussuf Nasir, a young intellectual educated in the U.S., who worked as a secondary school teacher in East Jerusalem.[88] The organization claimed to be a new West Bank leadership group. In its manifesto, published as a pamphlet at the end of 1970, the option of an independent Palestinian state in the West Bank and Gaza Strip was first laid down.

> **The National Palestinian Gathering's Manifesto**
> The manifesto was based on four principles: 1) rejection of the occupation; 2) unity of the Palestinian and Jordanian peoples, while clearly distinguishing between the Jordanian people and the regime, which had to be replaced by a regime of a 'national and democratic character which would represent the aspirations and will of both the Palestinians and the Jordanians'; 3) a just peace that would ensure the rights of the Palestinians in terms of international resolutions and their right to self-determination; 4) action on behalf of the Palestine cause by means of co-ordination between the Palestinians under occupation and those outside the occupied territories.
>
> In order to ensure the 'preservation of the Arab identity and character' of both the occupied territories and of the population itself, the group called for the placing of the West Bank, East Jerusalem and the Gaza Strip under a temporary U.N. administration after the withdrawal of the Israeli forces as a preliminary step towards the realization of their 'Palestinian idea'.

> Source: *Ma'ariv*, 26 November 1970 and *The New York Times*, 6 December 1970.

This concept differs decisively from the previous idea of a Palestinian entity in that the Palestinians outside the occupied territories are included and it insists on the right to self-determination, which a federation under Israeli or Jordanian control would exclude.

Manipulation from All Sides: the Elections of 1972
After a period of relative calm in the West Bank, the military administration felt it was possible to schedule municipal elections, which had continually been postponed since 1967. Israel wanted to use the elections to demonstrate the liberal nature of the occupation, but at the same time, did not want the traditional leaders to be defeated. On 26 November 1971, the military governor issued a decree for elections in four locations in the West Bank, more or less as a test for the other cities. The locations chosen for the elections were Jericho, where the public had requested elections, Tulkarm, where the more radical Hilmi Hanoun was mayor, as well as Qalqilya and Jenin. Because of resistance to this test run, a second decree provided for elections in all cities to be carried out in two stages. The new scheme also met with rejection, for the mayors feared the loss of their power. Generally, participation in elections under the military government was viewed as recognition of the occupation. It was not until Israel threatened to replace the mayors with Israeli officers,[89] that some of the traditional leaders changed their mind.

The leftist opposition fiercely attacked the elections and called for a boycott. Leaflets were circulated, demanding not only election boycotts but also punishments for those who ran as candidates. One reason for the decision to boycott was the Jordanian election law. According to this law, the right to vote was limited to male residents over the age of 21 who owned property and paid property taxes. Under these conditions and in view of the fact that the opposition was not yet completely united, candidates for the opposition would not have had much of a chance in the elections. An Arab intellectual from East Jerusalem commented: 'These elections won't change a thing. Under the conditions set by these reactionary laws, it will be just as it had been under Hussein, that is, the same leaders in the same positions.'[90]

The organizations of the Palestinian liberation movement also called for an election boycott. They saw the elections as an Israeli attempt to formally confirm a leadership group willing to collaborate, in order to be able to subsequently realize pseudo-autonomy under the Israeli military administration. These organizations threatened to take action against the traditional leaders if they ran.

King Hussein, who had fiercely attacked the idea of ballotting in the West Bank immediately after the election decree had been made, abandoned his opposition to the elections and let his followers know that he would do nothing to prevent them from participating.[91] Once convinced that the elections would definitely take place, the King feared a loss in the extent of his influence in the city councils; the notables loyal to him were in danger of being replaced by supporters of the 'entity' proposal.

Furthermore, there were rumours that Jordan and Israel had formed secret agreements as to how the elections should be carried out. In fact, they both had a stake in the election results. Both wanted to prevent the formation of a Palestinian state independent of Israel and Jordan. For this reason, they wanted to see the city council positions filled by the traditional leaders and notables loyal to Hussein. Israel needed traditional leaders willing to collaborate, to act as mediators between the military administration and the public and as 'democratic' figureheads. They would enable Israel to keep all its options open: a creeping annexation under the same form of military administration as was already in effect; plans for a West Bank 'autonomy' under Israeli supervision; and finally, the option of an agreement with Jordan.

There were repeated reports in the West Bank (but also in the foreign press) about Israeli-Jordanian contacts. Meetings between the diplomat Anwar Nuseibeh and Prime Minister Golda Meir, Defence Minister Moshe Dayan and the Minister of Police, Shlomo Hillel, were confirmed by all sides.[92] According to official statements, these discussions contributed to their mutual assessment of the elections and an agreement on prospects for the future.[93] According to other reports, Israel and Jordan agreed to allow only traditional leaders and those loyal to Hussein to have a chance.[94] Thus, Israel did not tolerate any propaganda against the elections and, in certain cases, arrested the instigators of election boycotts.[95]

Gradually, candidates were submitted in all West Bank cities. Only in Nablus did it come down to a confrontation of strength between Israel, the traditional leaders and the opposition. No candidates could be found. Even the former mayor and rich industrialist, Hamdi Kana'an, withdrew his name one week before the elections. The incumbent mayor, Ma'zuz Al-Masri, refused to the very end to run.

The conflict in Nablus, the centre of political resistance within the West Bank, was characteristic of that resistance. The Israeli military administration's reaction was soon to follow; several leading intellectuals from Nablus were threatened with deportation.[96] Hikmat Al-Masri, a relative of the mayor, was arrested for having contact with terrorists, a grave charge. The businesses of the Masri family were investigated and partially placed under surveillance.[97] In a talk with mayor Ma'zuz Al-Masri, Defence Minister Moshe Dayan threatened to place the city and all of its businesses under Israeli control and to put Lieutenant-Colonel Aaron in charge of the administration. Soon afterwards, Aaron himself appeared at the Nablus city hall, and at the same time, the military administration extended the deadline for submitting slates to the eve of the elections.[98]

Under massive pressure, the Nablus notables decided in favour of their business interests and declared themselves willing to run for office. Al-Masri assured Defence Minister Dayan that a sufficient number of candidates would be found. The economic restrictions on the city were lifted and the mayor's relatives were released. The second round in the power struggle went to Israel.

A final manoeuvre to support the traditional leadership was the federation plan for the West Bank, which King Hussein announced 14 days before the elections. In a speech outlining the status of the West Bank if a peace agreement were reached, the King spoke of new Jordanian plans for the West Bank.

> **King Hussein's Federation Plan (excerpts):**
> We are pleased to announce that the basic principles of the proposed new plan are:
> 1. The Hashemite Kingdom of Jordan shall become a United Arab Kingdom, and shall be thus named.
> 2. The United Arab Kingdom shall consist of two regions:
>   A. The Region of Palestine, which shall consist of the West Bank and any further Palestinian territories to be liberated and whose inhabitants opt to join.
>   B. The Region of Jordan, which shall consist of the East Bank.
> 3. Amman shall be the central capital of the Kingdom and at the same time shall be the capital of the Region of Jordan.
> 4. Jerusalem shall become the capital of the Region of Palestine.
> 5. The King shall be the Head of the State and shall assume the Central Executive Power, assisted by a Central Council of Ministers. The Central Legislative Power shall be vested in the King and in the National Assembly whose members shall be elected by direct and secret ballot, having an equal number of members from each of the two regions.
> 6. The Central Judicial Authority shall be vested in a 'Supreme Central Court.'
> 7. The Kingdom shall have a single 'Armed Forces' and its 'Supreme Commander' shall be the King.
> 8. The responsibilities of the Central Executive power shall be confined to matters relating to the Kingdom as a sovereign international entity ensuring the safety of the union, its stability and development.
> 9. The Executive Power in each Region shall be vested in a Governor-General from the Region, and in a Regional Council of Ministers also formed from citizens of the Region.
> 10. The Legislative Power in each Region shall be vested in a 'People's Council' which shall be elected by direct secret ballot. This Council shall elect the Governor General.
> 11. The Judicial Power in each Region shall be vested in the courts of the Region and nobody shall have any authority over it.
> 12. The Executive Power in each Region shall be responsible

> for all matters pertinent to it with the exception of such matters as the constitution defines to be the responsibility of the Central Executive Power.
>
> Source: *Journal of Palestine Studies*, summer 1972, Vol. I, No. 4, p. 167.

For the first time, King Hussein made concrete concessions to the West Bank in this plan. The traditional leaders therefore seized upon the plan immediately and interpreted it as 'a chance not to be missed, especially if it could bring about the end of the Israeli occupation'.[99] The P.L.O. vehemently attacked Hussein's plan the day following its publication and described it as a manoeuvre to deceive the population of the occupied territories.[100] The West Bank nationalist and leftist opposition reacted in a similar way, describing the plan as part of the Israeli-Jordanian agreements on the future of the West Bank.

Elections took place on 28 March in the north, and on 2 May 1972 in the south. Only in Hebron and Salfit was there no balloting; instead, the councillors of these two cities were confirmed for another term of office by the military government.[101] Although over half of the elected councillors were taking office for the first time, it was only a change of faces; the old traditional leadership remained in power. Only in the cities of Tulkarm and Ramallah was it any different. In Tulkarm, Hilmi Hanoun was confirmed in office. Although he did belong to the traditional leadership, he gradually felt himself drawn more to the political demands of the organizations of the Palestinian liberation movement. In Ramallah, Karim Khalaf, a member of one of the city's largest clans and a rich factory owner, was elected, and subsequently made no secret of his opposition to the rest of the traditional leaders.

The election was claimed a success by Israel as well as Jordan. The government press in Amman wrote that the elections were proof of 'the close connections between the East Bank and the West Bank and, in addition, were a slap in the face for the Fedayeen who opted for a Palestinian state'.[102] The military governor described the election results as 'a large step forward toward a normalization process'. He continued by saying that this was the first time in the five years of occupation that the public had participated in political decisions 'voluntarily and by their own choice and means'. In his opinion, the experiment was 'a complete success'.[103]

The large turnout for the election (85%, a good 10% above average) was particularly stressed. Voluntariness and freedom of choice probably played only a partial role in it. The passports of all those who went to the polls were stamped. Before the elections, the rumour was spread in the West Bank that in the future, only those with this stamp in their passport would be allowed to travel across the bridges to Jordan.[104] Nevertheless, Sheikh Al-Ja'abari published an announcement in bold print in Israeli newspapers, thanking Israel for its non-interference in the elections.[105]

From Protest to Resistance: 1972 to 1976

Even the 1972 elections could not disguise the fact that after five years of Israeli occupation, a vacuum had been created in the West Bank political leadership. The re-confirmed traditional leaders could pass themselves off as representatives of the people even less now than they could before. The elections did show, however, that the opposition did not yet have the personnel, organizational strength or political influence to stand against the traditional leaders. Up to this point, counteractions by the military administration and differences within the opposition itself had caused the failure of attempts to organize effectively. Nevertheless, young intellectuals and the Communist Party tried to form an opposition through existing and newly founded organizations such as youth clubs, professional and cultural associations, women's groups and labour unions.

The widespread sympathy enjoyed by the P.L.O. in the West Bank, especially since the Jordanian Black September, gave way to a more critical solidarity in the following years. The most important goal for the West Bank population (unlike the Palestinian organizations in exile) was the termination of the occupation. Therefore, the people of the West Bank were much more willing to compromise than the P.L.O. After five years of occupation, they considered Israel an opponent whose determination and military might were unquestionable. In addition, there were increasing signs of a perpetuation of the occupation − in statements by leading Israeli politicians, in the settlement policy and in the economic integration.[106] Under these circumstances, the P.L.O. still propagated military activities in 1972, neglected the political work in the occupied territories[107] and insisted on its all-or-nothing demands to replace the Zionist state with a democratic and secular state in Palestine. Within the P.L.O., this demand was beyond discussion, which guaranteed the co-operation of the various factions. In the West Bank, emotional and political criticism of the P.L.O.'s refusal to reconcile their demands with attainable goals, constantly became stronger. West Bank inhabitants became less willing to 'sacrifice themselves for an unattainable paradise'[108] and criticized the lack of consideration of their own views in the formation of policy within the P.L.O. This did not mean, however, that the P.L.O. lost any ground. A typical response to one of the polls taken in the occupied territories by the Paris newspaper *Le Monde* was that 'in spite of everything, the Fedayeen has given us back our honour, our pride in being Palestinians'.[109]

A chance for the West Bank population to have its views represented more strongly in the P.L.O. failed in 1972 because of united resistance from Israel and Jordan. The P.L.O. had invited about 100 people from the occupied territories (members of the traditional leadership as well as young intellectuals and representatives of the leftist opposition) to participate in the

Birth of a National Consciousness

'We Want Self-determination' – one of the many slogans in the West Bank

Tenth National Congress meeting in 1972 in Cairo. Jordan sharply attacked the P.L.O. and disputed its right to speak for all Palestinians. On the other side, the Israeli military governor announced that all who participated in the National Congress would forfeit their right to return to the occupied territories.[110] Yet the 1972 National Congress was important for the West Bank. It stressed the necessity of political struggle and, above all, of political organization in the occupied territories. In the West Bank a coalition of the groups which stressed the political struggle and the followers of the various factions of the P.L.O. now became possible.

The Founding of the National Front
Efforts to find a common organizational structure for the opposition forces led to the founding of the Palestinian National Front (P.N.F.) in August 1973. The P.N.F. considered itself an organizer of the political struggle against the Israeli occupation. Since the military government's security regulations prohibited all such political alliances, they had to work underground.

The Political Programme of the P.N.F. (A Summary)
The National Question
1) To resist Zionist occupation and to struggle for the liberation of the occupied Arab territories.
2) To secure the legitimate rights of the Palestinian people and, first and foremost, its right to national self-determination in its own land.
3) To reject all plans that aim to dissolve the national question of our people and ignore its rights, be they Zionist (e.g. the Allon Plan), Arab (e.g. the United Arab Kingdom of King Hussein), American, or any other defeatist and liquidationist solution that resembles them.

Economic, Cultural, and Civil Rights
4) To defend Arab lands and properties against measures of expropriation, arbitrary closure, and intimidation.
5) To protect our economy and to preserve our agricultural, industrial, and commercial institutions against the occupiers' attempts to destroy or absorb them.
6) To protect our culture and history from Zionist mockery and distortion, especially with regard to school programmes.
7) To defend our holy places from Zionist attempts to take them over or demolish them.
8) To revive our heritage of folklore and the literature of the resistance movement inasmuch as it represents our people's attachment to its land and its valiant struggle to defend it.
9) To help our militants, men and women, who are held in the Zionist prisons; to struggle for their release and the improvement of their conditions; and to provide care for their families and children.
10) To support our mass organizations such as trade and labour unions, student and women's associations, social clubs and religious groups; to defend them against the narrow interests of the élites representing them; and to strengthen them against Zionist attempts to infiltrate them.

Regional and International Affiliations
11) The Front affirms the unity of the Palestinian and Jordanian peoples, and proclaims its support of the Jordanian national movement struggling for the transformation of Jordan into a strong base that will sustain the fight against Zionism and imperialism.
12) The Front affirms that the Palestinian national movement, inside and outside the occupied territories, is part of the Arab liberation movement, as it also affirms that the continuation of

> Zionist occupation does not only threaten the rights and interests of the Palestinian people but also those of neighbouring Arab peoples.
> 13) The Front affirms that the Palestinian national movement is part of the progressive and revolutionary forces in the world and will act so as to strengthen its solidarity and co-operation with them and, especially, with the socialist countries.
>
> Source: *MERIP Reports*, No. 25, p. 22.

The members of the P.L.O. affiliated organizations, Communists, Ba'athists, Arab nationalists and also independents, were joined together in the P.N.F. alliance. Trade unions and professional, social and cultural associations were also represented in the Front. The National Front's aim was to create an effective political force in the West Bank in opposition to the traditional leadership. This political force, which considered itself to be part of the P.L.O., also was to formulate its own political objectives.

The goals set down in the P.N.F. charter are decisive for the formation of the broad alliance in the P.N.F. and for its autonomy within the P.L.O.[111] The charter does not mention the idea of a secular state in the whole of Palestine but only the right to self-determination and to repatriation for the refugees. In this respect, it goes way beyond the national charter of the P.L.O. and includes the possibility of a Palestinian state alongside Israel.

The Communist Party had played a particularly important role in the founding of the P.N.F. It was able to build upon its existing infrastructure and due to its political position it also had a central role in the formation of a broad alliance.[112] Factors outside the occupied territories also contributed to the success of the P.N.F. Within the P.L.O. there was a growing tendency to reconsider the all-or-nothing demand, which was evidenced in particular by the withdrawal of the Rejection Front from the P.L.O.'s executive committee. Activities on political and diplomatic levels gained increasing importance in the P.L.O.[113] Improvement in the ties between Moscow and the P.L.O. led to closer contacts with the Communist parties of Lebanon, Jordan and Iraq. In addition the West Bank Communist Party was willing to retract its recognition of U.N. Resolution 242 in favour of a broad alliance.

> **Interview with Two Leading Members of the National Front**[114]
> *Q.* When was the Palestine National Front formed?
> *A.* The front was formed in mid-August 1973, when its programme and formal political work began. The formation, however, was not sudden: it was based on years of political experimentation during the Israeli occupation. Immediately after the Israeli occupation began, a number of committees

sprang up based on the old membership of parties such as the Communist Party, the Ba'ath, branches of member parties of the P.L.O., and professional societies, all of which had existed in the Hashemite Kingdom. The committees undertook a variety of peaceful activities to protest occupation: petitions, resolutions, meetings and demonstrations. As the actions began to develop toward strikes, clashes grew between Arabs and Israelis. Israel began to arrest and deport Arabs it thought were organizing these protests. After the initial arrests, many people withdrew from these committees, and only the more revolutionary members, especially workers, women and students remained. Still, however, there was no real organization. There were many divisions; the resistance groups there stressed only armed struggle and not political struggle. This was a substantial obstacle to unifying the diverse groups.

But gradually, and especially after the September 1970 massacres in Jordan, the resistance organizations began to see how important unity was. Some commando groups even began to see the importance of political organization. This new trend appeared in the National Assemblies of 1972 and 1973, in the resolutions calling for formation of a National Front in the occupied territories.

At the beginning of 1973, various forces actively began to establish such a Front. A programme was written after consultations with a variety of trade union, student and women's groups and professional societies. Leaders of the Front were chosen from these groups and the Communist Party.

One of our first successes was the Front's campaigns against the September 1973 elections the Israelis held for the trade unions in Jerusalem. This was part of their policy to get Arabs to join Israeli unions. We organized a boycott of the election. Our estimates are that only 6% of the Arab workers voted.

Q. What kind of a political organization is the Front?
A. The P.N.F. is a member of the P.L.O. which is the sole representative of the Palestinian people. Our mission is to lead the struggle from inside the occupied territories.

Its base is very wide because it defends all classes of people. We believe the occupation weighs on all classes and strata. We help landlords oppose the expropriation of their land. We help the clergy oppose desecration of their holy places. We oppose any efforts to stamp out national culture. Even the Marxists have demonstrated against landlords' loss of land in Nablus. We support Archbishop Capucci, and he supports our struggle.

Q. Could a West Bank state survive?
A. Of course, the creation of a mini-state does not solve our problems because all refugees could not return to their homelands.

> To exist between two enemy states Israel and Jordan would be difficult. We will face many economic and social problems. But the establishment of such a state would enable us to rebuild ourselves culturally, politically. Freedom and independence are very important in themselves, whatever the problems.
>
> Source: *MERIP Reports*, No. 32, November 1974.

The October War and its Consequences

During the October War, the situation remained relatively calm. However, the P.N.F. successfully organized passive resistance. Tens of thousands of labourers from the occupied territories stayed away from work 'thereby paralysing numerous Israeli businesses'.[115] A resident of Nablus who lost one month's pay because of the war explained:

> Our task in the occupied territories is to protect the rest of Palestine. If we had used violent methods — for which we didn't have any means anyway — Israel would have used the opportunity and driven us out. Here, we're fighting for the land and we must hold on to it.[116]

The fact that King Hussein did not participate in the October War as well as the ensuing recognition of the P.L.O. by the Arab nations at the summit conference in Algiers[117] led to a new wave of sympathy for the P.L.O. The National Front even succeeded in persuading the conservative Islamic Council in Jerusalem, in which there were prominent Hussein supporters, to take a stand in favour of the P.L.O.[118] In view of the growing reputation of the P.L.O., the mayors one by one announced that they considered the P.L.O. to be the sole legitimate representative of the Palestinians. The nationalist and leftist groups were the main ones to promote agitation to the benefit of the P.L.O. All over the West Bank, slogans and Palestinian flags appeared on buildings. The Communist Party distributed leaflets which summoned the public to participate in the P.N.F. which was described as a part of the P.L.O.[119] The city council elections in Jerusalem at the end of 1973 showed just how much influence the P.N.F. had gained. The P.N.F. called for the citizens of East Jerusalem to boycott the elections, which an overwhelming majority did. Only 8% went to the polls.[120]

Israel's and Jordan's reactions once again demonstrated how their interests ran parallel paths. To the rest of the world, King Hussein did explain that it was up to the Palestinians to decide for themselves what their future should be.[121] At the same time, however, he undertook intense efforts to win the West Bank population over to his 1972 plan for a federation. In order to strengthen the ranks of his supporters, he sent millions of *dinars* across the Jordan.[122] Israel reacted to this new situation by returning to the policy of ruling with a heavy hand.[123] A spokesman for the military administration explained the Israeli measures used in connection with the closing of Bir Zeit University thus:

> The last straw was a demonstration, which took place in the institution last week, protesting against the deportation of eight eminent Arabs to Jordan. Once more the teachers and students were warned that they were exploiting Israeli freedom of speech too far, and when they did comply with the warnings it was decided to silence them.[124]

This proved to be unsuccessful, however.

The number of demonstrations increased and the P.N.F.'s influence continued to grow. In January 1974, the National Front sent a memorandum with signatures from hundreds of important persons as well as many social and cultural organizations and professional associations from the West Bank addressed to the Executive Committee of the P.L.O. In this memorandum, support of the P.L.O. was expressed, suggestions for modification of the P.L.O.'s position were submitted and participation of the West Bank population in the formation of political opinion within the P.L.O. was requested.[125] Within the occupied territories, the number of comments on, demands for and analyses of an independent Palestinian state in the West Bank and Gaza Strip multiplied.[126]

The military government tried to crush the P.N.F.'s influence, hoping to prevent an alternative to the traditional leaders emerging. Obviously, Israel considered the Communist Party especially dangerous because of its central role within the P.N.F., its well organized infrastructure and, above all, its political position which made the Israeli argument that Palestinians merely wanted to destroy Israel appear ridiculous.[127] In February and April 1974, another six leaders of the P.N.F. were deported, including the head of the West Bank's Communist Party, Suleyman Najjab.[128] In a wave of arrests at the end of April, 150 activists of the National Front were put into administrative detention.[129] According to an Israeli newspaper:

> The detainees included all active leaders of Jordan's illegal Communist Party. . . . They organized themselves as the 'Palestinian National Front' and began activities. . . . They are chiefly representatives of the class of young, educated Arabs — teachers, engineers and those active in underground professional associations.[130]

The reason the Israeli military government gave for the detentions clearly illuminate the 'liberal nature' of the Israeli occupying authority: 'The security forces explain that they were not arrested for their ideas, which, after all, can be heard all over the West Bank. The fact that they are organizing represents a danger to Israel since the Front also planned to realize its political ideas.'[131] Therefore, Israel tried to do everything it could to hinder the emergence of alternative leadership whose political concepts they would have had to confront.

The attempt to eliminate the P.N.F. by arresting and deporting Communists shows that Israel had assessed the nature of the movement incorrectly. The hope that there would be no backing by the middle class and the masses proved to be false. The National Front was primarily a national movement. It was precisely within the middle class that widespread solidarity developed and the P.N.F.'s influence increased even more.[132]

The Rabat Summit and its Results

Discussions within the Palestinian liberation movements about initiatives at a diplomatic level entered into an intensive phase following the October War of 1973. In this period, the developments in the occupied territories and the residents' demands played an important role. The majority of the organizations within the P.L.O. no longer tended toward a total rejection of any compromises as they had in 1967. Now they envisaged the founding of a Palestinian state in the occupied territories alongside Israel as a first stage. In its twelfth meeting, at the beginning of June 1974, the Palestinian National Council passed the Ten Point Programme which was sanctioned by the majority of the organizations. In a compromise formula, they expressed their aim to establish a Palestinian state 'in any part of Palestine from which Israel will withdraw or which will be liberated',[133] i.e. a state alongside Israel, while declaring that, strategically speaking, the founding of a democratic secular state in the entire area of Palestine still remained a long-term goal.

In the occupied territories, the stands taken in favour of the P.L.O. and against King Hussein became increasingly clear. Before the Arab summit conference in Rabat, the P.N.F. sent a petition signed by leading figures and representatives of social, cultural and professional associations which was addressed to the Arab heads of state and called for the official recognition of the P.L.O.

With this in mind and in view of possible peace negotiations in Geneva, the Arab leaders passed a resolution at their summit conference in October 1974 recognizing the P.L.O. 'as the sole legitimate representative of the Palestinian people' whose 'mission it is to establish an independent power in every liberated part of Palestinian territory'.[134] Three reasons could have induced the heads of state (primarily King Hussein's allies such as King Faisal, the Emir of Kuwait and King Hassan of Morocco) to choose the P.L.O. leader Yasser Arafat over the Hashemite monarch. Firstly, King Hussein's passivity in the October War had discredited him even in the eyes of many moderate Palestinians. Thus, the results of any Middle East negotiations connected with him would have been viewed very sceptically. Secondly, all peace negotiations would be dependent on concessions possibly endangering the positions of those making them. The Arab heads of state wanted to avoid this responsibility if at all possible by bringing those who would be affected the most (namely the Palestinians themselves) to the negotiating table. Thirdly, the Arab heads of state knew, perhaps even before the October War, that at least part of the Palestinian leadership was willing to compromise.

King Hussein, for whom this meant relinquishing the West Bank, also accepted this decision but only under the conditions that Jordan would retain jurisdiction over the West Bank until the liberation; that the West Bank's former status could be reinstated at any time should the Arab summit conference ever annul its decision; and that the residents of both the East and West Banks must decide what kind of ties the two areas would have after the liberation.[135] Thus, King Hussein tried to keep a loop-hole open for regaining rule over the West Bank sometime in the future. The conclusions he drew from the decisions of Rabat were just as ambiguous. The postponement of elections for the Jordanian parliament on the grounds that the West Bank residents would not be able to vote because of the occupation indicated that Jordan had not completely given up its claims to the West Bank. The recent reformulation of the economic plans, which no longer included the West Bank was due to economic problems in the East Bank.[136]

In the occupied territories these developments triggered a wave of declarations of support for the P.L.O. and protest demonstrations against the Israeli occupation. Israel reacted in the usual way, deporting four citizens accused of organizing the petition which had been sent to the Arab heads of state prior to the Rabat conference.[137] The United Nation's recognition of the P.L.O. and Yasser Arafat's speech before the U.N. General Assembly a week after the Arab simmit conference generated another high point in the demonstrations. In most of the cities, this led to long-lasting commercial strikes and demonstrations. Even the renewed use of deportation could not put a stop to them.[138]

After the October War, the traditional leaders continued to lose influence rapidly. A number of factors within the West Bank were responsible for this loss. The traditional leaders increasingly lost the economic basis of their power. The higher standard of living in the first few years of the occupation undermined their power base. The dependence of the numerous land workers and small farmers on the traditionally powerful local large landowners and money-lenders visibly decreased. The income of a worker who commuted to Israel daily often exceeded that of the *mikhtars*, who owned some land.[139]

The political positions which the traditional leaders took, often as a result of their collaboration with the military government, were increasingly rejected because of the growing political consciousness in the West Bank. Moreover, the traditional leaders stressed that only external forces – in their eyes, King Hussein – could improve the situation. Until that time, they continued, one would just have to live with the occupation.

Through the establishment of a large number of social and cultural organizations, professional associations and trade unions, a new élite was able to set up a power base and gain recognition and influence. They possessed a mouthpiece for their views in the East Jerusalem newspaper, *Al-Fajr*, founded in 1971 by its chief editor, Yussuf Nasir.

An essential element of the National Front's policy was to attempt to have a voice in the stands taken by the P.L.O., of which they consider themselves to be a part, and to advance the discussion begun within the P.L.O. on the concept of the 'democratic, secular state'. Typical for these efforts was the position represented by leading persons in the P.N.F. (who had recently been deported from the West Bank) at a convention of the Cairo newspaper, *Al-Tali'ah*, at the beginning of 1974:[140] 'The concept of a "democratic, secular, Palestinian state" is impractical and illogical, ... for the Israeli state exists by virtue of the 1948 U.N. resolution and the majority of the world's nations have recognized Israel.'[141] The Communist Party gained a special position within the P.N.F. because of its independent stand. Its criticism of the P.L.O.'s stand was particularly aggressive. An example of this is the editorial in its underground newspaper, *Al-Watan*, from January 1976. In it, the P.L.O. leadership is called upon to give up the idea of a secular state because it is 'unrealistic and wrong' and 'furthermore, because it has not won the agreement of an important segment of those to whom it is proposed',[142] i.e. the Palestinians of the West Bank and the Gaza Strip.

> *Al-Watan's* **Appeal to the P.L.O. (excerpts)**
> The Palestinian people have achieved important political successes over the past year. Most prominent among them was the U.N.'s recognition of its right to self-determination and of the P.L.O. as its legal representative to the Security Council and General Assembly, ...
>
> The Palestinian struggle at present faces a task more defined and less unclear: presenting a realistic solution to the Palestinian problem, one which will win wide international agreement and gain support of the various forces which participated in the achievement of present Palestinian successes and the achievement of world recognition of the Palestinian entity.
>
> Our people, especially in the conquered territories, who have suffered and suffer from the disgrace of conquest, its domination and its terror, and who have tasted and continue to taste the bitterness of banishment, prisons, confiscation of land and establishment of settlements close to their dwelling places and on their soil, sense the need to present such a realistic programme, and call upon the P.L.O. to assume its responsibility without hesitation or delay.
>
> Now is the time for the organisation to say to what it will agree and what it is willing to concede. The Palestinian struggle has arrived at a crossroads which requires the Palestinian national movement under the P.L.O.'s leadership to relate to existing facts and real components of the present state in the Palestinian and Arab struggle, and to the balance of forces in the region and in the world.
>
> Such conduct, in the interest of the Palestinian struggle, requires abandonment of the 'democratic, secular state' slogan, since it does not have the support of the forces which played an

> important role in attaining the Liberation Organization's political successes. And furthermore, because it has not won the agreement of an important segment of residents of the state to which it is proposed.
>
> Thus, insistence on this slogan while the movement holds its present position in the political arena means weakening the alliance of important and influential forces based on the Palestinian people's rights, and missing a valuable opportunity to increase Israel's isolation and to tighten the noose around the expansionist aggressive policy which relies on American imperialism.
>
> At the same time, we are aware of the reality of strong pressures on the P.L.O. leadership, and of extremist declarations from what is called the 'rejection front', but none of this justifies conflicting declarations and contradictory stands, or the occasional return to unrealistic slogans, whose hardness does not serve to advance the Palestinian struggle.
>
> The struggle has come to a stage where it must define clearly its stand regarding the form of its right of self-determination. The international community, represented by the U.N., recognized this right and now it is necessary to clarify this right as a political entity.
>
> Source: *New Outlook*, February/March 1976.

In October 1975, Israel stepped into the debates on political leadership in the West Bank and the new developments in the Palestinian liberation movement by proposing an 'administrative autonomy' for the West Bank as a first step in the realization of the Allon Plan, according to Israeli newspapers.[143] Defence Minister Shimm Peres, responsible for the plans, remarked that 'a new situation has arisen and the circumstances are favourable for granting the West Bank population self-administration'.[144] According to the Israeli Foreign Minister, the plans served to 'demand the crystallization of a leadership with which one can negotiate, when the time comes'.[145] By this he could only have meant the traditional leaders whom this proposal was to strengthen once again. Almost simultaneously, the Israeli government explained that it wanted to observe the schedule for voting as determined by Jordanian law and, therefore, planned elections for April 1976.

Both of these plans were assessed by the P.N.F. as a renewed attempt to legitimize and extend the duration of the occupation. In the National Front's charter, the idea of self-administration under Israeli occupation was completely rejected and Israeli plans which tended in this direction were fiercely attacked. The P.N.F. now discussed participation in the elections which would have meant a deviation from the strategy which the opposition to the traditional leadership had adopted in 1972. Within the P.N.F., the Communists in particular, argued for participation in the elections. The new political situation and a new election law were arguments for participation. Both opened up prospects of success for the leftist-nationalist forces.

A New Leadership Emerges: The 1976 Elections

Preceding the Elections

In accordance with the four-year election cycle prescribed by Jordanian law, the Israeli military government in the West Bank scheduled municipal elections for 12 April 1976. Since the last city council election in 1972 the situation in the West Bank had changed significantly. The 1973 war, the international recognition of the P.L.O. by the United Nations and King Hussein's verbal waiver of his right to the West Bank had strengthened the nationalist forces. Large segments of the West Bank population publicly aligned themselves with the P.L.O. and clearly expressed their opposition to the Israeli occupying authority through demonstrations and general strikes. In allowing the elections to be carried out, Israel counted on another effective demonstration of the 'liberal nature' of its military administration. They felt fairly certain of the results. Yitzhak Rabin's administration expected that the P.L.O. — as in the 1972 elections — would call for a boycott and that the moderate forces would once again be able to prevail.[146] Israel also counted on the influence of King Hussein who, it was rumoured, supported his followers with several million *dinars*.[147]

Israel had yet another expectation of the elections. Despite their assertions that the elections were only of local significance, it was hoped that a leadership could be affirmed which would be willing to collaborate with the military government and would be an opposing force to the P.L.O. International recognition of the P.L.O. and King Hussein's cession of the West Bank, which was valid at least at that time, had left a vacuum, dangerous for Israel. Hussein was no longer willing to speak for the West Bank Palestinians. That left only the P.L.O. with whom negotiation was to be avoided at all costs. In the eyes of Israel, the election of moderate forces could effectively be interpreted as rejection of the P.L.O. by the population of the occupied territories. It was hoped that these moderate forces could be established as representatives of the Palestinians in negotiations with Israel on limited qutonomy for the West Bank population, the so-called Peres Plan, being discussed at that time.

As soon as the candidates names were submitted, marking the start of the election campaign in April 1976, some of Israel's hopes proved to be misplaced. Among the 577 candidates running for the 205 offices, there were a large number of new faces. It was significant that several of the incumbent city councillors and mayors had chosen not to run, for instance the mayors of the West Bank's two largest cities: Sheikh Ali Al-Ja'abari from Hebron and Haj Ma'zuz Al-Masri from Nablus. They supported King Hussein and, as stated in the Israeli newspaper *Ha'aretz*, 'in most cases, both followed the directions of the [military] government'.[148] The majority of the candidates belonged to a new generation; three-quarters were less than 50 years old and 10% were even under 30. While in 1972 the traditional clan leaders had run for election, a new set of people consisting of lawyers, doctors, engineers and teachers on the one hand and 'ordinary people' such as craftsmen and salaried workers on the other was now running.[149] It was precisely among highly qualified professionals that frustration due to the occupation was greatest and resistnace to the military government was most obvious. Anyone belonging to this group who did not accept emigration as a solution, was, of necessity, to become radical as a result of the poor professional prospects.[150]

The main basis upon which candidates from different groups came together on the P.N.F. slates was their common goal to end the occupation and to establish a Palestinian state on the West Bank and Gaza Strip. Their precise conception of such a state was of less importance. In addition to the Communists who were the driving force within the National Front and made up about 20% of the candidates, there were also supporters of Fatah, the strongest faction in the P.L.O., and Ba'athists, supporters of Arab socialism. The candidates were not united in their political or in their social views. The percentage of representatives from the professional élite was especially high. There were also industrialists, such as Bassam Shak'a from Nablus, whose family is one of the richest clans in Nablus. Another example is the mayor of Ramallah, Karim Khalaf, a millionaire and owner of the local chocolate and Arak (liquor) factories.[151] There were also representatives of the trade unions, such as George Hasbun, who headed the list of candidates in Bethlehem. Many of the candidates were known to support the P.L.O.; many even publically declared their support for the P.L.O. or for the Communist Party. In numerous ambivalent statements, the P.L.O. called for neither a boycott of the elections nor participation in them.[152] Only the Rejection Front clearly spoke out against the elections. It was therefore left up to the candidates of the National Front themselves to decide whether or not they should run. The P.N.F. decided to participate.

After the National Front had submitted its slates shortly before the deadline, while many of the traditional leaders had not done so, the military governor extended the registration period. The *Jerusalem Post* commented:

> Officially this has been attributed to the 'pressure of numbers' but the deadline is believed to have been extended to enable more moderates to put forward their candidacy, with the aim of counterbalancing the radical tide which had swept the registration lists by the first deadline.[153]

At the same time, the military administration tried to persuade persons acceptable to it to run. The case of Sheikh Ali Al-Ja'abari from Hebron became very well known. A week before the opening of registration for candidates, Al-Ja'abari had already announced that he would not run. The Israeli morning paper *Ha'aretz* describes the efforts to persuade him to run as follows:

> ... the military government and local personages were said to have exerted pressure on Sheikh Ja'abari and Haj Ma'zuz Al-Masri [the mayor of Nablus] to submit their candidacy.... The Minister of Defence, Shimon Peres, met with Sheikh Ja'abari several times recently in an attempt to convince him to run in the elections. The adviser for Arab affairs in the military government, Dr Amnon Cohen, also met with Sheikh Ja'abari and Al-Masri in a similar attempt.[154]

The deportation of two National Front candidates on 28 March (14 days before the election) was also an attempt by the military authorities to influence election results in favour of the moderate forces. In Hebron, where one of them wanted to run against Sheikh Al-Ja'abari, the deportation was understood as an attempt to support Al-Ja'abari, which exposed him once and for all.

According to Jordanian law, the election campaign is to be limited to local issues. In April 1976, however, other topics were dominant. Posters for the P.N.F. candidates in Ramallah were printed in red, green, white and black, the Palestinian national colours. The mayor of Ramallah and candidate for the National Front, Karim Khalaf, said, 'We are for the P.L.O.; we say it in our speeches and that is the issue. In our public meetings people don't ask about fixing the streets or getting factories. They want to end the occupation.'[155]

Election Results

In all of the larger cities, with the exception of Bethlehem, the National Front coalition gained a majority on 12 April, in many cases by a large margin. In Bethlehem, it was the Communist candidate, George Hasbun, who received the highest number of votes, even though the P.N.F. coalition did not prevail. The incumbent mayor, Elias Freij, was barely able to claim a majority; six of his candidates were elected, while five were elected from the National Front. In Hebron, the candidates of the National Front, led by agronomist Fahad Qawasmeh, won all of the council seats. In Nablus, the 42 year-old candidate of the National Front, Bassam Shak'a, was at the top, winning along with seven other National Front candidates; the traditional leaders won only two seats. The results were similar in Ramallah, where Karim Khalaf, known as a resolute P.L.O. supporter, was re-elected as mayor. The nine seats in the city council were filled by eight candidates of the National Front and one traditional candidate. In all, the National Front won a majority in the city councils in two-thirds of the 24 localities where elections were held. Only one out of every five of the incumbent councillors was returned to his seat.

The successful candidates were quite different in appearance from the old group of traditional leaders, moderates and Hussein supporters. The new councillor was 30–40 years old, a leftist intellectual, usually a socialist or a sympathizer of the Jordanian Communist Party, having the explicit wish to end the Israeli occupation as soon as possible, and not hiding his support —

sometimes unlimited, sometimes with reservations — for Yasser Arafat's P.L.O. The important policy of most of the candidates was opposition to Israeli occupation and particularly to the plan for an 'autonomous administration' of the West Bank. Karim Khalaf, the re-elected mayor from Ramallah, summarized the importance of the election results as follows: 'Before the elections I was acting alone, there was no support [from the other West Bank mayors]. Now we can all protect each other.'[156]

Decisive for the results of the elections were not only the new candidates, but also the new voters. In 1976, about three times as many persons voted as had in 1972. For the first time, women could also vote, as a result of a change in the Jordanian election law in April 1973,[157] which the Israeli military administration adopted. It was also new that participation in the elections was no longer limited to those who paid property taxes. Now all those paying municipal taxes were also able to participate.

In the first reaction to the election results, the Israeli newspaper *Ha'aretz* wrote in its editorial two days after the elections: 'The elections became a "national" demonstration — that is an anti-Israeli demonstration.'[158] Karim Khalaf asked: 'Could the message be more clear? The vote shows the whole world that the West Bankers are Palestinians who want to establish their own national entity and put an end to the Israeli occupation.'[159] With these election results, the phase of re-orientation of the West Bank population had reached its climax; the P.N.F.'s leadership position was confirmed by the elections. Following the 1973 war, when Israel's invulnerability proved to be a myth, the resistance in the occupied territories against the occupation grew. The regularity and intensity of protest activities, which went as far as general strikes, were new. The activities also had a new direction: the support of the P.L.O., the rejection of Hussein, and, with the establishment of the P.N.F., the attempt at formulating their own political positions. Previously, one had hoped for a change from the outside. With the April 1976 elections, the people of the West Bank decided in favour of a leadership which took the affairs of the West Bank Palestinians into its own hands. The new generation did see their partner and representative in the P.L.O., yet at the same time, maintained a certain independence in their acts and tried actively to influence discussions within the P.L.O.

In Israel, the P.N.F.'s landslide victory was a shock. Characteristic of the atmosphere was the warning of liberal circles against exhausting the arsenal of British laws from the time of the Mandate, and deporting the mayors who had been elected. On the contrary, the Israeli government, one day after the elections, was expected to 'make the best out of a bad situation and to play the democratic card'.[160] At the same time, Israel admitted that 'the new municipal leadership that has appeared is a result of nine years of Israeli rule in the territories and is undoubtedly an authentic leadership'.[161] In comments on the elections, two things were especially lamented. One was that Israel had not succeeded in establishing a moderate leadership group which would also have been acceptable to the public. The second was that they had neglected to negotiate with King Hussein in time over the future of the West Bank. A prominent Israeli expert on Arab affairs stated: 'The argument that the Palestinians themselves have never voted for the P.L.O. can only draw smirks of ridicule now.'[162]

The elections were a clear rejection of King Hussein. No official statement was issued from Amman. The Arab newspaper, *Al-Kuds*, which is published in East Jerusalem and is known to be loyal to Hussein, merely attempted to play down the importance of the elections. It wrote: 'The municipalities are not a parliament.'[163] However, the new mayors did not break with Jordan. Jordan was too important as the only bridge to the Arab world and possibly indispensable for later negotiations with Israel. Some time after the elections, Hebron's mayor, Fahad Qawasmeh, characterized the relation of the new mayors to Jordan in this manner: 'As long as money flows into the West Bank from Jordan, it is our ally. After the events in Lebanon, the Jordanians probably believe that the P.L.O. is at an end; that is their right, but they are wrong. In the meantime, we are profiting from their money and their friendly attention.'[164] The Jordanian Prime Minister explained that his country 'does not intend to shirk its responsibility toward the West Bank localities and that Jordan would do its utmost to help the residents of the occupied territories'.[165] Jordan tried to regain its influence in the West Bank by offering generous financial support. In connection with preparations for resuming the Geneva Conference, which had been under discussion since the middle of 1976, the Arab countries also assumed that Jordan would participate in any peace negotiations. In view of Israel's and the U.S.'s vetoes of P.L.O. participation in negotiations, the Arab states envisaged Palestinian participation in the form of joint Arab-Jordanian-Palestinian representation. This plan ran into opposition in the P.L.O. as well as among the residents of the West Bank and their representatives in the city councils. Finally, because of pressure put on the P.L.O. by the Arab states, February 1977 saw the first discussions between the P.L.O. and Jordan since Black September in 1970. According to a Jordanian communiqué these discussions ended with the agreement that a 'connection should exist'[166] between a future Palestinian state and Jordan.

A New Era: After the Elections

Immediately following the elections, it became obvious that Israel was faced with a new political force in the city councils in the West Bank.

One week after the elections, the nationalist-religious movement, Gush Emunim, organized a march from Israel through the occupied territories. The two-day procession was approved by the Israeli government directly following the elections and was protected by the army. Over 30,000 Israelis, including some Knesset deputies, took part in the Eretz Israel March (so named by the sponsors) whose declared objective was 'to get to know new areas in the West Bank and to pressure for their settlement as soon as possible'.[167]

This Land is Our Land

Gush Emunim advertisement calling for participation in the Eretz Yisrael March

Birth of a National Consciousness

The West Bank mayors tried to develop a common strategy against the Israeli occupation. Having just been confirmed in their offices by the spokesman for the military government, Karim Khalaf in Ramallah, Bassam Shak'a in Nablus, Hilmi Hanoun in Tulkarm, Amin Ibrahim in Qalqilya and Fahad Qawasmeh in Hebron considered having a counter-march, if possible, even into the heart of Israel. However, the march which was to take place two weeks after the Gush Emunim march, was forbidden by the military administration. During the two-day procession sponsored by Gush Emunim, there were school strikes and demonstrations in all of the larger cities, and businesses closed down. The newly elected mayors sent joint protest telegrams to Defence Minister Shimon Peres and U.N. General Secretary Kurt Waldheim. The East Jerusalem daily, *Al-Fajr*, commented:

> If those who permitted the march thought that it was a suitable response to the municipal election results on the West Bank, they were mistaken. The voters knew that those who were elected would not be able to prevent the Gush Emunim march.[168]

Whereas in previous years the West Bank population had only sporadically protested against Israeli rightists organizing similar processions through the West Bank, they now presented a united front. The public and the city administrators found themselves on the same side. The mayor of Nablus refused to accept responsibility for the unrest in his city and responded to Defence Minister Peres that, 'the city council could not be responsible for law and order because in the final analysis a situation of conqueror and conquered exists in the town'.[169]

In the first few weeks of the new mayors' terms of office it became clear that they were pursuing a new line toward the Israeli occupying authority: 1) They co-ordinated their actions in all cities of the West Bank; 2) They rejected all co-operation with the military authorities; 3) They openly protested against the Israeli occupation in general and against individual measures taken by the military government; 4) They worked with the public and no longer passed on pressure from the military government down to the people; 5) They took advantage of the fact that they were the sole democratically-elected representatives of Palestinians (and that they were numerically and politically a significant part of the Palestinian people) to express their opinions to the P.L.O. and to the Arab countries.

> When we were campaigning in the streets, we told the people, 'Don't expect us to be able to do anything for you or to take on large projects. We don't have any money and we're not promising you anything. We'll only work against the Israeli occupation. If you want to help us, please do.'[170]

That was, according to Karim Khalaf, the starting point for the work of the new city councils.

Two things brought about the confrontation between the West Bank

Palestinians and Israel in 1976 and 1977:[171] first, the conflict over the Israeli settlements and, over the 'historical right' of the Jews to 'Judea and Samaria', as shown by the dispute over the Patriarch's Tomb in Hebron; and second, the binding of the West Bank to the Israeli economy, as evidenced by the introduction of the Israeli value-added tax in the West Bank. Both create fears in the West Bank, that Israel is seeking to make the occupation irreversible and that Israeli policy amounts to a creeping annexation.

The role played by the city councils in this conflict with Israel differed fundamentally from that of their predecessors. The newly elected representatives supported the public by being a mouthpiece for their protests and by trying to publicize the events in the occupied territories internationally. From the very beginning of their terms in office, they stated that issues such as tax problems, the Israeli settlements and detainees definitely concerned the city councils. During the conflicts concerning the value-added tax, the mayors of various West Bank cities even called a strike. This had never happened under their predecessors.[172]

Hebron 1976: Who does the West Bank Belong to?

In September 1976, the conflicts in Hebron at the Patriarch's Tomb, a mosque which the Jews have claimed as a synagogue, led to serious incidents. 'This is a pogrom. They curse us. They throw stones at the Jews while they pray. They kick the *Torah* with their feet. A pogrom, I tell you. . . .'[173] This is how an Israeli Jew described his resentment to the incidents in the mosque. The destruction of the Jewish scrolls had, however, been preceded by the desecration of Islamic objects of worship by the zealous settlers of Kiryat Arba.[174] The term 'religious war' does not accurately define this new climax in the altercations between the Jewish settlers from Kiryat Arba and the residents of the neighbouring city of Hebron. For the settlers, as well as for the Arab population, the problems lie much deeper.

The settlement of Kiryat Arba, established by Israel in 1970[175] has a different history from the other settlements in the West Bank. While the other settlements in the Jordan Valley have been justified by Israel's 'security needs' and at first were passed off as military installations, this does not apply to Kiryat Arba. The settlers of Kiryat Arba connect their presence in the West Bank with their historical claim to this territory. In answer to the question whether or not the settlers would be willing to live by the laws of a Palestinian state in the West Bank, the leader of Gush Emunim in Kiryat Arba replied, 'Of course not! Hebron is just as much a part of Israel as Shekhem [Nablus], as Jericho and as the rest of Judea and Samaria [thus, the entire West Bank].'[176] Therefore, in the conflicts in Hebron, nothing less than the land, the Palestinian rights to the West Bank and the Jewish claim to dominion of it are at stake.

The activities of Gush Emunim steadily increased in the second half of the 1970s and found growing support in Israel. As far as the West Bank population was concerned, the Israeli Labour coalition governments also protected Gush Emunim's settlement activities, since it did not put a stop to them. The residents of Hebron were particularly defenceless against the occasionally violent encroachments by the settlers of Kiryat Arba.

The fact that more was at stake than just the Patriarch's Tomb can also be seen from the arguments on both sides: 'The synagogue of the Patriarch's Tomb was built for King Herod, the last great Jewish King. It wasn't until 900 years later, after the Arab conquest, that the mosque was erected on the foundations of the synagogue,'[177] said the Israeli chief rabbi Shloma Goren. The zealous settlers also give the same reasons for their 'historical rights' in Hebron. The city's mayor, Fahad Qawasmeh responded to this: 'The Al-Ibrahim Mosque was built over 1,000 years ago. Before 1967, the Jews never prayed there,[178] not even during the time of the British Mandate.[179] In order to put an end to the unrest, the Jews must stop praying in the mosque.'[180]

The residents and the mayor of Hebron agree on the public rejection of the 'historical rights' to the West Bank as proclaimed by Gush Emunim. Fahad Qawasmeh's position on the matter is as clear as it is complex. It is not directed against Jewish presence in the West Bank, but rather against Israel's claim to rule the West Bank. The settlers in Kiryat Arba point out that Jews lived in Hebron before the founding of the state of Israel in 1948. Mayor Fahad Qawasmeh made the following comment on this:

Monuments of the Occupation – the Kiriyat Arba settlement above Hebron

> I think it's normal that the Jews want to restore their synagogue and pray there. I also understand why they want to return to their homes in Hebron and live there. Furthermore, I even invite them to do so. And if their houses are destroyed, we'll build them new ones. But only on one condition — that the Palestinian refugees can likewise return to their homes in Lod, Ramleh and Yafo.[181]

The protests of the West Bank population against the settlements have, since the 1976 election, been fully supported by the mayors, and have become considerably stronger. They are aimed less at the presence of the Jews than they are at the creeping annexation of the West Bank. In the eyes of the residents, this annexation is connected with the settlement activity. When the Likud bloc, led by Prime Minister Menachem Begin, came into power in May 1977, there were renewed protests by the Hebron residents, as well as an increase in the provocations by the Jewish settlers toward the Arab population. The new administration supported Gush Emunim and announced, soon after taking office, the establishment of a large number of new settlements.[182]

The Introduction of the Value-Added Tax

Toward the end of 1976, the Israeli government decided to introduce the value-added tax (V.A.T.) in the West Bank, which had already been put into effect in Israel in July of the same year. The West Bank population resisted this new tax (which had not existed under Jordanian rule) for several reasons. To begin with, according to the Geneva Convention, an occupying authority does not have the right to change existing tax laws. Other fears were even more instrumental in the protests. For instance, the growing economic integration of the West Bank into the Israeli economy added to the fear of the perpetuation of the Israeli occupation. Besides objecting to the price increase resulting from the V.A.T. (the initial tax set at 8% was increased to 12% by the Begin administration), they also objected to the use of the tax, as the West Bank population was not to profit from it.[183]

The protests against V.A.T. led to the worst disturbances since the elections and even spread to cities such as Hebron, which were traditionally considered calm. Even the normally reserved and conservative chambers of commerce supported the strikes and called on their members to close their shops. This change could be attributed not only to the economic losses which the businessmen feared; beyond this, many wanted to use the opportunity to regain ground lost in the 1976 elections by presenting themselves as a radical force. At the same time, the traditionalists attempted to disrupt the protest actions in order 'to demonstrate the incapability of the newly elected representatives'. The Jordanian media also gave the struggle considerable attention and even called for resistance. The city councils answered by convening meetings, in which all groups in the city were to take part, and appealed to the residents to permit the organization of a total but peaceful strike which did then occur.

Based on the new possibility of organizing civil resistance on a wide basis, the protest demonstrations in 1976 differed fundamentally from those in earlier years in extent and, above all, in their expansion over the entire West Bank. Foreign observers compared the situation in the occupied territories in 1976 with that of former colonies. 'Today, the situation [in the occupied territories] is comparable to the revolt of the national liberation movements in a number of former colonial countries.'[184] The Israeli military government reacted to the new situation primarily by intensifying the confrontation between the population and the army. As a result, six West Bank residents, including two children, were shot during the five weeks following the municipal elections.[185] In a Knesset debate concerning the criticism from home and abroad on the actions of the military administration, Moshe Dayan described the revolts as a 'popular movement' and drew the conclusion, as summarized by the Israeli newspaper, *Ha'aretz*, 'that we [the Israelis] must influence the mass of Arabs, and as an effective method, must consider cutting off basic services (water, gas, electricity).'[186]

The Israeli Counter-Strategy
Late in the summer of 1976, the adviser on Arab affairs to the military governor in the West Bank was replaced. Accompanying the change in personnel was a change in Israeli strategy. The new man taking up the post, Dr Menachem Milson, who had just been promoted to General, sought above all to weaken the political base of the new mayors. Up to that point, the mayors had been entitled to the right of representing their constituents to the military government. But from that time on, they were to limit their work to technically administrative matters.

This became apparent in various practical ways. Previously, the military governor had sought out the mayors in their city halls when he wanted to talk with them. Now, they were summoned to the headquarters of the military governor, sometimes even by military order. Also, the mayors now never received written confirmation of any agreements with the military governor. The only time contracts were signed for was Israeli loans; however, the binding version was in Hebrew, the legal venue was Jerusalem, and Israel could unilaterally terminate these contracts at any time. Under these conditions, the city councils chose to forgo loans from the military government.[187]

The military government's interventions in the mayors' attempts to provide the cities with a vital infrastructure and projects for city development weighed even more heavily. Virtually all projects proposed by the city councils were delayed, often rejected or approved in an initial phase and then stopped after costly preparations had already been made. One example is the construction of the Ramallah sewage system approved in 1974. The city administration invested millions of Israeli pounds in the excavation of the ditches and the laying of the first pipes before the project was stopped by the military government. Since then, work has not resumed.[188] In another case, Israel put a stop to the construction of a school in Nablus shortly before it would have been finished.[189] Likewise, delegations from the cities which wanted to request financial aid from Arab countries for development projects were refused exit visas.[190] Furthermore, the new city councils were denied any improvements in the water system, even when the necessary capital could be supplied. The same was true for power stations. The mayors refused to connect up to the Israeli power system, as they feared that Israel would then have a means of exerting pressure on the population.

The declared aim of the strategy of the military government was to discredit the new city councils and to take the popular support away from them. While hindering the representatives elected by the people, the military government was also trying to keep its contacts with the traditional and moderate leaders and to build up these persons in the public eye as contacts who could facilitate their dealings with the military government. The elected mayors did not receive answers, for example, to their inquiries regarding the grounds for arrest or the whereabouts of prisoners. If one of the traditional leaders did ask, however, he was usually given an immediate answer. These leaders were able to help with daily problems, such as obtaining exit visas, whereas if the elected mayors intervened in such matters, the military government told them their sole task was to see to 'order and sanitation'.

The daily newspaper *Ha'aretz*, closely connected with the Labour Party, described the government policy thus:

> Dr Milson, with the approval of the commander of the territory, General David Hagoel, and the co-ordinator of activities in the [occupied] territories, General Abraham Orly, attempted to enlarge the power of other representative bodies in the West Bank, for example, of the chambers of commerce, thereby limiting the influence of the elected city councils as the only representatives of the people.[191]

The mayor of Ramallah commented on the situation as follows:

> In this way, the Israeli authorities are trying to stop the city councils from involving themselves with the people's problems. They want to show the people, 'What kind of mayors and city councils are they, anyway? They don't do anything for you at all.'[192]

The P.N.F. and the P.L.O.

The National Front demonstrated, with its decision to have candidates run in the 1976 city council elections, that it was fighting (politically) on the P.L.O.'s side against the Israeli occupation but, on the other hand, it did not wait for instructions from remote headquarters.

The P.L.O., which before the elections had not been able to make a decision on a call for participation, celebrated the victory of the progressive nationalist forces:

> There is no doubt that the decision of the nationalists to fight the

elections was a courageous step; far from being a mere reaction, it was an attempt to gain the initiative. This was bound to embarrass the occupation authorities and to impede Israeli moves which are usually based on the assumption that the opposing party is non-existent and ineffective.[193]

For the Rejection Front which had called for an election boycott, the results were a clear defeat.

The newly elected city councils tried to represent the interests of the West Bank population even beyond the West Bank borders, to the P.L.O. and the Arab states. The positions which the mayors adopted on this matter corresponded to those of the P.N.F. In an interview with *Le Monde*, mayor Fahad Qawasmeh outlined their major goals:

> We have confined ourselves to a demand for a small state which will emerge in the territories Israel has occupied since 1967 and which it must evacuate. The problem of the refugees must be dealt with when the occupation is over. Then the refugees must be given the choice to return to their homeland or to receive financial compensation.[194]

The mayors had been elected on the basis of this political stand. The position of the city councils differed from the P.L.O.'s official position in that it included the recognition of Israel; but the P.L.O. was developing more and more in the same direction. In answer to the question whether the P.L.O. would approve of a state in the West Bank and Gaza Strip, mayor Qawasmeh replied, 'I don't believe they'd stab us in the back. I can't imagine that the P.L.O. would be opposed to a solution which would mean the end of the occupation.'[195] The differences in the stands taken by the West Bank population and their representatives on the one side, and the P.L.O. on the other, can be attributed to the differences in their respective situations. While the P.L.O. exists outside of the Israeli sphere of influence, the West Bank population has been confronted with the Israeli occupation daily since the takeover in 1967.

A member of the National Front and the city council of Ramallah described their relationship to the P.L.O. as follows: 'We are for the P.L.O. but not just any P.L.O.!'[196] The city councils try to influence the positions of the P.L.O.; this, however, should not be viewed as an attempt to divide the Palestinian ranks. The council's support of the P.L.O. has been too clear for that. Having been elected by the vast majority of Palestinians in the West Bank, the mayors of the National Front did try, however, to take full advantage of their strong position.

Israel prohibited the West Bank residents and especially the mayors from participating personally in the meetings of the P.L.O. bodies. The Israeli government announced in November 1976, that any resident of the occupied territories taking part in the Thirteenth National Congress of the P.L.O. in March 1977 would not be permitted to re-enter the occupied territories.[197]

Thus, the only possible way left to the people of the occupied territories and their mayors to express their opinions was in the form of petitions, which they did use extensively. Prior to the Thirteenth National Congress, thousands of signatures were collected in the West Bank for a petition to the P.L.O. in which the people of the West Bank expressed their support of the plan for a Palestinian state (within the 1967 borders) alongside Israel. In addition to 20 West Bank mayors, representatives of almost all other groups (trade unions, youth groups, co-operatives, women's and professional associations, and representatives of university and school students) signed the petition. In it, the P.L.O. was asked to endorse the establishment of a Palestinian state alongside Israel, which would mean recognition of the existence of the State of Israel.[198]

The Communist Party once again defined its position unequivocally in an article on the meeting of the National Congress:

> We, the members of the Palestinian Communist Organization in the West Bank, [the organization succeeding the Jordanian Communist Party in the West Bank] declare clearly and frankly, that we are struggling for the existence of a Palestinian state in the West Bank and the Gaza Strip, following a complete Israeli withdrawal from all the territories conquered in June 1967 and for the repatriation of all Palestinian refugees from 1948 to their homes.[199]

In the West Bank, leaflets were distributed and sent to the mayors, in which the P.L.O. and the Arab states were requested not to make any agreements without first consulting the population of the occupied territories. Beyond this, the leaflets called for the creation of a body in the occupied territories whose task it would be to lead consultations with the P.L.O. and the Arab states.[200] The purpose of the numerous petitions sent by the mayors and various organizations of the West Bank to the Arab heads of state was (especially in view of the civil war in Lebanon) to strengthen the position of the P.L.O. and to call upon the Arab heads of state to do the same.[201]

The events in Lebanon in the summer of 1976, gained increasing significance for the West Bank and were the occasion for demonstrations chiefly against Syria's intervention. A central issue was the fall of the Palestinian refugee camp, Tel a-Za'ator, which had been besieged by Christian militias. The population, which had committed itself to the P.L.O. in the city council elections with a large majority, interpreted this blow to the P.L.O. as their own defeat. The Arab daily newspaper from East Jerusalem, *Al-Fajr*, commented on the seizure of the camp, pointing out that 'even if the case of Tel a-Za'atar is repeated a thousand times over, they will not liquidate the Palestinian revolution'.[202] But the euphoria which existed directly following the elections receded because of this massive attempt to undermine the military and political position of the P.L.O. The view that the defeat of Tel a-Za'atar was due to the tolerance and even support by the apparent allies, who had recognized and supported the P.L.O., particularly after the 1974 summit meeting in Rabat, was one of the reasons for the active support for the P.L.O. in the occupied territories.

The Lebanese civil war strengthened the realization that a Palestinian state was necessary. A founding member of the National Front, deported in 1974, commented on the situation following the war in Lebanon thus: 'We Palestinians . . . resist the control of other states, be they Arab countries, Syria or Israel. We have the right to determine our own future, to establish a state and to possess an independent fatherland just as any other people.'[203]

In the Backyard of History: The Gaza Strip

The 1947 U.N. Partition Plan provided for the Gaza Strip as well as the West Bank to be a part of the Palestinian state in the Mandate Territory of Palestine. The history of the Gaza Strip in the period following the first Middle East war in 1948 up until the Israeli occupation in June 1967 differs greatly from the development in the West Bank.

After the 1948 war, a wave of 160,000 to 180,000 refugees flowed into the Gaza Strip which had been occupied by the Egyptian army. The lower class of Palestinian society (farm workers, small tenant farmers and craftsmen) gathered in the refugee camps. Refugees of a higher class had either gone into the West Bank and other countries or left the crowded Gaza Strip as soon as a possibility arose.[204]

Most of the people in the Gaza Strip were unable to leave. Unlike the West Bank, the Gaza Strip was not annexed but was simply administered by an Egyptian military government. The residents of the Gaza Strip were, therefore, 'stateless', that is, they were only granted exit visas with special permission from Egyptian authorities. In general, life was strictly regimented; for example, nightly curfews were maintained for 20 years.[205]

The economic situation was a catastrophe. Approximately 70% of the population, especially refugees, lived on rations from UNRWA, and the unemployment rate was almost 50%.

Political structures were unable to develop. All high administrative posts were filled by Egyptians; city councillors, put into office by the military government, and the traditional *mukhtar* maintained contact with the population. However, they were responsible for administrative matters only (for example, marriages, taxes and electricity and water supply) and did not have any political authority.[207] Not only were the traditional leaders divided but, in contrast to the West Bank, they did not have a base among the refugees in the Gaza Strip and, therefore, among the largest part of the population. The latter did not have resolute leadership and began a life of hopelessness: in camps, without prospects of being integrated, no chance economically, and crowded together in a small amount of space.[208] Their only chance lay in a struggle against Israel. The Gaza Strip developed into a centre of Palestinian resistance — at least that part which was under the control of the Arab governments. First, the Palestinian Liberation Army

(P.L.A.) was stationed in Gaza, and secondly, the P.L.O. was founded in the Gaza Strip with support of the Arab League. Under the leadership of Ahmad Shukeiry, it had the structure of the old nationalist movement led by the notables.

The Israeli takeover of the Gaza Strip met with fierce armed resistance. Unlike Jordanian groups, Egyptian and Palestinian units resisted vehemently.[209] Remnants of the Palestinian units went underground in the Gaza Strip. They had a large supply of weapons, ammunition and explosives, and quickly took up armed resistance against the occupying power.

The Army, Refugees and the Fedayeen

Soon after the occupation, Israeli politicians let it be known that they wanted to annex the Gaza Strip.[210] The plans provided for the original inhabitants of the Gaza Strip, that is those who had been living there since before the 1948 war, to become Israeli citizens. The refugees, i.e., those residents who had fled the territory of the state of Israel in 1948, were to emigrate or to be resettled in northern Sinai or the West Bank.[211] An initial step in the realization of these plans was for 40,000 people to leave the Gaza Strip (with Israeli support) for Jordan during the first six months of the occupation.[212]

The occupying authrotiy's goals were unmistakable. It was equally clear how the Palestinians would react. The resistance movement organized a guerilla war against the Israeli army, against establishments of the Israeli administration and against Gaza residents who co-operated with Israel in any way, shape or form, be it simply having a job in Israel.[213] Their base was in the refugee camps over which they had complete control.[214] The Israeli army used every means to fight the Fedayeen: retention of the night curfews, collective punishment such as the destruction of houses and the detention of Fedayeen family members in camps in the Sinai,[215] official permission to shoot 'perpetrators', even if they were in the middle of a crowd of innocent bystanders. Another characteristic of the hard confrontation was the methods which the Israeli military government used against the demonstrators. There were deaths and injuries, especially in 1969, when the Israeli army shot into demonstrating crowds.[216] As in the West Bank, most of the demonstrations were started by school students and women.

Using the fight against the Fedayeen as grounds, the military government began 'thinning out' the overcrowded refugee camps in the beginning of 1971. First, the army made the camps more accessible for their vehicles and restricted the Fedayeen's freedom of movement by making wide passages through the camps. Frequently, the houses they planned to demolish were not condemned until shortly before the destruction. After the residents had packed up their belongings, the bulldozers would begin their work. The refugees had the choice either to move to El Arish in north Sinai (i.e. outside the Gaza Strip), where the Israeli government would issue them houses of Egyptians who had fled in 1967; to go to the West Bank; or to find their own lodging in the Gaza Strip.[217]

In this connection, the Palestinians continually raised the accusation that the resettlement did not have anything to do with security considerations, but was a part of the Israeli plan to rid the Gaza Strip of the refugees.[218] This accusation was supported not only by the fact that the thinning out continued long after the Fedayeen had been defeated, but also by statements made by Israeli politicians and military personnel. In 1971, the military governor for the Gaza Strip at that time, General Shlomo Gazit made the following comment on the initial resettlement phase: 'The goal is to evacuate thousands of people for whom the Gaza Strip is too poor and too crowded.'[219] During the second resettlement phase in 1973, alternative apartments were built for the Gaza Strip residents in the Gaza Strip itself, but also in El Arish and in other locations in northern Sinai. The Prime Minister at that time, Yitzhak Rabin, defined Israeli hopes when he proposed that the 'conditions be created so that within the next ten years a natural migration of the people to East Jordan takes place. . . . The problem of the refugees in the Gaza Strip should not be solved in Gaza or in El Arish but rather chiefly in East Jordan.'[220] In November 1976, the U.N. General Assembly (with the vote of the U.S.) requested Israel to stop the refugee resettlement in the Gaza Strip and to allow the refugees as soon as possible to return to their former camps.[221]

While the Fedayeen was in control in the refugee camps and in the poorer quarters of Gaza until 1972, the old notables, who had remained in office, decided to collaborate with the Israeli authorities. Although they rejected the actions of the Fedayeen, they also spoke out against Israeli plans for annexation. The traditional leaders, most of whom were merchants or owners of citrus plantations, were even less worthy of the term 'representatives of the people' in the Gaza Strip than they were in the West Bank.

In addition to the notables, who were rather isolated politically, and the Fedayeen, who exclusively sought military confrontation with Israel until 1973, other politically active groups (for example the Communist Party) remained of minor importance.

From Armed Struggle to Political Struggle

Since 1972, the P.L.O. has been involved in the political struggle in the occupied territories.[222] The defeat of the Fedayeen against the superiority of Israel, the lack of support from the population and the P.L.O.'s new line made the Palestinian organizations in the Gaza Strip change their tactics.[223] In the past few years, the field of action for political groups has expanded.

The first result of the new situation was the participation of the Gaza Strip population in the National Front founded for both the West Bank and the Gaza Strip.[224] However, the roots and support of the P.N.F. were much weaker in the Gaza Strip than in the West Bank. There were never any elections in the Gaza Strip. The degree of organization in professional and other associations, which in the West Bank had played such an important role in the effectiveness of the National Front, was very small. The formation of a broad alliance was also hindered by the conditions dictated by the Gaza Strip social structure.[225]

Just as it had done in the West Bank, the P.N.F. tried to anchor itself to the local institutions in the Gaza Strip. An example of this is the Red Crescent Society[226] whose chairman is Dr Haider Abdel Shafei, one of the most important advocates of the P.L.O. who is closely connected with the Communist Party: 17 of the 21 recently elected members of the executive council of the Red Crescent in Gaza have the same nationalist, pro-P.L.O. political leanings as Dr Shafei himself.[227]

As in the West Bank, the P.N.F. is on one side and on the other are the traditional leaders. Today, the latter have been placed in local positions by Israel (just as Egypt had done previously) to act as intermediaries between the military government and the public. However, the contrast between the two groups is not as pronounced in the Gaza Strip as it is in the West Bank. The notables do have ties with Jordan, but at the same time always keep an option under P.L.O. leadership open to them. The most prominent representative of this group is the mayor of Gaza, Rashed Al-Shawa, placed in office by Israel. He is considered, despite all his verbal signs of support for the P.L.O., 'King Hussein's uncrowned representative in the Gaza Strip'.[228] Just as other owners of citrus plantations are dependent on export to and through Jordan, so is he. As the mayor of Gaza, he procures export licences for Gaza products which are exported to Jordan and issues the residents of the Gaza Strip the only travel documents made available to them, Jordanian passports. With Al-Shawa at the head, King Hussein is trying to build up a group of pro-Jordanian leaders in the Gaza Strip, who would be in a position, should the opportunity arise, to bring the Gaza Strip into a Jordanian-Palestinian federation under the Jordanian monarch's leadership.[229]

It was not until the P.N.F. was founded that the political struggle in the Gaza Strip began to develop similarities to that in the West Bank. In the past few years, the Gaza Strip has also taken part in the discussions for a Palestinian state in the occupied territories. However, for the majority of refugees, the question of returning to their villages in Israel and of compensation for lost property, is much more important than for the refugees in the West Bank, the majority of whom have been integrated. Organizationally, the new political common ground is shown today in the fact that the National Guidance Committee, which was founded in 1978 and which co-ordinates all political activities in the occupied territories, also has a representative from the Gaza Strip, Dr Haider Abdel Shafei from the Red Crescent.[230] The common political interests became clear during the discussions on the Sadat initiative and the Israeli proposal for 'autonomy'.

Notes

1. Cf. *Sinai/Pollack 1977*, p. 27.
2. Cf. *Djeghloul 1979*, pp. 14–18; see in particular, the depiction of the social basis of the early Palestinian National Movement.
3. With the exception of Jordan, all Arab governments recognized this government in exile.
4. *Lexikon 1979*, p. 145.
5. It was not until 31 May 1950, when Jordan conveyed to the Arab League that the annexation did not represent an anticipation of the final solution, that it was able to escape impending exclusion from the League. Indeed, in the second part of the Jordanian law (on the unification of the two banks of the Jordan), it is also stated that 'this unity shall in no way be connected with the final settlement of the just Palestinian cause within the limits of national hopes, Arab co-operation and international justice'. (Cf. *Commission 1977*, p. 36.)
6. Belonging to this group are, for example, the Nashashibi family from Jerusalem, the Tuqan clan from Nablus and the Jiyyusis from Tulkarm.
7. A typical representative of this group was Ahmad Tuqan, a former civil servant of the British Mandate administration from Nablus. He — or representatives of his clan — were members of seven out of the first eight Jordanian cabinets.
8. There were protests against annexation of the West Bank in 1952 and at the end of 1959 only, especially in the northern part of the West Bank. The Communist Party in the West Bank, which in 1947 had recognized the U.N. Partition Plan and advocated founding a Palestinian state alongside Israel, joined with the Communist Party of Transjordan. Responsible for this development was, above all, the position of the Arab Communist Parties which were characterized by an international and pan-Arab position. (On this issue and in general on Jordanian rule over the West Bank cf. *Be'eri 1978*, p. II ff.)
9. Cf. *Sinai/Pollack 1977*, p. 57. Also cf. information on the Jordanian policy of oppression in the West Bank.
10. During the Suez crisis of 1956, the government of Nabulsi declared its solidarity with Nasser and cancelled its contract with Great Britain concerning British military bases in Jordan.
11. As to the role of the West during the conflicts of 1956/57, cf. *Henle 1972*.
12. A group of notables in the West Bank had already demanded equal economic treatment of the West Bank and Transjordan in 1952. (Cf. *Stendel 1968*, p. 42.)
13. Concerning this matter, cf. Chapter 4.
14. Regarding the course of the war and the occupying of East Jerusalem, cf. *Schleifer 1971; Churchill 1967; Hussein 1969*.
15. Cf. *Le Monde*, 5 July 1969; *Gussing 1967*, p. 93 ff.; *Israel & Palestine*, No. 43, October 1972.
16. Cf. the report of U.N. representative Gussing in *Gussing 1967*, p. 92 ff. The story of the city of Qalqilya, whose residents were only permitted to return to their city as a result of massive international pressure,

became especially well-known.
17. Cf. *Weber 1968*, p. 29.
18. Cf. *Gussing 1967*, p. 91. Israel continued to provide buses for transporting refugees to the Jordan, after they had signed a document stating that they were leaving the area voluntarily. For further details on this and other similar measures, cf. *Gussing 1967*; *Ha'aretz*, 14, 16, 18 and 25 June 1967, as well as *New Outlook*, June 1972, p. 21. As to the motives for fleeing, also see *Dodd/Barakat 1968*.
19. Cf. *Le Monde*, 13 June 1967.
20. These figures are more or less identical to those in *Le Monde*, 26 December 1967. Israeli figures and those of the American embassy in Amman are lower by about 25%. Regarding the UNRWA figures, cf. U.N. Document A/6713/Supplement 13 and A/SPC/SR 584. As to the Israeli figures, cf. *Ha'aretz*, 29 September 1967. The difference between the two figures can be explained primarily by the different times of calculation; most of the refugees did not leave the Gaza Strip until long after the end of the war.
21. Cf. U.N. Document A/6713/Supplement 13.
22. *MER 1967*, p. 226.
23. Cf. *Nahumi 1968*, for more details see Chapter 2.
24. *Le Monde*, 12 December 1967.
25. *Rouleau 1968*, p. 497.
26. *The Jerusalem Post*, 29 October 1967.
27. Cf. *Nahumi 1972 (a)*, p. 16 ff. and p. 28 ff. Only the small communist opposition group, Rakach, advocated the complete withdrawal of Israeli troops from all of the occupied territories. This change was also soon expressed in official terminology. Whereas originally one had spoken of 'occupied territories', officially they were soon referred to as 'the territories' or as 'Judaea and Samaria'. Even the term 'liberated territories' was quickly adopted, especially by right-wing groups. (Regarding the introduction of the use of 'Judaea and Samaria' in official terminology, cf. *MER 1967*, p. 278).
28. Cf. *Le Monde diplomatique*, January 1969. Although the plan was never defined as official government policy, it determined the practical policy of the Labour government starting in 1968, cf. *Davar*, 22 December 1968.
29. Cf. *Le Monde diplomatique*, January 1969.
30. According to Menachem Begin, cf. *ibid.* An opinion poll in the middle of 1968 revealed that 47% and 97% of those questioned wanted to keep the entire West Bank and Jerusalem, respectively. (Cf. *Le Monde*, 3 May 1968). Concerning the positions of the inner-Israeli opposition, see Chapter 9.
31. Regarding the conflict over this in Israel, see Chapter 2 and Chapter 4.
32. *Ha'aretz*, 9 November 1967. Dayan made a similar statement in a conversation with Palestinian notables, to whom he declared that anyone who did not agree with Israeli control of the West Bank could emigrate; cf. *The New York Times*, 29 October 1968.
33. This policy manifested itself particularly in the Israeli settlement and economic policies: for further details see Chapters 2 and 4.

34. Statement by a Palestinian in an interview with the authors, September 1977.
35. Cf. *The New York Times*, 4 September 1967.
36. *MER* 1967, p. 285.
37. Cf. *Rejwan 1973*, p. 18.
38. *The Jerusalem Post*, 15 June 1967.
39. *Ha'aretz*, 10 August 1967.
40. *Peretz 1968*, p. 57.
41. For a detailed treatment of the disagreements over the schoolbooks within Israel as well as between the West Bank population and the occupying authority, cf. *Fried 1975*, p. 90 ff.
42. Cf. *Ha'aretz*, 8 October 1967; see also Chapter 3
43. *Nahumi 1968*.
44. *MER* 1968, p. 450.
45. Cf. *Ma'ariv*, 9 March 1969, and *New Middle East*, May 1969.
46. The *International Herald Tribune*, 2 December 1969.
47. *The Times*, 24 October 1969.
48. The protest activities selected were taken exclusively from reports in Israeli newspapers and *Le Monde* which are documented in *MER* 1968 and 1969.
49. In 1969, for instance, the region of Hebron, at the peak of the harvest, was forbidden to trade with Jordan. More than 100,000 people were affected by this ban (cf. *MER* 1969/70, p. 365).
50. *The New York Times*, 29 October 1968.
51. Cf. *Lesch 1979*.
52. For a complete list of the deportations and an analysis of the reasons for them, cf. *Lesch 1979*.
53. See Chapter 5.
54. See also Chapter 3.
55. *Ha'aretz*, 20 November 1967; also cf. *The Jerusalem Post*, 10 September 1967.
56. Cf. *MER* 1967, p. 283.
57. Cf. *Bailey 1978*.
58. Cf. *Ma'ariv*, 10 February 1969.
59. As a result, Hamdi Kana'an, mayor of Nablus, received, for instance, I£200,000–300,000 to support pro-Jordanian activities up to the beginning of 1969 (cf. *Sinai/Pollack 1977*, p. 221). All Jordanian employees in the West Bank continued to receive their salaries.
60. As to the other pro-Jordanian notables who were deported, cf. *Lesch 1979*.
61. Cf. *Nahumi 1968*.
62. *Kapeliouk 1967 (a)*.
63. *The Jerusalem Post*, 23 January 1968.
64. Cf. e.g. *MER* 1969/70, p. 391.
65. *MER* 1968, p. 220.
66. Cf. *The Jerusalem Post*, 17 March 1969.
67. Cf. e.g. the interview with a leader of the Communist Party in *New Outlook*, September/October 1967.
68. Cf. e.g. the signatories of the resolution against the annexation of East Jerusalem.

69. Cf. *MER* 1968, p. 598 ff., and *New Middle East*, November 1971.
70. Cf. e.g. *MER* 1967, p. 283, and *MER* 1968, p. 598 ff.
71. Cf. *Al-Anwar*, 2 February 1969, also *MER* 1969/70, p. 379.
72. Cf. *Ha'aretz*, 5 March 1974.
73. Cf. *ibid.*, *Ma'ariv*, 31 December 1970; *MER* 1968, p. 449; *MER* 1969/70, p. 379, and *Al Hamishmar*, 25 January 1980.
74. *Al-Dastur*, 2 February 1969. In 1970, reports of contacts between the Communists in the West Bank and in Israel appeared in Israeli newspapers. It was pointed out that both groups were planning joint activities against the occupation.
75. Cf. e.g. the interview with a leader of the National Front in *MERIP Reports* No. 32; and *Al Hamishmar*, 25 January 1980.
76. Cf. *Le Monde*, 22 and 23 December 1967.
77. Cf. *Lesch 1979*.
78. Cf. Chapter 3.
79. Cf. *MER* 1969/70, p. 434.
80. Cf. *The Jerusalem Post*, 3 March 1969.
81. *Al-Anwar*, 2 February 1969.
82. *Ibid.*
83. The battle of Karameh, a small village in Transjordan, was one of the first military attempts by the Israeli army to eliminate the Palestinian resistance. The battle on 21 March 1968 between the Israeli army and the Fedayeen resulted in substantial Israeli losses. It was celebrated as a victory in the Arab world and became a symbol of the Palestinian opposition. It is a semantic coincidence that the name of the small village Karemeh is the Arab word for 'dignity'.
84. In the autumn of 1970, Jordan began a campaign of annihilation against the Palestinian civilian population and the liberation movement in Jordan; this became known as Black September; cf. e.g. *Hollstein 1977*, p. 235 ff.
85. It contained, e.g. the demand to punish Hussein for his 'war crimes' and expressed the obvious rejection of Hussein by the West Bank population.
86. *The Jerusalem Post*, 23 October 1970.
87. The Jordanian monarch actually declared his willingness to grant the Palestinians a status 'which could go as far as autonomy' (*Le Monde diplomatique*, November 1970). In the same breath, he offered Al-Masri, the mayor of Nablus, the position of prime minister.
88. Yussuf Nasir later became editor-in-chief of the newspaper, *Al-Fajr*, founded in East Jerusalem in 1971. *Al-Fajr* advocated a Palestinian state alongside Israel right from the very beginning (cf. *Rejwan 1973*, p. 17) and became the organ of the National Front for a long time.
89. Cf. *Kapeliouk 1972*.
90. *Ibid.*
91. Cf. *ibid.*
92. Cf. *Neue Zürcher Zeitung*, 22 February 1972, and *Süddeutsche Zeitung*, 12 February 1972.
93. Cf. *ibid.*
94. Cf. *Israel & Palestine*, No. 8, March 1972.
95. Cf. *Cygielman 1972*.

96. Cf. *ibid.*
97. Cf. *Kapeliouk 1972* and *Cygielman 1972.*
98. Cf. *Kapeliouk 1972.*
99. *Cygielman 1972.*
100. Cf. reply of P.L.O. spokesman, Kamal Nasser, concerning Hussein's plan, *Journal of Palestine Studies*, summer 1972.
101. According to the Jordanian election law, candidates on a slate are considered to be automatically elected if there is no opposition candidate. This was the case in the districts mentioned.
102. *Cygielman 1972.*
103. *Neue Zürcher Zeitung*, 5 May 1972.
104. Cf. *Kapeliouk 1972* and *Cygielman 1972.*
105. Cf. Al Ja'abari's advertisement in *The Jerusalem Post*, 28 April 1972.
106. In addition, there were the futile attempts to form a settlement: the Rogers' initiative (1970) and the initiative by U.N. representative, Jarring, (1971).
107. Cf. *Djeghloul 1979*, p. 28.
108. *Rouleau 1975.*
109. The *Le Monde* poll was carried out at the end of 1972; cf. *Rouleau 1975.*
110. Cf. *Cygielman 1972.*
111. Cf. the Charter, *Sirhan 1975*, p. 74 ff.
112. The Communist Party of Jordan (the West Bank branch operated under this name until 1975 and since then has called itself the Palestinian Communist Organization), which had already recognized the U.N. Partition Plan and Israel in 1947 and 1948 respectively, took no part in armed actions (cf. *Ha'aretz*, 5 March 1974) and advocated the establishment of a Palestinian state alongside Israel.
113. The Eleventh National Congress of the P.L.O. in Cairo in January 1973 recognized primarily the significance of the political struggle — in addition to the armed one.
114. The interview with Jiryis Qawwas and Arabi Awwad took place in Beirut in September 1974. Both had been deported from the West Bank in December 1973.
115. Cf. *Kapeliouk 1975*, p. 214 ff.
116. *Ibid.*, p. 214.
117. In the final document of the conference, the recognition of the P.L.O. was not mentioned. King Hussein, the only Arab head of state to do so, abstained from the ballot and, therefore, the decision remained a secret for the time being. (Cf. *Abu Ijad 1979*, p. 205 ff.)
118. Cf. *Ha'aretz*, 4 December 1973, and *Lesch 1979.*
119. Cf. *Zo-Haderekh*, 21 November 1973, and *Ha'aretz*, 5 March 1974.
120. Cf. *Kapeliouk 1975*, p. 215.
121. Cf. e.g. the interview with Hussein in *Le Monde* (English edition), 15 December 1973.
122. Cf. *Neue Zürcher Zeitung*, 13 December 1973. King Hussein resumed payment of the salaries which had been stopped three years before.
123. Cf. *Ha'aretz*, 13 December 1973, and *Kapeliouk 1975*, p. 216 ff. For the first time in a long time, curfews were again imposed, the Bir Zeit University was closed for several weeks and on 10 December 1973,

eight citizens were deported Communists, the mayor of Al-Bireh and a member of the Islamic Council of Jerusalem. The number of security prisoners reached a new high at the end of 1973. According to figures given in Israeli newspapers, the number amounted to 1,825 including mainly members of the Communist Party (cf. *Yediot Aharanot*, 5 September 1974).

124. Quoted from *Yediot Aharanot*, 17 December 1973, taken from *Israleft*, No. 31, 30 September 1973.
125. Cf. *Ashab 1977*.
126. Cf. e.g. the position paper of the Communist Workers League from February 1972, *Israleft*, No. 38, 15 April 1974; the description of positions of the West Bank population in 'What do the Palestinians want?', *New Outlook*, February 1974; as well as the description of the Communist Party and its activities in the 70s, *Al Hamishmar*, 25 January 1980.
127. The Communist Party had recognized the 1947 U.N. Partition Plan, spoke out for a Palestinian state alongside Israel and was critical of armed action; cf. *Al Hamishmar*, 25 January 1980.
128. Cf. *Lesch 1979*.
129. For administrative detention and its conditions see Chapter 3. The administrative detention, applied without a court decision. trial or charge, was lengthened several times in these cases. Cf. *Ha'aretz*, 5 November 1974, and *Davar*, 2 March 1975. The political character of the detention was again affirmed in the February 1975 trials of the P.N.F. members. 'Not at a single trial of the P.N.F. people were charges of sabotage either proven or even alleged.' (*Israleft*, No. 57, 1 March 1975). Cf. for the political and non-military character of the P.N.F., also *Kapeliouk 1975*, p. 216.
130. *Davar*, 1 September 1974.
131. *Ibid.*
132. In view of the Israeli repressive measures, the Communist Party had temporarily to halt the publication of its underground newspaper, *Al Watan*. However the National Front came out of the conflict even stronger, cf. also *Israel & Palestine*, No. 53/54, September 1976, p. 10.
133. *Israel & Palestine*, No. 81, September 1980; also cf. *Djeghloul 1979*, pp. 28 ff. and 43; also see Chapter 8, pp. 000.
134. *Le Monde diplomatique*, November 1977, Supplément Jordanie.
135. Cf. *ibid*.
136. Cf. *ibid*.
137. Cf. *Lesch 1979*. Included in those deported was the publisher of the East Jerusalem daily paper, *Al-Sha'ab*, who, avoiding the censorship, wrote articles for the P.L.O.
138. Deportation of five citizens, including a member of the Ramallah city council and chamber of commerce, as well as the president of Bir Zeit University.
139. See Chapters 4 and 5.
140. Of the eight leading personalities of the P.N.F. deported in December 1973, three were taken up into the executive committee of the P.L.O.
141. *Al Hamishmar*, 22/23 May 1974; *Amit 1976*.
142. The text of the article can be found in *New Outlook*, February/March

1976. Cf. also *Ha'aretz*, 28 January 1976. Within the West Bank, the appeal to the P.L.O. was distributed as a leaflet. For the development within the P.L.O., see also Chapter 8.
143. Cf. e.g. *Ha'aretz*, 21 October 1975.
144. *Al Hamishmar*, 23 October 1975.
145. *Ha'aretz*, 21 October 1975. For these plans, cf. for details, *Journal of Palestine Studies*, No. 17/18, autumn 1975/winter 1976, p. 185 ff.
146. Cf. *Ha'aretz*, 5 April 1976.
147. Cf. *Financial Times*, 15 April 1976.
148. *Ha'aretz*, 2 April 1976.
149. Cf. *Ansprenger 1978*, p. 252.
150. See Chapters 4 and 5.
151. As a result of the lack of a national industrial policy and customs barriers, the West Bank industries were defenceless against the Israeli competition and, therefore, the few industrialists of the West Bank became definite opponents of the Israeli economic policies.
152. Cf. *Rabab 1976*.
153. *The Jerusalem Post*, 2 April 1976.
154. *Ha'aretz*, 1 April, 1976.
155. *Herald Tribune*, 12 April 1976.
156. *Financial Times*, 20 May 1976.
157. Cf. *Le Monde diplomatique*, November 1977, Supplément Jordanie.
158. *Ha'aretz*, 14 April 1976.
159. *Herald Tribune*, 14 April 1976.
160. *Ha'aretz*, 13 April 1976.
161. *Davar*, 16 April 1976.
162. *Financial Times*, 15 April 1976.
163. *Watad 1976*.
164. *Ha'aretz*, 27 August 1976.
165. *Yediot Aharanot*, 11 November 1976.
166. Cf. *The New York Times*, 24 February 1977.
167. *Ha'aretz*, 19 April 1976.
168. *Al-Fajr*, 17 April 1976.
169. *Israleft*, No. 84, 15 May 1976, p. 4.
170. Interview by the authors, September 1977.
171. For a detailed documentation of the events and protest actions in the West Bank, cf. the summary of the Israeli media in the *Israleft* information service. For the period following the 1976 elections, cf. No. 82, 15 April 1976, and subsequent issues.
172. Cf. *The Jerusalem Post*, 15 December 1976.
173. *Nouvel Observateur*, 18 October 1976.
174. Cf. *ibid*.
175. Cf. *Fried 1975*, p. 315 ff. For the conflicts (which began in 1968) over the founding of Kiryat Arba cf. *Lesch 1970*, p. 66 ff.
176. *Nouvel Observateur*, 18 October 1976.
177. *Ibid*.
178. *Ibid*.
179. *Le Monde*, 22 October 1976.
180. *Nouvel Observateur*, 18 October 1976.
181. *Ibid*.

182. See Chapter 2,
183. For the use of the taxes lifted by Israel, cf. the testimony of mayor Qawasmeh in 1979 before the U.N. Human Rights Commission, U.N. Doc. A/AC. 145/RT. 279, p. 15 ff.
184. *Rabab 1976.*
185. Cf. the chronicles of the events in the Middle East in *Middle East Journal*, here for the period from 16 April to 15 August 1976.
186. *Ha'aretz*, 12 April 1976.
187. Cf. the testimony of mayor Qawasmeh in 1979 before the U.N. Human Rights Commission, op. cit., p. 16.
188. Interview by the authors, September 1977.
189. *Ha'aretz*, 17 July 1977.
190. Cf. *Yediot Aharanot*, 3 June 1977, and *Ha'aretz*, 17 July 1977.
191. *Ha'aretz*, 3 August 1977, an article on the one-year service period of Dr Milson. The Israeli attempts to establish institutions other than the city councils as the active representatives of the population also included religious institutions, in particular to establish a front against the leftist forces.
192. Interview by the authors, September 1977.
193. *Filastin Al Thaura*, 25 June 1976, quoted from *Journal of Palestine Studies*, No. 19/20, spring/summer 1976, p. 227.
194. *Le Monde*, 10 October 1976.
195. *Ibid.*
196. Interview by the authors with a member of the city council. See also Chapter 8.
197. Cf. *Ha'aretz*, 3 December 1976, and *Yediot Aharanot*, 15 December 1976.
198. Cf. the summary of the Petition, *Yediot Aharanot*, 1 February 1977.
199. Appeal in the underground newspaper of the Communist Party, *Al Watan*, quoted from *Israleft*, No. 99, 1 February 1977.
200. Cf. *Yediot Aharanot*, 18 November 1976. In October 1978, this committee, the National Guidance Committee, which came out of the National Front, was established in connection with President Sadat's initiative and the Camp David negotiations.
201. Cf. e.g. the appeal of mayor Khalaf in the name of the West Bank population to the leaders of the Arab governments, *Davar*, 3 November 1976.
202. *Al-Fajr*, 16 August 1976.
203. Testimony from Abdul Hak, *Nouvel Observateur*, 30 August 1976.
204. *New Middle East*, April 1973.
205. *Nahumi 1968.*
206. *Nahumi 1972*; the figures are for 1967.
207. *Aviram 1967.*
208. *New Middle East*, April 1973.
209. *Ibid.*
210. See Chapter 2, and MER 1968, p. 253. The Israeli government conducted a psychological campaign in order to make it clear that the army would not pull back again as in 1956/57. Cf. *Le Monde*, 12 December 1967.
211. Cf. the testimony of Israeli Prime Minister Levi Eshkol in *The Jerusalem*

Post, 3 March 1968; cf. further *MER* 1968, p. 253.
212. Cf. *Kanovsky 1970*, p. 181.
213. Especially since 1970, as the P.F.L.P. dominated in the Gaza Strip and increasingly took action against those who worked in Israel. Cf. *The Times*, 3 September 1971.
214. *New Middle East*, February 1972.
215. At the beginning of 1971, 12,000 relatives were interrogated, cf. *Christian Science Monitor*, 3 December 1971.
216. *MER* 1968, p. 395.
217. Cf. *The Times*, 3 September 1971; *Le Monde* (English weekly edition), 21 August 1971. Up to August 1971, according to a report of the International Red Cross, 14,700 refugees were moved from the Gaza Strip to El Arish.
218. *Neue Zürcher Zeitung*, 25 August 1971; *Le Monde* (English weekly edition), 21 August 1971.
219. *Ma'ariv*, 20 August 1971; at the same time there was room for the establishment of Israeli settlements. See also Chapter 2.
220. *Ma'ariv*, 16 February 1973.
221. *NLG Report* 1977, p. 24 ff. Cf. also p. 21 ff.: a detailed account of the resettlement activities as well as an assessment of the Israeli arguments and the discussion of the admissibility of such methods in accordance with international agreements.
222. See also Chapter 8.
223. With the exception of the P.F.L.P.
224. *Brönner 1979*, p. 255.
225. Polarization of the marginalized refugees and resident population; absence of the declassed petit bourgeoisie and the threatened industrial bourgeoisie; 'stabilization' of the refugee camps through employment in Israel resulted in relative stability of the social structure also under the occupation. See also Chapter 5.
226. The Red Crescent is the Palestinian Red Cross.
227. *The Middle East Newsletter*, 28 January 1980, p. 6.
228. *The Jerusalem Post*, 4 January 1978.
229. The basis for this is the Jordanian federation plan from 1972; see also Chapter 6.
230. *The Jerusalem Post*, 11 October 1979.

7. Peace Without the Palestinians? International Peace Initiatives

A Desperate Mission: The Sadat Initiative

Anwar Sadat, compromise candidate for a collective group of leaders, was elected in 1970 to succeed Nasser. At his inauguration Sadat was faced with a situation which had not changed fundamentally since the Israeli takeover of Arab territory in the 1967 June War. The policies of Israel and the United States were aimed at preserving the status quo. Both countries evidently found the present circumstances preferable to an unstable peace. The myth of Israeli invincibility and the creeping annexation, which proved to be advantageous for Israel, made it easy for the latter to dismiss cautious Egyptian offers for negotiation while substituting their own unrealistic demands as prerequisites. The Israeli policy of delaying and rejecting all types of negotiations was assured unconditional American support, as opening the Suez Canal at that time would only have facilitated the movement of Soviet troops to Vietnam.

The situation was much more difficult for Egypt. Following the war of attrition along the Suez Canal (1969-70), Sadat attempted to break the stalemate; in February 1971 he declared his willingness to forgo the demand for a complete withdrawal of the Israeli forces from the occupied territories. Instead, by offering to open the Suez Canal, he hoped to achieve a partial Israeli withdrawal from the Sinai Peninsula. However, this initiative failed because of the Israeli demand for a comprehensive non-aggression pact.

For Egypt, the state of 'neither peace nor war' became increasingly intolerable. The economic situation worsened. Defence spending rose threateningly, making urgently needed social and economic reforms impossible. Dissatisfaction grew among workers and students. Growing military and political dependence on the Soviet Union restricted political movement. Ending the confrontation with Israel was, therefore, in Sadat's opinion, the prerequisite for the necessary and desired economic recovery.

According to the political strategy of the Egyptian President, the United States was expected to play a key role in solving dis
of the Egyptian economy was to be overcome with the help of Western, in particular North American, capital. However, the opening of Egypt to Western investors depended on two prerequisites: 1) dissolving the close

relations with and forms of dependence on the Soviet Union; and 2) ending the conflict with Israel, for the constant threat of a new military conflict in the Middle East was not exactly conducive to a good climate for investment.

Sadat took the first steps in this direction. In a surprise move in 1971, he removed all pro-Soviet members from the Egyptian collective leadership. Then in June 1972, he expelled the Soviet military advisers from Egypt (approximately 17,000). At first, this manoeuvre appeared to be a serious mistake since neither the American nor the Israeli government understood the far-reaching implications of this change of course.

In 1973, domestic difficulties in Egypt intensified. The October War was a desperate step by the Egyptian President to bring an end to political stagnation, domestic and foreign. From a military standpoint, the war was anything but a raging success, yet politically, Sadat was clearly the victor. In particular, the war-related oil boycott imposed by the O.P.E.C. countries on many Western nations and the subsequent rises in oil prices made the danger to American interests in the Middle East incalculable, if the United States continued its unconditional support of Israel. No longer could Israel's military superiority alone guarantee the political and economic interests of the U.S. indefinitely.

The securing of oil supplies became a permanent and essential political factor in the consciousness of the Western world. In future, U.S. policy in the Middle East would have to ensure access to Arab oil supplies. In other words, the United States dared not gamble with the oil-rich Arab states' willingness to co-operate by maintaining its complete partisanship with Israel. Furthermore, due to their growing oil profits, the Arab countries were becoming increasingly attractive to American industry as a market for U.S. products.

In the light of irreconcilable differences between Israel and the Arab states, a comprehensive solution to the Middle East conflict seemed to be a long way off. Yet Sadat had achieved the essential political objective of the October War; the fronts which had been paralysed for years had been set in motion again. By mediating the two Sinai Disengagement Agreements (18 January 1974 and 10 October 1975) through Henry Kissinger's shuttle diplomacy, the U.S. government began its policy of small steps with which it hoped to defuse the Middle East powder-keg.[1]

In 1976, the new American President, Jimmy Carter, took office. Sadat's domestic difficulties coincided with the ambitions of the Carter administration to initiate a comprehensive peace agreement in the Middle East under U.S. auspices.

At first, everything pointed to a reconvening of the Geneva Conference. The main obstacle was the question of how the Palestinians should be represented. Israel still fought against the representation of the Palestinian people by the P.L.O. The Soviet-American working paper from 1 October 1977, appeared to be the breakthrough to a new round of negotiations. The joint statement stressed that 'vital interests' of the peoples of the Middle East 'urgently dictate' that the Geneva Conference, which was to meet again in December 1977, be reconvened as the only way to 'a just and lasting settlement', that is, 'comprehensive, incorporating all parties concerned and all questions'. It called for decisions worked out by 'representatives of all parties . . . including those of the Palestinian people'.[2] Whereas the P.L.O. welcomed this declaration, Israeli representatives described it as 'not acceptable',[3] since the recognition of the legitimate rights of the Palestinian people would imply the establishment of a Palestinian state.

The hopes of the Palestinians, which were bound to this joint declaration of the U.S. and the U.S.S.R., were dashed a few days later by an American-Israeli working paper, in which the American government, at Israeli Foreign Minister Dayan's instigation, virtually disavowed the Soviet-American declaration. The Israeli government did acknowledge, for the first time in this paper, the political nature of the Palestinian issue (previously it had been handled strictly as a humanitarian, refugee problem) and declared its willingness to take part in future negotiations with Palestinian representatives. Still, in comparison to the declaration of the superpowers, which was barely a few days old, these Israeli-American agreements represented a clear step backwards. Once again they spoke only of bilateral negotiations, in which the Palestinian issue would only be 'discussed' but not negotiated.[4]

A few weeks later, Sadat surprised the world with his trip to Jerusalem. Neither the Arab countries nor the P.L.O. had been consulted. In recent years and months, the Palestinians and the Arab governments concerned had frequently shown their growing willingness to negotiate, but Sadat's lone attempt made a concerted Arab action impossible. With his initiative, Sadat crushed the hopes for a comprehensive peace agreement, which could only come into being through the co-operation of all parties involved in the conflict. The negotiation process, which should have led to the reopening of the Geneva Conference, was stopped.

This initiative excluded Egypt from the Arab camp and, as a consequence, Sadat was criticized even by the governments of Jordan, Saudi Arabia and the Gulf states, which had always supported him up until then. This made his vulnerability clear. The fact that desperation rather than political courage was behind his initiative was also recognized by Israel. Through his policies, Sadat had put himself under so much pressure to achieve success that he had to be prepared to make substantial concessions. Since he was more concerned with a quick end to the Egyptian-Israeli confrontation than he was with a comprehensive settlement of the conflict, Israel saw the chance to realize its long cherished wish for a bilateral agreement with Egypt.

Whereas the visit of the Egyptian President to Jerusalem was greeted with euphoric approval in many parts of the world, the Palestinian reaction was, above all, one of uncertainty. At the beginning, P.L.O. leader Arafat announced cautious approval and some mayors in the occupied territories followed suit. The mayor of Hebron, Fahad Qawasmeh, (as well as Elias Freij and Rashed Al-Shawa, the mayors of Bethlehem and Gaza, respectively) praised the 'extraordinary political courage' of Sadat.[5] Yet even before Sadat's arrival in Israel, rejection outweighed approval. 'We Palestinians do not support Sadat's move. His visit means the official recognition of Jerusalem as the capital of Israel',[6] stated Hilmi Hanoun, mayor of Tulkarm, thus expressing the prevailing mood among the Palestinian population.

Despite Israeli efforts to stop them, there were already protests and demonstrations before the visit. Strikes were organized in various schools, and leaflets appeared in the cities condemning the Sadat visit.[7] The P.L.O. called for a 'day of mourning'. As the Egyptian President stepped onto Israeli ground on 19 November 1977, there, to greet Sadat as representatives of the Palestinians, were only a few old pro-Jordanian and pro-Egyptian notables (for example, the former mayor of Hebron, Sheikh Ali Al-Ja'abari).[8] It became evident that, in the final outcome, only the traditional notables supported the Sadat initiative.[9] Even those leaders labelled as pro-Jordanian, such as Elias Freij, Hikmat Al-Masri and Anwar Al-Khatib emphasized during a meeting with Sadat that the P.L.O. was the only legitimate representative of the Palestinian people. Most of the mayors of the West Bank and other representatives of the Palestinian National Front expressed their opposition to the Sadat initiative by boycotting all invitations to meet with the Egyptian President.

'No More War'

Despite the wave of disapproval, nearly all Palestinians in the West Bank and Gaza Strip watched television on 20 November 1977, in order to follow the anxiously awaited speech of Sadat before the Israeli parliament, the Knesset. The essential elements of his speech were:[10] 1) the recognition of the state of Israel; 2) the demand for an end to the Israeli occupation, including Jerusalem; 3) the demand for the realization of the legitimate rights of the Palestinian people, including the right to establish their own state; 4) the right of all the states in the region to live within secure and recognized borders on the basis of appropriate international guarantees; 5) the commitment of all states in the region to regulate mutual relations in accordance with the goals and principles of the U.N. Charter and to resolve all conflicts by peaceful means; 6) an end to the state of war.

Sadat called on Israel to give up 'for ever the dream of conquest' and described the Palestinian problem as the 'nucleus of the Middle East conflict'. Likewise, he emphasized that he had not come to Jerusalem to sign a separate agreement between Israel and Egypt. The most important aspect of his speech was, however, what was not said — there was not even a single reference to the P.L.O.

Begin, in his reply before the deputies in the Knesset, spoke solely of the history of the Jewish people marked by discrimination, persecution and extermination and of Israel's right to exist, but did not respond at all to the proposals of the Egyptian President for a comprehensive solution to the Middle East conflict.

Thus, Sadat left Israel without having received any concrete signs of a willingness to co-operate from the Israeli government. The unity between the Egyptian and Israeli leaders seemed to be limited to a common vow of 'no more war' and the willingness for further negotiations. Certainly, Sadat was celebrated as a hero in the Western world, yet he had not been able to move the Israeli government to make a single concession; indeed, he could not have expected to make such a breakthrough himself. The primary target of his trip was American opinion rather than the Israeli public and their government. Sadat's visit at last untied the American President's hands so he could make a political change of course — to end the U.S. policy of unconditional support of Israel. After the visit, no one could still maintain that there was no party among the Arab nations willing to negotiate peace. Egypt had demonstrated that it was ready for a peace agreement and that, at this stage, Israel's withdrawal from the occupied territories was required before Egypt would recognize it. An American president who, in this situation, was not willing to support Egypt's position and, if necessary, to expedite the peace process by exerting considerable pressure on Israel, would have U.S. public opinion against him.

By making the trip to Jerusalem, thus recognizing Israel, by showing willingness to make peace and to normalize political and economic relations, by failing to mention the P.L.O., and by making the vow that there should never again be war, Sadat placed Israeli Prime Minister Begin under pressure to make a choice — peace or territories. The Egyptian President had not anticipated an immediate response from Begin, rather he had sought the maximum publicity possible for his ultimatum. For years, the Israeli government and the Zionist lobby in the United States had evaded having to come to terms with this choice on the pretext that there was a basic lack of will for peace on the part of the Arabs. President Carter, who aimed at weakening these groups, in order not to endanger the political and economic interests of the United States in the Middle East, was likewise given the chance to distinguish himself as a peacemaker by supporting the Egyptian policy.

Reasonable as this clear 'peace or territories' strategy of the Egyptian leader appeared at first glance, it still ignored the main problem in the Middle East conflict — the Palestinian issue. Peace would not have been achieved by Israel simply returning the occupied territories. Sadat's failure to mention the P.L.O. in his Knesset speech caused great disappointment in the occupied territories. The danger of a separate agreement could, despite Sadat's assertions to the contrary, no longer be overlooked. It was apparent to the Palestinians that they would have to pay the price.

The opposition to Sadat's initiative in the occupied territories finally began to organize itself after his visit. Many Palestinian dignitaries and notables, who had adopted a wait-and-see attitude at first, could now be counted among the ranks of the opposition.[11] Several days after Sadat's return to Cairo, the West Bank city councils and various professional organizations and trade unions passed a declaration in which the Sadat visit was condemned, and demands were made for the founding of a Palestinian state under the leadership of the P.L.O. and the complete withdrawal of all Israeli armed forces.[12] Demonstrations continued; in Nablus, in Ramallah and at the Bir Zeit University, the Palestinian population vented its bitterness toward the 'traitor Sadat'.[13]

By failing to mention the P.L.O. in his Knesset speech and in other public declarations, Sadat aimed to split the Palestinian liberation movement and to weaken the P.L.O. leadership. He hoped to convince the Palestinian people with his peace offer to Israel that their continued support of the P.L.O. and their extreme demands could only bring damage to them. But this attempt failed. Solidarity within the occupied territories and with the P.L.O. was seldom so high. Nearly the entire group of leaders in the occupied territories which had emerged from the local elections in 1976 was united in its rejection of the Sadat initiative.

The Label Swindle: Begin's Autonomy Plan

Sadat's policy forced the Israeli government to act. The entire world was waiting for Israeli Prime Minister Begin to reciprocate the peace gesture in order to keep the negotiation process, which had finally begun, in motion.

In view of the forthcoming consultations with Sadat in Ismailia, and following consultations with the American government, Begin proposed the so-called autonomy plan, which he presented to the Knesset on 28 December 1977. This 26-point plan 'for Palestinian Arabs, residents of Judea, Samaria and the Gaza district', includes, among others, the following provisions:

> 1. The administration of the military government in Judea, Samaria and the Gaza district will be abolished.
> 2. In Judea, Samaria and the Gaza district administrative autonomy of the residents, by and for them, will be established.
> 3. The residents of Judea, Samaria and the Gaza district will elect an administrative council composed of eleven members. The administrative council will operate in accordance with the principles laid down in this paper.
> 10. The administrative council will operate the following departments: (a) education; (b) religious affairs; (c) finance; (d) transportation; (e) construction and housing; (f) industry, commerce and tourism; (g) agriculture; (h) health; (i) labour and social welfare; (j) rehabilitation of refugees; (k) administration of justice and the supervision of local police forces; and will promulgate regulations relating to the operation of these departments.
> 11. Security and public order in the areas of Judea, Samaria and the Gaza district will be the responsibility of the Israeli authorities.
> 14. Residents of Judea, Samaria and the Gaza district, not possessing citizenship, or who are stateless, will be granted free choice of either Israeli or Jordanian citizenship.
> 19. A committee will be established of representatives of Israel, Jordan and the administrative council to examine existing legislation in Judea, Samaria and the Gaza district, and to determine which legislation will

continue in force, which will be abolished, and exactly what the powers of the administrative council will be in implementing regulations. The rulings of the committee will be adopted by unanimous decision.

20. Residents of Israel will be entitled to acquire land and settle in the areas of Judea, Samaria and the Gaza district. Arabs, residents of Judea, Samaria and the Gaza district who, in accordance with the free option granted them, become Israeli citizens, will be entitled to acquire land and settle in Israel.

21. A committee will be established of representatives of Israel, Jordan and the administrative council to determine norms of immigration to the areas of Judea, Samaria and the Gaza district. The committee will determine the norms whereby Arab refugees residing outside Judea, Samaria and the Gaza district will be permitted to immigrate to these areas in reasonable numbers. The rulings of the committee will be adopted by unanimous decision.

24. Israel stands by its right and its claim of sovereignty to Judea, Samaria and the Gaza district. In the knowledge that other claims exist, it proposes, for the sake of the agreement and the peace, that the question of sovereignty in these areas be left open.

26. These principles will be subject to review after a five-year period.[14]

The goal of Begin's peace proposals was unmistakably to make the Israeli occupation permanent. It was a plan, in other words, for 'Palestinian Arabs, residents of Judea, Samaria and the Gaza district', not for the occupied territories. This formulation was designed to make it clear that only the *residents* would be granted *cultural autonomy*, which was limited to matters of education, religion and daily life. The *territorial autonomy*, which Israel reserved for itself, included control of the country's resources, the state land and its use.

Begin's autonomy plan was wholly unacceptable to the Palestinian population. Although Israeli military control in the occupied territories was to be terminated (point 1), the preservation of 'security and public order' — in other words, the exercising of the actual authority — would remain under Israeli responsibility (point 11). Israeli citizens would be conceded the right to settle in the occupied territories (point 20), but the return of any Palestinian to his homeland would be subject to Israeli approval (point 21). The apparently generous right to acquire land in Israel for Palestinians who had decided to become Israeli citizens (point 20) existed only on paper. In response to the anxious question from Knesset representatives as to whether this did not open the door for the sale of all of the Jewish land to Arabs, which the rich oil-producing countries would finance, Foreign Minister Dayan stated that 92% of Israeli land belonged solely to the Jewish National Fund, which was forbidden by law to sell Jewish land to non-Jews.[15] Besides, any potential Arab buyer would first have to find a Jew who would be willing to sell his land to a Palestinian. The administrative council which was to be elected (points 3–12) had practically no importance, for it was not supposed to have any legislative functions; even the council's right to announce ordinances is subject to Israel's approval (point 19).

To conceal the powerlessness of the administrative council and to fill out the meagre plan somewhat, certain self-evident points were included, such as the administrative council's right to elect its own chairperson (point 12) and to convene its first meeting 30 days after the announcement of the election results (point 13). Even the concluding regulations of this so-called autonomy plan, providing for a re-examination of the regulations after five years (point 26), did not offer the Palestinians any reason for hope, for this re-examination was, according to Begin's conception, in no way to degenerate into new negotiations — as declarations by the Israeli government quickly made clear. The proposed autonomy was, therefore, to represent not an interim solution or preliminary phase for the establishment of a Palestinian state, but rather a legalization of the existing state of occupation.

Foreign Minister Dayan elucidated Israel's intentions in a speech before the Knesset:

> The basis of our proposal . . . is a dual one: to free ourselves of the situation in which we are ruling over one million Arabs who do not want our rule and regard us as foreign occupiers: to free ourselves — not them — from this situation, which we neither need nor want . . . . At the same time to ensure Israel's security and our relation with our homeland, namely Judea and Samaria: not to disavow it and not to sever ourselves from it. . . . This is not a provisional settlement, in the sense that it is not a settlement we are proposing for a five-year period. What we are proposing is within the framework of the peace treaty . . . and after five years, when the re-examination takes place, no changes will be introduced . . . without our agreement. . . . There is a possibility that one day a part of this population will declare itself to be Palestinian, as an independent state — and that we do not want to allow to happen, and that is why we said: only two alternatives: either Jordanian or Israeli. . . .

When asked by a Knesset deputy how he would prevent a Palestinian state from arising, Dayan answered:

> By force of the army. . . . Any agreement can be broken and there is no court to look after our interests except ourselves. How will I prevent their refusal to sell land to Jews? How will I prevent the influx of hundreds of thousands of refugees from Lebanon against our will? By force of the Israeli army![16]

The fact that Begin was interested in hindering a compromise on the future of the occupied territories was emphasized by his administration's resolutions to intensify the settlement activities, despite worldwide protests. Thus, while Begin was discussing his 'peace plan' with President Carter, the

Knesset's finance committee allocated I£89 million for 'rural settlements' on the other side of the 'green line'.[17] On 10 January 1978, the Knesset committee on foreign affairs and the committee on security approved the establishment of four new settlements in Samaria for military purposes. In addition, work was started on three new settlements in the northern part of the Sinai.[18]

'Less than Bantustans'

As soon as the first details of the autonomy plan became known, there was a storm of public protest in the occupied territories. The former president of the Jordanian parliament, Hikmat Al-Masri, certainly not suspected of being a partisan of the P.L.O. and initially open-minded towards the Sadat initiative, said the plan was outdated and had already been rejected 10 years earlier.[19] Since even the West Bank politicians who were considered moderate and not simply those belonging to the National Front rejected the plan outright, it had absolutely no chance of finding approval within any segment of the population.

At a meeting of several West Bank mayors and representatives of the trade unions, Begin was accused of wanting to create a contract which would ensure that the illegal occupation was perpetuated. The autonomy plan unmasked the Israeli government's intentions to colonize the occupied territories and denied the Palestinian people the right to self-determination.[20]

In Yasser Arafat's reaction to the publication of these proposals, he alluded to the similarities between the autonomy which Begin wanted to grant the Palestinians in the occupied territories and the 'independence' in the 'homelands' established by the South African apartheid regime for the population.

> Finally, Begin comes along and announces this formula which Premier Rabin and the Labour Party had already offered to the West Bank mayors. They had rejected it. That was five years ago. What is Begin offering us now? Bantustans, nothing more. Even less than Bantustans, Swaziland has more rights than we would have.[21]

The Israeli delegation entered the negotiations at the second Middle East summit conference in Ismailia (Christmas 1977) with this autonomy plan. The political strategy of these proposals corresponded to the principle 'divide and conquer'; by largely satisfying Egypt's territorial claims, that is, by withdrawing from the Sinai Peninsula under certain conditions, the Israelis hoped to persuade Sadat to sign a separate agreement, thereby severing him from the united Arab front. The general declaration of the principles of a peace solution was intended to enable Sadat to present himself as trustee of Arab-Palestinian interests, but, at the same time, to effect a postponement of the Palestinian problem.

Sadat rejected Begin's proposals. A complete withdrawal from the Sinai, i.e. the abandonment of all Jewish settlements and military installations on the penisnsula (the Israeli government was unwilling to go along with both at that time) was the minimum Egypt required for a joint agreement with Israel. The failure of the summit conference in Ismailia could not be disguised by setting up two Israeli-Egyptian negotiating commissions which were to deliberate on political and military issues. Due to the fundamentally opposing interests which persisted, the commissions did not survive very long. After the Israeli representatives showed no more signs of willingness to make concessions at the talks in Cairo and Jerusalem, the Egyptian president recalled his delegation. The Israeli-Egyptian negotiations had reached an impasse.

The Coup: Camp David

It was precisely this lack of results which brought in the American government. At the beginning of January, President Carter travelled to Cairo and declared in a press conference that a peace settlement in the Middle East would have to take the legitimate rights of the Palestinians into consideration and give them the possibility to take part in planning their future.[22] However, the statements of the U.S. government remained vague and contradictory and did not make their positions clear. They served more to appease the other Arab states (which had been critical of the Sadat initiative and any American attempt to mediate) than they did to influence Israel. The U.S. repeatedly assured the Israeli government that comments on the 'legitimate rights of the Palestinian people' or a 'Palestinian homeland' did not indicate any substantial change in the American Middle East policy.

Various attempts at reviving the peace talks through the mediation of American diplomats were unsuccessful. In spring and summer 1978, the euphoria created by Sadat's visit to Jerusalem had completely vanished. Peace in the Middle East seemed even more remote than ever; Palestinian organizations intensified their terrorist attacks in Israel. The Israeli army's invasion of southern Lebanon contributed to a further aggravation of the situation and seemed to mean an end to all hopes for peace. There were fierce demonstrations and strikes in Nablus, East Jerusalem, Bir Zeit, Al Bireh, Jericho and Gaza Strip cities, in which the Palestinian population protested against the Israeli invasion of Lebanon.[23] Again, thousands of Palestinians became refugees. How could peace be concluded with a government which started a new war when peace negotiations were in progress?

The Palestinians had absolutely no reason to hope that Sadat would be the one to fight for their rights. He had broken off relations with the P.L.O., deported many Palestinians because of their opposition to his policy, and now stated publicly that he was no longer demanding an independent state, but rather was in favour of a Palestinian entity connected with the Jordanian Kingdom.[24]

President Carter believed that the only solution to the impasse in the negotiations was a summit conference in the U.S. to which he would invite

Sadat and Begin. He was not without hopes of improving his own sagging image by acting as a peacemaker for the Middle East.

The Agreements
On 17 September 1978, after 13 days of closed meetings at the Camp David presidential retreat, Carter, Begin and Sadat presented a whole package of agreements in Washington: the Framework for the Conclusion of a Peace Treaty between Egypt and Israel and the Framework of Peace in the Middle East.

The content of the Israeli-Egyptian treaty is clear and unequivocal. President Sadat declared his willingness to conclude a peace treaty and to enter into diplomatic, economic and cultural relations with Israel in exchange for the Sinai Peninsula, i.e. the Israeli armed forces would be withdrawn from the area and the existing Jewish settlements would be dissolved.

The contents of the second document, Framework of Peace in the Middle East, are much more complicated and vague. In it, Israel recognizes the legitimate rights of the Palestinian people and agrees to the 'transfer of authority' to the West Bank and the Gaza Strip. Within a transition period of five years, the residents of the occupied territories are to be granted 'full autonomy'. The Israeli military government and its civilian administration are to be removed and replaced by an administrative council to be elected by the inhabitants. Egypt, Israel and Jordan (which is to be invited to participate in negotiations) will determine how this administrative council is to be formed. These states and representatives of the West Bank and the Gaza Strip residents are to start negotiations on the final status of the territories in the third year of the interim period at the latest.[25]

The Barter
Throughout the Western world, these resolutions were immediately welcomed with a big sigh of relief and occasionally with jubilation, while in the Arab countries, they were greeted with harsh criticism.

The negotiations were steadfastly condemned with particular vehemence by the states of the Arab Front. At a special meeting in Damascus in which Algeria, Libya, South Yemen and the P.L.O. participated, they decided to break off economic and political relations with Egypt, and called for more co-operation with the socialist countries, especially the Soviet Union.[26]

King Hussein's reaction was cautious. Jordan's isolation in the Arab camp as a result of the resolutions of the 1974 Arab summit conference in Rabat (at which the right to represent the Palestinian people had been removed from King Hussein) had been overcome for the most part, and relations with neighbouring Syria, which had been very strained for many years, had improved greatly. With no prospect of recovering Jordanian sovereignty over the West Bank and East Jerusalem, the invitation to participate in the peace negotiations merely endangered Jordan's recently stabilized position in the Arab camp. The Jordanian monarch therefore stated that he felt himself in no way legally or morally tied to the Camp David agreements.

However, he stressed continued Jordanian willingness to examine all possibilities which could 'serve the Palestinian cause, Arab rights and a just peace ... through intense and comprehensive contacts with Arabs and at an international level',[27] thereby leaving all options open for the future.

On 18 September 1978, one day after the announcement of the Camp David agreements, a special meeting of the P.L.O.'s executive council was held in Beirut. In a declaration they stated:

> The results of the Camp David summit represent the most dangerous conspiracy against the Arab nation since 1948. It also represents what Zionism and U.S. imperialism have tried to achieve over the past 30 years. This is now offered to them by Sadat through accepting all the conditions for liquidating the Palestinian and Arab cause.[28]

In particular, the nature of the agreements was criticized as a 'Pax Americana' which not only was to be thrust upon the Arabs but also offered manifold possibilities for American intervention in the Middle East. Sadat was accused of full capitulation to Israel's expansionist goals and collaboration with American imperialism.

The major significance of the Camp David agreements was that, in essence, they constituted the framework for a separate treaty between Israel and Egypt. In this respect, Israeli hopes and Arab-Palestinian fears had been fulfilled. There were absolutely no connections between the two documents. The planned conclusion of an Egyptian-Israeli peace treaty was to take place quite independently of agreements over the future of the other occupied territories. In this way, Israel had attained the most important goal of its strategy. In exchange for the return of the Sinai Peninsula to Egyptian administration and a certain amount of relaxation in its control over the occupied territories, it received a peace treaty with Egypt, thereby removing its most dangerous enemy from among the ranks of the opposing Arab states and enabling it to secure its occupation of the West Bank and Gaza Strip for the time being. The decisive concessions on the part of Israel were the withdrawal from the Sinai and the relinquishing of the Jewish settlements in the territory, which had always been considered indispensable.

Israel did recognize (according to the treaty) the legitimate rights of the Palestinian people and agreed to the participation of Palestinians in the negotiations on the final status of the West Bank and Gaza Strip which were to be conducted during the interim period; however, the entire provision was dependent on Jordan's participation. This and the lack of temporal and legal linkage between the two framework agreements gave Prime Minister Begin the opportunity to conclude a separate treaty with Egypt. The sole prerequisite was the refusal of King Hussein to join the negotiation process, thereby hindering an arrangement on the occupied territories, and freeing Begin to conclude a peace treaty with Sadat without having to fear Egyptian objections. It was therefore necessary for the Israeli government to thwart Jordanian approval of the Camp David resolutions.

The ink was barely dry on the treaty documents, which also provided for a temporary pause in the settlement activities in the West Bank, when Begin announced the continuation of the settlement policy. Even though 'transitional arrangements' and the 'transfer of authority' in the West Bank were stated in the agreement, the leader of the Israeli government made clear that 'Jerusalem is one city indivisible, the capital of the State of Israel' and he would 'never' agree to Jordanian sovereignty over parts of the city.[29] As expected, the response of the King in Amman to the Camp David invitation was negative. As long as the withdrawal of Israeli armed forces from the West Bank and the return of East Jerusalem to Arab sovereignty were categorically rejected and the expansion of Jewish settlement in the occupied territories not curtailed, he saw no reason to take part in the peace negotiations.

Empty Words

Instead of documenting a compromise between opposing Egyptian and Israeli positions, many of the provisions contained in the framework agreement are actually evidence of Israeli-Egyptian disagreement, carefully disguised by means of clever formulations. On some controversial points, participating legal advisers were unable to formulate statements capable of bridging the gap between the two standpoints, so that essential problems remained completely unmentioned.

Following shortly on the end of the summit meeting, the participants tried to legitimize the conclusion of the agreements to their critics by means of contradictory interpretations. To begin with, only a few days after the signing of the agreements, the Israeli Prime Minister apparently could no longer remember the length of the halt to settlement agreed upon. A major concession made by the Israeli delegation to the negotiation, namely the recognition of the legitimate rights of the Palestinian people, was revealed to be a farce. In one of the six supplements to the framework agreement, President Carter confirmed that Prime Minister Begin had declared to him that:

> The expression 'Palestinians' or 'Palestinian people' are being and will be construed and understood as 'Palestinian Arabs', which, according to official Israeli policy, means that the agreements only refer to the residents of the territories which, for Prime Minister Begin, are part of the historic fatherland of the Jews.[30]

The Israeli interpretation of the term 'West Bank' does not correspond with conventional usage either: 'The expression "West Bank" ... is being and will be understood by the government of Israel as Judea and Samaria'[31] only, therefore excluding East Jerusalem; according to general interpretation, the term 'West Bank' includes East Jerusalem. Furthermore, members of the Israeli cabinet clarified that although the withdrawal of the military government from the occupied territories had been agreed to, this did not mean

Peace Without the Palestinians?

Everyday reality – Palestinians controlled by Israeli soldiers

the former would be dissolved. It was certainly conceivable that the headquarters of the military government would be transferred to Tel Aviv.[32] Besides the setting up of a 'strong local police force which may include Jordanian citizens', it is envisaged in the treaty that 'Israeli and Jordanian forces will participate in joint patrols and in the manning of control posts to assure the security of the borders'. Foreign Minister Dayan interpreted this passage thus: 'If the local police cannot keep the residents under control in the case of a demonstration, we will call in our armed forces to help the police restore order.'[33] In this connection, Begin pointed out for example, that Israel has the right 'to build roads in West Jordan [i.e. the West Bank] and the Gaza Strip, according to its needs. The Israeli armed forces fight against terrorism everywhere using every available means'.[34]

On the other hand, Sadat not only emphasized the forthcoming recovery of the Sinai Peninsula, he also praised the agreements as a substantial step toward the realization of the Palestinian right to self-determination. He promised he would not conclude a separate treaty and that the prerequisite to the conclusion of a peace treaty would be to take the legitimate rights of the Palestinians into account. Of course, he was also able to refer to the letters accompanying the Camp David agreements, in which he described East Jerusalem as part of the Arab West Bank, thereby affirming the existing claim to Arab sovereignty. Yet even this could not obscure the fact that there was no link between the two sets of treaties and that the search for the words 'Palestinian right to self-determination' or 'independence' was in vain.

Two other words were also missing from the treaty entirely: Jerusalem and the P.L.O. The incompatibility of the Egyptian and Israeli views toward the future of the 'City of Peace' was clear in the correspondence, yet the P.L.O. was apparently not even a topic of discussion in the negotiations. Two central issues in the Middle East conflict were thus excluded from the agreements. Yet, unless these issues are resolved, peace in the area is inconceivable.

'Big Brother': The United States

The agreements of Camp David were said to have been reached through the mediation of President Carter; but 'mediation' is a euphemistic description of the actual role played by the United States during the negotiations.

Sadat's visit to Jerusalem led to a change not only in U.S. government and administration opinion but also in public opinion. The uppermost objective of the Middle East policy was no longer unconditional support of Israel; it was now a comprehensive settlement for peace, which would also require the Jewish state to make sacrifices. It became clearer and clearer that the Carter administration followed a course which essentially corresponded to the political recommendations of the Brookings Report. This 1975 report was based on six-month studies done by a commission consisting of 16 Middle East experts including presidential advisers Zbigniew Brzezinski and William Quandt. Even though Brzezinski did not often take part in the commission's meetings,[35] the statements in this report[36] were certainly in keeping with the views of Carter's most important adviser on foreign affairs.[37]

In the 'basic assumptions' named in the report, American interest in a peaceful solution to the Middle East conflict is stressed,[38] since a new Arab-Israeli war could lead to a confrontation between the U.S. and the U.S.S.R. and to a renewed oil embargo. 'It would be imprudent and unsafe to attempt to leave the situation "frozen" for any prolonged period'[39] because 'basic conditions are now more propitious for a settlement than they have been or may be again for some time.'[40] Besides, 'the United States remains the great power best fitted to work actively with the parties in bringing about a settlement'[41] yet, 'as much as possible, a settlement should be negotiated and agreed upon by the parties on their own initiative'.[42] The report gives the following as the most important elements for a comprehensive solution: 'The primary basis for a settlement must be a negotiated and agreed trade-off between the Israeli requirement for peace and security and the Arab requirement for evacuation of territories occupied in 1967 and for Palestinian self-determination.'[43] The necessity of a settlement concerning Jerusalem is emphasized just as strongly, as 'binding reciprocal commitments by all parties to the settlement to respect the sovereignty, independence, and territorial integrity of the others'.[44] The members of the commission not only demanded Israel's withdrawal from the occupied territories,[45] but also the realization of the Palestinians' right to self-determination, either by means of 'an independent Palestinian state accepting the obligations and commitments of the peace agreements, or [through] a Palestinian entity voluntarily federated with Jordan but exercising the extensive political autonomy King Hussein has offered'.[46] This type of peace settlement 'should be implemented in clearly defined stages, particular [Israeli] steps of withdrawal being matched with security measures'.[47]

In this, the Brookings Report greatly resembled an outline for the negotiations at Camp David. Indeed, the report urged a solution within the framework of the Geneva Peace Convention. Yet the U.S. government's signing of the working paper (written by Carter and Dayan) on 5 October 1977, which negated the joint American-Soviet communiqué of 1 October 1977, made a settlement which included the Soviet Union impossible.

Despite the strong appeal for peace from Camp David, it was not merely Carter's love of peace which drove him to attempt to mediate. It was very clearly stated in the Brookings Report what was at stake in the Middle East — oil, securing sources of energy for the Western states, and the containment of Soviet influence in the region. Brzezinski had already written in 1974 that 'without a settlement of the issue [i.e. the Middle East conflict] in the near future, any stable arrangement in the energy area is simply not possible'.[48] This concern became more and more acute with the failure of Carter's energy programme, the inflation within the American economy, the rising consumption of oil by the superpower and the rising oil prices.

Although the comprehensive peace settlement envisaged in the Brookings Report was not realized at Camp David, a fact which could not be obscured even by the American President's statements to the contrary, the agreements can certainly be interpreted as a step in the direction of a comprehensive solution. However, in reality, the embryo of a separate Egyptian-Israeli treaty was conceived at Camp David, although peace in the Middle East is inseparable from the realization of the right of the Palestinians to self-determination. Despite this knowledge, it was precisely this connection which was ignored by all three parties to the treaty at Camp David.

Complete Rejection: Reactions in the Occupied Territories

The almost total rejection of these agreements on the part of the population in the West Bank and Gaza Strip came as no surprise. The representatives of the National Front and many other leading personages condemned the agreement from the very beginning. At numerous assemblies, resolutions were passed in which any participation on the part of Palestinians to realize the plans for the occupied territories worked out at Camp David was rejected.[49]

'Complete Rejection of the Camp David Agreements'

In a declaration by an assembly of representatives of all trade unions, professional associations and organizations, which took place in East Jerusalem at the end of September 1978, it was stated:

1. Those assembled here declare their complete rejection of the Camp David agreements.

2. The Camp David agreements are contradictory to the Arab nature of the struggle and represent a separate peace between Egypt and Israel as a first step towards breaking Egypt away from the Arab front and towards transforming the struggle for Palestine into a struggle for a part of the occupied Egyptian territory. . . .

5. The agreement has shaken Arab unity and strengthened the Zionist principle of bilateral negotiations with every Arab country. The separatist logic contained therein has done considerable damage to the Palestinian cause.

6. The Camp David accord does mention the rights of the Palestinian people; it fails, however, to name the P.L.O. as their sole legitimate representative and to secure their right to repatriation, self-determination and the establishment of an independent, free nation in their own territory.

7. The agreement . . . does not obligate Israel to withdraw from Arab Jerusalem, the West Bank, the Gaza Strip and the remaining Arab territories. It openly proposes self-administration, which means permanent establishment of the occupying rule, the incorporation of the occupied territories and the intensifying of Israeli control over the Palestinian people.

8. . . . The future of the region must be viewed as a unit, even if hostile forces seek to obstruct it. The Palestinian people from within and outside of the occupied homeland are likewise an indivisible unit under the leadership of the P.L.O., the sole legitimate representative of the people. . . .

10. . . . There will be no peace in the region if the Palestinian people are not able to exercise their sovereignty in Jerusalem, in the West Bank and in the Gaza Strip. . . .

12. We urge all residents of the occupied territories to close their ranks in face of the attempt to win their approval of the proposal for self-administration, sought by the Camp David agreements. Each and every attempt in this direction must be repelled.

Source: *Palästina Bulletin*, Bonn, 12 October 1978.

Despite almost complete opposition, the Israeli authorities first tried to gain the support of individuals, mayors and notables for the proposed self-administration. Yet none of these attempts was successful. 'When the Israelis want to talk about rights, we always answer, "We want our own Palestinian state alongside Israel, and the P.L.O. is the only organization of the Palestinian people that can negotiate the matter!" ' said the mayor of Ramallah.[50]

When Begin presented the autonomy plan in the winter of 1977, a new phase in Israeli policy with respect to the occupied territories was launched. Whereas a tight rein had been kept on Palestinian representatives in the city councils elected in 1976 – the military government forbidding them to do almost everything and greatly hindering local activities – now there was a more liberal period. The mayors of the large cities of Hebron, Ramallah and Nablus were permitted to travel to several Arab countries and collect financial donations for the development of their cities. Suddenly, the city administrations were allowed to purchase their own generators, thereby freeing them from their dependence on the Israeli power system; they were allowed to carry out plans for a sewage system and to build houses and schools. Even prison visits as well as joint meetings of the mayors were permitted. However, this step taken by the occupying authority under Defence Minister Ezer Weizman only meant a change in method. 'Politically, nothing has changed', said Hebron's mayor, Fahad Qawasmeh, 'they used to put us under constant pressure to show the population that the mayors and city councils which they had elected couldn't do anything for them. Now we can work almost completely undisturbed.' However, the mayors did not conceal their speculation that this new 'policy of dialogue' with them was designed to discredit them as collaborators in the P.L.O.'s eyes and to make the autonomy proposals attractive to them.

Springboard or Fig-leaf?

The call by the political leaders in the occupied territories to close ranks in opposition to Camp David was opposed very little by the public. In all groups and organizations in the territories, the advantages and disadvantages of the autonomy plan were actually discussed intensively. Many supporters of the Palestinians from all over the world and even from Israel called on them to learn from history, to pursue a 'moderate' course and to cease rejecting every proposal automatically.[51] A representative of the National Front, Mayor Qawasmeh, rejected this argument:

> We are not that naive. Sadat did not succeed in getting us the right of self-determination in his discussions with Begin. How could we a Palestinians, controlled by Israel, have more power to wrest from the Israeli leaders our rights and succeed where President Sadat failed? We prefer to live under occupation for another ten years. Under the military occupation government we remain a fishbone in Israel's throat and a problem for the world. If we accept self-rule, Israel can claim that

the Palestinian problem in the West Bank and Gaza is solved or being solved; no more military government, the Palestinians are ruling themselves. In reality, we will only provide a cover for a more stealthy, but permanent Israeli domination over our people and territories.[52]

It soon became apparent that the agreements could not be a springboard to self-determination for the Palestinian people; it was only a fig-leaf behind which the Egyptian-Israeli separate treaty was to be hidden. Not only did the publication of the supplementary protocol and letters agreed upon at Camp David contribute to the disillusionment of the supporters of the 'springboard' theory, but circles within the Israeli government announced more and more clearly their intention to eliminate the risk of the establishment of a Palestinian state in the West Bank and Gaza Strip. In addition, a government committee was formed to work out the details of the autonomy plan, the outcome of which soon leaked out despite Israeli Foreign Minister Dayan's warning against public discussions on the form of the administrative autonomy: 'If the Egyptians knew Israel's intentions concerning autonomy, they would not sign the pact.'[53]

First, new Israeli plans for intensifying settlement activities in the West Bank were announced. With 54 billion Israeli pounds, new settlements for approximately 27,000 Jewish families were to be financed in the next five years. Israel argues that these settlements 'contribute to a *rapprochement* between the Jewish and Arab populations'.[54] According to General Dayan:

> With the military government's help, even more land should be confiscated. The Prime Minister must give the Defence Minister the instructions and he, in turn, must order the fencing in of the required areas. The Minister of Justice must proclaim the necessary laws and Mr Ehrlich, the Finance Minister, should allocate the necessary funds. And if the Egyptians or Americans are opposed? Too bad, we are not willing to sign a peace treaty that only satisfies them.[55]

In spite of autonomy, the administration of the water resources, which are of vital importance especially for agricultural development in the occupied territories, was to remain under Israeli control. In the past few years, Israel has already helped itself freely to the water resources in the occupied territories, yet has only approved a few Palestinian requests to drill for water.

The self-administrative council which was to be formed was not to receive any legislative or financial authority whatsoever. It was not empowered to impose customs duty, to regulate the exchange of goods and capital, or to have control over the currency and the emigration of workers. Israel was to contribute substantially to the budget of the local administration, thereby having another instrument of control in its power.[56]

'No Palestinian state will ever come into being. None.' This is how the Israeli head of government summarized his position:

The Israeli army has the job of preventing this. It is not by chance that the governing council to be elected will be called an administrative council. Administration and nothing more! We have proposed autonomy, not sovereignty. And the difference between the two is enormous.[57]

First the Carrot, Then the Stick
Once the opposition to Camp David in the occupied territories had taken shape and winning the public and their political representatives over to the autonomy plan seemed hopeless, the Israeli military government no longer saw any reason to continue the liberal 'policy of dialogue'. Since November 1978, a wave of arrests had gone through the occupied territories. Dozens of Palestinians, including many students, were taken at night from their beds and carried off to the military stations without any warrants for their arrest. All indications suggested that these measures were not the usual interrogations and detentions which had become a part of everyday life for the Palestinian population. These arrests were not meant merely to intimidate the residents and make them feel insecure; this was obviously a calculated blow struck by the Israeli military authorities in connection with the Camp David agreements and Begin's autonomy plan. Evidence for this was the searching of houses, a measure not commonly employed up to that time; most of the individuals involved were young Palestinians active in youth and athletic clubs, church, cultural and social organizations — the only form of organization permitted in the occupied territories. The main objective of the interrogations was to extract information as to who thought what about the autonomy plan.

This wave of arrests naturally set off further bitterness among the people, particularly since the arrests had soon reached such proportions that even the Bir Zeit University felt forced to inform the public about what was going on by means of a press conference. Since the deportation of its president in 1974, the university administration had decided to be politically cautious so as not to endanger the educational process. However, the large number of arrests of students and assistant professors and their treatment led to the discontinuation of this policy. The only chance to exert pressure on the military government was by informing the public, especially since the accusations of brutal interrogation methods used in the prisons multiplied again during this period. A resolution from the university pointed to the escalation of repressive measures by the occupying authority:

> Israeli authorities are using methods of thought control, the confiscation of legally permitted literature, beating and torture to create an atmosphere of terror which makes a free university education virtually impossible. There has emerged a new pattern in the interrogation of the students seized in this most recent round-up. They are being asked to provide specific information concerning the position of individual students and faculty members on the Israeli-sponsored autonomy plan. ... What is happening at this moment to the University of Bir Zeit

is only a part of the general pattern of harrassment and intimidation directed against Arabs throughout Palestine.⁵⁸

A Student Meeting at Birzeit University

A Dead End: the Egyptian-Israeli-American Peace Treaty

A year and a half after Sadat's trip to Jerusalem and seven months after the Camp David agreements, Sadat and Begin, in the presence of U.S. President Carter, signed the peace treaty during a festive ceremony in front of the White House in Washington. The signing of the treaty on 26 March 1979 had been preceded by extensive negotiations, which had characteristically taken place, for the most part, in the American capital, so that the U.S. could influence the negotiation delegations when they chose to do so.

The treaty, which consisted of a preamble, nine articles, three supplements, four letters and three protocols,⁵⁹ confirmed in essence the agreements made at Camp David. Egypt's departure from the rest of the Arab front was formally secured. In return it regained the Sinai Peninsula, which was to be evacuated by the Israelis according to a fixed schedule within the next three years. This withdrawal was to take place on condition, however, that Egypt was only allowed to station a limited number of troops in the region and that in the future, Israel would be supplied with oil from wells tapped there.

At the same time, a gradual normalization of bilateral relations between the two states, politically as well as culturally and economically, was agreed upon; for Israel, this meant breaking the Arab boycott. Of special importance for Israel was Sadat's concession in Article VI, Paragraph 2 of the peace treaty, in which both parties to the treaty bound themselves 'to fulfil in good faith their obligations under this Treaty, without regard to action or inaction of any other party and independently of any instrument external to this Treaty'. This very clause made it clear that even in the event of a military conflict between other Arab states and Israel, Egypt would not intervene militarily.[60]

The issue of the Palestinians' right to self-determination was largely left out of this document. Only in the correspondence which was part of the treaty did the parties agree to enter into negotiations within one month of the exchange of the instruments of ratification. 'The purpose of the negotiations shall be to agree ... on the modalities for establishing the elected self-governing authority (administrative council)' in the West Bank and the Gaza Strip. These negotiations, which were 'to provide full autonomy to the inhabitants' were to be concluded within one year.

The Egyptian-Israeli-American Treaty: A Joint Letter from Sadat and Begin to President Carter

Dear Mr President:

This letter confirms that Egypt and Israel have agreed as follows:

The Governments of Egypt and Israel recall that they concluded at Camp David and signed at the White House on September 17, 1978, the annexed documents entitled 'A Framework for Peace in the Middle East Agreed at Camp David' and 'Framework for the conclusion of a Peace Treaty between Egypt and Israel'.

For the purpose of achieving a comprehensive peace settlement in accordance with the above-mentioned Frameworks, Egypt and Israel will proceed with the implementation of those provisions relating to the West Bank and the Gaza Strip. They have agreed to start negotiations within a month after the exchange of the instruments of ratification of the Peace Treaty. In accordance with the 'Framework for Peace in the Middle East', the Hashemite Kingdom of Jordan is invited to join the negotiations. The Delegation of Egypt and Jordan may include Palestinians from the West Bank and Gaza Strip or other Palestinians as mutually agreed. The purpose of the negotiations shall be to agree, prior to the elections, on the modalities for establishing the elected self-governing authority (administrative council), define its powers and responsibilities, and agree upon other

> related issues. In the event Jordan decides not to take part in the negotiations, the negotiations will be held by Egypt and Israel.
>
> The two Governments agree to negotiate continuously and in good faith to conclude these negotiations at the earliest possible date. They also agree that the objective of the negotiations is the establishment of the self-governing authority in the West Bank and Gaza in order to provide full autonomy to the inhabitants.
>
> Egypt and Israel set for themselves the goal of completing the negotiations within one year so that elections will be held as expeditiously as possible after agreement has been reached between the parties. The self-governing authority referred to in the 'Framework for Peace in the Middle East' will be established and inaugurated within one month after it has been elected, at which time the transitional period of five years will begin. The Israeli military government and its civilian administration will be withdrawn, to be replaced by the self-governing authority, as specified in the 'Framework for Peace in the Middle East'. A withdrawal of Israeli armed forces will then take place and there will be a redeployment of the remaining Israeli forces into specified security locations.
>
> This letter also confirms our understanding that the United States Government will participate fully in all stages of negotiations.
>
> > Sincerely yours,
> > Mohammed Anwar el-Sadat
> > Menachem Begin
>
> Source: *New Outlook*, September 1979, p. 52.
>
> NB: President Carter, upon receipt of this letter, added to the American and Israeli copies: 'I have been informed that the expression "West Bank" is understood by the Government of Israel to mean "Judea and Samaria".

Considerable financial concessions by the U.S. had made the conclusion of the treaty possible.[61] The agreements foresaw U.S. participation in the autonomy negotiations, a fact which would enable it to influence the results these negotiations would have. Palestinian participation was only hinted at as a possibility.

Arab Reactions

In all of the Arab countries, the Egyptian-Israeli-American agreements were judged for what they were: a separate treaty between Israel and Egypt in which the rights of the Palestinian people were in no way taken into account. Even though there was a consensus among all of the states in the Arab League concerning rejection of the Egyptian policy, they could not agree on a united effective stand to take against Egypt.

At the Baghdad Conference in November 1978, they threatened comprehensive political and economic measures which were to lead to complete isolation of Egypt in the Arab world. The agreed breaking off of diplomatic relations with Egypt was, in fact, carried out by almost all of the Arab countries. Also the headquarters of the Arab League, whose policy had largely been formed by Egypt in the past, was moved from Cairo to Tunis and Egypt's membership in many pan-Arab organizations was frozen.[62]

The 'sanctions' decided upon by the Arab states remained, however, restricted to demonstrative political actions. The proposed economic sanctions did not have any lasting effect, since in this area the Gulf states — Saudi Arabia in particular — contended themselves with verbal assertions of Arab solidarity. Saudi Arabia, which up to this point had paid the largest percentage of Arab financial and economic aid to Egypt, only withheld a portion of its allocations. The trade boycott imposed on Egypt remained an ineffective weapon, as a mere 6% of Egypt's foreign trade was transacted with the Arab states. Egyptian specialists and 'exported labour' (of which there were about 1.7 million) working in other Arab countries, whose transfer of money to their homeland is an important factor in the Egyptian balance of payments, were still welcome in their host countries and were allowed to transfer their earnings to their homeland.[63] Egypt's moderate financial losses brought on by the fragmentary Arab boycott were in part balanced by American and international financial aid, so that the Egyptian economy, which was in a difficult situation, did not suffer too greatly by the measures taken by the Arab states.

This inconsistent policy of the Arab states revealed the conflict between the states of the Rejection Front and the reactionary governments of the Gulf countries. The common opposition to the Egyptian-Israeli separate treaty cannot conceal the obvious interest the Gulf countries have in a continuation of the pro-American policy of the Egyptian government. A danger to the Sadat government could —especially since Iran is no longer the preserver of American interests in the Middle East — upset the balance of power in the region and also their own governments as a result. The events in Mecca at the beginning of 1980 showed that, for instance, the Saudi dynasty is no longer so firmly established as had generally been assumed. In contrast to the states of the Rejection Front, the policy of the oil-producing countries, therefore, is not directed against Sadat's attitude toward the U.S., but only against the form and content of the peace agreements.

The P.L.O. spoke out harshly against the treaty[64] and announced a heightening of the resistance against the 'Zionist state'. As a result of the separate peace, there was *rapprochement* — for the first time since Black September 1970 — between the P.L.O., the Fatah faction in particular, and

Jordan, in order to deliberate jointly on the struggle against the treaty.

Dialogue of the Deaf and Dumb! The Autonomy Negotiations

The time limit of one year, which was set for the negotiations on the 'autonomy' of the population of the West Bank and the Gaza Strip in the separate treaty, expired on 26 May 1980 with no result. In endless rounds of negotiations, Israel and Egypt continually confirmed their unaltered positions. The Egyptian President interrupted the talks several times because the Israeli government under Menachem Begin repeatedly announced its inflexibility and made it clear through provocative acts that it was in no way willing to ease its control over the occupied territories. The euphoria over the concluded peace treaty evaporated very quickly and although Israel's withdrawal from the Sinai Peninsula was carried out as planned, the borders between the two states were opened and diplomatic relations were established, the negotiation climate deteriorated rapidly. Particularly responsible for this were the following: 1) the continuation of the settlement policy in the occupied territories, which became more and more provocative because of the establishment of new Jewish settlements nearby or in Arab cities; 2) statements by Israeli cabinet members which made a farce out of the autonomy negotiations; 3) an increasing swing to the right within the Israeli government, so that Begin, after the resignations of his ministers, Dayan and Weizman, who had been considered moderates, was only able to keep his coalition (which had shrunk to a bare majority) in power by maintaining a particularly uncompromising policy; and 4) the growing repression of all political endeavours in the occupied territories, where a conflict of almost civil war dimensions was developing due to arrests and deportations, attempted assassinations and terrorist attacks.

In August 1980, negotiations came to a complete halt. The Israeli parliament passed the so-called Jerusalem Law, constitutionally reinforcing Jerusalem's status as the eternal and indivisible capital of Israel.[65] Actually, the status of Jerusalem was not changed by the law, yet coupled with Begin's announcement that he was going to move his administrative seat from Jewish West Jerusalem to Arab East Jerusalem, the passage of this law represented such a provocation during the negotiations with Egypt that Sadat felt obliged to break off the talks.[66] Another very important factor in the termination of the negotiations was certainly that President Carter — who, in 1980, preoccupied with the Soviet invasion of Afghanistan and the hostage crisis in Iran — was condemned to inaction in the Middle East situation because of the forthcoming presidential election.

In the past several years, the growing isolation of Israel has become more and more evident. In the emergency session of the U.N. General Assembly in July 1980 regarding the Palestine problem, only six countries (the United States, Norway, Canada, Australia, Guatemala, and the Dominican Republic) voted against a resolution calling for Israel's withdrawal from the occupied territories by 15 November 1980, condemning the Jewish settlement policy and stressing the Palestinian right to self-determination and the role of the P.L.O. as the legitimate representative of the Palestinian people.[67] The countries of the European Common Market in particular abstained from voting. They are distancing themselves more and more from Israeli policy and are attempting to develop their own initiatives towards a peaceful settlement of the conflict — despite opposition or at least scepticism on the part of the United States.

This reveals, to a growing extent, the process of change in the Middle East, the effects of which have become clearer in the past several years. Israel had particularly enjoyed the military and financial protection of the Western world in the past few decades. The Western world imposed few or no limitations on the 'local conflict existing between Israel and the Arabs when it was in its interest to use Israel to threaten nationalist Arab governments, even militarily'.[68] The old opposition between the industrial countries of the West and the Arab nations of the Middle East no longer exists in its old form. Today, a new political strategy is needed in order to secure access to raw materials in those countries, but also to ensure the flow of Arab capital to the West and to avoid endangering the already unstable world currency system and the capitalistic world market. Israel — inasmuch as it was able to gain support from the West, profited from the expansion of the conflict which originally had only been between the Zionists and Palestinians into an opposition between the Western and the Arab states and occasionally even into a conflict between East and West — has now more or less lost its function as protector of Western interests in the Middle East. As Western interests in the Middle East cannot be safeguarded by military means alone, the new political strategy of the West is aimed at integrating the Arab states, rich in raw materials, into the world economic system. Thus, Israel's military superiority no longer has any economic function. On the contrary: in the long run, the Israeli settlement policy and occupation will endanger Western interests in the Middle East, and will cause the United States and the Common Market countries to increase their pressure on Israel in the future.[69]

Peace Out of Sight: The Situation in the Occupied Territories

The peace agreement between Israel and Egypt met unanimous rejection by all political groups and their representatives in the occupied territories. There were demonstrations and a general strike which lasted several days.[70] All political organizations in the West Bank were in agreement as seldom before and announced their opposition to the 'autonomy' solution which Israel sought.

The National Guidance Committee
Following the Camp David accords, the National Guidance Committee (N.G.C.) was founded on 1 October 1978 in Beit Hanina, a suburb of East Jerusalem, and has proved to be of special importance for the co-ordination of all political activities in the occupied territories. The first year after its

founding, the N.G.C. was able to build upon an already existing organizational structure and to gain political influence and importance which has exceeded, by far, that of all other organizations and alliances. The aim of this committee has been to co-ordinate and mobilize the opposition of the Palestinian population in the occupied territories. The committee calls strikes and demonstrations, publishes statements on its positions and holds meetings. Today, there are local guidance committees modelled on the N.G.C. in all the larger cities in the West Bank and Gaza Strip, and these co-ordinate local activities. The alliance represented by the N.G.C. goes beyond the political spectrum of the Palestinian National Front.[71] Nevertheless, the N.G.C. was not founded because of any failure on the part of the P.N.F., but rather as a result of the new situation following Camp David and the Egyptian-Israeli separate agreement.

Two developments created the conditions under which the N.G.C. emerged from the National Front. The first was that Anwar Sadat's trip to Jerusalem, the Camp David conference and the Israeli-Egyptian peace treaty offered the Palestinians no prospects for their taking part in the negotiating process. In the autumn of 1978 and the following spring, Palestinian leaders were therefore concerned, above all, with spreading the opposition to the American-Israeli-Egyptian initiative to an international level and to broaden the base in its own ranks as much as possible. One element of this policy was the resumption of contacts between the P.L.O. and Jordan — which had been interrupted since Black September in 1970 — within the framework of the Arab Rejection Front. The policy of *rapprochement*, which was pursued in the P.L.O. especially by the Fatah, had a temporary climax in the establishment of a joint Palestinian-Jordanian Committee for the Occupied Territories. The new co-operation between the P.L.O. and Jordan was reflected in the occupied territories by discussions on this issue in the National Front. This new Fatah line was not supported by all of the other organizations, because it meant an upgrading of the position of the followers of King Hussein, who had been forced to lead a shadow existence ever since the elections in April 1976.

The second development was the shift in the balance of power and the points of crystallization in the political life in the occupied territories. The left, which at that time, consisted primarily of the Popular Democratic Front (P.D.F.L.P.) and the Communist Party (the Popular Front came later) had centred their activities on political involvement in trade unions, universities, professional associations, charity organizations and other associations. This policy had also become evident in the increasing number of activities in the villages. Whereas the strongholds of the National Front had been situated in the cities, where the P.N.F. had campaigned in the 1976 elections with its own slates, the organizations of the left had tried to gain influence in the villages by founding associations and expanding the nationalist organizations. Their aim was to lessen the influence of traditional structures, which had continued to be quite extensive in rural areas. The politicizing of the village population had definitely increased as time went on.[72] A major reason for this was the growing frequency of abuse and provocation directed at villagers by the Gush Emunim[73] and the growing wave of land expropriations by the military government.

The National Front had worked particularly within the framework of the city administrations. The expanding of political activities to grass-root organizations provided them, and the organizations which backed them up, with greater influence in the political structure of the left.

The founding of the National Guidance Committee was a reaction to these new circumstances — the differences in opinion in the National Front concerning co-operation with Jordan and the new balance of power in the political life of the occupied territories.

Whereas the P.N.F. represented an alliance of various political groupings, the composition of the committee was based on different principles. The 22 members of the N.G.C. were chosen according to regional and political considerations. Today, in their entirety, they represent large segments of Palestinian society in the West Bank and Gaza Strip. Criteria for belonging to the N.G.C. is not so much membership in a political organization as representation of a segment of Palestinian society (for instance, city or village population, interest groups and other groups in the society).

In the committee are: two representatives delegated by the trade unions; the nine mayors of the West Bank who had all been elected from the National Front slates — the most prominent among them being Bassam Shak'a from Nablus, Karim Khalaf of Ramallah and the mayor of Hebron, Fahad Qawasmeh, deported in May 1980; the editors-in-chief of the daily paper, *Al-Fajr*, (supportive of the Fatah) and the Communist weekly paper, *Al-Tali'ah*, representatives of the Palestinian press in the occupied territories; and representatives from the students. The groups mentioned above were already working together in the National Front and are joined in the N.G.C. by the following representatives of the traditional Palestinian associations: the bar association, the chambers of commerce, charity and women's organizations and the Muslim council, each designating one representative. The final two members of the N.G.C. are from the Gaza Strip: the president of the Red Crescent and the chairman of the medical association.[74] This composition accounts for the influence and importance of the committee — in the occupied territories as well as externally, when dealing with the P.L.O. and the Arab states.

> **'We are Asking for our Rights!'**
> Interview with Fahad Qawasmeh, mayor of Hebron (deported on 3 May 1980, by the military government):
>
> *Q.* Mr Qawasmeh, could you describe the position of the N.G.C. in more detail? Would you accept a Palestinian state in the West Bank and Gaza Strip alongside Israel?
> *A.* The problem is not where the borders of a Palestinian

state will be some day. The point is that the world and Israel must acknowledge our rights, our right to self-determination and our right to establish an independent Palestinian state – our right to have our own flag, the right to our own identity. As far as the borders are concerned, that is a decision which will have to be reached by the Palestinians later. But it must be acknowledged beforehand that the Palestinians have rights.

Q. Should the rights of the Palestinians be recognized, could you imagine the Palestinians as being open to co-existence and being able to accept a Palestinian state alongside Israel?

A. As I've already said, that isn't the problem right now. At the moment, there are no negotiations. Mr Begin has made it clear that he will never accept a Palestinian state. The problem is whether or not Israel is prepared to acknowledge our rights. The Security Council has recognized these rights; the United Nationas and most countries in the world have done so. But the U.S. and Israel refuse to acknowledge these rights. So the ball is not in the Palestinian court, it's in Israel's.

Israel refuses to acknowledge Palestinian rights, it refuses to call a halt to settlement activity, it refuses to carry out the U.N. resolutions. It is against a Palestinian state. What is there to negotiate, what should we talk about with Israel? About schools, hospitals, food? Those aren't our problems; those aren't our demands. We're asking for our rights!

Q. Mr Qawasmeh, the Communists from the West Bank were a major force within the National Front. What role do they play in the N.G.C.?

A. Yes, they are represented in the N.G.C.; they take part just like every other party. The policy of the N.G.C. is to link all the groups which are against the 'autonomy' plan.

Q. To clarify the question: in several articles in their underground paper, *Al-Watan*, and in posters in the West Bank, the Communist organization requested the P.L.O. among other things, to accept a Palestinian state alongside Israel. Do the Communists promote this position in the N.G.C. too? For instance, by way of a statement acknowledging the right of the Jews to their own state?

A. No, we aren't discussing this question now, because it's a matter for the P.L.O. And, as I told you before, this point is not on the agenda at the moment, it's not our immediate problem. Why should we guarnatee this right to Israel today, when at the same time, it denies us the same right, when they continue to build settlements and deny us our own state? As long as they don't change their strategy and methods, no one can demand that we recognize Israel without demanding that Israel recognize the rights of the Palestinians.

> *Q.* What role do you accord Jordan? There are rumours that the N.G.C. criticizes the P.L.O.'s *rapprochement* with Jordan.
> *A.* That's not correct. We must try to gain the support of all countries, in particular the Arab ones; especially from our neighbours.
> *Q.* Does that mean you would agree to Jordan's participation in future negotiations?
> *A,* No, that's not what I meant. There's a difference between relations with a country and negotiations in our name. We deny anyone the right to represent us. That right belongs solely to the P.L.O.
>
> Source: Interview by the authors in Geneva in May 1980, printed in the Berlin *Tageszeitung*, 12 June 1980

The founding of the N.G.C. broadened the base of the National Front alliance. As the most important member organization of the P.L.O., Fatah has a great amount of influence in the committee. Since leftist groups often head the social organizations in the occupied territories, and it is these

Ma'aleh Adumim settlement on the Jerusalem Jericho road, planned to house 10,000 Jewish settlers

organizations which send representatives to the N.G.C. leftist forces also play a significant role. Their representatives (such as Ibrahim Dakak, chairman of the engineers' union, or Bashir Barghouti, the publisher of the Communist weekly newspaper, *Al-Tali'ah*, and the chairman of the Red Crescent in the Gaza Strip, Dr Haider Abdel Shafi) are considered to be especially influential and initiate many of the N.G.C.'s activities.[75] For example, Ibrahim Dakak, a Communist, is called the 'mayor or mayors' because of his influence.[76]

The fact that the N.G.C. pursues an independent policy is due in particular to the influence of leftist forces. It has made clear again and again that the P.L.O. is the sole legitimate representative of the Palestinian people and acknowledges its leadership role without reservation. Nevertheless, the committee has proved repeatedly that, in local disputes with the occupying authorities, it prefers to rely on its own assessment of the situation than on the advice of the distant P.L.O.'s Department of the Occupied Homeland.[77] This became especially clear during the so-called Shak'a affair in November/December 1979, when the mayor of Nablus was threatened with deportation from the West Bank. Whereas the P.L.O., along with Jordan and conservative circles,[78] spoke out against the collective resignation of the mayors in the occupied territories, the N.G.C. saw in this the step which would lead to the release of the prominent mayor and pushed through the collective resignation.[79] It was not until much later that the P.L.O. conceded and advised the conservative mayors, who, in their characteristic manner, were waiting for a recommendation by the P.L.O., to follow the strategy decided upon by the N.G.C.

Part of the P.L.O., but not *the* P.L.O.
Interview with Fahad Qawasmeh, mayor of Hebron:

Q. Can you describe the relationship of the N.G.C. to the P.L.O.?
A. Let's put it this way, the N.G.C. is an arm of the P.L.O. in our region. The committee considers itself to be part of the P.L.O., but it does not represent the P.L.O. in the occupied territories.
Q. Mr Qawasmeh, Israel is trying to classify the N.G.C. in the same group as the Rejection Front within the P.L.O. Is such a classification correct?
A. No, that's not correct. The vast majority of N.G.C. members want a genuine peace, a just peace. We want an end to the settlements and an end to the occupation. But the Israelis don't want to see moderates, they want to see extremists — because they want to show the world that the Palestinians are extremists. that they want to destroy Israel and will do this and that. Whenever we talk to military personnel in the occupied territories, they try to accuse us of such things in order to destroy us. They

> only want to see and show Palestinians extremists but they won't succeed. Together with our people, we will continue to demand a genuine and just peace.
>
> Source: Interview by the authors in Geneva in May 1980, printed in the Berlin *Tageszeitung*, 12 June 1980.

Ever since the *rapprochement* between the P.L.O. and Jordan, the difference between the supporters of King Hussein and those of the Fatah have lost significance in the occupied territories. Today, Fatah representatives in the West Bank often join with pro-Jordanian forces, although the latter are not represented in the N.G.C. and have been the traditional opponents of the national P.N.F. alliance. Notables, such as Elias Freij, and Rashed A-Shawa, the mayors of Bethlehem and Gaza respectively, who, as so-called 'moderate forces', had consistently conceded the leadership role to the P.L.O. in the past few years, re-emphasized even more clearly than before the importance of Jordan in a peace process. The co-operation between the P.L.O. and the Hashemite throne was also instrumental in strengthening the position of these forces.

> **Jordan and the P.L.O.**
> Interview with the mayor of Bethlehem, Elias Freij:
>
> *Q.* You are regarded by many as pro-Jordanian. What would be Jordan's role in the efforts to find a solution to the Palestinian problem?
> *A.* First of all it must be made clear that terms such as 'pro-Jordanian' are obsolete. Today there is no difference between Jordan and the P.L.O., between King Hussein and Yasser Arafat, where the way to a solution to the conflict in our region is concerned. The same applies to the occupied territories. We are all united in our basic demands for a Palestinian state under P.L.O. leadership, removal of the settlements, etc. As to the form of the future regime, I think that a referendum should be held among the Palestinians on the form of the link with Jordan once the Palestinian state is established. I am for a confederation between the two states in which the independence of each would be preserved. Jordan will certainly have an important role to play in the efforts to solve the Palestinian problem because more than half its population is composed of Palestinians.
>
> Source: *New Outlook*, January/February 1980

After years in which the unity of the nationalist forces was the top priority, the P.L.O. (Fatah)-Jordan coalition had created a new basis for political discussion in the occupied territories. Generally, leftist organizations have criticized co-operation with Amman, even though the Communist Party has come to terms with the situation for tactical reasons. The criticism by their speakers in the N.G.C. is directed primarily at the policy of the Joint Committee for the Occupied Territories, through which, under Palestinian-Jordanian direction, money for the support of the population of the occupied territories is channelled into the West Bank and the Gaza Strip. The Joint Committee administers a $150 million fund which was placed at its disposal by Arab governments. In practice, it functions as a rival to the N.G.C.[80] A portion of the money does benefit the city administrations, but part is also allocated to individual projects. The criteria for allocation usually depend on the recipient's political connection with the Palestinian and Jordanian administrators of the fund. For this reason, the Joint Committee is becoming a tool for strengthening the influence of the Fatah and Jordan in the occupied territories. When the N.G.C. requested that the administration of the monies be turned over to it, the conflict came out into the open. The subsequent refusal of the Joint Committee led to heated protests by the N.G.C. The Joint Committee was accused of 'underestimating the significance of the national organizations within the occupied territories'.[81] 'For', said Mohammed Milhem, mayor of Hahul, who was deported in May 1980, 'it is those institutions which can judge the true needs of the occupied territories better than any other.'[82]

The left had also to realize that they themselves are occasionally a direct target of the coalition between Fatah supporters and pro-Jordanian forces. The conservative circles in the occupied territories try to diminish the influence of leftist forces in the committee by demanding, for instance, that the N.G.C. be stacked with representatives of their political persuasion. For example, the East Jerusalem daily paper, *Al-Kuds*, started a campaign in March 1980 against the leftist forces, in which it criticized the 'politicizing of the patriotic organizations' in a series of articles.[83] The leftist newspapers, *Al-Tali'ah* and *A-Sha'ab*, replied 'that the attacks from the right were aimed at transferring the leadership to those who are willing to implement a solution *à la* Sadat, Begin and Carter', and that those 'who claim that they do not belong to any group are in reality collaborators'.[84]

Therefore, since the Camp David agreements, the forming of the Rejection Front and the reconciliation between the Fatah and Hussein, the disagreements in the occupied territories were no longer between the pro-Jordan camp and the supporters of the P.L.O. but rather between a progressive and a conservative camp. These discussions bring the representatives from Fatah and the traditional leaders, who had once been considered to be pro-Jordan, closer together. As seen from the outside, this widened the front against Camp David even further and also expanded the circle of those who today advocate the participation of the P.L.O. in a peace settlement.

The heightening of tensions in the occupied territories during 1980 did make the work of the N.G.C. more difficult but it could not destroy it. Despite the bomb assaults on Bassam Shak'a and Karim Khalaf, despite the deportation of Fahad Qawasmeh and Mohammed Milhem, despite the restriction on the freedom of movement for the mayors and the ban on their meetings and on press conferences, and despite constant warnings by the military government, the N.G.C. is still the organ which plans, announces and co-ordinates the political activities in the occupied territories and therefore which enjoys broad support and a great amount of trust from the population.

> **'Let us Revive the Anniversary of the Land Day'**
> **(30 March 1981): Leaflet of the N.G.C.**
> ... The fifth anniversary of the Land Day — a symbol of the hold our people have on their land and their rights, and a symbol of their willingness to make sacrifices — comes at a time in which Israeli authorities are escalating their campaign to confiscate Arab land in order to establish settlements there. Up to now, this escalation has been a standard result of the practices of various Israeli governments. It serves the purpose of securing Zionist rule over Arab land and, moreover, of emptying these areas of their esidents and landowners by disregarding their most basic rights.
>
> This campaign is intended to establish a *fait accompli* in the conquered territories, thus preventing the establishment of an independent national Palestinian state. The American-Israeli-Egyptian Camp David agreements and the bilateral accords between Egypt and Israel have given Israel the unique opportunity to continue its oppression of the Arab people by means of a policy of stealing and confiscating land, of establishing settlements and making assassination attempts on national figures as well as by means of restriction of freedoms and the attempt to destroy the academic institutions and unions. All of these methods, as well as others which try to destroy the will of the people with a firm hand have been unsuccessful. The people have continued their struggle and resistance against the conqueror in order to gain their national independence and to establish their own independent state led by the P.L.O., their sole, legitimate representative. This struggle is becoming more and more intense.
>
> Let us make this day an occasion to renew and confirm our ties to our holy land. Let us hold mass events: congresses and meetings in which we reject the settlement policy. Let us make this day a day of work in order to regain and cultivate every patch of earth in our land, where every inch of soil is threatened by the settlement policy. Let us establish a

> committee for the protection of the land in every town and in every village in order to organize the defence of our people and their land. And let us use this day to strengthen our hold on the P.L.O. as the sole, legitimate representative of out people and let us insist on our right to self-determination and to establish a national state under the leadership of the P.L.O.
>
> Source: National Guidance Committee, 27 March 1981.

Polarization

The year 1980 was characterized by a growing polarization in the occupied territories as well as in Israel. In the West Bank, the conflict between the Palestinian population and the occupying authority took on, to some extent, the proportions of a civil war. In view of the obvious failure of all negotiations, bitterness is growing among the Palestinians. In the eyes of many observers, the Palestinian attack on six Jewish seminarians in Hebron[85] — the first in a long time for which the P.L.O. accepted responsibility — and the bombing attacks of mayor Shak'a of Nablus and mayor Khalaf of Ramallah by Jewish extremists[86] have signalled a new phase in the struggle.[87]

The situation was especially aggravated by provocative actions of the Gush Emunim settlement group and the Jewish militant extremist organization, Kakh, which pursue more and more openly a strategy of confrontation in the occupied territories in order to encourage the Palestinians to leave the country and to make it clear to the whole world that Jews and Arabs cannot live together peacefully.[88] Vandalism of Palestinian institutions and private property as well as the terrorizing of entire villages and refugee camps by armed troops — such actions are part of the programme of these extremist organizations.[89]

In no way does the military government merely rely on the initiative of Jewish settlers to take these actions; it has increased its own repressive measures against the population. Repression of all kinds, intended to crush the growing Palestinian opposition, and the brutal oppression with which the military government is attempting to establish 'security' in the occupied territories has become so widespread that even soldiers and officers have felt the need to inform the public about the daily violation of human rights.[90] While the brutality of the measures of the Israeli military government continues, there is a horrifying lack of response to the provocative acts of violence by Jewish extremists.

Menachem Begin's administration completely lost its political freedom of movement when the the more moderate forces left the coalition and the parliamentary survival of his government depended solely on the support of the right-wing parties. Under pressure from the extreme right and following the resignation of Foreign Minister Moshe Dayan, who was usually labelled a moderate, Begin was only able to appoint one man, Yihak Shamir, who has rejected the Camp David agreements.

Up to this time, Begin has been unable to find a successor for Defence Minister Weizman (another representative of the 'moderate' wing in the coalition, who also resigned) because the office was claimed by right-wing Minister of Agriculture Sharon,[91] of whom even one of his own government colleagues maintained: 'Should General Sharon ever come to power, he would dissolve parliament and declare a military dictatorship, maybe even set up camps for political prisoners.'[92] This process of decay in the Israeli government was hidden, with great effort, by a demonstration of toughness and strength towards the Egyptian negotiators as well as towards the Palestinian population in the occupied territories.

The escalation of violence in the West Bank and Gaza Strip corresponds to a political polarization in Israel. The Israeli public is increasingly critical of government policy,[93] and warnings on the negative effects of the occupation policy on Israeli society are becoming loud.

'The reality,' stated the Israeli daily paper, *Ha'aretz*, in an editorial, 'which we cannot change through words, settlements or legal arguments, is that in the West Bank and Gaza Strip, one nation is trying to rule another against its will.'[94] A representative of the social democratic Labour Party said:

> Opposition creates repression, and repression strengthens the opposition, which, in turn, increases the repression. And one fine day we Israelis are going to look in the mirror and will not be able to bear the hideous and repulsive face reflected there. Not only do we want to free the Palestinians from the military occupation, but we also want to free ourselves from its consequences.[95]

Whether or not Begin's critics are willing and able fundamentally to change this reality remains to be seen.

'The Labour Party has a Fundamentally Different Philosophy'
Interview with Abba Eban of the Israeli Labour Party. Eban was Minister of Foreign Affairs in the government of Golda Meir. He was the candidate for this office in the 1981 election team of Shimon Peres.

Q. Mr Eban, today there are more than 100 Israeli settlements in the occupied West Bank. How will the Labour Party deal with this fact supposing it is in power after the elections in June 1981?
A. The most important question is not the question of the settlements but the political future of the area itself. It is the political determination that will decide the future of the settlements and it is not the settlements that will decide the political future. Here the Labour Party has a diametrically contrary

policy and philosophy to that of the Likud. The Likud regards the whole area and all the population as a part of Eretz Israel. We regard them as a separate people from whom we should part, if there is a peace settlement. In other words: we base our policy on the idea of partition. It is not the partition that existed before the Six Day War, but the principle that there are two peoples in the area between the Jordan River and the Mediterranean. Therefore there cannot be a unitary political structure. We express this in the principle that we enunciate in our conference resolutions that we do not want to exercise permanent Israeli rule over the million and a quarter Arabs in the West Bank and Gaza. We would like them to join with the rest of the Palestinians on the other side of the Jordan in a Palestine-Jordanian state. Since we do not regard these areas as being permanently a part of Israel we therefore have a different policy on settlements. The Labour Party's policy is: why put settlements in places which you do not believe will be a permanent part of Israel, except those security measures one might want to take for temporary reasons? Therefore we are not impressed by Mr Sharon's policy. In my opinion it does not create a stable situation. After all there was a much bigger Israeli settlement policy in Sinai, Sharm el Sheikh and in Yamit. But when there was a political decision ... what happened? In other words: he is wrong in believing the creation of physical facts necessarily determines the political future. Yamit was one of the greatest ventures. It was prosperous, it was solid, people had homes, there was a tremendous trade. And yet it was not politically realistic to stay there, and therefore it's being dispersed.

The tragedy of Sharon's policy is that he is investing a lot of effort and emotion in places where there is no guarantee whatever of permanence. That is the first point. The second point is that I don't accept the idea that there has been a fundamental change. After 14 years of Israeli possession of the area, we end up with a situation in which, if we take the West Bank and Gaza together, there are 1.2 million Arabs and 20,000 Israelis. There isn't any way of changing the Arab predominance in the area concerned. If the result of four years of Likud was that the Israelis in the area were going up from 12,000 to 20,000 ... I wouldn't call that a historic change in the social composition of the area. So what will have to be decided in June is between these two philosophies. Are we going to try to impose ourselves permanently on another people or are we prepared to reach a compromise which will enable most of them to live within the Arab world. Once we make a decision on the political future the settlement question is subsidiary.

Q. Does this mean, you are in favour of eventually dismantling the settlements?

A. I must tell you this: we don't see any reason why there cannot be Israeli villages on that side, because there are so many Arab villages in Israel. I don't accept the idea that if a certain territory is outside of Israel there cannot be any Israelis there. I reject the idea that the removal of settlements is inevitable, if there is peace. If there isn't peace, then there is nothing to talk about. If there is peace we should get used to the idea of being more in contact with each other.

Q. But it certainly depends on the status these Israeli settlements would have in that case. For example whether the Arab 'autonomous authority' would be in charge of them or whether they would claim a kind of extra-territorial status . . . .

A. It depends on the decision, on the agreement. For example: The Likud had peace negotiations with Egypt. The Israeli settlements were a subject for negotiation. If they are a subject for negotiation there then they cannot be excluded from the negotiations on this side. I hope that we will succeed more in the negotiations than the Likud did.

Q. What do you mean by 'security measures'? The party's resolutions talk about a 'territorial compromise'.

A. Our opening position is something very much like the Allon Plan, which excludes from Israel the populated areas and takes care of the boundary situation in the unpopulated areas, especially in the Jordan Valley. But, honestly, what happens will be the results of negotiations. But the important part of the idea is that it does not include the populated Arab areas in Israel. And that, of course, is a completely different concept of Israel than the Likud concept. They put the stress on geographical unity. And we put our stress on the Jewish and democratic nature of Israel.

Q. As a party to the negotiations you are thinking of Jordan. Why should King Hussein join the talks?

A. I think if they really believe that we would be willing to give up our jurisdiction over the populated areas they will find it very hard to stay out. Because they have an opportunity of being the instrument for freeing an Arab population from Israeli rule. To have the opportunity and not to use it would be a very serious matter. If Jordan wants to be responsible for the maintenance of Israeli rule, that will be very surprising. So the Arab world sometime in 1981 will decide: do they want to bring these people and their territories into the Arab world? If so, you cannot avoid the Palestinian-Jordanian integrality. Or is it so important to them not to do this? Then they are

> responsible for the status quo. They have never really faced that situation. The Likud doesn't create that situation, because the Likud doesn't offer them the option of entering the Arab world.
>
> *Q.* How do you consider the attitude of the West Bank and Gaza Palestinians towards Jordan? Usually they tend to speak out in favour of the P.L.O. rather than in favour of King Hussein.
>
> *A.* I would say this: If they have a choice between three possibilities: to stay under Israeli rule, to come into a Jordanian framework or to have a separate state, they prefer a separate state. If, however, the choice is to stay under Israeli rule or to come under Arab rule with Jordan, they will prefer Arab rule with Jordan. So everything depends on how the options appear. And those two are the only options. The option of a P.L.O. state doesn't exist because Israel is against it. That means it doesn't exist.
>
> Source: Interview by the authors in Herzliya Pituach, Israel, 9 April 1981.

Notes

1. Cf. *Safran 1978*, p. 506 ff. and *Hollstein 1977*, p. 305 ff.
2. *MERIP Reports*, No. 64, February 1978, p. 10.
3. *The New York Times*, 3 October 1977.
4. *The Washington Post*, 8 October 1977.
5. *Yediot Aharonot* and *Al Hamishmar*, 17 November 1977.
6. *Ibid.*
7. *Davar*, 14 November 1977.
8. *Yediot Aharonot*, 20 November 1977.
9. *Ibid.*
10. Cf. speech in *The Jerusalem Post*, 20 November 1977.
11. *Davar*, 19 December 1977.
12. *Zo Haderekh*, 23 November 1977.
13. *Al Hamishmar*, 9 December 1977; *Davar*, 12 December 1977; *Yediot Aharonot*, 19 December 1977.
14. Quoted from the pamphlet 'Self Rule', Israel Information Centre, Jerusalem, 1978.
15. *The New York Times*, 30 December 1977.
16. *The Jerusalem Post*, 1 January 1978.
17. *Al Hamishmar*, 21 December 1977.
18. *The Jerusalem Post*, 1 January 1978.
19. *Yediot Aharonot*, 19 December 1977.
20. *Yediot Aharonot* and *Al Hamishmar*, 20 December 1977.

21. *The Guardian Weekly*, 3 January 1978.
22. *The New York Times*, 5 January 1978.
23. *Yediot Aharonot*, 16/19 March 1978; *Davar*, 17/19/21/23 March 1978.
24. *International Herald Tribune*, 4 January 1978; *Le Monde*, 5 January 1978.
25. *New Outlook*, November/December 1978.
26. Cf. *Palestine – P.L.O. Information Bulletin*, 15/30 November 1978.
27. Cf. the government's statement from 19 September 1978, *Middle East International*, October 1978.
28. *Palestine – P.L.O. Information Bulletin*, 30 September 1978.
29. Begin on Israeli television on 18 September 1978, quoted from *Israel & Palestine*, No. 70, October 1978.
30. *New Outlook*, November/December 1978, p. 34.
31. *Ibid.*
32. *Ma'ariv*, 3 November 1978.
33. *Ha'aretz*, 27 September 1978.
34. *Ma'ariv*, 8 December 1978.
35. 'Carter's Long Middle East Ordeal', *New York Times Magazine*, 15 January 1978.
36. *Brookings Report 1975*.
37. Cf *Brzezinski 1974–75*.
38. *Brookings Report 1975*, p. 5.
39. *Ibid.*, p. 7.
40. *Ibid.*
41. *Ibid.*, p. 21.
42. *Ibid.*, p. 22.
43. *Ibid.*, p. 10.
44. *Ibid.*, p. 9.
45. *Ibid.*, p. 11.
46. *Ibid.*, p. 10.
47. *Ibid.*, p. 13.
48. *Brzezinski 1974–75*.
49. *The Jerusalem Post*, 17 October 1978; *Ha'aretz.*, 25 September 1978; *Davar*, 8 November 1978.
50. Interview by the authors, 10 September 1978.
51. Cf. Uri Avnery in *Ha'olam Hazeh*, 21 October 1978; Danny Rubinstein in *Davar*, 5 October 1978; Maxim Ghilan in *Israel & Palestine*, No. 70, October 1978, p. 2; Harold Beely in *Middle East International*, No. 89, November 1978.
52. *New Outlook*, October 1978.
53. *Al Hamishmar*, 19 December 1978.
54. *Davar*, 29 November 1978.
55. *Ma'ariv*, 24 November 1978.
56. *Le Monde diplomatique*, January 1979.
57. *Ma'ariv*, 1 November 1978.
58. *Israleft*, No. 138, 1 December 1978; cf. Rifkin 1979, p. 21 ff., and *3. Welt Magazin*, January/February 1979, p. 50.
59. *New Outlook*, July/August 1979, p. 51.
60. *Ibid.*, p. 53.
61. Cf. *Spiegel*, 26 March 1979, No. 13/79.

62. Cf. *Blätter des iz3w*, No. 77, May 1979, p. 8; *Süddeutsche Zeitung*, 28 April 1979.
63. Cf. *Tages-Anzeiger*, 30 April 1979; *Handelsblatt*, 17 March and 9 May 1979; *Spiegel*, 9 April 1979, No. 15/79; *Le Monde*, 3 April 1979.
64. Cf. *Palestine – P.L.O. Bulletin*, 16–31 March 1979.
65. Cf. *Frankfurter Rundschau*, 31 July 1980; *Spiegel*, 28 July 1980; *Süddeutsche Zeitung*, 23 July 1980.
66. *Frankfurter Rundschau*, 4 August 1980.
67. *Frankfurter Rundschau*, 31 July 1980.
68. *Diner 1980 (a)*, p. 171.
69. Cf. for detail *Diner 1980 (a)*, p. 169 ff.
70. Cf. *Neue Zürcher Zeitung*, 28 March 1979; *Palästina Bulletin*, 5 April 1979.
71. Also see Chapter 6.
72. Also see Chapter 5.
73. Cf. for details on the abuse, e.g. the statement by Mohammed Milhem (the mayor of Halhul who had been deported) before the U.N. Special Committee in May 1980, U.N. Doc. A/AC. 145/Rt 305 and 306.
74. Cf. the complete list of N.G.C. members and their functions, *Le Monde diplomatique*, June 1980.
75. Cf. *Middle East International*, 9 May 1980.
76. *Ibid.*
77. Cf. *Le Monde diplomatique*, op. cit.
78. Cf. *New Outlook*, January/February 1980; *Middle East International*, op. cit.
79. Cf. *Al Hamishmar*, 25 January 1980.
80. Cf. *Le Monde diplomatique*, op. cit.; *Israel & Palestine*, No. 79, March 1980.
81. *Al-Watan* (Kuwait), 7 March 1980.
82. *Ibid.*
83. Cf. *Al-Kuds*, 4 March 1980.
84. *Al-Scha'ab*, 13 March 1980.
85. Also see Chapter 2.
86. *Frankfurter Rundschau*, 2 June 1980.
87. Cf. e.g. Brumlik, *Links*, June 1980, p. 6.
88. Cf. e.g. *Le Monde diplomatique*, December 1979; *Yediot Aharonot*, 2 November 1979; *The Jerusalem Post*, 5 May 1980; for details see also Chapter 2.
89. Cf. *Al Hamishmar*, 13 June 1980; *Ha'aretz*, 16 and 18 June 1980.
90. Brutal and humiliating arbitrary measures taken by the army against the Palestinian population are described by Israeli soldiers and officers in a letter to the Knesset Deputy (Sheli) Uri Avnery, *Middle East Inter- atio national*, 6 June 1980; also cf. *Middle East International*, 23 May 1980; Amnon Kapeliouk, *New Outlook*, June/July 1980, p. 14 ff.
91. For his role of representative of an expansive settlement policy see also Chapter 2. Sharon, of course, became Defence Minister.
92. *Frankfurter Rundschau*, 10 and 16 June, 1980.
93. Cf. e.g. *Israleft*, No. 171, 1 July 1980 and *New Outlook*, June/July 1980, with a selection of critical comments from the Israeli press.
94. *Ha'aretz*, 28 April 1980.
95. M. Yossi, *Ha'aretz*, 30 October 1979; cf. Amos Kenan in *Yediot Aharonot*, 2 May 1980, who labelled Gush Emunim 'Israel's worst enemy'.

8. Dream and Reality: An Independent Palestinian State alongside Israel

> **Palestinians Without a Country**
>
> We are better understood when we explain that what every Palestinian wants above all is a place to turn to as a haven, however small it may be, a consulate to which he can turn when he feels injured or threatened. Would we be less worthy citizens of one of the Gulf Emirates? Most of the Arab states refuse to grant citizenship to the Palestinians. So be it. We do not complain. They do us a service, perhaps unknowingly. For thereby they contribute towards preserving our authenticity and strengthening our determination to regain our homeland. The day we succeed in instituting our own state in the liberated territories of the West Bank and Gaza we shall begin to issue our own identity papers. It is quite possible that many Palestinians may, for reasons of practical convenience, decide not to live in the new state. But does that really matter? They will be able to live in the Arab state of their choice without complexes of anxieties. At last they will be treated as equals with all those who have passports to display. And if ever they should feel threatened, for one reason or another, they will always have the possibility of packing their bags and going back to Palestine where they do not run the risk of being treated like outcasts.
>
> Source: Abu Iyad, 'Palestinians without a Country', *New Outlook*, January/February 1979, p. 55.
>
> NB: Abu Iyad, alias Salah Khalaf, is a charter member of the Fatah and is on its central committee. He is also head of the intelligence service of the P.L.O.

The idea of dividing Palestine into Jewish and Arab-Palestinian states is not new. In the 1930s, British investigation commissions proposed this division, which was to ease the conflict between the resident Palestinians and the Jewish immigrants.[1] The U.N. Partition Plan of 1947 proposed a modified version of these recommendations as a 'solution' to the Middle East conflict.[2]

Since the beginning of Jewish immigration into Palestine at the end of the last century, the Palestinians have protested against the division of their land. To them, all of the division plans had a single direction, namely to secure and legitimize the presence of the Zionist settlers in Palestine and to limit the right of residence of the native Palestinians.

The region has been through five wars. Israel is militarily the strongest state in the Middle East. Today 1.3 million Palestinians live in exile scattered throughout the entire world. Now for the first time, a proposal to divide Palestine has come from the Palestinians themselves; they seek the establishment of an independent Palestinian state alongside Israel in the West Bank and in the Gaza Strip. Instead of returning to Haifa or Jaffa, many Palestinians today would be willing to settle for a home in the West Bank or Gaza Strip in exchange for Israeli recognition of the new state and some form of compensation for the refugees of 1948.

Only by looking back at the long distance that has been covered can one understand the harsh disputes over the idea of a Palestinian state alongside Israel among the Palestinian people themselves and within their liberation movement. What people in the history of the world has given up half of its homeland virtually from one day to the next without resistance? The discussion on the West Bank/Gaza Strip state solution is by no means over. Today, the situations in which Palestinians live all over the world are so different that the proposed state in the West Bank and Gaza Strip cannot appear to all to be the only acceptable solution.

Homeland and Exile: The Background to Different Palestinian Concepts

> **'We Want to go Back!'**
> We completely refuse a state on the West Bank and Gaza. . . .
> We want to go back to the territories occupied in 1948. If we all die we will accept nothing less than to go back to our country. If the Palestine state is created in spite of us, we will continue fighting. If the West Bank people go back, what about us?
> Even if we were given land we would feel it was not our motherland. I will not leave the camp until I can move directly to Palestine.'
> — a woman refugee in Shlila refugee camp.
>
> Source: Rubin, 'What do the Palestinians Want?', *New Outlook*, March/April 1975, p. 50.

Dream and Reality

Approximately 600,000 Palestinians who fled from the territory which is now Israel at the end of the 1940s, are still living in refugee camps in Syria, Jordan, Lebanon, the West Bank and the Gaza Strip. For many of them, the West Bank/Gaza Strip state is not an acceptable solution. With the founding of such a state, even if the rights of repatriation and compensation for lost property were recognized by Israel (which the Palestinian advocates of the mini-state solution demand), these refugees would only be able to live in their homeland under Israeli sovereignty. They would have to choose between returning to their homeland or living in a Palestinian state.

For the refugees from the territories now occupied by Israel, it is a different story. For them a Palestinian state in the West Bank and Gaza Strip would make both their repatriation and the realization of their national aspirations possible.

Homeless – Jabalia Refugee Camp in the Gaza Strip

Important in this discussion are the Palestinians who fled Galilee and the coastal plain and then managed to work their way out of the refugee camps — a majority compared with those who are still under the care of the UNRWA. Today, one million refugees live in Arab states, approximately 30,000 in Europe, the U.S. and Latin America, and 380,000 in the West Bank and Gaza Strip. Many are sceptical about a Palestinian state in the West Bank and Gaza Strip. As a rule, their life is no longer as difficult as that of their countrymen in the camps but, nevertheless, they do not understand why they should simply give up their right to their homeland. 'Why should Israel exist on my rights? Why should they stop me going to Haifa and living on my land?'[3] asks a dentist who was born in Haifa and lives in Beirut. On the other hand, others could imagine living in the West Bank even though their homes had originally been in what is now Israel. A rich Palestinian businessman in Beirut, for example, paints an optimistic picture of the choices for a West Bank/Gaza Strip state: 'If the Arab countries gave 20% of their present war budgets we would be all right.' Besides, a new state would be an attraction for many educated Palestinians who live today in exile. 'Then we will export technology!'[4] continues the businessman.

By contrast, a small merchant who owns a shop in the Wahdat refugee camp in Amman voices yet a third opinion: 'If I don't return to my old town I see no point in going to the West Bank.' He comes from Zarnuka near Jaffa. 'Once the political issue has been resolved, then one has to live wherever one can make a living. If there is a mini-state, I shall wait and see what happens there. I have my shop now, but if the living is good in the new place, then perhaps I'll go.'[5]

For many Palestinians, a Palestinian state alongside Israel would be the solution to their worst problem; 1.2 million Palestinians in the occupied territories, 280,000 of whom are in refugee camps, would be liberated from Israeli occupation. Daily, they experience the occupation at first hand and see how the gradual annexation is changing their country. The longer this occupation lasts, the more difficult it will be to undo. 'Why should I sacrifice myself for the repatriation of others when I'm already settled here? I want to get rid of the occupation!' says an Arab farmer in Tubas.[6] The Palestinians in the occupied territories are the ones most directly confronted with the military strength of the Jewish state. It is not by chance that demands to orient the P.L.O. strategy to the reality of the situation and the military balance of power came from the West Bank.[7]

> **Realities**
> Interview with a Palestinian professor from the Bir Zeit University near Ramallah:
>
> *Q.* What is the major aim of the population of the occupied territories?

> *A.* We want to get rid of the Israeli occupation at any price. If this were done by establishing a Palestinian state on the West Bank and the Gaza Strip, or by any other means, we would agree to such a solution.
> *Q.* Do you think, that if a Palestinian state were set up, your problems would be solved?
> *A.* A Palestinian state in the West Bank and the Gaza Strip will not solve the problem for all Palestinians: it will, however, do so for some of them. For example, it will not solve the problem of our rights in historic Palestine.
> *Q.* What do you mean by 'our rights in historic Palestine'?
> *A.* I mean Palestine with its borders before 1948. We have rights in every part of it. I want to make it clear that this is not the same as the idea contained in the slogan 'the Arabization of Palestine'. Reality has taught us that this is not possible. There are three million Israeli Jews living there. They are here and they are part of this land, whether we like it or not.
>
> Source: Fouzi el'Asmar, 'Talking to Palestinians', *Middle East International*, March 1977, p. 22 ff.

The Position in the Occupied Territories

In the West Bank and the Gaza Strip, the concept of a Palestinian state alongside Israel had been discussed since the beginning of the 1970s. The first public allusion to the concept was in a publication of the Palestinian National Gathering, a group of East Jerusalem intellectuals. In the winter of 1970, they circulated their manifesto in the West Bank on which the Israeli press reported: 'The group called for the placing of the West Bank, East Jerusalem and the Gaza Strip under a temporary U.N. administration after the withdrawal of the Israeli forces as a preliminary step towards the realization of their "Palestinian idea".'[8] In addition, the Communist Party, above all other groups, spoke out repeatedly for an independent Palestinian state alongside Israel and clearly urged the P.L.O. to change its policy accordingly.[9]

When the alliance of the Palestinian National Front finally got off the ground before the 1976 elections,[10] the plan for a Palestinian state alongside Israel also appeared in the proclamation of this group, the most important political factor in the occupied territories. As shown by the 1976 elections, this position was based on widespread consensus in the occupied territories. It was expressed by the representatives of the P.N.F. in P.L.O. bodies as well as in statements on P.L.O. policy.

In such statements, the representatives of the occupied territories were clearly contradicting the position of the Rejection Front, which would not accept any negotiated solution, and were to be categorized with the 'moderates' within the P.L.O.

In the past few years, some members of the former pro-Jordan camp have also reconsidered their position toward the P.L.O. and on the issue of an independent Palestinian state. Previously, Elias Freij, mayor of Bethlehem, had been considered part of the camp which had opted for King Hussein and he had collaborated with the other mayors elected in 1976, reluctantly, if at all. Today, he often co-operates with his colleagues. A major reason for this change of attitude was the occupying authority's heightened repression of the Palestinian population and their mayors. In response to the detainment of Bassam Shak'a, mayor of Nablus, in November 1979 and the threat to deport him, Freij said:

> What did Shak'a say? He expressed himself as I or Karim Khalaf or the other mayors would. He, like us, supports a Palestinian state led by the P.L.O., the sole and legitimate representative of our people. He, like us, demands an end to the occupation and Israeli withdrawal from occupied territories including the Arab part of Jerusalem.[11]

Not only can the new alliance between the Hussein supporters and the forces of the P.N.F. be attributed to the fact that the two groups came together in solidarity against the occupying authority, but it also reflects how relations between the Jordanian King and the P.L.O. leadership have changed. In the autumn of 1978, Yasser Arafat met with the Hashemite monarch for the first time since Black September. In addition, Jordan and the P.L.O. set up a joint committee to co-ordinate activities in the West Bank.[12] The resumption of relations with King Hussein was intended to join the Jordanian regime to the front which was against the Camp David agreements and Israeli autonomy plans. It facilitated co-operation between the progressive and the pro-Jordan forces, without, however, eliminating the actual differences of opinion.

The pro-Jordan groups do support the demand for an end to the occupation, but do not unconditionally support the demand for an independent Palestinian state in the West Bank and the Gaza Strip. For many of them, any kind of ties between Jordan and the future state appear undesirable. In view of almost unanimous recognition of the P.L.O. by the population of the occupied territories, and widespread agreement on the demand for a Palestinian state in the West Bank and Gaza Strip, Elias Freij and other pro-Jordan forces would lose their political backing if they did not publicly affirm both.

The Communists and other leftist forces are, therefore, sceptical about co-operating with those sympathetic to Jordan. Political parties are still forbidden in Transjordan. Because of Jordan's connections to the western world, Hussein supporters expose themselves to suspicion that they would accept an 'American peace'.[13]

The most important political body within the occupied territories today

Dream and Reality

is the National Guidance Committee. The demand for an independent Palestinian state alongside Israel is also the centre of their political conceptions.

> **The Mood in the West Bank**
> Interviews with Bassam Shak'a, mayor of Nablus, Karim Khalaf, mayor of Ramallah, and Fahad Qawasmeh, mayor of Hebron until 1980.
>
> *Q.* What do you consider would be the necessary elements of a peace settlement in the Middle East? How could it be brought about?
> *Shak'a*: 1) We ask for the right to self-determination for the Palestinian people, i.e., the right of the Palestinians to an independent Palestinian state on Palestinian land on the West Bank, Gaza and Jerusalem; 2) We ask for the recognition of the P.L.O. as the sole representative of the Palestinian people; 3) We ask for the Palestinians' right to return to their homes; 4) Our future relationship with the Jewish people depends on how they will relate to us as a Palestinian people. Will they treat us as equals in a friendly, co-operative manner or will they deal with us as they do now — as second-class people subordinate to the Jewish people. Our goals must and can be achieved by our armed struggle and our diplomacy on the international level. The Zionists must come to understand that we are a people here to stay and that we are fighting for our basic human rights.
> *Khalaf*: Today, our demands are the following — and I've also explained them to the P.L.O.: Israel should withdraw from the territories occupied in 1967 including East Jerusalem. Then we would establish an independent state under our own direction. The refugee problem should be resolved according to the relevant U.N. resolution. We want self-determination. Self-determination means that our people decide whether or not they want to enter into a confederation with a particular state or even with Israel. It depends on what our people want. And without it, there will never be peace. The only other choice is war, not necessarily in the next three years, but in 20, 30 or 40 years. And who will be the loser? Not us, the Israelis. We, as Palestinians, have already lost everything. The next time, the Israelis will be the losers. The United States won't remain the way it is, and the positions of the European countries are also showing signs of change. Time is on our side, not Israel's. My advice to the Jews, if they want peace, is to convince their leaders to withdraw from the occupied territories, to recognize the P.L.O. and the rights of the Palestinians, and to allow the

> founding of a Palestinian state.
> *Qawasmeh*: There are two requirements: 1) To recognize the P.L.O. as the representative of the Palestinian people. 2) To recognize that the West Bank, Gaza and Jerusalem are Palestinian land. The peace process can only start if Israel accepts these two axioms. There are our minimum requirements for peace negotiations. The Israelis speak a lot about peace but do not really want it, and are preparing for war.
>
> So far we have had a lot of success on the first point. The great majority of the international community recognize the P.L.O. as our representative. We are also struggling on the military level, for war is the continuation of politics by other means. And it is only due to our military struggle that we have achieved our present political status as a Palestinian people.
>
> Sources: The statements by Shak'a and Qawasmeh were taken from the *Journal of Palestinian Studies*, No. 33, Fall 1979; the statements by Khalaf from an interview by the authors on 10 September 1978.

The Position of the P.L.O.

The concept of a separate Palestinian state alongside Israel is clearly supported in the West Bank; it is just as clear that this attitude is in no way directed against the P.L.O. The West Bank's policy cannot be separated from the P.L.O.'s for two reasons. On the one hand, the P.L.O. speaks for all Palestinians – including the Palestinians living in the territories occupied in 1967. On the other hand, the P.L.O. leadership has to take the opinions of the Palestinian population in the occupied territories into consideration, for approximately one third of all Palestinians live there, the largest intact Palestinian community in the only remaining part of Palestine that has preserved its Arab-Palestinian nature.

Not only is this numerically the most important sector within the Palestinian community, it also represents the majority of those for whom an end to the occupation appears to be the most pressing. In its decision-making, the P.L.O. has to take into consideration the international balance of power, to which it reacts very sensitively, as well as the opinions of the Palestinian citizens in exile and those in the occupied territories. With this in mind, the concept of an independent Palestinian state alongside Israel has been discussed in the P.L.O. and has been generally accepted in the past few years.

At the Twelfth National Council which took place in Cairo in June 1974, the P.L.O. decided in its Ten Point Programme to establish a national authority in 'every part of Palestinian territory that is liberated' instead of waiting for the 'total liberation of all occupied Palestine'.[14] This formu-

Dream and Reality

lation, which paved the way for the establishment of an independent Palestinian state, was fiercely debated by the Fatah, As-Saika and the Democratic Front on the one side and the Popular Front and the Popular Front — General Command on the other.[15] The argument of the majority that the organization had to pursue a realistic policy if they wanted to attain anything at all was opposed by the Rejection Front which included George Habash's Popular Front for the Liberation of Palestine. The latter argued, in turn, that as soon as the P.L.O. accepted a negotiated solution, it would lose all international support for long-term goals because the Palestinian problem would be considered by the whole world to be resolved. They further argued that the founding of a Palestinian state in the West Bank and Gaza Strip would, once and for all, amount to the Palestinian people relinquishing the right to their homeland in its entirety. Even today, this split between the 'moderates' and the Rejection Front in the Palestinian umbrella organization has not been reconciled, at least not in this respect.[16]

This decision by the National Council which opened the option for an independent Palestinian state alongside Israel and which was finally reached despite considerable opposition, cannot be attributed exclusively to the influence of certain groups within the P.L.O. The fact that the Arab states had changed their political stance after the October War was also responsible for the breakthrough. After the partial victory against Israel, which along with the oil boycott had strengthened their position, they now strove for a negotiated solution. The line of the P.L.O. which had been compromising up to this point only promised perpetuation of the state of war. Thus, the P.L.O. ran the danger of becoming isolated in the Arab camp if it did not adapt to the new political situation.

The decision of the Twelfth National Council was promptly rewarded. In October 1974, the Arab summit conference in Rabat recognized the P.L.O. as the 'sole and legitimate representative of the Palestinian people'. The P.L.O. was the first liberation movement to receive observer status in the U.N. This was followed by Yasser Arafat's speech before the U.N. General Assembly on 13 November 1974 and by growing diplomatic recognition of the P.L.O. worldwide.

In his speech before the United Nations, the chairman of the P.L.O. said:

> ... you must now share my dream. I think this is exactly why I can ask you now to help, as together we bring out our dream into a bright reality, our common dream for a peaceful future in Palestine's sacred land .... So let us work together that my dream may be fulfilled, that I may return with my people out of exile. ...
>
> In my capacity as chairman of the Palestine Liberation Organization and commander of the Palestinian revolution I proclaim before you that when we speak of our common hopes for the Palestine of tomorrow we include in our perspective all Jews now living in Palestine who choose to live with us there in peace and without discrimination.[17]

These words made the vision of a 'democratic secular state' sound like a dream, a wish, a distant goal, not an intention which was to be realized by means of an armed struggle in the near future. By doing this, Yasser Arafat left the way open for intermediate solutions — which, as he later explained, had been his intention. 'Certainly I have said that I dream of a united democratic Palestine — I emphasize the word dream. Is dreaming forbidden? Is it forbidden to imagine the evolution that there could be in the coming years?'[18]

> **Said Hammani: A Palestinian Strategy for Peaceful Co-existence**
> We make no apology for our opposition to the Zionist state as it exists today. We have every right and every reason to oppose it and we shall continue to do so, so long as it retains its present Zionist structure and denies to the indigenous Palestinians the rights it confers automatically on Jewish immigrants from anywhere else in the world. Let there be no doubt about this . . . .
>
> I am myself a man of peace and I deplore violence in political affairs, particularly when it involves innocent people who are not a party to the conflict. But by the normal and accepted standards of patriotic duty I do not believe that anyone can justly condemn Palestinians for taking up arms against Israeli oppression. . . . The practical question for our Palestinian leadership in the context of possible peace negotiations is whether a continuation of the armed struggle against Israel is the most *effective* method to be pursued. In particular, if we assume that a probable outcome of any peace settlement is likely to be the establishment of some kind of Palestinian state on territory recovered from Israel, it seems to me that a very necessary and useful subject for discussion is whether we may then hope to pursue our unaltered, ultimate aim of a 'state in partnership' covering the whole area of Israel/Palestine by non-violent and evolutionary means rather than by a continuation of armed struggle. . . .
>
> Source: *New Outlook*, March/April 1975, p. 56 ff.
>
> NB: Said Hammami was the P.L.O. representative in London and one of the most prominent advocates of the separate state concept. He was assassinated, supposedly on orders from Iraq.

The decision made by the Twelfth National Council was only a first step. The Thirteenth National Council in March 1977 continued along this line, in that it recognized the political struggle as being equal to the armed struggle. Further, it expressly agreed to the establishment of an 'independent national state' and announced its willingness for a negotiated solution to the Palestinian conflict.[19] This confirmed the stand which the population of the occupied territories had taken in countless resolutions and petitions to the P.L.O.[20]

The outcome of the Fourteenth National Council held in January 1979 represented a new hardening in this respect. In view of the negotiations between Begin and Sadat, it was necessary to organize the broadest possible alliance in opposition to the Egyptian-Israeli separate peace. Thus, the Popular Front led by George Habash, which had been considered part of the Rejection Front up until then, was again accepted into the ranks of the P.L.O. and the reconciliation with Jordan, which was at hand, was approved. In spite of the solidification and radicalization visible within the Palestinian organizations, the concept of an independent Palestinian state was still valid and was taken up again in the Council's resolutions on the formula of an 'independent state'.[21] The radicalization of publicly proclaimed P.L.O. positions also continued in 1980, especially since the West Bank mayors who were sympathetic to the P.L.O. had been deported by the Israeli government and had become targets for assassination attempts by radical Israelis. The escalation of violence, which has been visible in the occupied territories for some time, does not even leave the moderate forces in the P.L.O. room to advocate compromises. However, the P.L.O. has not revised the decisions made by the Twelfth or the Thirteenth National Councils.

What was merely implied by Arafat before the United Nations, has become increasingly clear in the statements of other Palestinian leaders in the past few years. Diplomatic representatives of the P.L.O. have stated in all parts of the world that the establishment of an independent state in the West Bank and Gaza Strip was the next aim of the P.L.O. and simultaneously implied other political concessions; yet they never left any doubt that peace did not mean capitulation.

An exponent of this majority position is Sabri Jiryis. He used to live in Israel but had to leave because of political difficulties following the publication of a book on the situation of the Arabs in Israel. Today, he is a member of the Palestinian National Council.

'I am for a Palestinian State'
An interview with Sabri Jiryis.

Jiryis. I came out strongly against the so-called armed resistance and the popular war. That was criticized very much, even by some who would not consider themselves Rejection Front people. I said that there are other ways to solve the Palestine problem besides armed struggle and armed resistance. That was criticized from many quarters.

Some of the Palestinian organizations say that the only way is to go on with the armed struggle. I say that first of all, the

Palestinians do not have enough power to solve the problem by force. Not even Israel, Egypt, Syria or the others can solve it by force, so how can we? There must be some kind of a peaceful settlement.

Q. Could you be more specific about other approaches you advocate instead of force?

A. The basic question is: are you for a Palestinian state or not? I am for it. I belong to that faction of the P.L.O. which would really like a Palestinian state. To explain, let me first analyse the criticisms against such a strategy;

This state would mean an end to armed struggle. That does not bother me, I think it is good. Such a state could be a tool for solving the Palestinian problem, for those who will inhabit it and those who will live elsewhere. I do not see why the emphasis should not be shifted towards economic, social and even political activities. This is the heated discussion among Palestinians, going on since the October War: for or against a Palestinian state.

Q. What percentage of Palestinians lean in your direction?

A. I think we have a majority. We have a numerical majority of the Palestine National Council, and I think that the majority of the people are for this state, too. Roughly, there are three million Palestinians. About half live in the territories occupied since 1967 or inside Israel. The other half live outside, in Lebanon, Syria, Kuwait, etc. If you let the people inside the occupied territories choose between life under occupation and the establishment of a Palestinian state, I think 95% would be for the Palestinian state. It is in their interest.

Outside, we are divided, but still a good number really support it. For example, about 300,000 Palestinians in Kuwait or elsewhere, connected with the West Bank, would support such a move. The P.L.O., as you know, adopted the so-called Ten Point Programme. It was explained everywhere, rightly, as a move towards agreement to such a state.

Q. What about contacts after the state is established?

A. Eventually, there will be recognition. Otherwise, how can the Palestinian state be established? How could they live with each other? But we cannot extend complete recognition to Israel now; no Palestinian can do it and be respected. Full recognition would mean giving up rights to lands and homes inside Israel and abandoning the democratic state idea.

Q. If they recognize you, would you . . .

A. I don't think they will. Why? Because we would then come up with a list of our claims inside Israel, like compensation for land which was taken. There are some four million *dunams* of agricultural land, there are homes, the refugees who have been away for 25 years: it is a big problem. Simply to say: 'We recognize you and that's that' — the Israelis cannot do it and we cannot do it.

Q. How can this Palestinian state defend itself? It is hard to see Israel accepting a state on its borders, that ...

A. The Israelis ask for guarantees, and we shall, too, though we do not like guarantees any more than the Israelis do. Personally, this problem does not bother me; I have a broad view. Egypt, Syria and Jordan, with all their wealth, can only with great difficulty fight Israel and Israel fight them, as seen in 1967. To think that a Palestinian state could continue to fight Israel after it was established is simply a joke, even if it wants to. In other ways, economic, social and political, perhaps. But our people know that even if they say the fighting will go on, it simply cannot be.

Q. Do you view the two state solution as permanent?

A. Our declared aim, as you know, is a single state in all of Palestine. I do believe in it, theoretically. But practically, I am against it. I would not like to see a single state now in Palestine. The reasons are very simple, connected more with us than with the Israelis. On the West Bank and Gaza Strip, the people are almost of one social class, either agricultural workers or day labourers. Even if we had a single democratic state now, the Arabs would be of a lower class, attached to the Israeli economy.

Also, we have our own Palestinian problems. A single state of Arabs and Jews could not do much for Palestinians on the outside. So I prefer two states now, Israeli and Palestinian. Perhaps after 10, 15, 20, or even 25 years, when political circumstances change and a state of development is attained enabling us to deal with social, economic and other problems, then the time may be ripe to discuss a single state. By then the war situation will have changed so that people will not discuss it the way they do now.

I am trying to be realistic and am saying it openly: even if the Israelis agreed to a single state now, we could not bear it. What could we do? We have no university on the West Bank. We have no industry. We have nothing. Every Palestinian knows this, especially the leadership. There is a lot to do, to solve the problems of the refugees, so now and for 20 or 25 years we should keep away from the Israelis.

Source: *New Outlook*, September 1975

Of course, not many Palestinians have so far spoken out this clearly for an independent Palestinian state alongside Israel. Yet Sabri Jiryis is not just anybody. A sign that his statements do not completely contradict Palestinian leadership is that he is now director of the P.L.O. research centre in Beirut.

Yasser Arafat himself has, in a number of statements, endorsed an independent Palestinian state in exchange for the end of the armed conflict with Israel and the *de facto* recognition of the Jewish state. Examples of these are his statements (chosen here because of their semi-official nature) to Paul Findley, a U.S. Congressman. Twice in 1978, Findley made trips to the Middle East to find out from the P.L.O. leadership how they felt about a Palestinian state in the West Bank and Gaza Strip. The question of what the P.L.O.'s attitude would be if such a Palestinian state came into being was a primary topic of the discussions. Arafat made it clear in the talks that the new state 'would live at peace with all its neighbours' and would recognize Israel *de facto*.[22]

> **'Moderate Balance'**
> From the records of congressman Paul Findley from his discussions with Yasser Arafat on 5 January 1978.
>
> Arafat sets forth more clearly than ever before his willingness to have a U.N. peacekeeping force in the new State of Palestine; he states his desire to end the state of belliigerency with Israel; he states his desire to pursue a moderate course, states the difficulties this position poses for him and his hope that the U.S. will not force him into a corner but instead help him to maintain his 'moderate balance'.
>
> Source: *Israel & Palestine*, June 1978.

The opponents of the P.L.O., especially those in Israel, do not believe Palestinian statements of this kind. They point out that the P.L.O.'s national charter exclusively contains the strategic goal of a 'democratic, secular state'. In order to attain this goal, 'armed struggle' is the only tactic named in this official document.[23] To this day, the national charter has not been changed. As long as this does not occur, opponents of the P.L.O. argue, peaceful assertions cannot be trusted.

In the summer of 1977, the P.L.O. leadership expressed its position towards this issue in a memorandum sent to President Carter via Saudi Arabian intermediaries. The charter would be revised to read 'peaceful means' instead of 'armed struggle' as soon as the national rights of the Palestinian people in a state in the West Bank and Gaza Strip were secured.[24] In this memorandum, which was soon to be labelled the P.L.O.'s 'peace plan', the P.L.O. leadership also pointed out:

> ... it can be said, that Israel itself has not yet defined its frontiers or proclaimed its constitution. ... If the Palestine national charter is to be scrutinized, so must the charter of the World Zionist Organization. It is to be assumed that a commitment would be made that, after the Palestinians secured the primary rights they are demanding, the means of achieving the aims of the charter would become subject to change — a change in the nature of the struggle, so that these aims would be achieved by peaceful means. If a state came into being the body representing the Palestinian people would issue a constitution for this state, taking into account existing realities and agreements.
> ... As regards military operations, these were undertaken to achieve a political purpose. If they are to be suspended because of a truce or negotiations, this can only come about under certain conditions, among them that the 'other side' [Israel] recognizes Palestinian sovereignty in a certain form, ceases its persecutions and arrests, and releases detainees.[25]

This moderate line of the P.L.O. has been labelled as a 'feint' by Israelis. To prove this, they cite a number of statements made by prominent Palestinians in which no such willingness to compromise can be found and the 'democratic, secular state' is the only clearly defined goal. It is indeed not difficult to find contradictory statements with which to reproach various P.L.O. leaders.

Those who only hear the belligerent voices and never the ones ready for compromise seem themselves to be uninterested in a peaceful settlement to the conflict. The natural 'partner' in the P.L.O. for the Israeli hawks is the Rejection Front, since in Israel the bellicose and irreconcilable words of George Habash, the leader of the Popular Front for the Liberation of Palestine, are politically more usable than the vague and, very often contradictory statements of Yasser Arafat.

An assessment of the P.L.O. policy of the past few years must take the following factors into account. Firstly, the balance of power within the umbrella organization: on the international scene, the leadership can put forward its moderate line, which it feels to be the most realistic, only as far as it does not upset the inner balance of power. Secondly, the policy of the Israeli opponent: the worse the confrontation with Israel is, the less room there is for compromise on the part of the Palestinians. To refugees in a Lebanese camp, who are constantly exposed to attacks from Israeli planes, or to West Bank residents, whose elected representatives are the targets of assassination attempts made by radical Israelis, how and why they are supposed to live in peace with Israelis is probably not clear. The P.L.O. leadership has to take this into account. The third aspect of P.L.O. policy is the organization's dependence on various Arab states: the Palestinians have often been at the mercy of Arab interests. The Arab countries secure their influence over the P.L.O. by means of financial dependence and through groups in the P.L.O. which they control (for example, As-Saika for Syria and the Popular Front — General Command for Iraq). Today, about one-third of all Palestinians live in Arab countries. The fact that they are unwanted guests there has been made evident by the bloody events in Jordan and Lebanon. International recognition of the P.L.O. as the sole legitimate representative of the Palestinian people would certainly not have progressed so far if the P.L.O. had insisted on continuation of the armed struggle exclusively and on the concept of the 'democratic, secular state'. This position does not fit into the strategy of the Arab states affected by the conflict; they would prefer to reach a negotiated solution.

Diplomatic customs also affect P.L.O. policy: peace in the Middle East will be the result of negotiations. None of the parties involved will make concessions without negotiating. Once something has been relinquished, it can no longer be used to negotiate with. By recognizing Israel and completely abandoning the armed struggle, the P.L.O. would already have played its trump card before negotiations had even begun. Regarding the future of the West Bank and the Gaza Strip, the Palestinian liberation movement has already shown more willingness to compromise than all of the Israeli governments put together.

In spite of the often inconsistent statements made by Palestinian leaders, it can be said that hardly anyone in the P.L.O. had publicly spoken out for the mini-state before the October War of 1973. Since the Twelfth National Council, the P.L.O. has followed a new policy on this issue — even the fact that there is still a faction within the P.L.O. which rejects all compromise does not make this assessment incorrect.

Future Problems: The Viability of a Separate Palestinian State

Since the concept of a Palestinian state is being discussed again on a political level, the economic viability of such a 'mini-state' is being doubted, especially on the part of Israel, who thereby declares a step of this kind towards a solution to the Middle East conflict impossible.

A series of American, Israeli and Arab studies have investigated this issue in recent years.[26] Although the viability of a Palestinian state of widely differing designs and with very varied conditions and limitations, is affirmed in almost all analyses, the hypothetical nature of such studies must be considered. 'To ask whether a West Bank–Gaza Strip state could be viable is to pose the wrong question. For this, as for other territories about which the question might be asked, the answer is neither Yes nor No. The only realistic answer is "Only if . . ."'.[27]

Too many questions which can substantially influence economic prospects for the future have still not been answered today. For instance: What political and economic structures will the new Palestinian state have? What forms of political and economic co-operation will there be between this state and other neighbouring countries? How many refugees will repatriate? Will the refugees receive compensation from Israel? From whom and to what

Table 12
Registered Refugees and Palestinians Living in Camps (in May 1976)

	Total Palestinians (in 1973)	Registered Refugees	Number of Camps	Number of Camp Residents
West Bank	670,000	296,628	20	74,941
Jordan	900,000	644,669	10	216,245
Gaza Strip	364,000	339,824	8	201,960
Lebanon	240,000	198,637	15	102,136
Syria	155,000	188,447	10	54,965
Kuwait	140,000			
Egypt	33,000			
Saudi Arabia	20,000			
United Arab Emirates	15,000			
Iraq	14,000			
Libya	5,000			
Federal Republic of Germany	15,000			
USA	7,000			
Latin America	5,000			

Source: *Brönner 1979*, p. 20.

extent will the state receive financial support? In what form will Jerusalem belong to this state?

Economic viability is a relative concept. If one understands that to mean autarky, not very many countries in the world are viable. Even if viability refers to a fundamental independence from foreign aid, there are few countries, especially in the Third World, which are viable. There is hardly any other country as dependent on financial support from abroad as Israel itself, yet no Israeli would doubt the viability of the state because of that.

The concept of economic viability is thus used particularly in reference to an independent Palestinian state as an argument in the political struggle. Political concepts are hidden behind the apparently objective and scientific prognosis. Whoever rejects the establishment of a Palestinian 'mini-state' because he considers it to be economically stillborn, must ask himself whether he also questions the right of the other numerous small states in Europe, Africa and Asia to exist.

An independent Palestinian state alongside Israel would certainly have vast economic problems. The economic development in the West Bank and Gaza Strip during the occupation has added to the problems considerably. The economic start of a Palestinian state would be acutely impeded by I Israel's economic entanglement in the occupied territories, which has been pursued by the occupying authority at the expense of the local Arab population. Still, the economic viability substantially depends on political factors which can not yet be determined; 'viability is not inherent, it has to be achieved'.[28]

> **Viability and Independence**
> To summarize, economic viability is a function of a complex of characteristics and behaviour patterns which enable the economy to cope with demographic change, to generate and sustain a standard of living progressively approaching the expected level, and to withstand outside economic pressure for a reasonable period of time. The levels of technology and education, the banking institutions, the transportation system, and the stability of government are all among the characteristics of viability....
>
> A state of Palestine of the West Bank and Gaza (including East Jerusalem) can be economically viable.... We estimate that the state of Palestine can support far more than the two and a half million people expected in the first few years.... And we expect the Palestinians to be able to realize fully their confidence of identity if the chance prevails....
>
> A state of Palestine would be more likely to achieve its confidence of identity and economic viability if it stays independent and refrains from integration with its neighbours. Integration with Israel and/or Jordan carries the risk of economic imperialism by one party or another, and a threat to the confidence of identity of the new state of Palestine. After the state had achieved viability, large-scale integration with other economies may be considered.
>
> Source: *Tuma 1978*, pp. 32/115.

Notes

1. Cf. for details *Hollstein 1977*, p. 89 ff.
2. Cf. *ibid.*, p. 125; *Cattan 1973*, p. 39.
3. *Smith 1977*, p. 13.
4. *Ibid.*
5. *Ibid.*
6. Interview with the authors, September 1978.
7. See Chapter 6.

8. *Ma'ariv*, 26 November 1970.
9. See Chapter 6.
10. See Chapter 6.
11. *Al Hamishmar*, 7 December 1979.
12. *MERIP Reports*, No. 83, December 1979, p. 17; as early as 1977 there had been various contacts preceding the committee, which served to co-ordinate the strategy for the Geneva Conference which, however, never came about as a result of the Sadat initiative.
13. Cf. the report on the situation in the Palestinian Communist Party, *Al Hamishmar*, 25 January 1980.
14. *Djeghloul 1979*, p. 29; *MERIP Reports*, No. 80, September 1979, p. 5.
15. For a summary of the individual Palestinian organizations which belong to the P.L.O. umbrella organization, cf. *Tophoven 1975*, p. 30 ff., and *Abu Ijad 1979*.
16. In October 1978 (after the Camp David agreements), the P.F.L.P. once again took part in an executive committee meeting, and in 1979 for the first time participated again in the meeting of the National Council which, in view of the Israeli-Egyptian separate agreements, was aimed at re-establishing 'Palestinian unity'. Cf. *Agraham 1979*, p. 5 ff.
17. *Journal of Palestinian Studies*, No. 14, Vol. IV, No. 2, winter 1975, p. 191.
18. *Le Monde*, 7 January 1975.
19. Cf. *PNC Resolutions 1977*; *Abu Lughod 1977*, p. 10 ff.; *Sommer 1977*, p. 16 ff.; *Ashab 1977*, p. 28 ff.
20. Cf. for example, Yediot Aharonot, 1 February 1977; see also Chapter 6
21. *PNC Programme of National Unity 1979*; cf. also *Israel & Palestine*, February 1979.
22. Cf. *Israel & Palestine*, December 1978, p. 14.
23. The complete text of the charter is printed in *Ibrahim 1973*. The charter was agreed upon in 1968. Its predecessor was the so-called Palestinian Contract of 1964. In Article 9 of the charter it states: 'Armed struggle is the only way to liberate Palestine. Thus it is the overall strategy, not merely a tactical phase.' Article 21 states: 'The Arab Palestinian people, expressing themselves by the armed Palestinian revolution, reject all solutions which are substitutes for the total liberation of Palestine and reject all proposals aiming at the liquidation of the Palestinian problem, or its internationalization.'
24. This memorandum was printed in the Beirut newspaper, *Al-Nahar*, cf. David Hirst, 'Peace and the P.L.O.', *Guardian Weekly*, 7 August 1977; *Abraham 1979*, p. 7 ff.
25. *Guardian Weekly*, op. cit.
26. *Bull 1975*; *Tuma 1978*; *Sayigh 1970*; *Shahar 1971*; R. Ward in *Peretz 1970*; *Ward 1977*; *Abu-Shilbaya 1977*; *Zarki 1977*; *Darin-Drabkin 1975* and *1978 (b)*.
27. *Arkadie 1977*, p. 153 ff.
28. *Tuma 1978*, p. 32.

9. 'Better A Land of Peace than A Piece of Land': Israeli Opposition to the Occupation

To the distant observer, Israel appears to be a monolith. Western media present the picture of a right-wing extremist government which can pursue an expansive settlement policy more or less unchallenged. Reports of opposition movements seldom reach the public. It is true that there is a broad consensus in Israel regarding all questions of national security, a fact that can only be explained by the history of the Jewish people. Due to the experience of mass murder in Auschwitz, a feeling, often called 'security trauma' has developed in Israel. Never again do the Jewish people want to be so helplessly delivered up to their enemies. Thus, it is held to be imperative for the state of Israel, which is so militarily and strategically vulnerable, to safeguard itself by any and every means available. According to Israeli consciousness today, the enemy — particularly the Arabs and Palestinians — has only one desire, like the Nazis, to exterminate the Jewish people. The conflict with the Arab states, smouldering for more than 30 years and continually breaking out into war, has only intensified this security trauma.

The Palestinians are seen as the incarnation of the threat to the Jewish state. Palestinian attacks on Jewish citizens and institutions are taken again and again as proof of their desire to exterminate the Jewish people. Thus, the measures taken by the Israeli military government in the occupied territories serve *a priori* as a self-defence. Military strength is the only guarantee of security and security is the only guarantee of the survival of the Jewish people in Israel. Security is becoming a magic word in the daily practices of the military government and is used to justify certain measures and to develop long-term perspectives for a peace settlement giving them 'secure borders'. For this reason, no broad movement of solidarity with the Palestinians has developed in Israel — in the eyes of many Israelis, the residents of the West Bank and Gaza Strip still represent too great a security risk.

But, for many Jews, Palestinians are not just potential terrorists. The mere recognition of their existence as a people with all the rights the Jews claim for themselves, challenges the legitimacy of the Jewish state for, whoever accepts the right of the Palestinians to their homeland, implies that the Israeli people, through mass immigration and the establishment of the state of Israel in Palestine, has violated the rights of the Arab population.

Nonetheless, there is an intense discussion going on in Israel concerning the future of the occupied territories and harsh criticism of the policy of the Begin administration, although the opposition social-democratic Labour parties do not criticize expansion in itself as much as the manner in which the settlement policy is carried out and its political usefulness. The broad parliamentary opposition questions neither the settlement practice nor the Jewish right to their homeland in all of historical Palestine. It simply feels that the government, in the establishment of settlements, should be motivated less by religious considerations and more by the security policy. Thus, the social democrats do reject the settlements of Gush Emunim in Hebron and near Nablus,[1] yet they defend the paramilitary settlements, for instance, in the Jordan Valley which are meant to safeguard the future border between Israel and Jordan. It is therefore no surprise that the opposition sometimes tries to surpass the government on the right.

It violently criticizes, for example, the discontinuation of the settlements in the northern Sinai, whose establishment was not due to religious considerations, but exclusively part of the security policy.[2] Therefore, in the 1981 election campaign, Shimon Peres, the Labour Party's candidate for the office of Prime Minister, repeatedly guaranteed voters that if elected, he had no intention of giving up any of the settlements. On the other hand, other leading Labour Party members, such as Foreign Minister of the Shadow Cabinet, Abba Eban, let it be known that the continued existence of certain settlements could very possibly be the object of negotiations.

Nevertheless there is a basic difference between the 'peace solution' proposed by Begin's administration and Labour's ideas on the future of the occupied territories. Whereas Begin and his supporters cannot assent to a return of even a part of the territories as a matter of principle and advocate instead an 'autonomy' settlement for the Palestinians under the occupation, the Labour Party endorses, in principle, a partition. In particular, the part of the West Bank in the Samarian and Judean highlands and the northern part of the Gaza Strip which are densely populated by Arabs are, according to negotiations, to be returned to Jordan. However, in Article 30 of the Labour Party manifesto for the 1981 Knesset elections, parts of the region considered to be 'vital to the security of the state of Israle' are claimed as 'part of the sovereign territory of Israel'. These areas, which correspond generally to the 'security areas' mentioned in the Allon Plan, are thus to be annexed and the rest returned to Jordan.

When the Labour Party was in power, these negotiation proposals were often offered under the heading 'territorial compromise'. However, in the 1981 election campaign, this policy of the Labour Party, which was advocated for almost a decade without success, is called the 'Jordanian option', because it is designed to exclude the P.L.O. and involve the Jordanian King in the negotiating process. Yet Jordan has repeatedly rejected negotiations on this basis. The P.L.O. pointed out that the so-called 'security areas' which Israel, according to the Labour Party, would like to incorporate into its own state territory, comprise '40% of the total area of the West Bank and Gaza Strip', but at the same time 'approximately 90% of the arable land as well as the largest part of the natural resources'. 'The Labour Party', according to Issam Sartawi, member of the Palestinian National Council:

> consequently aims to confiscate the greater part of the Palestinian population's means of existence. Ultimately this will only cause misery and a new wave of emigration. In other words, the programme being presented to us as humane and positive is merely a plan to depopulate and to desiccate.[3]

The Palestinians' devastating criticism of the Labour Party's offer of negotiation is only understandable in light of Article 18 of this party's manifesto in which 'active defence against the P.L.O. on a military, political and ideological level' is characterized as 'the duty of each and every Israeli administration'. At the same time, Article 27 emphasizes Israel's right to be militarily active beyond its own borders, which means a continuation of the war against the P.L.O. and its organizations.

In the current political dispute, the Labour Party's policy appears to rely first, on the rejection of the autonomy concept of the bourgeois-nationalist party block around Begin, because a) it perpetuates the problem of the rule of 1.2 million Palestinians in the occupied territories; and b) it involves the danger of laying the foundation for a Palestinian state alongside Israel. This is why Israel strives to annex as much land as possible with as few (Arab) people as possible. In this way, the demographic problems of the occupation and those of the security policy are to be solved. Added to this are the statements of almost all Palestinians who see a Jordanian occupation as the lesser of two evils (as compared with an Israeli occupation). By establishing Arab sovereignty over certain parts of the occupied territories, the Labour Party hopes to take the edge off the Palestinian movement.

These proposals are accompanied by hopes of a way out of the current impasse in negotiations. The 'Jordanian option' is meant to break up the united front of the Arab states and the Palestinians against the Camp David agreements. It is expected that sooner or later King Hussein and the pro-Jordanian forces in the occupied territories will be willing to negotiate and will assert themselves against the leftist and nationalist forces. To make the Jordanian option more appealing to the Palestinians, it is pointed out that Jordan is already a majority Palestinian state anyway. By returning the densely populated regions of the West Bank and the Gaza Strip to the Jordanian state, the Palestinian segment of the population would only be increased and it would then be up to the Palestinians to bring their interests to bear in this state.

In spite of this fundamental difference in the ideas for a solution between the conservative nationalist party block around Begin's Herut Party and the social-democratic Labour parties, the broad national consensus is characterized by the so-called 'four no's'. 1) No to a withdrawal to the borders of 4 June 1967; 2) No to the return of Jerusalem; 3) No to negotiations with the P.L.O.; and 4) No to a Palestinian state between Israel and Jordan.

Therefore, only those groups and persons who reject these four no's (which have determined Israeli policy since 1967) can be described as actual opposition to the occupation. These forces, generally regarded as the 'peace camp', demand the right to determine their own political future for the Palestinians as well as for the Jewish people. They consider territorial compromises to be insufficient and instead hold the view that one must recognize the Palestinians' right to self-determination in order to reach a solution to the problems of the Palestinian people brought about by the mass immigration of Jews and the establishment of the state of Israel. This opposition consists of a variety of different parties, groups and individuals who do indeed influence the political discussion in Israel in no small way although their parliamentary representation is very small. In order to judge the prospects for peace in the Middle East, it is important to know that these groups exist in addition to the chauvinism of the right and the short-sighted 'security' pragmatism of the Israeli social democrats.

Leftist Zionists
A small party which marks the left fringe of the spectrum of Zionist parties and which then had only one representative left in the Israeli parliament is S.H.E.L.I. (Peace and Equality for Israel). It consists chiefly of former members of social-democratic, socialist and communist parties[4] which strive, in particular, for reconciliation with Arabs inside as well as outside Israel. Their platform includes: 1) the recognition of the Palestinians' right to self-determination including the right to their own state; 2) complete withdrawal of Israeli troops from the occupied territories; and 3) the discontinuation of settlements if they 'present an obstacle to peace'.[5] As a Zionist party, S.H.E.L.I. accuses the ruling political groups of a false understanding of Zionism:

> The ideal of Zionism was the renaissance of the Jewish people. The Zionist movement tried to reach this goal by establishing a sovereign state in Israel in which it was supposed to be possible for the Jewish people, who were living as a persecuted minority in many countries, to establish a society based on freedom and justice.... Today the primary task of the Zionist movement is to achieve peace between Israel and its neighbours in order to make the Jewish state the safe port it is supposed to be.... The attempts of Israeli chauvinists to make mountains and valleys sacred, as if they were more precious than peace and freedom, endanger the future of the State of Israel. No nation is free when it rules another....[6]

In this way, S.H.E.L.I. criticizes what is today called neo-Zionism in Israel. The conception of Zionism as a 'movement which originated as an answer to the needs of the Jews' is 'turned into the language of an ideology of power',[7] which 'welds the historical peaks of political power and territorial rule together' in order to 'create political arguments for current territorial claims'.[8] Whereas Zionism was designed to liberate the persecuted Jewish people, neo-Zionism is aimed at 'liberating' the territories 'taken from the Jewish people' by the Palestinians. According to S.H.E.L.I., a just solution to the competing claims of two peoples to Palestine/Israel can only exist in a geographical partition. This is necessary in order to guarantee the survival of the Jewish state and its moral and humanistic base.

In addition to the conflict over the 'correct' Zionism, another element determines the argument of these leftist Zionists, namely, security. In the long run, they say, military security which is based solely on force and superiority cannot secure peace. Political security which is based on peace treaties and mutual recognition is essential. Thus, in their eyes, peace cannot be gained through security, but rather security only through peace.

Non-Zionists and Anti-Zionists

The Communist Party of Israel (C.P.I.), which had joined together with other socialist and communist groups since the 1977 elections to make up the Democratic Front for Peace and Equality and which then had five representatives in parliament, also advocates the complete withdrawal of Israel from the occupied territories and the founding of a Palestinian state alongside Israel.[9] The policy of the C.P.I. is essentially determined by two elements: the dependence on the Soviet Middle East policy and its almost exclusively Arab electorate in Israel. Although the C.P.I. and S.H.E.L.I. agree on basic ideas of a peace policy in parliament, they are on opposite sides of the dividing line between Zionists and non-Zionist groups. Whereas S.H.E.L.I. demands the continued existence of the Jewish State of Israel, the C.P.I. demands a complete turning away from Zionism. In their opinion, this is not a national liberation movement of the Jewish people but an imperialistic instrument which, because of its dependence on American capital, not only serves to suppress the Arab peoples in this region, but also hinders the natural relationship between the Jewish and Arab working class. Moreover, they feel that the Jews in Israel have the right to their own state, just as the Palestinians do, but not to a Zionist state, since this would inevitably mean discrimination against Arabs living in Israel.

The significance of this difference can hardly be underestimated since, for Zionist Israel, the supporters of the C.P.I. are on the other side of the national consensus. According to the prevailing understanding of many leftist Zionists, political co-operation with this party is not even possible on a limited basis. In its 'peace plan' passed in January 1981, the C.P.I. demands an independent Palestinian state alongside Israel based on the 4 June 1967 borders. Furthermore, East Jerusalem should be under Palestinian sovereignty and West Jerusalem should become the capital of Israel; the establishment of a joint administration for both parts of the city would guarantee free access to the holy places. The plan also states that peace negotiations should take place under the auspices of the U.N. with the participation of the U.S., the U.S.S.R. and other interested states as well as the P.L.O.[10]

Some other non-Zionist and anti-Zionist groups are decidedly more isolated and without any parliamentary representation. Matzpen (Compass) is the name generally used for the Israeli Socialist Organization (and is the title of its official publication), which describes itself as explicitly anti-Zionist.[11] It rejects the differentiation made by the C.P.I. and other non-Zionist groups between Zionism, the movement and its ideology on the one hand, and Israel as a result of this movement on the other hand. It considers Israel to be a colonialist and racist state in which the European Jews, as representatives of American imperialism, oppress the oriental Jews and the Palestinians. It also feels a solution to the national and social problems in the region can only be reached by means of a socialist revolution in all states in the area, out of which a democratic and secular state under the leadership of the working class should emerge. Today, Matzpen and its splinter groups[12] have some hundred members and supporters.

The number of supporters of S.I.A.C.H. (New Israeli Left), an undogmatic leftist group which emerged especially from among young and disillusioned members of MAPAM after the June War in 1967, appears to be substantially larger.[13] Its ideas for bringing about a synthesis of socialism and Zionism have never been put before the electorate, since this would have inevitably led to a division. The support of a Palestinian state and the demand for an Israeli withdrawal from all occupied territories mark, however, the minimal consensus which enables the Zionists (who usually support S.H.E.L.I. in election campaigns) as well as the non-Zionists (who reject Zionism, but recognize Israel's right to exist and thus support the alliance of the Democratic Front led by the C.P.I.) to act jointly in their political efforts against the occupation.

New Forces?

The Committee for a Just Peace and the Israeli Council for an Israeli-Palestinian Peace are loose associations of people from various fields, including politics, the sciences, arts and media, who repeatedly make public appeals and declarations as a means to promote a peaceful solution to the conflict within Israeli society. These groups have drawn attention to themselves especially since the mid-70s when they broke a taboo in Israeli politics by meeting and talking with the P.L.O.[14]

The Committee, which united Zionist and non-Zionist personalities, had existed since 1971. But in 1975 the Zionist forces broke away with the hope of increasing their political influence within Israel by founding the exclusively Zionist Council. In addition, especially as Zionists, they wanted to come into contact with representatives of the P.L.O. Today the Council is heavily influenced by S.H.E.L.I., while the members belonging to the C.P.I. largely determine the policies in the Committee.

Through their contacts with the P.L.O. and political representatives of the Palestinian population from the West Bank and Gaza Strip, these two groups have made Israel's direct negotiations with the Palestinians a subject for internal discussion and have shaken hitherto rigid thought patterns. Especially influential in this discussion have been 'patriots of merit', such as

Reserve General Mati Peled; former secretary of the Labour Party, Lova Eliav; the respected professor, Dani Amit; and the famous journalist, Uri Avnery. The initiatives of these groups also created dialogue partners for the P.L.O. in Israel. Such partners provide important backing for the moderates in the P.L.O., which, in discussions on the willingness of the Palestinian liberation movement to compromise, can at least point to some Zionists with whom, from the Palestinian point of view, discussions would be possible.[16]

The Peace Now! movement arose out of Sadat's visit.[17] This movement brought 100,000 people into the streets in the summer and autumn of 1978 on the eve of the Israeli-Egyptian negotiations to demonstrate for an Israeli policy which would be more open to compromise. The political stance of the movement is very vague and this is the prime reason why it enjoys such wide support. The Jewish nature of Israel and the historic right of Jews to Judea and Samaria are not questioned. The right to national self-determination of the Palestinian people is not expressly recognized by Peace Now!; This 'movement, unsuspected of leftist tendencies',[18] is a 'liberal, middle-class, reformist group, which strives in an almost anxious way to publicly emphasize its faithfulness to the nation and its commitment to the values and norms of Zionism'.[19] Its central cause is the appeal to the government to demonstrate its willingness to compromise in the negotiations with Egypt. Concrete ideas of a peace settlement have never been expressed by the group.

It is precisely this character of a broad protest movement which makes reaching the status of a political party in terms of content and organization impossible. As the 1981 Knesset elections approached, the movement disappeared from the political scene. Its activists joined the broadest variety of parties and slates as a means of putting the mark of their political convictions on the existing political structures.

The enormous support which the Peace Now! movement has gained in the last few years cannot be allowed to obscure the fact that the peace forces in Israel are in a difficult position. In addition to the organizations and parties already mentioned, which mark the most important ideological positions within the peace movement, there are a number of other smaller groups.[20] Representatives of the peace forces in parliament are not only found in S.H.E.L.I. and the C.P.I.; there are also 'doves' in the small socialist United Labour Party (MAPAM), the social-democratic Labour Party (M.A.P.I.); the National Religious Party and in factions of the Democratic Movement for Change, a citizens protest party which has, for the time being, disbanded. The peace conceptions of the United Labour Party and the leftist Zionists from S.H.E.L.I. in particular have certain points in common.

However, the peace forces and the leftists have so far not been able to join together to become an influential political factor. The Israeli government has always been able to secure the support of a wide majority by continually pointing out the ever-present danger of extermination by the Arabs. With the existence of Israel at stake, the preservation of this fated community must not be further endangered by criticism from within. There has always been ample evidence of the Arab desire to exterminate the Jews to be found in the statements of Arab representatives. The external danger has served as a means of internal political discipline. In this situation, the peace forces have suffered, particularly for their sympathies for the rights of the Palestinians put them outside the broad national consensus and made them a 'security risk'.

This fact did not bring about wide solidarity and political co-operation among the leftists, but rather brought about their fragmentation. In particular, the Zionist forces, which called for a withdrawal from the occupied territories and supported the right of Palestinians to self-determination, were anxiously engaged in distancing themselves from the non-Zionists. The split between the leftist Zionists and non-Zionists was, and still is, so great that continuing political co-operation between, for example, S.H.E.L.I. and the C.P.I. seems impossible. In most cases, the Zionist leftists in parliament prefer to vote in alignment with the religious and nationalist conservative parties than to run the risk of being thrown into one pot with the non-Zionists, i.e. the C.P.I. The Communists and other non-Zionist groups have the image of travellers without a home. Anyone who co-operates with such groups must expect to be accused of undermining the foundations of the Zionist state. Out of fear of losing their Jewish electorate, the leftist Zionists shy away from an alliance with the anti- and non-Zionists.

As contradictory and fragmented as the peace movement is, it is still the only force in the Jewish state seeking a lasting and just peace which also recognizes the legitimate rights of the Palestinian people. The opposition to Begin's policy of no compromise has definitely grown in the last few years. The number of Israelis who believe that a solution to the Middle East conflict must include consideration of the Palestinian question has also grown.

The common interests and views of the peace forces among the Jews and among the Palestinians cannot be overlooked, yet they are far from becoming negotiating partners or even allies in the struggle for a just peace in the region. The daily violence of the occupation and of the resistance has repeatedly interrupted the cautious contacts between them. The national issue dominates in both camps, and that emphasizes the differences. It is worth noting that certain forces in the P.L.O. are seeking contacts with Israeli peace groups to a much greater extent. At the meeting of the Palestinian National Council in 1977 it was decided to initiate a dialogue with democratic forces inside and outside Israel. Even Zionist forces such as S.H.E.L.I. or people connected with the magazine, *New Outlook*, are included in this dialogue, which up to now, however, has consisted solely of informal talks. Within international Communist bodies, contacts between the C.P.I. and the P.L.O. have grown stronger.

Today, these talks, which are certainly not supported by all factions within the P.L.O., are not only no longer conducted in secret, but are published for the Arab and Palestinian public and referred to even by Yasser Arafat.[21] A few years ago this would have been inconceivable. These modest beginnings of a dialogue between Israeli and Palestinian groups have certainly not yet led to a breakthrough, but they have begun to create some flexibility of thought on the periphery. Whether or not this movement will gain ground, however, remains to be seen.

Notes

1. Cf. *Süddeutsche Zeitung*, 25 March 1980.
2. Regarding the policy of the Labour Party, cf. Chapter 2.
3. *Le Monde*, 6 February 1981.
4. The history of the political parties in Israel is a chain of splits, founding of new parties, re-unifications, combining of slates, etc., which is hard to overlook. This chapter cannot go into all the parties and groupings of the left-wing party spectrum. We have focussed on the most important groupings, the essential ideological views they represent, their significance for the peace policy, as well as their differences and their similarities. Unfortunately, simplifications cannot be avoided.
5. 'S.H.E.L.I.'s stand on Zionism 1978', Information paper of S.H.E.L.I.
6. *Ibid.*, also see *Peretz 1977*, p. 260 ff.
7. Lamm, Zvi, 'The Path of Zionism from Realism to Autism', *Dispersion and Unity*, edited by the Jewish Agency, No. 12/22, Jerusalem 1973/74.
8. Naaman, Shlomo, 'The Emergence of Neo-Zionism', *ibid.*
9. Regarding the Communist Party of Israel, cf. *Schnall 1977*, p. 167 ff. for further references, and *Lockman 1976*, p. 11 ff.; the Communist Party of Israel is often called Rakah (New Communist List), as after the split of the old Communist Party of Israel in 1965, it formed a slate for the Knesset elections using this name.
10. Cf. *Information Bulletin of the Communist Party of Israel*, January 1981, p. 19 ff.
11. Cf. *Schnall 1977*, p. 163 for further references, and *Lockman 1976*, p. 13 ff.
12. For details cf. *Lockman 1976*, p. 14 ff.
13. *Ibid.*, p. 15; *Israleft*, Biweekly News Service published by *Siach*, Jerusalem.
14. The first official talks between former Major-General Mattityahu Peled, the chairman of the Council and P.L.O. representatives took place on 31 December 1976, and 1 January 1977, in Paris and London, respectively; cf. *Abraham 1979*, p. 6; *New Outlook*, January/February 1977.
15. On the position of this Council, cf. *DIAK 1978*, p. 19.
16. Cf. *Abu-Lughod 1977*.
17. Regarding the political background and the forerunners of this movement cf. in great detail, *Bernstein 1978*, p. 67 ff.
18. Bernstein in the Introduction to *DIAK 1978*, p. 6.
19. *Bernstein 1978*, p. 67.
20. For example, the Movement for another Zionism and the group Power and Peace, which is made up mainly of practising Jews; cf. *DIAK 1978*, p. 30 ff.
21. Cf. the interview with Issam Sartawi, member of the Palestinian National Council; moreover, the speech by Uri Avnery in the Knesset on 2 February 1981, citing the various Arab publications in which Arafat and other Palestinian representatives comment on dialogue with Israeli peace groups. Cf. *Israel & Palestine* political report (Supplement), February 1981.

Bibliography

Newspaper articles have not been included in the bibliography; these are cited solely in the notes. Articles which appeared originally in Arabic or Hebrew were, in general, available to the authors in either English, French or German translations which they took from various periodicals, information services and publications pertinent to the Middle East conflict, in particular the following: *New Outlook, Isvaleft, Al-Fajr, Middle East International, Middle East Newsletter, The Middle East Journal, Middle East Record, Israel & Palestine* in English, *EURABIA* and the *Info-Service des Deutsch-Israelischen Arbeitskreis für Frieden im Nahen Osten* in German. All these publications contain translations from the Israeli press more or less regularly.

Bibliographical entries appearing in the notes and as sources are listed below.

Abraham, Sameer, 'The P.L.O. at the Crossroads — Moderation, Encirclement, Future Prospects'. *MERIP Reports*, No. 80, September 1979.
Abu-Ayyash, Abdul-Ilah, 'Israeli Regional Planning Policy in the Occupied Territories'. *Journal of Palestine Studies*, No. 19/20, spring/summer 1976.
Abu Ijad, *Heimat oder Tod,* Düsseldorf/Vienna 1979 (English edition: *Palestinians Without a Country*).
Abu-Lughod, Ibrahim, 'P.N.C. — Maps Out', *MERIP Reports*, No. 57, May 1977.
Abu-Shilbaya, Mohammed, 'On Palestine's Viability', *New Outlook*, June/July 1977.
Adams, Michael, 'Israel's Treatment of the Arabs in the Occupied Territories'. *Journal of Palestine Studies*, No. 22, winter 1977.
Al-Adid, Ibrahim, *Human Rights in the Occupied Territories*, Beirut 1970.
Al-Khatib, Ruhi, *The Judaization of Jerusalem*, P.L.O. Research Centre, Beirut 1970.
Amad, Adnan, ed., *Israeli League for Human and Civil Rights*, (The Shahak Papers), Beirut 1973.
Amit, Daniel, 'Israéliens et Palestiniens — Le double refus', *Le Monde diplomatique,* March 1976.
Amnesty International, *Annual Report*, London, various years.
Amnesty International, *Jahresbericht 1979*, Frankfurt 1980.
Ansprenger, Franz, *Juden und Araber in Einem Land*, Mainz/Munich 1978.
Arkadie, Brian van, *Benefits and Burdens — A Report on the West Bank and*

Gaza Strip Economies Since 1967, Washington D.C. 1977
Ashab, Naim el, 'Die Entwicklung der P.L.O. und der Kampf gegen die Okkupation', *Antiimperialistisches Informations Bulletin*, 6/77.
Aviram, Alexander, 'Civil Administrator for Gaza', *New Outlook*, December 1967.
Avnery, Uri, 'Should the Palestinians Change the Charter?', *New Outlook*, March and April 1980.
Bailey, Clinton, 'Changing Attitudes Toward Jordan in the West Bank', *The Middle East Journal*, spring 1978.
Bank of Israel, *The Economy of the Administrated Areas 1969*, Jerusalem 1971.
Becker, Abraham S., *Israel and the Palestinian Occupied Territories: Military-Political Issues in the Debate*, RAND Corp., Santa Monica, Calif.
Be'eri, Eliezer, *The Palestinians Under Jordanian Rule – Three Issues*, Jerusalem 1978.
Bernstein, Reiner, 'Die Bewegung "Frieden Jetzt": Alternative von links?', *Tribüne– Zeitschrift zum Verständnis des Judentums*, No. 68, 1978.
Bishara, Ghassan, 'The Human Rights Case Against Israel: The Policy of Torture'. *Journal of Palestine Studies*, No. 32, summer 1979.
Blum, Yehuda, 'Israelische Siedlungen und das internationale Gesetz', *Emuna/Israel-Forum, No. 3, 1978*.
Blum, Yehuda, 'The Missing Reversioner: Reflections on the Status of Judea and Samaria', *Israeli Law Review*, vol. 3, 1968.
Boyd, Stephen M., 'The Application of International Law to Occupied Territories', *Israel Yearbook on Human Rights*, vol. 1, Tel Aviv 1971.
Brecher, Michael, 'Jerusalem – Israel's Political Decisions 1947–1977', *Middle East Journal*, winter 1978.
Bregman, Arie, *Economic Growth in the Administered Areas 1968–1973*, Bank of Israel, Research Dept., Jerusalem 1975.
Bregman, Arie, *The Economy of the Administered Areas 1974–1975*, Bank of Israel, Research Dept., Jerusalem 1976.
'Towards Peace in the Middle East', *Brookings Report*, 1975.
Brönner, Wolfram, *Der Nahost-Konflikt und die Palästinafrage*, Frankfurt 1979.
Bruno, Michael, *Economic Development Problems of Israel 1970–1980*, RAND Corp., Santa Monica, Calif., 1970.
Brzezinski, Z., 'Recognizing the Crisis', *Foreign Policy*, No. 17, winter 1974/75.
Bull, Vivian, *The West Bank – Is It Viable?*, Toronto/London 1975.
Cahana, Shamai, *Human Rights in the Areas Administered by Israel* – Statement on behalf of Israel in the Special Political Committee of the General Assembly of the U.N. on 13 December 1971, Ministry for Foreign Affairs: Jerusalem 1972.
Cattan, Henry, *Palestine, the Arabs and Israel*, London 1969.
Cattan, Henry, *Palestine and International Law*, London 1973.
Israel Central Bureau of Statistics, *The West Bank, Gaza Strip and Northern Sinai, Golan Heights – Census of Population*, Jerusalem 1967.
Churchill, Randolph S. and Winston S., *The Six Day War*, London 1967.
International Commission of Jurists, 'Israeli Settlements in Occupied Territories', *The Review of the International Commission of Jurists*, No. 19, December 1977 (Geneva).

Coone, Tim, 'Union Power', *The Middle East*, March 1980.

Cygielman, Victor, 'Hussein's Proposal and the West Bank Municipal Elections' A Post-Mortem', *New Outlook*, March/April 1972.

Cygielman, Victor, 'Palestinians at the Crossroads', *New Outlook*, October 1978.

Dajani, N.I., *Economic Impact of the Israeli Aggression*, Ministry of Culture and Information, Amman 1969.

Darin-Drabkin, Haim, 'Is a Palestinian State Viable?', *New Outlook*, May/June 1975.

Darin-Drabkin, Haim, 'From Settlement to Colonisation', *New Outlook*, February/March 1978.

Darin-Drabkin, Haim, 'The Economic Viability of a Palestinian State', *New Outlook*, April 1978.

Davies, Philip E., 'The Educated West Bank Palestinians', *Journal of Palestine Studies*, No. 31, spring 1979.

Davis, Uri, 'Settlements and Politics Under Begin', *MERIP Reports*, No. 78, June 1979.

Dayan, Moshe, *New Map – New Relations*, Tel Aviv 1969.

Decter, Moshe, 'Settlements in Judea and Samaria. History, the Jews and Israel', *Midstream*, December 1979.

Dershovitz, Alan, 'Preventive Detention of Citizens During a National Emergency – A Comparison Between Israel and the U.S.', *Israel Yearbook on Human Rights*, vol. 1, Tel Aviv 1971.

Deutsch-Israelischer Arbeitskreis für Frieden im Nahen Osten, 'Schonzeit für Vernunft – Gusch Emunim und die Folgen, Dokumentation', *Info-Service des DIAK*, various years.

Deutsch-Israelisher Arbeitskreis für Frieden im Nahen Osten, 'Aktivisten des Friedens – Gruppen und Parteien in Israel', *Info-Service des DIAK*, May 1978.

Dib, George, and Jabbar, Fuad, *Israel's Violation of Human Rights in the Occupied Territories – A Documental Report*, Beirut 1970.

Diner, Dan, *Die Palästinafrage im Vorderen Orient*, John Bunzl (ed.) *Israel/Palästina*, Hamburg 1980.

Diner, Dan, *Israel in Palästina*. Königstein/ts. 1980.

Dinstein, Yoram, 'The International Law of Belligerent Occupation and Human Rights', *Israel Yearbook on Human Rights*, Tel Aviv 1978.

Diskin, A. and Wolffsohn, M., 'Die organisatorische und ideologische Entwicklung der politischen Parteien in Israel', *Orient*, vol. 1, Hamburg 1979.

Djeghloul, Abdèlkader, *Nahost: kein Friede ohne Palästinenser, Wurzeln und Perspektiven des Palästinensischen Befreiungskampfes*, Zurich 1979.

Dodd, Peter and Barakat, Halim, *River without Bridges, Study of the Exodus of the 1967 Palestinian Arab Refugees*, Institute for Palestine Studies, Beirut 1968.

Drori, Moshe, 'The Legal System in Judea and Samaria – A Review of the Previous Decade with a Glance at the Future', in *Israel Yearbook on Human Rights*, Tel Aviv 1978.

Etzioni-Halevy, Eva, and Livne, Moshe, 'The Response of the Israeli Establishment to the Yom Kippur War Protest', *The Middle East Journal*, summer 1977.

Evron, Boaz, 'The New Israeli Peace Movement', *New Outlook*, September 1978.

Feinburg, Nathan, 'The West Bank's Legal Status', *New Outlook*, October/November 1977.
Fried, Melvin, *Israels Besatzungspolitik 1967-1972*, Diss. Tübingen 1975.
Gans, Jonathan B., 'Journey to the Occupied West Bank', *Journal of Palestine Studies*, summer 1979.
Gerson, Allan, *Israel, the West Bank and International Law*, London 1978.
Goldstein, Michael, 'Israeli Security Measures in the Occupied Territories: Administrative Detention', *The Middle East Journal*, winter 1978.
'Bericht des UN-Sonderbeauftragten Gussing vom 2. Okt. 1967', U.N. Document S/8158.
Hadar, Zvi, 'Administrative Detentions Employed by Israel', *Israel Yearbook on Human Rights*, vol. 1, Tel Aviv 1971.
Hammami, Said, 'A Palestinian Strategy for Peaceful Co-existence', *New Outlook*, March/April 1975.
Henle, Hans, *Der neue Nahe Osten*, Frankfurt/Main 1972.
Hilal, Jamil, *The West Bank: Its Economic and Social Structure 1948-1974*, (Arabic) Beirut 1975.
Hilal, Jamil, 'Class Transformation in the West Bank and Gaza', *MERIP Reports*, No. 53, December 1976.
Hollstein, Walter, *Kein Frieden um Israel*, Bonn 1977.
Hussein, King, *My War with Israel*, New York 1969.
Ibrahim, S., 'Zur Genesis des Palästinensischen Widerstandes 1882-1972', *Blätter für Deutsche und Internationale Politik*, No. 5, 1973.
International Committee of the Red Cross, *Annual Report*, Geneva, various years.
International Committee of the Red Cross, 'The Middle East Activities of the ICRC, June 1967-June 1970', *International Review of the Red Cross*, August 1970.
International Labour Office, *Action Taken on the Resolution Adopted by the International Labour Conference at Its 59th to 64th Session*, Appendix: Report of the Mission sent by the Director General to examine the situation of workers of the occupied Arab territories/International Labour Conference 65th Session 1979, Geneva 1979.
International Labour Conference, *66th Session 1980, Report of the Director General*, Appendix III, Geneva 1980.
Institute for Palestine Studies, *The Resistance of the Western Bank of Jordan to Israeli Occupation*, Beirut 1967.
Ministry of Defence (Israel), *The Israeli Administration in Judea, Samaria and Gaza – A Record of Progress*, Tel Aviv 1970.
Ministry of Defence (Israel), *Development and Economic Situation in Judea, Samaria, the Gaza Strip and North Sinai 1967-1969*, Tel Aviv 1970.
Ministry of Defence (Israel), *Three Years of Military Government 1967-1970: Civilian Activities in Judea and Samaria, the Gaza Strip and Northern Sinai*, Tel Aviv, June 1970.
Ministry of Defence (Israel), *Four Years of Military Administration 1967-1971*, Jerusalem.
Embassy of Israel, *Human Rights in the Administered Territories*, Washington, D.C. June 1978.
Israel Information Centre, 'Facts about the Administered Areas', *Information Briefing*, No. 28, Jerusalem.

Israel Information Centre, *Human Rights in the Administered Territories*, Jerusalem 1976.
Ministry of Labour and Social Affairs (Israel), *A Survey of Activities and New Developments in Labour and Employment during 1978*, Jerusalem, February 1979.
Jiryis, Sabir, 'A P.L.O. Moderate Speaks Out', *New Outlook*, September 1975.
Jones, S. Shepard, 'The Status of Jerusalem: Some National and International Aspects', *The Arab – Israeli Conflict*, see Moore 1977.
Kanovsky, Elijahu, *The Economic Impact of the Six Day War*, New York 1970.
Kapeliouk, Amnon, 'Talking on the West Bank', *New Outlook*, July/August 1967.
Kapeliouk, Amnon, 'First of all Evacuate the Occupied Territories', *New Outlook*, September/October 1967.
Kapeliouk, Amnon, 'Les Israéliens ont misé sur les élections pour normaliser la situation en Cisjordanie', *Le Monde diplomatique*, April 1972.
Kapeliouk, Amnon, *Israel – la fin des mythes*, Paris 1975.
Kapeliouk, Amnon, 'A qui appartient la Cisjordanie?', *Le Monde*, 14 September 1977.
Kapeliouk, Amnon, 'Die besetzten Gebiete und der Frieden', *DIAK Info-Service*, March 1979.
Kapeliouk, Amnon, 'L'aggressivité de l'extrême droite Israélienne', *Le Monde diplomatique*, December 1979.
Kapeliouk, Amnon, 'Autonomy as Viewed by Israel', *New Outlook*, April 1979.
Khouri, Rami G., 'Israel's Deportation Policy', *MERIP Reports*, No. 65, March 1978.
Langer, Felicia, 'Israeli Violations of Human Rights in the Occupied Territories', *Palaces of Injustice*, Americans for Middle East Understanding, Public Affairs Series No. 7, city and year unknown.
Langer, Felicia, *Mit eigenen Augen*, Bonn 1977.
Langer, Felicia, *These are my Brothers – Israel and the Occupied Territories*, London 1979.
Laqueur, Walter Z., *Der Weg zum Staat Israel*, Vienna 1975.
Lesch, Ann Mosley, *Israel's Occupation of the West Bank: The First Two Years*, RAND Corp., Santa Monica, Calif. August 1970.
Lesch, Ann Mosley, 'Israeli Settlements in the Occupied Territories 1967–1977', *Journal of Palestine Studies*, No. 25, autumn 1977.
Lesch, Ann Mosley, 'Israeli Deportation of Palestinians from the West Bank and the Gaza Strip, 1976–1978', *Journal of Palestine Studies*, spring 1979 and winter 1979.
Steinbach, Udo, Hofmeier, Rolf, and Schönborn, Mathias, eds., *Politisches Lexikon Nahost*, Munich 1979.
Lockman, Zachary, 'The Left in Israel – Zionism vs. Socialism', *MERIP Reports*, No. 49, July 1976.
Lorch, Netanel, Statement at the 'Symposium on Human Rights, July 1–4, 1971', *Israel Yearbook on Human Rights*, vol. 1, Tel Aviv 1971.
Mansour, Atallah and Stock, Ernest, 'Arab Jerusalem and Annexation', *New Outlook*, January 1971.

Mathiot, Elisabeth, *Die kulturelle Unterdrückung in den besetzten arabischen Gebieten*, Deutsch-Arabische Gesellschaft, Bonn, year unknown.
McPeak, Colonel Merril A., 'Israel: Borders and Security', *Foreign Affairs*, April 1976.
Dishon, Daniel, ed., *Middle East Record*, Jerusalem, vol. III – 1967, (1971); vol. IV – 1968 (1973); vol. V – 1969–1970 (1977).
Monroe, Elizabeth, 'The West Bank: Palestinian or Israeli?', *The Middle East Journal*, autumn 1977.
Moore, John Norton, The Arab-Israeli Conflict – Readings and Documents, Princeton, N.Y. 1977.
Nahumi, Mordechai, 'Policies and Practice of Occupation', *New Outlook*, May 1968.
Nahumi, Mordechai, 'Israel as an Occupying Power', *New Outlook*, June 1972.
Nahumi, Mordechai, 'Dayan and the Politics of Creeping Annexation', *New Outlook*, November/December 1972.
Nakhleh, Khalil and Zureik, Elia, *The Sociology of the Palestinians*, London 1980.
National Council of the Churches of Christ, *Report of the Deputation to the Middle East (July 19-31, 1968)*, City unknown, 1968.
Neumann, H., Seewald, R., Seewald, U. and Sterzing, C., *Alltag ohne Frieden*, Berlin 1977.
National Lawyers Guild, *Treatment of Palestinians in Israeli Occupied West Bank and Gaza: Report of the National Lawyers Guild, 1977 Middle East Delegation*, New York 1978.
'Resolutions of the 13th Palestine National Council Cairo', *Journal of Palestine Studies*, No. 23, spring 1977.
'14th Palestinian National Congress', *Palestine – PLO Information Bulletin*, 15 February 1979.
Peretz, D., *Israel and the Palestine Arabs*, Washington 1956.
Peretz, Don., 'Israel's New Arab Dilemma', *The Middle East Journal*, winter 1968.
Peretz, D., Wilson, Evan M. and Ward, Richard J., *A Palestinian Entity?*, Washington D.C. 1970.
Peretz, D., 'The Earthquake – Israel's Ninth Knesset Elections', *The Middle East Journal*, summer 1977.
Pfaff, Richard H., 'Jerusalem: Keystone of an Arab-Israeli Settlement', *The Arab-Israeli Conflict*, see Moore 1977.
Quiring, Paul, 'Israeli Settlements and Palestinian Rights', *Middle East International*, September and October 1978.
Rabab, Arthur, 'La levée palestinienne en Cisjordanie', *Le Monde diplomatique*, May 1976.
Rejwan, Nissim, 'The Palestinian Press under Israeli Administration', *Midstream*, November 1973.
Rifkin, Lena, 'Wave of Political Arrests After Camp David', *MERIP Reports*, No. 74, January 1979.
Rouleau, Eric, 'Hawks and Doves in Israel's Foreign Policy', *The World Today*, 1968.
Rouleau, Eric, 'Le peuple palestinien – Histoire d'une conscience nationale', *Le Monde diplomatique*, January 1975.
Ryan, Sheila, 'Israeli Economic Policy in the Occupied Areas: Foundations

of a New Imperialism', *MERIP Reports*, No. 24, January 1974.
Ryan, Sheila, 'Political Consequence of Occupation', *MERIP Reports*, No. 74, January 1979.
Safran, Nadav, *Israel – The Embattled Ally*, Cambridge, Mass. and London 1978.
Sayigh, Y.A., 'Palestinian Peace', *The Middle East Newsletter*, June/July 1970.
Schleifer, Abdullah S., 'The Fall of Jerusalem', *Journal of Palestine Studies*, No 1, autumn 1971.
Schnall, David J., 'Native Anti-Zionism: Ideologies of Radical Dissent in Israel', *The Middle East Journal*, spring 1977.
Schölch, Alexander, 'Zum Selbstverständnis und zu den politischen Bestrebungen der Palästina-Araber seit 1967', *Aus Politik und Zeitgeschichte* (insert in the weekly paper, *das parlament*), 15 December 1979.
Schroeter, Leonard W., 'The Status of East Jerusalem', *Midstream*, August/September 1972.
Shahar, H.B., Berglas, E., Mundlak, Y. and Sadan, E., *Economic Structure and Development Prospects of the West Bank and Gaza Strip*, RAND Corp., Santa Monica, Calif. 1971.
Shamgar, Meir, 'The Observances of International Law in the Administered Territories', *Israel Yearbook on Human Rights*, vol. 1, Tel Aviv 1971.
Sharif, Regina, 'The United Nations and Palestinian Rights 1974-79', *Journal of Palestine Studies*, No. 33, autumn 1979.
Shefi, Dov, 'The Protection of Human Rights in Areas Administered by Israel: United Nations Findings and Reality', *Israel Yearbook on Human Rights,* vol. 3, Tel Aviv 1973.
Shehadeh, Raja, *The West Bank and the Rule of Law*, ed. by The International Commission of Jurists, Geneva 1980.
Sheskin, Aryeh, 'Economic Structure of the West Bank', *New Outlook*, September/October 1967.
Sinai, Anne and Pollack, Allan, *The Hashemite Kingdom of Jordan and the West Bank*, New York 1977.
Sirhan, Bassem, *Die Generation der Befreiung*, Basel 1975.
Smith, Colin and Andrews, John, *The Palestinians*, London 1977.
Sommer, Birgit, 'Unabhängigkeit und nationale Einheit – Zur Sitzung des 13. Palästinensischen Nationalrates', *3. Welt Magazin*, April 1977.
The Human Rights Reports Prepared by the Department of State in Accordance with Section 502 (B) (b) of the Foreign Assistance Act of 1961 as Amended (March 1977), Washington, D.C.
Country Reports on Human Rights Practices, Report Submitted to the Committee on International Relations, U.S. House of Representatives and Committee on Foreign Relations, U.S. Senate, by the Department of State in Accordance with Sections 116 (d) and 502 (B) (b) of the Foreign Assistance Act of 1961 as Amended (Feb. 1978), Washington, D.C.
Central Bureau of Statistics (Israel), *Statistical Abstracts of Israel*, Jerusalem, various years.
Central Bureau of Statistics (Israel), *Family Expenditures – Survey in the Administered Territories*, Jerusalem 1976.
Stendel, Ori, *Arab Villages in Israel and Judea/Samaria*, Jerusalem 1968.
Tawil, Raymonda, *Mein Gefängnis hat viele Mauern*, Bonn 1979. (English

edition 'My Home, my Prison').

Teveth, Shabtai, *The Cursed Blessing – The Story of Israel's Occupation of the West Bank*, New York 1969.

Tophoven, Rolf, *Fedayin – Guerilla ohne Grenzen*, Munich 1975.

Tophoven, Rolf, 'PLO – zwischen Terror und Diplomatie', *Aus Politik und Zeitgeschichte* (insert in the weekly paper, *das parlament*), 15 December 1979.

Tuma, Elias H. and Darin-Drabkin, Haim, *The Economic Case for Palestine*, London 1978.

'Die UN-Resolutionen zum Nahost-Konflikt', trans. Arnold Harttung, *Völkerrecht und Politik*, vol. 5, Berlin 1978.

United Nations, Report of the U.N. Special Committee to Investigate Israeli Practices Affecting the Human Rights of the Population of the Occupied Territories, New York, published annually. U.N. Documents: A/8039 (1970), A/8384 (1971), A/8828 (1972), A/9148 (1973), A/9817 (1974), A/1027 (1975), A/31/218 (1976), A/32/284 (1977), A/33/356 (1978), A/34/631 (1979).

U.S. House of Representatives, 59th Congress, Israeli Settlements in the Occupied Territories – Hearings before the subcommittee on international organizations and on Europe and the Middle East of the Committee on International Relations, September/October 1977, Washington, D.C. 1978.

U.S. Senate, 59th Congress, The Colonization of the West Bank Territories by Israel – Hearings before the U.S. Senate subcommittee on Immigration and Naturalization(Committee on the Judiciary), October 1977, on 'Question of the West Bank Settlements and the Treatment of Arabs in the Israeli Occupied Territories', Washington D.C. 1978.

Wagner, Heinz, *Der Arabisch-Israelische Konflikt im Völkerrecht*, Berlin 1971.

Ward, R.J., *A Palestinian State – A Rational Approach*, New York 1977.

Watad, Muhammad, 'Reflections on West Bank Elections', *New Outlook*, April/May 1976.

Weber, Hans C., 'Israels Politik in den besetzten Gebieten', *diskussion*, No. 24, February 1968.

Weigert, Gideon, *Sie pflügen neue Felder. Die Landwirtschaft im Westufergebiet 1970–1975*, Jerusalem 1975.

Yaniv, Avner, 'Schwierige Alternativen im arabisch-israelischen Konflikt – Zwischen einer zweiten Teilung und einem dritten Palästina Staat', *Aus Politik und Zeitgeschichte* (insert in the weekly paper, *das parlament*), 15 December 1979.

Additional Bibliography

During the course of the preparation of this book, a further bibliography, too long to be included here, on the development of the West Bank and the Gaza Strip was put together. In addition to those included in this book, it contains approximately 250 listings. It is relatively comprehensive, although it can be assumed that there is a great amount of literature in Arabic and Hebrew on the occupied territories which was not available to the authors

The additional bibliography can be obtained directly from:

    Christian Sterzing
    Bahnhofstrasse 148
    D-6732 Edenkoben
    Federal Republic of Germany.

Please enclose £2.00.

MIDDLE EAST TITLES FROM ZED PRESS

POLITICAL ECONOMY

SAMIR AMIN
The Arab Economy Today
(with a comprehensive bibliography of Amin's works)
Hb

B. BERBEROGLU
Turkey in Crisis:
From State Capitalism to Neo-Colonialism
Hb and Pb

SAMIR AMIN
The Arab Nation:
Nationalism and Class Struggles
Hb and Pb

MAXIME RODINSON
Marxism and the Muslim World
Pb

GHALI SHOUKRI
Egypt: Portrait of a President
Sadat's Road to Jerusalem
Hb and Pb

CONTEMPORARY HISTORY/REVOLUTIONARY STRUGGLES

KAMAL JOUMBLATT
I Speak for Lebanon
Hb and Pb

GERARD CHALIAND (EDITOR), A.R. GHASSEMLOU, KENDAL, M. NAZDAR, A. ROOSEVELT AND I.S. VANLY
People Without a Country: The Kurds and Kurdistan
Hb and Pb

ROSEMARY SAYIGH
Palestinians: From Peasants to Revolutionaries
Hb and Pb

BIZHAN JAZANI
Capitalism and Revolution in Iran
Hb and Pb

PEOPLE'S PRESS
Our Roots are Still Alive
Pb

ANOUAR ABDEL-MALEK (EDITOR)
Contemporary Arab Political Thought
Hb

MICHAEL JANSEN
The Battle of Beirut:
Why Israel Invaded Lebanon
Hb and Pb

REGINA SHARIF
Non-Jewish Zionism:
Its Roots in Western History
Hb and Pb

HUMAN RIGHTS

JAN METZGER, MARTIN ORTH AND CHRISTIAN STERZING
This Land is Our Land:
The West Bank Under Israeli Occupation
Hb and Pb

GERARD CHALIAND AND YVES TERNON
The Armenians: From Genocide to Terrorism
Hb and Pb

WOMEN

ASMA EL DAREER
Woman, Why do you Weep?
Circumcision and Its Consequences
Hb and Pb

AZAR TABARI AND NAHID YEGANEH
In the Shadow of Islam:
The Women's Movement in Iran
Hb and Pb

RAQIYA HAJI DUALEH ABDALLA
Sisters in Affliction:
Circumcision and Infibulation of Women in Africa
Hb and Pb

INGELA BENDT AND JAMES DOWNING
We Shall Return:
Women of Palestine
Hb and Pb

MIRANDA DAVIES (EDITOR)
Third World — Second Sex:
Women's Struggles and National Liberation
Hb and Pb

NAWAL EL SAADAWI
The Hidden Face of Eve:
Women in the Arab World
Hb and Pb

JULIETTE MINCES
The House of Obedience:
Women in Arab Society
Hb and Pb

Zed press titles cover Africa, Asia, Latin America and the Middle East, as well as general issues affecting the Third World's relations with the rest of the world. Our Series embrace: Imperialism, Women, Political Economy, History, Labour, Voices of Struggle, Human Rights and other areas pertinent to the Third World.

You can order Zed titles direct from Zed Press, 57 Caledonian Road, London, N1 9DN, U.K.